On Walter Benjamin

Studies in Contemporary German Social Thought
Thomas McCarthy, General Editor

On Walter Benjamin

Critical Essays and Recollections

edited by Gary Smith

The MIT Press, Cambridge, Massachusetts and London, England

This book was set in Baskerville by Achorn Graphic Services Inc. and printed and bound by Halliday Lithographic in the United States of America.

Library of Congress Cataloging-in-Publication Data

On Walter Benjamin.

(Studies in contemporary German social thought)
Bibliography: p.
Includes index.
1. Benjamin, Walter, 1892–1940. 2. Authors, German—
20th century—Biography. I. Smith, Gary. II. Series.
PT2603.E455Z77 1988   838'.91209 [B]   87-37825
ISBN 0-262-19268-3

Contents

Preface

"The Kabbalah relates," so Benjamin tells us, "that in every instant G-d creates an immense number of new angels whose only purpose is, before they dissolve into naught, to sing His praise before His throne for a moment. Mine [Klee's *Angelus Novus*] was interrupted in doing so." Not all the accolades of Benjamin's own angels, however, have remained inaudible. While most of his interpreters have shared the ephemeral character of those Talmudic messengers, a number of critical essays and recollections endure because they serve as reference points for—if not measures of—subsequent readings.

The essays in this volume are such texts. The wide range of topics they address provides an emphatic indication of the great breadth of Benjamin's concerns. But despite the recent efflorescence of Benjamin criticism in English, the full scope of his themes and concerns may come as a surprise to most Anglo-American readers. It could hardly be otherwise, as the English translations of Benjamin's writings occupy little space when placed next to the seven volumes of his *Gesammelte Schriften* and hundreds of published letters. Since Charles Rosen's complaint a decade ago about the dearth of Benjamin's writings in English, only the collection *Reflections* has appeared, along with one of eighteen extant autobiographical texts (the *Moscow Diary*). In that same span in Germany, the edition of Benjamin's collected writings has been completed, making available several thousand pages of primary literature.

This collection reflects the contexts of Benjamin criticism on the Continent.[1] The sustained, often fulminating, interest in his ideas across the Atlantic has not been matched in the United States. This circumstance is by no means limited to the reception of Benjamin's works. In general, recent discussions of theory and criticism in the United States have been decidedly influenced by French theory, while there has been little access to some of the best German sources.[2] Paradoxically, those sources have been more available in France and have been regularly transmitted to the United States by way of French theorists, who are avid interpreters of the Germans, and of Benjamin. Examples range from the Benjaminian traces in the writings of Malraux, Klossowski, and even Bataille in the 1930s, to Derrida's sustained study of Benjamin's writings over the last decade. It is reasonable to suppose that among the German theorists who could make a substantial contribution to—if not change the terms of—parallel discussions in the United States, Benjamin is the single most important.[3] But his inclusion continues to be frustrated by the intermittency of translations of his works.

The reception of Benjamin's writings in West Germany is embedded in the moraine of their postwar publication history. The present collection follows the chronology of these publications. Several of the essays were written as introductions or afterwords, though they bear nothing of the character of occasional pieces, or were used as such by the publisher, Suhrkamp Verlag. Adorno's two essays introduced Benjamin's *Schriften* and *Briefe,* in 1955 and 1966, respectively. Szondi's "Walter Benjamin's *Städtebilder*" (1963) followed a collection of Benjamin's travel pieces under the same name, which was published in the now famous series "edition suhrkamp" in its first year. Another early volume in that series, *Über Walter Benjamin,* reprinted the recollections by Bloch and Selz. In 1972 the publisher sponsored a colloquium to mark the occasion of Benjamin's eightieth birthday and to celebrate the publication of the first volumes of the *Gesammelte Schriften.* The publication which resulted from that event, *Zur Aktualität Walter Benjamins,* featured Scholem's "Walter Benjamin and His Angel" as well as Habermas's lecture and included the recollection by Sahl. That same year, Schweppenhäuser's propaedeutic prefaced a collection of Benjamin's writings entitled *Über Haschisch.* And when the fragments of the legendary Arcades Project were finally published a decade later as volume five of the *Gesammelte Schriften*, Tiedemann's skillful introduction served as a guide to many of the project's passageways.

The need to make more Benjamin literature available in English extends to the best interpretations and criticism of his work. This collection presents a selection of the most indispensable items from the secondary literature—readings that have themselves been influential and have benefited from the diffusion of a more comprehensive familiarity with his works.

The editor owes a considerable debt to Tom McCarthy, whose advice and other observations were always most valuable, and to Larry Cohen, whose equanimity can only be admired. The editor also wishes to express his gratitude to Debbi Edelstein, Jeremy Gaines, Deborah Johnson, John McCole, and Hans Puttnies for editorial contributions and excellent suggestions on a number of points.

Notes

1. Although two of the authors, Charles Rosen and Irving Wohlfarth, wrote their essays in English, both have a firm position in the European discourse. Rosen's essay was translated in the influential French journal *Critique* (no. 370, March 1978). Wohlfarth's effort is a further canto in his ongoing tribute to Benjamin, portions of which have appeared in German, French, and English.

2. Obvious exceptions include the writings of Adorno, Heidegger, and Nietzsche.

3. Nietzsche and Heidegger have already entered these discussions via France.

Sources and Acknowledgments

We gratefully acknowledge the following sources for permission to reprint the essays in this volume:

Adorno
"Einleitung zu Benjamin's *Schriften.*" In Benjamin, *Schriften,* ed. Theodor W. Adorno and Gretel Adorno in collaboration with Friedrich Podszus. Frankfurt a.M.: Suhrkamp, 1955, 9–27.

"Benjamin, der Briefschreiber." In Benjamin, *Briefe,* ed. Gershom Scholem and Theodor W. Adorno. Frankfurt a.M.: Suhrkamp, 1966, 14–21. "Benjamin the Letter Writer" will preface Howard Stern's translation of *Briefe,* forthcoming from the University of Chicago Press.

Bloch
"Erinnerungen an Walter Benjamin." *Der Monat* 18, 216 (September 1966): 38–41.

Habermas
"Consciousness-raising or Rescuing Critique," trans. Frederick Lawrence. In J. Habermas, *Philosophical-Political Profiles.* Cambridge, MA: MIT Press, 1983, 29–63. First published as "Bewußtmachende oder rettende Kritik—die Aktualität Walter Benjamins" in S. Unseld, ed. *Zur Aktualität Walter Benjamins.* Frankfurt a.M.: Suhrkamp, 1972, 173–223.

Jauss
"Nachtrag (zu dem Kapitel: 'Die Moderne' in Walter Benjamins Baudelaire-Fragmenten)." In H. R. Jauss, *Literaturgeschichte als Provokation.* Frankfurt a.M.: Suhrkamp, 1970, 57–66.

Klossowski
"Entre Marx et Fourier." *Le Monde* (May 31, 1969).

Mayer
"Walter Benjamin und Franz Kafka: Bericht über eine Konstellation." *Literatur und Kritik* 140 (1979): 579–597.

Menninghaus
Unpublished German typescript, 1983. French translation in Heinz Wisman, ed. *Walter Benjamin et Paris* (Paris: Cerf, 1986), 529–558.

Sources and Acknowledgments

Missac
"Walter Benjamin: De la rupture au naufrage," *Critique* 36, 395 (April 1980): 370–381.

Rosen
"The Ruins of Walter Benjamin." *New York Review of Books* 24, 17 (October 27, 1977): 31–40; "The Origins of Walter Benjamin." *New York Review of Books* 24, 18 (November 10, 1977): 30–38.

Sahl
"Walter Benjamin im Lager." *Der Monat* 18, 219 (December 1966): 86–91.

Scholem
"Walter Benjamin and His Angel." In G. Scholem, *On Jews and Judaism in Crisis: Selected Essays.* New York: Schocken, 1976, 198–236. First published as "Walter Benjamin und sein Engel" in S. Unseld, ed. *Walter Benjamin zu ehren.* Frankfurt a.M.: Suhrkamp, 1972, 77–124.

Schweppenhäuser
"Die Vorschule der profanen Erleuchtung." In Benjamin, *Über Haschisch,* ed. Tillman Rexroth. Frankfurt a.M.: Suhrkamp, 1972, 9–30.

Selz
"Walter Benjamin à Ibiza." *Les Lettres Nouvelles* 2, 11 (January 1954): 14–27.

Szondi
"Walter Benjamins Städtebilder." Afterword to Benjamin, *Städtebilder.* Frankfurt a.M.: Suhrkamp, 1963, 79–99.

Tiedemann
"Dialektik im Stillstand: Annäherungen an das *Passagen-Werk.*" In R. Tiedemann, *Dialektik im Stillstand. Versuche zum Spätwerk Walter Benjamins.* Frankfurt a.M.: Suhrkamp, 1983, 9–41. Slight revision of "Einleitung des Herausgebers," in Benjamin, *Gesammelte Schriften,* Bd. V, ed. R. Tiedemann. Frankfurt a.M.: Suhrkamp, 1982, 9–41.

Wohlfarth
Unpublished typescript, 1981. Revised 1986.

Critical Essays

Introduction to Benjamin's *Schriften*

Theodor W. Adorno

In view of the commercial failure of the first edition of Walter Benjamin's Berliner Kindheit um Neunzehnhundert (1950), *it is not surprising that Adorno had such a difficult time persuading his publisher, Peter Suhrkamp, to invest in a two-volume edition of his friend's writings. Suhrkamp's characterization of the book—in a 1951* Spiegel *article about the year's best- and worst-selling German books—foreshadowed his resistance: he ascribed its failure to "the compressed miniatures . . . which open themselves to the reader only with difficulty, all the more since their form of speech is so precise, seamless, and harsh. . . . These pieces will likely remain undigested for a long time." Nevertheless, the subsequent two-volume edition of* Schriften *(1955) ran nearly 1200 pages; it contains practically every text we know in English, including those collected in* Illuminations *and* Reflections, The Origin of German Trauerspiel, *and "Central Park" as well as some still untranslated texts, such as Benjamin's dissertation on the concept of* Kunstkritik *in early German Romanticism and his essays on Goethe's* Elective Affinities *and two poems by Friedrich Hölderlin.*

In addition to the formidable task of justifying such an extensive edition, Adorno's introductory essay had to bear the freight of both Benjamin's philosophical-literary diversity and his obscurity after 1933. Taking up this charge, Adorno introduced Benjamin's great themes while presenting a synoptic view of his oeuvre. *Benjamin's works were of exceptional significance for Adorno's own thinking; the early affinity he had discovered between his own work and Benjamin's led to a continuing exchange of ideas, although many would argue that this exchange was basically one-way. So, while the occasion called for a* Gesamtinterpretation, *or an overview of the* oeuvre, *Adorno was also implicitly listing his debts to Benjamin. Many of the ideas he focused on can be projected back onto a reading of his own works; hence Adorno's virtually exclusive attention to the philosophical moments in Benjamin's thought. In this sense, Adorno's essay can be read not only as a perspicacious introduction to Benjamin, but also as a crystallized instance of a process underway within his own "life's work"—the persistent effort to define his work against Benjamin's.*

The publication of an extensive edition of Walter Benjamin's writings should do justice to their real significance.[1] Here the intention is not to assemble the "life's work" of a philosopher or scholar, neither is it to make amends to one who died a victim of National Socialist persecution and whose name has been repressed from Germany's public consciousness since 1933. The nineteenth-century idea of a "life's work" does not apply to Benjamin; indeed it is questionable whether a life's work—the culmination of an undisrupted life, fulfilled according to its own measure—is granted to anyone today. It is certain, however, that the historical catastrophes of his time denied Benjamin's work any consummate wholeness and condemned to the fragmentary not only the major project of his later years, on which he staked everything, but also his entire philosophy. For precisely this reason the attempt to protect him from the threat of oblivion would be legitimate: the quality of texts such as "Goethes *Wahlverwandtschaften*"[2] or *The Origin of German Trauerspiel*—long familiar to a small circle—is reason enough to make accessible once again what has been lost for decades. Yet such an attempt at spiritual reparation would be marked by a helplessness that no one would have sensed more deeply than Benjamin himself, who had heroically fought off any childish faith in the ahistorical immutability and permanence of works of the spirit. Rather, what motivates the decision to publish an *oeuvre*—which its author would have much preferred buried in "marble vaults" and exhumed on a better day—is a promise that emanated from Benjamin the writer and the person, a promise that it becomes all the more urgent to recollect now that the overwhelming powers of the status quo have clearly sworn never again to permit anything comparable to Benjamin's unique fascination to recur. This fascination arises not only from spirit, fullness, originality, and profundity. Rather, Benjamin's thoughts radiate a color that hardly ever occurs in the spectrum of concepts and that belongs to an order to which consciousness instinctually blinds itself so as not to be sickened by the world as it is and its purposes. What Benjamin said and wrote sounded as if it were conjured up out of a secret depth. Its power, however, came from its evidentness. It was free of any affectation of occult doctrine, the preserve of initiates. Benjamin never practiced "privileged thinking."[3] Admittedly, one could easily picture him as a magician with tall pointed hat, and he did sometimes present thoughts to his friends like precious and fragile magic charms; yet all these thoughts, even the strangest and most quixotic, always tacitly included something like a notice that its insights could be mastered by an alert consciousness provided that it were sufficiently wide awake. His statements did not appeal to revelation but to a type of experience that distinguished itself from the usual only by its indifference to the limitations and taboos to which a well-adjusted consciousness normally bows. Benjamin never once acknowledged the boundary taken for granted by all modern thought: the Kantian commandment not to trespass into intelligible worlds or, as Hegel riposted, to where there are "houses of ill repute." Benjamin's thought no more renounces the sensuous happiness banned by the traditional work ethic than its spiritual counterpart, the relation to the absolute. For the supernatural is inseparable from the fulfillment of the natural. Therefore, Benjamin does not weave a relation to the absolute out of concepts, but rather seeks it through corporeal contact with the material. For Benjamin everything habitually excluded by the norms of experience ought to become part of experience to the extent that it adheres to its own concreteness instead of dissipating this, its immortal aspect, by subordinating it to the schema of the abstract universal. Benjamin thereby placed himself in stark opposition to all modern philosophy, with the possible exception of the peerless Hegel—who knew that to establish a limit always also means to overstep it—and made it easy for those who dispute the rigor of his thought to dismiss it as scattered insights, as merely subjective, merely aesthetic, or as merely a metaphysical world view. He was so at odds with these criteria that it never even occurred to him to defend himself against them as Bergson did, just as he disdained laying claim to a special intuitive source of knowledge. What is fascinating about him is that the standard objections to the self-evident quality of his experience—experience that was in no way retraceable in all its steps, yet often compelling—acquired a foolishly gesticulating and apologetic aspect, a tone of "yes, but . . . ." They sound like the tired efforts of conventional minds to affirm themselves in the face of the irrefutable, of a source of light (more profound) than the protective shell of a rationality indentured to the status quo. Without polemics, Benjamin's philosophy (which is anything but irrational), nevertheless convicts such rationality of its own stupidity by virtue of its very existence. It was not for want of knowledge or out of willful fancy that he ignored the philosophical tradition and the current rules of scientific logic, but rather because he suspected something sterile, futile, and worn out about them, and because the undiminished, unadjusted truth was too powerful a force within him for him to allow himself to be intimidated by the raised warning finger of the intellectual supervisor.

Benjamin's philosophy invites misreading: it dares the reader to consume and reduce it to a succession of desultory *aperçus*, governed by the happenstance of mood and light. This must be challenged not only by the tensely spiritual character of his insights, entirely contrary to all mollusk-like reactions even amid the most sensuous objects: every one of his insights has its place within an extraordinary unity of philosophical consciousness. The essence of this unity, however, is its centrifugal direction, its effort to gain itself by relinquishing itself to the manifold. The measure of experience, which fills out every one of Benjamin's sentences, is the relentless force setting the center in the periphery instead of developing the peripheral out of the center as demanded by standard philosophical practice and traditional theory. Just as Benjamin's thought does not respect the boundary line between the conditional and the unconditional, neither does it, conversely, claim definitive self-completion—a claim raised wherever thought marks out its own circle, the kingdom of subjectivity, in order to reign supreme within it. Paradoxically, Benjamin's speculative method intersects with the empirical method. In the preface to the *Trauerspiel* study, he undertook a metaphysical rescue of nominalism: throughout, inferences are made not from top to bottom but rather, in an eccentric manner, "inductively." Philosophical fantasy is for him the capacity for "interpolation into the most minute," and a cell of well-studied reality—again in his own words—carries a greater importance than the rest of the world. Benjamin stands as far from the presumptuousness of the system as from resignation to the finite; indeed, they strike him as intrinsically identical: systematic philosophy sketches the futile *trompe l'oeil* of that truth, sedimented in theology, which Benjamin is bent on faithfully and radically translating into the secular. Corresponding subterraneously to his power of self-relinquishment is a mole's burrow of tunnels linking everything together. He profoundly mistrusted any classifying organization of the superficies: he feared that in it, as the fairy tale warns, the best is forgotten. Just as Benjamin's dissertation was dedicated to a central theoretical problem of early German Romanticism, his whole life remained indebted to Friedrich Schlegel and Novalis for the conception of the fragment as a philosophical form that—precisely because it is fractured and incomplete—retains something of the force of the universal that evaporates in all-inclusive projects. That Benjamin's work remained fragmentary is thus not simply to be ascribed to his adverse fate; rather, it is implicit from the start in the structure of his thought, in his fundamental idea. Even his most extensive work, *The Origin of German Trauerspiel,* is so constructed that, despite the most meticulous overall architectonic, each of the tightly woven and internally seamless sections pauses, as it were, for breath and begins anew rather than flowing directly into the next section as required by the schema of a gapless train of thought. The claim of this principle of literary composition is nothing less than that of expressing Benjamin's idea of truth itself. No more for him than for Hegel is truth the mere *adequatio intellectus et res*, not a jot of Benjamin's work obeys this criterion; rather, truth is a constellation of ideas that together constitute the divine name, and these ideas crystallize within the detail, their force field.

Benjamin belongs to the philosophical generation that tried in every way to break out of idealism and systematic philosophy, and there is no lack of contact with the older representatives of these efforts. He is linked to phenomenology, particularly in his youthful work, by the antinominalist definition of essences through objective semantic analyses rather than through the arbitrary positing of a terminology. The "Critique of Violence" exemplifies this approach. Benjamin always commanded an archaically rigorous power of definition: from that of fate as the "guilt-context of the living"[4] right up to his final definition of "Aura."[5] What Benjamin owed to George's school—more than may be superficially gleaned from his writings—is a spellbinding, philosophical gesture that freezes the animate, that monumentality of the momentary, which constitutes one of the decisive tensions of the form of his thought. He is related to the antisystematic Simmel by his effort to lead philosophy out of the "frozen wasteland of abstraction."[6] and carry thought over into concrete historical images. Among those of his own generation, he is allied with Franz Rosenzweig in his tendency to allow philosophical speculation to reverse into theological doctrine; and he was allied as well with the Ernst Bloch of the *Spirit of Utopia* through the conception of "theoretical messianism," through the indifference to the Kantian restrictions on philosophy and the intention to interpret inner-worldly experience as a cipher for transcendental experience. Yet Benjamin distanced himself most energetically from precisely those contemporary philosophemes with which he seemed to be in agreement. He preferred to incorporate thought that was foreign and dangerous to him as a sort of innoculation rather than entrust himself to some look-alike in which he, incorruptible, discerned complicity with the extant and official even when one behaved as if day were just breaking and one were starting anew. As to Husserl—whose speculative audacity was oddly coupled with vestiges of an academic neo-Kantianism, indeed even with scholastic terminology—Benjamin was fond of saying that he did not understand him; and with regard to Scheler, Benjamin (along with Scholem) harbored the scorn of the Jewish theological tradition for the resurrection of metaphysics in the marketplace. But what essentially distinguished Benjamin from any and every similarity he had with his epoch was the specific gravity of the concrete in his philosophy. He never degraded the concrete to an example of the concept, not even to a "symbolic intention," to the trace of the messianic in the helplessly fallen natural world. Rather, he took the concept of the concrete, which had degenerated into ideology and obscurantism, so literally that it became simply useless for all those manipulations that it is currently made to serve in the name of "mission," "encounter," "concern," "honesty," and "authenticity." He was relentlessly vigilant against the temptation of using concrete statements to camouflage illegitimate concepts as substantial and experientially full while the concrete is silently passed off as an example of its preconceived concept. To the extent that it is in the power of thought, he consistently focused on those points where the concrete is most densely, inextricably, knotted together. With tenderest devotion to the material, his philosophy relentlessly cracks its eye teeth on the kernel. To this extent it is allied with Hegel: the constant effort of the concept, devoid of any faith in the automatic mechanisms of a categorizing that simply spins a web over its objects. Completely contrary to contemporary phenomenology, Benjamin—when he is not expressly dealing with intentions like that of allegory, as in his study of the baroque— does not want to reproduce intentions in thought, but rather crack them open and thrust them into the intentionless, if not, in a kind of Sisyphean labor, decipher the intentionless itself. The greater the demand that Benjamin places on the speculative concept, the more entirely—one could almost say, the blinder—is his thought subordinated to its material. He once said, not coquettishly but with the greatest seriousness, that he needed a fair dose of stupidity to be able to think a worthwhile thought.

The material to which he dedicated himself was historical and literary. When he was still quite young, in the early twenties, he made it his maxim never to spin thoughts up out of the blue, as he put it, "amateurishly," but rather always and exclusively to think in relation to already existing texts. Benjamin recognized idealist metaphysics as deceptive in its identification of existence and meaning and, at the same time, for him, every unmediated statement about such meaning, about transcendence, is historically prohibited. This gives an allegorical character to his philosophy. It aims at the absolute, but desultorily, mediately. All creation becomes for him script that must be deciphered though the code is unknown. He immersed himself in reality as in a palimpsest. Interpretation, translation, critique are the schemes of his thought. The wall of words that he percusses gives his homeless thought authority and shelter; he on occasion spoke of his method as a parody of philology. Even here, a theological model is unmistakable: the tradition of Jewish and particularly mystical biblical interpretation. The inspection of profane texts as if they were sacred is not least among the operations of the rescue of theology through its secularization. This is Benjamin's elective affinity with Karl Kraus. But the ascetic restriction of his philosophy to what intellect has already produced, to "culture"—even where he provocatively plays off the concept of barbarism against this term—this restriction to what spirit has produced, the renunciation of philosophical concern for any immediacy of existence and any so-called primordiality, attests at the same time that it is precisely the world of the humanly made and socially mediated, that, totally occupying his philosophical horizon, has inserted itself as a totality in front of "nature." It is for this reason that in Benjamin the historical itself appears as if it were nature. The centrality of the concept of "natural history" in his interpretation of the baroque is not accidental. Here as elsewhere Benjamin distills the essence of recondite material. The historically concrete becomes for him an "image"—the prototype both of nature and the supernatural—just as, conversely, nature becomes a metaphor of the historical. "The incomparable language of the skull: complete lack of expression—the black of its eye sockets—united with the wildest expression—the grinning rows of teeth," as he says in *One-Way Street*.[7] The peculiar imagistic quality of Benjamin's speculation, what might be called his mythicizing trait, has its origin in his melancholy gaze, under which the historical is transformed into nature by the strength of its own fragility and everything natural is transformed into a fragment of the history of creation. Benjamin circles about this relation tirelessly; as if he wanted to elucidate the enigma which staterooms and gypsy wagons present to childlike wonder, and under his eye, as for Baudelaire, everything becomes allegory. Only in the intentionless would such devoted concentration find its limit, only in it would the concept be finally extinguished; this is why he elevates the thought-image (*Denkbild*) to an ideal. Yet as little as Benjamin aimed at an irrational philosophy—for only cognitively distinguished elements are capable of being assembled in these images—they are just as distant from such mythical imagery as that toward which Jung's psychology aspires. Benjamin's images do not present invariant archetypes that are to be extracted from history; rather, they shoot together precisely by means of the force of history. Benjamin's micrological gaze, the unmistakable hue of his manner of concretion, is directed toward the historical in direct opposition to *philosophia perennis*. His philosophical interest is indifferent to the ahistorical, but focuses precisely on the temporally most determinate, the irreversible. Thus the title: *One-Way Street*. Benjamin's images are bound to nature not as elements of an ever self-identical ontology, but in the name of death, of transcience as the highest category of natural existence toward which Benjamin's speculation progresses. Only the transient is eternal in them. He correctly called the images of his philosophy dialectical: the plan for the book *Pariser Passagen* envisages as much a panorama of dialectical images as their theory. The concept of a dialectical image was meant objectively, not psychologically: the presentation of the modern as at once the new, the already past and the ever-same was to have been the work's central philosophical theme and the central dialectical image.

The uncommon difficulties in front of which Benjamin sets the reader are not primarily those of presentation, although at least in the earlier texts this exacts an effort because of its doctrinal tone, a language that in and for itself, by the force of naming, claims authority and, not unlike phenomenology, largely rejects the stipulation of assumptions and argumentation. The greater difficulties, however, are those arising from the philosophical content. It requires the suspension of those expectations with which the philosophically educated commonly enter texts. First of all, Benjamin's antisystematic impulse determines this technique much more radically than is otherwise the case even among antisystematists. His trust in experience—experience in that particular sense that can hardly be defined but only gained through familiarity with Benjamin's work—forbids the articulation of so-called fundamental principles and the logical deduction of all further thoughts from them. Still, it is hard to make out to what extent Benjamin himself radically rejected the concept of fundamental principles or to what extent he conceals them all the better to potentiate their effect: concealed, their light illuminates phenomena, whereas they would blind whomever stared directly into them. Whatever the case, Benjamin was readier to put his cards on the table—to use his own expression—in his youth than later on. He himself always thought particularly highly of the short essay, "Fate and Character"[8] and regarded it as a sort of theoretical model of what he had in mind to do. Whoever wants to become acquainted with him would do well to first study this essay intensively. One will also notice Benjamin's deep and vaguely antiquarian bond with Kant, above all with Kant's sharp distinction between nature and the supernatural, and note as well the involuntary reshaping and alienation of such concepts under Benjamin's saturnine gaze. For it is precisely character, which Benjamin with equal emphasis separates from the moral order as from fate, that is for Kant the "intelligible" character, the autonomously posited determining ground of moral freedom. And here, clearly, there is an echo of Benjamin's thesis that in character the supernatural or the human wrests itself away from the mythically amorphous. Although the effort to produce an ontological interpretation of Kant continued long after this relatively early work had been written, today it is evident that antecedent to these efforts Kant's thoroughly functional thinking, aimed at "activities," had already petrified into a kind of ontology under Benjamin's medusan, fixating gaze. The concepts of the phenomenal and noumenal, which are bound together in Kant by a selfsame reason and which reciprocally determine each other even in their opposition, became for Benjamin spheres of a theocratic order. In this spirit he transformed all culture that entered his vicinity, as if the form of his mind and the melancholy with which his nature conceived of the idea of the supernatural, of reconciliation, had to give everything he apprehended a shimmer of death. Even the concept of dialectics, toward which he inclined in his later materialist phase, is marked by this trait. It is not by accident that this dialectic is one of images rather than progression and continuity; it is a "dialectic at a standstill," the name that, incidentally, he hit upon without knowing that Kierkegaard's melancholy had long since conjured it up. He escaped the antithesis of the eternal and the historical through a micrological technique, a concentration on the most minute, in which historical movement halts and sediments into an image. Thus, one only understands Benjamin correctly when one senses behind every one of his sentences the sudden reversal of utmost movement into something static, indeed into the "static" idea (*Vorstellung*) of the movement itself; this reversal is also responsible for the specific essence of his language. In the decisive theses "On the Concept of History,"[9] which belong to the complex of the late work *Pariser Passagen,* he finally spoke candidly of his philosophical idea (*Idee*) and in doing so surpassed dynamic concepts such as progress by virtue of his incomparable experience, similar only perhaps to the photographic snapping of an instant. If other keys to Benjamin's work are sought beyond the early treatise and the theses, written with infinite effort and in the face of the ultimate danger, it would be necessary to mention first the "Critique of Violence,"[10] in which the polarity of myth and reconciliation powerfully emerge. By disassociating into the shapeless and subjectless on one hand, and into what has escaped all natural order, that is to say justice, on the other hand, everything that constitutes the middle world of the humans dissipates in Benjamin's works: dynamic, development, and freedom. By virtue of this disassociation, Benjamin's philosophy is indeed inhuman: man is the site or arena of this philosophy rather than a being for himself, originating in himself. The shudder that this provokes is in fact what defines the innermost difficulty of Benjamin's texts. Intellectual difficulty rarely stems from a simple lack of comprehension; it is usually the result of a shock. That person will recoil from Benjamin who will not entrust himself to thoughts in which a mortal danger to familiar self-consciousness is sensed. Reading Benjamin is fruitful and felicitous only for one who looks this danger in the eye without balking because he wants nothing to do with such denaturalization of life. In Benjamin's work hope truly appears only where there is danger.

The inner composition of his prose is also unsettling in the concatenation of its thoughts, and nowhere is it more necessary than here to clear away false expectations if one is not to be led astray. For the idea of Benjamin's work, rigorously conceived, excludes not just fundamental themes but all analytical techniques of composition, development, the whole mechanism of presupposition, assertion, and proof, of theses and conclusions. Just as the uncompromising representatives of the New Music tolerate no "development," no distinction between theme and elaboration, and instead require that every musical idea, indeed its every note, stands equally near to the center, so too is Benjamin's philosophy "athematic." It too is dialectic at a standstill to the extent that it admits of no period of development (*Entwicklungszeit*), but rather gains its form from the constellation of its particular enunciation. Hence its affinity to aphorism. At the same time, however, the theoretical element of his thought continually requires extensive intellectual construction. He compared its form to a woven fabric, and its extreme self-enclosure is dependent on this: the particular themes are adjusted to, and entwined with, each other without regard either to portraying a train of thought by their concatenation, to communicating anything, or to persuading the reader: "Persuasion is fruitless."[11] Disappointment is unavoidable if one seeks results from Benjamin's philosophy; it satisfies only one who broods over it long enough to find what inheres in it: "Then one night, it comes alive," as in George's *Tapestry*.[12] In his later years, under the influence of materialist infusions, Benjamin wanted to exclude the unrestrainedly uncommunicative element which he unyieldingly pursued in the earlier texts, and which gained its most compelling expression in "The Task of the Translator."[13] "The Work of Art in the Age of Mechanical Reproduction"[14] not only describes the historico-philosophical situation that dissolves the uncommunicative element, but also secretly contains a program for Benjamin's own work that the treatise "On Some Motifs in Baudelaire"[15] and the theses "On the Concept of History" attempted to realize. What he had in mind was the communication of the uncommunicable by means of lapidary expression. A certain simplification of language is unmistakable. But as so often in the history of philosophy, simplicity deceives; nothing changed in Benjamin's intellectual focus, and although the strangest insights are expressed as if they were simple common sense, their strangeness is only increased:

nothing could be more Benjaminian than the response he once gave to a request for an example of healthy common sense: "The later the evening, the more beautiful the guests." As in his youth, his style again took on something authoritarian, something of the inverted proverbs, perhaps out of the desire to balance his kind of spiritual experience with the intention of broader communication. Without a doubt, it was not the theoretical content of dialectical materialism that appealed to him but the hope it offered of an authorized and collectively authenticated discourse. He no longer believed, as in his youth, that he could draw on mystical theology without sacrificing the idea of doctrine: here again, the theme of the rescue of theology through its relinquishment, its complete secularization, is expressed. This configuration of the unreconcilable, and at the same time this intransigence toward what he had always rejected, gives the later philosophy of Benjamin its painfully fragile depth.

The need for authority in the sense of a collective guarantee was not, furthermore, as foreign to Benjamin as might be presumed from his turn of mind, inimical to any conformity. On the contrary, it was precisely the incommensurable in his thought and its bearer, individuated to the point of the most painful isolation, that from the very first sought self-expression, even in the obviously hopeless attempt to fit into communities and various organizations. Benjamin was certainly one of the first philosophers to notice the following antagonism: that the bourgeois individual who thinks becomes problematic to the core, yet without the existence of anything supra-individual in which the isolated subject could gain spiritual transcendance without being oppressed; it is this that he expressed in defining himself as one who left his class without, however, belonging to another. His role in the youth movement, which at that time was, of course, extremely different from its later manifestations (he was among the chief contributors to *Der Anfang* and was a friend of Wyneken's until the latter became an apologist for World War I) and perhaps even his propensity for theocratic notions is of the same cast as his type of Marxism, which he adopted in an orthodox fashion as a doctrinal corpus, without suspicion of the productive misunderstandings he thereby set in motion. It is not difficult to recognize the futility of all these escape attempts, efforts of helpless assimilation to newly rising powers, whose horror no one would have sensed more acutely than Benjamin: "It was as if I refused under any condition to build a front, not even with my own mother," he could still write in *Berliner Kindheit*.[16] He knew the impossibility of fitting in and yet never renounced the desire to do so. But this contradiction by no means points back merely to the weakness of an isolated individual; truth is registered in it: the recognition that private reflection is deficient as long as it is separated from social movements and praxis that aim at changing the situation. This deficiency damages even one who makes himself into a seismograph of the moment, as did Benjamin to an extraordinary degree. Benjamin, who admitted thinking in fragments, did not shy away from the greatest extremity; he assimilated into himself the mortally foreign and even renounced the form of harmony possible for him: that of the monad which, while windowless, nevertheless "represents" the universe. For he knew that recourse to preestablished harmony was no longer tenable, if indeed it ever had been. No less can be learned from the *tour de force* upon which he embarked without any great illusions as to its possible success than from the masterly texts he completed. When he entitled an essay "Wider ein Meisterwerk" (Against a Masterwork),[17] he also wrote against himself, and precisely this ability is inseparable from his productive force.

This contradiction is the origin of Benjamin's melancholy, his "character" in the sense that he himself gave the word. Sadness—which is different from the simple fact of being sad—was his nature, as Jewish awareness of the permanence of danger and catastrophe as well as the antiquarian tendency to see the present transformed into the ancient past, as if by enchantment. Benjamin, inexhaustibly inventive and productive, at every waking moment of his life in complete control of his spirit and completely commanded by spirit, was nevertheless anything but what the cliché of spontaneity passes off as such; just as his speech was letter perfect, his characterization of the elderly Goethe as the Chancery clerk of his own interior applied to Benjamin himself in every regard.[18] The preponderance of spirit radically alienated him from his physical and even his psychological existence. As Schoenberg once said of Webern, whose handwriting was reminiscent of Benjamin's, he had put a taboo on animal warmth; friends hardly dared put a hand on his shoulder, and even his death may have to do with the fact that, during the last night in Port Bou, out of shyness the group with which he fled arranged for him to have a single room, with the result that he was able to take unobserved the morphine he had reserved for the utmost emergency. Nevertheless, his aura was warm, not cold. He had a unique capacity to delight that left all simple bonhomie infinitely far behind: that of giving without reserve. What Zarathustra praises above all else, the virtue of giving, was Benjamin's to the degree of overshadowing everything else: "Uncommon is the highest virtue and useless; it is gleaming and gentle in its splendor."[19] And although he named his chosen emblem, Klee's *Angelus Novus,* the angel that takes rather than gives,[20] even this fulfills one of Nietzsche's thoughts: "Such gift-giving love must become a robber of all values," for "the earth shall yet become a place of convalescence! And a new scent, one bringing salvation, already surrounds it—as does a new hope."[21] Benjamin's speech gave witness to this hope, his fairy-tale, soundless, disembodied smile, and his silence. Every instant spent with him restored what has otherwise been irretrievably lost: the holiday. In his presence one felt like a child at Christmas the instant the door is cracked open to the living room and an overwhelming flood of light fills the eyes with tears; a light more shattering and certain than any dazzling light seen directly when one is finally called to enter the room. The whole power of thought assembled in Benjamin to prepare such instants, and to them alone has passed what theological doctrines once promised.

Translated by R. Hullot-Kentor

Notes

My task in preparing this translation was rendered easier by the preliminary efforts of Eric Krakauer and Thomas Levin, to whom I am grateful.

1. Adorno's original references were to the two-volume edition of Benjamin's *Schriften,* ed. Theodor W. Adorno and Gretel Adorno in cooperation with Friedrich Podszus

Introduction to Benjamin's *Schriften*

(Frankfurt a.M.: Suhrkamp, 1955), which his essay introduced. All notes, most of which referred to texts in this edition, have been replaced by references to the scholarly edition of Benjamin's *Gesammelte Schriften*, as well as English translations, whenever possible. Several notes have also been added.

2. I:123–201.

3. III:315–22.

4. *Reflections*, 308.

5. Cf. *Illuminations*, 188ff., 224f.; *One-Way Street*, 250f.

6. T. W. Adorno, *Negative Dialectics*, trans. E. B. Ashton (London: Routledge & Kegan Paul, 1973), xix.

7. *One-Way Street*, 70.

8. *Reflections*, 304–11.

9. *Illuminations*, 255–66.

10. *Reflections* 277–300.

11. *Reflections*, 63. [German: "Überzeugen ist unfruchtbar."]

12. Cf. Stefan George, "The Tapestry of Life," in *The Works of Stefan George*, trans. O. Marx and E. Morwitz (Chapel Hill: University of North Carolina Press, 1974), 185.

13. *Illuminations*, 69–82.

14. *Illuminations*, 219–53.

15. *Illuminations*, 157–202.

16. IV:287.

17. III:252–259.

18. Cf. "Deutsche Menschen. Eine Folge von Briefen," IV:211.

19. Friedrich Nietzsche, *The Portable Nietzsche*, ed. Walter Kaufmann (New York: Viking, 1980), 186.

20. *Reflections*, 273.

21. Cf. Nietzsche, 187, 189.

Walter Benjamin's City Portraits

Peter Szondi

For Rudolf Hirsch

In 1962 Suhrkamp Verlag commissioned the literary historian Peter Szondi to write an afterword to a collection of Benjamin's travel pieces. A year earlier, Szondi had published a talk entitled "Hoffnung in Vergangen: Walter Benjamin und die Suche nach der verlorenen Zeit,"* which had been his inaugural lecture as Germany's first Professor for Comparative Literature at the Free University of Berlin. Szondi treated the project of Benjamin's Berliner Kindheit *alongside both Proust's* Remembrance of Things Past *and Benjamin's own writings on Proust. In his view, the central difference between their respective undertakings is their relation to the past: whereas Proust essentializes the past as such, Benjamin attempts to locate "prophetic" moments in what is past—moments that anticipate the future or await "redemption" in the future ("hope in the past"). What links that lecture with the essay below is Szondi's attention to a theme that almost no serious study of Benjamin's thought has since left untouched: his theory or metaphysics of experience. Szondi uses the occasion of the collection of Benjamin's* Städtebilder *(city portraits)† to examine Benjamin's reflections on the differences between the foreigner's and the native's experience of cities. Szondi pays close attention to distance and nearness, foreignness and familiarity. He situates Benjamin's* Berliner Kindheit *against the context of the earlier city portraits and speculates on the reasons why Benjamin ceased to write travel pieces once he was forced into exile. Here, as well as in reflections about Benjamin's use of memory and metaphor, Szondi turns again to Proust, both as witness and as guide.*

1

It was perhaps no accident that Benjamin reflected upon ways of describing cities in 1929, the year that lies midway between his city portraits and his reminiscences of Berlin. For his remarks bear precisely on the difference between portraits of

cities by foreigners and those by natives. Seeking to explain why
the latter are so much less common than the former, Benjamin
wrote:

The superficial inducement, the exotic, the picturesque has an effect
only on the foreigner. To portray a city, a native must have other,
deeper motives—motives of one who travels into the past instead of
into the distance. A native's book about his city will always be related
to memoirs; the writer has not spent his childhood there in vain.
(III:194)

It is natural to look at Benjamin's city portraits in the light of
this assertion. Their contours might thus become more sharply
delineated and reveal whether in this observation, which appeared in a book review, Benjamin is not in essence writing
about his own works. Is he not looking back critically at his
descriptions of Naples (1925), Moscow (1927), and Marseilles
(1929) and forward to his projected book *Berliner Kindheit um
Neunzehnhundert*? In this perspective, two things become clear.
While Benjamin's characterization exactly fits the book on Berlin that he intended to write at the time, his judgment regarding portraits of foreign cities hardly applies to those he had
already produced. The motives underlying them scarcely differ
from those that marked the book of reminiscences—in no way
could the terms "superficial" and "profound" be used to classify
Benjamin's own descriptions. More likely, it seems that in his
portraits of foreign cities he wished to demonstrate the
superficiality of a distinction made on the basis of the author's
birthplace. It is evident also that his remark is not merely an
elucidation of the images of cities (*Städtebilder*), but requires its
own elucidation in turn. Benjamin's city portraits provide this
commentary.

2

Anyone who describes his own city must travel into the past
instead of into the distance. One might ask why this journey is
necessary at all, why the native cannot remain in the present.
The *Berliner Kindheit um Neunzehnhundert* suggests in its very
title that the answer is to be found in the affinity of such books

with memoirs. At the same time, it shows that the journey into the past is a journey into the distance as well. For without distance there can be no description, except that of mere *reportage*. The portrait of one's own city is torn from this lower realm by the adult's painful separation from the scenes of his childhood. The city is still there, but that early period lies irrecoverably within it; this is a paradox, which sharpens not only our pain but also our perception. Gone, therefore, is our familiarity with streets and houses, though they may still surround us; we see them with a doubly alien view: with the view of the child we no longer are and with the view of the child to whom the city was not yet familiar. Benjamin's Berlin book is proof of the constitutive role of distance. In this respect it is like Gottfried Keller's *Der grüne Heinrich,* which was written not in Zurich but abroad; like *Buddenbrooks,* which was written in Italy; and like the novel of Dublin, which could be written only on the Continent because its author believed that absence is the highest degree of the present. So, too, Flaubert found himself at the foot of an Egyptian pyramid when he conceived the name Bovary, which was to stand as a monument to the petty narrowness of the French provinces.

All the same, *Berliner Kindheit* differs in one crucial respect from all other works whose mainspring is memory, and thus also from the book to which it is closest and which Benjamin translated into German: Proust's *Remembrance of Things Past.* For Benjamin's work is devoted not so much to memory itself as to one of its special gifts, which is captured in a sentence from his *One-Way Street:* "Like ultraviolet rays, memory shows to everyone in the book of life a script that invisibly glosses the text as prophecy" (*Reflections,* 89). The adult's glance does not yearn to merge with the child's glance. It is directed toward those moments when the future first announced itself to the child. In *Berliner Kindheit* Benjamin writes of the shock "with which a word startles us like a forgotten muff in our room. Just as the latter allows us to infer that some unknown woman has been there, so certain words or pauses allow us to detect the presence of that invisible stranger, the future, who left them behind with us" (IV:252). Everywhere in the city, in the streets and parks, the Berlin book is on the trail of such shocks, the memories of which are preserved by the child until the adult can decipher them. Thus the Tiergarten is not merely a playground but also the place where the child "first grasped, never to forget it, what only later came [to him] as a word: love" (IV:237). Unlike Proust, Benjamin does not flee the future. On the contrary, he deliberately seeks it out in the emotional turmoil of certain childhood experiences, where it went, as it were, into hibernation, whereas upon entering the present it passes into its grave. His "lost time" is not the past but the future. His backward glance is on the shattered utopia which can kindle "the spark of hope" only "in the past."[1] Benjamin, who in the years approaching the Third Reich could neither close his eyes to reality nor give up the promise of a time worthy of humanity, welded a paradoxical bond of hope and despair. It is only in this light that we can understand his plan for a "Prehistory of the Modern"; and the same may be said of his anthology of letters, *Deutsche Menschen,* on the origins of the German bourgeoisie, which—no less paradoxically—appeared as Noah's ark to the socialist driven out of Germany.[2]

3

The remark quoted at the beginning of this essay was made at the expense of foreign cities. How little Benjamin's city portraits display the qualitative difference he notes can be seen from the very first sentence of his early text on the Russian metropolis: "More quickly than Moscow itself, one gets to know Berlin through Moscow" (*Reflections,* 97). This new perspective on his own city is the most tangible of Benjamin's gains from his stay in Russia. Things foreign do not lure the visitor into self-forgetfulness; he does not become intoxicated by the picturesque and exotic but rather sees his own life, sees himself with an estranged vision. The effect of a journey into the distance is no different from that of a journey into the past, which is likewise a journey into the distance. Still, it is only because Benjamin goes even further that he can write on foreign cities. While he explores them, the same forces are at work which will

later lead him to embark on the journey into his own childhood. From Benjamin's first impressions of Moscow we learn
that to the newcomer the city is a labyrinth, and the Berlin book
begins: "Not to find one's way about in a city is no great thing.
But to get lost in a city, as one gets lost in the woods, requires
practice" (IV:237). A foreign city fulfills this strange wish more
easily than does one's own. But why this wish? Benjamin once
described the labyrinth as the home of the tarrier and said it is
the "right path for one who, in any event, always arrives early
enough at his destination" (I:668). The labyrinth is thus in
space what memory, which seeks hint of the future in the past,
is in time. For the path whose milestones are the shocks of
which he speaks ought confidently to choose hope as its destination; it will never reach it and so will never be proved false.

In *One-Way Street* Benjamin writes of one's first glimpse of a
village or city in the countryside; it is "so incomparable and so
irrecoverable" because "in it distance resonates in rigorous connection with nearness. Habit has not yet done its work." The
glance that the adult casts on his childhood is determined not
least by the wish to escape from the ordinary. The journey,
however, is not into something entirely different; it is into that
time when the habitual was not yet habitual, into the experiences of the "for the first time." "Once we begin to find our way
about a place, that earliest image can never be restored" (*Reflections*, 83). This earliest image, which is a promise, comes to the
adult not only from early childhood, but also from distant
cities.

There is yet another factor linking the description of these
cities with the Berlin book. The foreign surroundings do not
just replace the distance of childhood for the adult; they turn
him into a child again. Many passages in Benjamin's writings
evince this feeling. Of San Gimignano we read that the town
"does not look as if one could ever succeed in approaching it.
But once one does, one is drawn into its lap and is unable to
concentrate on oneself because of the humming of crickets and
the shouting of children" (IV:364). Here the children's real
screaming illustrates the process intended by the metaphor, but
it simultaneously interrupts this process as well. The conclusion
of the section on Moscow's transport system, in contrast, is

more straightforward. There he describes the low sledges which afford no downward view but only "a tender, rapid skimming along stones, people, and horses," and he remarks that on them "one feels like a child gliding through the house on a stool" (*Reflections,* 112). That this is more than a chance association is shown by an observation at the beginning of the description of Moscow: "The childhood stage starts right upon arrival. On the thick sheet ice of these streets walking must be learned anew" (*Reflections,* 99). The intensity of the melancholic happiness accompanying these sentences, without being explicitly expressed, is first revealed in a page of *Berliner Kindheit* that later provided a commentary on the passage. There the adult writes of the child's set of reading boxes.:

The longing that it awakens in me proves how much a part of my childhood it was. What I am really seeking in it is the latter itself; my entire childhood, as it lay in the grasp with which the hand slid the letters along the ledge on which they were lined up. The hand can still dream of this grasp, but can never awake and execute the gesture. In like manner, many an individual may dream of how he learned to walk. But that is of no help to him. He can walk now, but never again learn to walk.

The repetition of the "for the first time," the return to the earliest image: both of these experiences seemed to be lost forever, but they still exist in the shelter of foreign lands.

4

Benjamin's descriptions of foreign cities thus derive from impulses that are no less personal than those underlying *Berliner Kindheit.* This does not mean, however, that he was insensitive to foreign reality. Indeed, a foreign city can fulfill its secret task of turning the visitor into a child only if it appears as exotic and as picturesque as the child's own city once appeared to him. When abroad Benjamin surrenders with astonishment and curiosity to all the impressions streaming in upon him, like a child standing wide-eyed in a labyrinth he cannot fully compass. The images he offers the reader could hardly be richer, more colorful, or more precise. And yet, *what* he experiences seems just as relevant to his "Search for Lost Time" as the way in which he experiences them. Unlike Proust's search, Benjamin's is borne along by historical and sociological impulses. He is seeking a way out of sclerotic late-bourgeois society, enslaved to the principle of individualism, back to the lost origins of society itself. The protest that the young Hegel and Hölderlin raised against "positivity" in the name of living becomes audible again in Benjamin. This accounts for his participation in the German Youth Movement, as his essay "The Life of the Students" attests (II:75–87). From this point of view, the links between Benjamin's portraits of such different cities as Naples and Moscow become evident. In the South—in Marseilles, Naples, and San Gimignano—he encountered a collective life that had not yet become alienated from its origins (and that was the very opposite of the isolation he coldly describes at the beginning of "Nordische See"). In the Soviet Union of 1926, on the other hand, he was able to observe a society in the process of formation. All the same, archaic and revolutionary seemed more closely related than the usual distinction between conservative and progressive would have it. And here he was not thinking solely of that idea of primitive communism which the Russia of the 1930s, already becoming a police state, betrayed with a positivity that mocked dialectical theory. The old in Naples and the new in Moscow are linked by more than just the fact that "to exist is a collective matter," as the following lines on Naples make clear:

The architecture is as porous as this stone. Building and action interpenetrate in the courtyards, arcades, and stairways. In everything they preserve the scope to become a theater of the new, unforeseen constellations. The definitive, the stamped, is avoided. No situation appears intended forever, no figure asserts it's "thus and not otherwise." This is how architecture, the most binding part of the communal rhythm, comes into being here. (*Reflections*, 165f.)

This picture stands in bold contrast to the meticulousness characteristic of the North. Benjamin notes, for example, that the typical house in Bergen "still has strict boundaries." At the same time, the Naples portrait finds its analogy in the movement into which everything in Moscow has been plunged. Benjamin describes in detail the programmed "Remonte," which likewise did not tolerate anything definitive and which, as it

were, stretched life out "on the laboratory table." "In this dominant passion there lies as much naive will to do good as boundless curiosity and playfulness. Little is more decisive in Russia
today. The country is mobilized day and night" (*Reflections,*
106). Private life, which had scarcely been allowed to develop in
the South, has been "abolished" by bolshevism. There is a
strange similarity in Benjamin's descriptions of the apartment
houses in Moscow and in Naples. Once again, the children
form the noisy background. They fill the streets and courtyards
in countless hordes, as if they did not belong to individual
families. The adult whose lonely youth was spent in a villa, as a
"prisoner" of Berlin's old West End (IV:287), seems to cast a
longing glance at the community these children enjoy. And it is
not only the children who are childish here. The Russians,
Benjamin says, are constantly playing, no matter what the situation. "If a scene for a film is being shot on the street, they forget
where they are going and why, tag along for hours, and arrive
at the office in a state of bewilderment" (*Reflections,* 110f.). It is
only the last word of the sentence that reminds the reader that
it is adults, not children, who are being described. And since
even the adults are like children, it becomes necessary to call
upon Lenin's authority for that astonishing maxim "time is
money."

Benjamin returned from his trip "with mixed feelings at
best," as Friedrich Podszus reports in his biographical sketch.[3]
Reading Benjamin's description of early Soviet Russia, we can
sense his suspicion that this dynamism would turn into stasis
and the freedom into terror. In particular, the display of images of Lenin seems to have intensified Benjamin's suspicion,
and the last section of his essay is devoted to the cult that was
growing up around them. "In corners and niches consecrated
to Lenin, they appear as busts; in the larger clubs, as bronze
statues or reliefs; in offices, as life-size half-length portraits; in
kitchens, laundry rooms, and storerooms as small photographs" (missing from *Reflections,* cf. IV:348). An even clearer
indication of Benjamin's premonition of the threat to the living
inherent in the new positivity of the dead image is his observation that babies are called *Oktyabr* (October) "from the moment
they are able to point to Lenin's picture "(*Reflections,* 103). No

less revealing is the metaphor in the final sentence describing the market on the Sucharevskaya: "Since the selling of icons is considered a branch of the picture and paper trade, these booths with pictures of saints tend to be located near paper goods stands, so that everywhere they are flanked by pictures of Lenin, like a prisoner between two policemen" (*Reflections*, 102).

5

It is metaphor that makes Benjamin's city portraits what they are. It is the source of their magic and, in a very precise sense, their status as poetic writing. The very purpose of these texts, to convey the experience of alienation and of being a foreigner, is first accomplished through the medium of language, which here is a language of images. The quest for lost time and for what takes its place is no less bound to language than the attempt to take possession of what one has already found. Name and image are the two poles of this field of force. In the labyrinth of the foreign city "every step one takes . . . is on named ground. And where one of these names happens to fall, in a flash imagination builds a whole quarter about the sound. This will long defy the later reality and remain brittly embedded in it like glass masonry" (*Reflections*, 99). While one is waiting for reality, it is preceded by its name, which functions as its surrogate. The name, however, creates its own reality. The competition between the two always ends, to be sure, with the victory of objective reality, but this is very often a Pyrrhic victory: its name is disillusion. Many pages of Proust's novel are devoted to this same theme, which already appears in the Romantic writers and which is revived by Benjamin.

The counterpart of this theme is the process by which reality becomes an image. "Finding words for what lies before one's eyes—how hard that can be! But when they do come they strike against reality with little hammers until they have knocked the image out of it, as out of a copper plate" (IV:364). Thus begins Benjamin's description of San Gimignano, which, not without reason, is dedicated to the memory of the author of the "Lord

Chandos Letter" and written in the year of his death. The potential field in which reality oscillates between name and image requires a separation; it requires the distance of time or of space. For the ordinary has long since absorbed its name and dispelled expectation; it will never again be transformed into an image. But whoever voyages into his past finds that reality and name constantly break apart again. It may be that the name has outlived the reality and now takes its place in memory as its phantom; it may be that in those "for the first time" experiences the name was there before the reality was experienced or that the experience was there before it received a name, so that it remained there without being understood, like the prophetic writing which invisibly glosses the text in the book of one's life. Whether he described the Berlin of his childhood or some foreign city, the consciousness of this separation rarely left Benjamin. It is difficult to say, though, if this was more a source of joy or of pain to him. In any case, it is only against this background that we can understand the following episode from his voyage on the North Sea:

In the evening, heart heavy as lead, full of anxiety, on the deck. For a long time I follow the play of the gulls. . . . The sun has long since gone down, and in the east it is very dark. The ship travels southward. Some brightness is left in the west. What now happened to the birds or—to myself?: that occurred by virtue of the spot that I, so domineeringly, so lonely, selected for myself in my melancholy in the middle of the quarter-deck. All of a sudden there were two flights of gulls, one to the east, one to the west, left and right, so entirely different that the name gull fell away from them. (IV: 385f.)

Melancholy sees only the dark side of everything. The tension between name and reality, which is the origin of poetry, is only experienced painfully, as the distance separating man from things. The experience that Benjamin reports, without reflecting upon it, breaks through this pain. The chiaroscuro of the sky tears reality asunder and abolishes the identity which made naming possible in the first place. The gulls' name falls away from them; they are now only themselves, but as such they are perhaps closer to man than if he possessed them by virtue of knowing their name.

6

These remarks do not yet adequately convey the meaning of this experience, which also brings to light the inverse of that which gives rise to metaphor in Proust as well as in Benjamin. Here the name falls away from the gulls because the sky divides them into groups, and the difference becomes greater than that which unites them, while in metaphor two different things cease to be identical to themselves because they are superimposed through an analogy discovered by the writer. As Proust himself came to realize, metaphor aided him in his search for lost time. Like the experience with the madeleine, metaphor should lift man beyond temporality through the bond it creates between a moment in the present and a moment in the past. In Benjamin as well simile can assist memory when it seeks tokens of the future in the past. In such instances, the two members of the simile are related as a text that one actually experiences is related to its prophetic commentary, which is first deciphered by memory. We may take as an example the "Pilfering Child" of *One-Way Street* (72f.), who becomes the first-person narrator of *Berliner Kindheit*. "His hand," we read, slipped through "the chink of the barely open larder . . . like a lover through the night." Yet in Benjamin metaphor is no more restricted to a single function than it is in Proust; on the contrary, it serves as a rule for the descriptive process itself. Benjamin seems to have shared Proust's view that the enumeration of objects in a description can never lead to truth and that truth first appears at the moment when the author takes two different objects and reveals their essence by linking them in a metaphor based on a common property.[4]

The only thing that seems foreign to Benjamin's intentions here is the mention of "essence," for his frequent use of metaphor and simile in portraying foreign cities derives from other grounds. The language of images makes it possible to understand unfamiliar things without their ceasing to be unfamiliar. Simile brings distant things near while at the same time freezing them in an image protected from the ravaging force of habit. Metaphor helps Benjamin paint his city portraits as miniatures, much like his preferred form, the fragment.

Moreover, in their linking of nearness and distance, in their withdrawn existence, such miniatures resemble those favorite objects of Benjamin's: glass globes in which snow falls on a landscape. His figurative language evinces supreme artistic understanding. Benjamin was a master in the creation of twofold definitions through images:

What is sentimentality if not the flagging wing of feeling, which settles down anywhere at all because it can go on no further, and what, then, its opposite, if not this tireless movement, which so wisely holds itself back [and] settles down on no experience or memory, but rather remains hovering, grazing one after the other.[5]

Benjamin is often dissatisfied with simple metaphors, so he creates entire compositions with them, as in his description of Notre Dame de la Garde in Marseilles or in his evocation of the conflict between that city and its surrounding landscape. As each new image carries the comparison further, the danger grows that the bridge might not reach the other bank, and yet the link between the two banks becomes stronger with each new span. Sometimes, too, the image does not leave the language unaffected. Thus, Benjamin writes of Bergen, "Just as the inhabitants of remote mountain villages intermarry to the point of sickliness and death, so the staircases and corners of the houses have become intertwined." The new images are what make the comparison evident, although they themselves become possible only as a result of the comparison. Sometimes Benjamin resorts to the metaphoric conditional tense, which in its suggestion of experiment betrays the whole playful awareness and fragility of the metaphor. For example, "If this sea is the Campagna, then Bergen lies in the Sabine Hills" (IV:383). Despite such artistry, Benjamin never uses figurative language without real commitment. Indeed, it is largely responsible for an effect aptly characterized by T. W. Adorno: "What Benjamin said and wrote sounded as if it were conjured up out of a secret depth. Its power, however, came from its evidentness."[6]

Neither the secret nor the obviousness would be possible if it were true, as Hugo Friedrich asserts, that "the fundamental vocation of metaphor lies not in recognizing existing similarities but rather in inventing nonexistent ones."[7] Metaphor's achievement lies beyond this alternative. It is not concerned, of course, with what is at hand, but neither is it interested in inventing similarities; it seeks, rather, to find them. Metaphor originates in the belief that the world is built up of correspondences that can and should be recognized. In his description of Weimar, Benjamin writes:

In the Goethe-Schiller Archives the staircases, drawing rooms, display cases and reading rooms are white. . . . The manuscripts are bedded down like patients in hospitals. And yet, the longer one exposes oneself to this harsh light, the more one believes that he discerns a reason, unconscious of itself, underlying such institutions. (IV:353)

The metaphorist's glance proves to be that of the theologian's. Benjamin is a student of the baroque emblematists, whom he treats in his work *The Origin of German Trauerspiel*. And what is true of them is equally true of himself: what seems to be artistry and was once learned from books is nothing less than the exegesis of the Creation.

7

The city portraits are products of the years between 1925 and 1930; *Berliner Kindheit* was written after 1930. Anyone familiar with Benjamin's biography and works will grasp the significance of these dates. From the period before 1925, we may mention an essay he wrote at the age of twenty-two on Hölderlin, a work that would have marked a new epoch in the study of that poet had it become known at the time. (The essay was first published in 1955). Then came the great study of Goethe's *Elective Affinities* (1924) along with the major work on German baroque drama (1923–25), with which Benjamin vainly sought to qualify as a university lecturer at Frankfurt. It was only after Benjamin was obliged to give up the prospect of an academic career (his mind having been judged to be insufficiently academic) that he became a man of letters and a journalist. To earn a living, he began to write the articles for newspapers and journals that today contribute as much to his reputation as does his scholarly work. It is among these that we find the city portraits. Nothing earlier in his life had hinted at this activity, as becomes clear, for example, in reading a letter written in his student days in Berne (October 22, 1917), in which he told Gershom Scholem of his plans for the future (*Briefe*, 55). It would thus appear that it was the university, whose representatives rejected him, that was responsible for Benjamin's becoming the kind of writer it suspected him of being.

The fact that Benjamin wrote no more city portraits in the period after 1933 can also be explained by the date in question. At that time a story was circulating in the emigrant community about a Jew who planned to emigrate to Uruguay; when his friends in Paris seemed astonished that he wanted to go so far away, he retorted, "Far from where?" With the loss of one's homeland the notion of distance also disappears. If everything is foreign, then that tension between distance and nearness from which the city portraits draw their life cannot exist. The emigrant's travels are not the kind one looks back upon; his map has no focal point around which foreign lands assume a fixed configuration. After he had finished his book of reminiscences about Berlin, Benjamin did, it is true, devote the last ten years of his life to a work on Paris, the city in which he had long felt at home. This work, however, has nothing in common with the earlier city portraits. Benjamin had frequently written about Paris even while he was still living in Germany, but he had never tried to capture the city's traits in a miniature ("too near," he remarked in a note reporting a dream about Paris).[8] The path he entered on in Paris in search of Paris was thus the same one that—in the remark quoted at the start of this essay— he urged upon whoever undertakes to write about his native city: a journey into the past. The projected book, a montage of historical texts presented as if the city were writing its own memoirs, was to be called *Paris, Capital of the Nineteenth Century*.

Translated by Harvey Mendelsohn

Peter Szondi

Notes

* Translated as "Hope in the Past: On Walter Benjamin" by Harvey Mendelsohn, *Critical Inquiry* 4, no. 3 (Spring 1978): 491–506.

† Keeping in mind that one translation of *Bild* is "image," *Städtebilder* can also be read as a play on Benjamin's *dialektische Bilder*.

1. *Illuminations*, 257. Cf. also P. Szondi, "Hope in the Past: On Walter Benjamin," trans. H. Mendelsohn, *Critical Inquiry* 4, no. 3 (Spring 1978): 491–506.

2. This is how Benjamin expressed it in a dedication, cf. Szondi, ibid.

3. F. Podszus, "Biographische Notiz," in *Illuminationen* (Frankfurt a.M.: Suhrkamp, 1961), 44.

4. M. Proust, *A la Recherche du temps perdu* (Paris. Pléiade, n.d.), III, 8.

5. Benjamin, *Deutsche Menschen* (Franklin a.M.: Suhrkamp, 1962), 75f.

6. T. W. Adorno, "Introduction to Benjamin's *Schriften*," this volume, 3f.

7. H. Friedrich, "Nachwort" to K. Krolow, *Ausgewählte Gedichte* (Frankfurt a.M.: Suhrkamp, 1962).

8. Cf. IV:356ff. and IV:567ff.

Propaedeutics of Profane Illumination

Hermann Schweppenhäuser

For Rolf Tiedemann

The decision to publish Benjamin's writings on hashish in 1972 cannot be explained solely by the date of its appearance. The texts collected in Über Haschisch,* *now in the sixth volume of* Gesammelte Schriften, *bring together the residues of one of Benjamin's own publication plans. Four decades earlier, in response to Scholem's birthday wishes, Benjamin presented a state of the* oeuvre *report:*

Although many—or a sizeable number—of my works have been small-scale victories, they correspond to large-scale defeats. I do not wish to speak of the projects that had to remain unfinished, even untouched, but would like to name here the four books that mark the site of the ruins or disasters, the furthest boundary of which I am still unable to discern when I let my eyes roam over the next few years of my life. They include the Paris Arcades, the Collected Essays on Literature, the Letters, and **a truly exceptional book about hashish.** Nobody knows about the last subject, and for the moment it would be better if it remained between us.†

The 1972 volume includes all of Benjamin's writings on hashish. Two of them he published in fashionable places in 1930 and 1932; the remainder were unpublished texts.

In the following essay, Hermann Schweppenhäuser, one of the editors of Benjamin's Gesammelte Schriften, *approaches the writings on hashish as a philosopher-sleuth: he stalks the dialectic of subject and object in Benjamin's hashish-related activities and closely observes the separations of self in his "profane illumination." He is at his best when he shows the reification of aura in Benjamin's experiments. All of these themes critically probe traditional notions of experience, as Benjamin had in 1918 in his critique of Kant's "narrow" concept of experience. And Schweppenhäuser's reflections serve as a reminder that Benjamin—whether talking about "aura" or "illumination"— is treating lifelong concerns, which are ultimately accessible only by taking account of the full breadth of his writings.*

1

The essays and notes that Benjamin devoted to the characteristics of narcotic intoxication (*Rausch;* also "trance," "ecstasy") are, despite their fragmentary nature,[1] among the most authentic ever put to paper. He owed the insights wrested from this realm to his double perspective as a participant who gives himself willingly to the intoxication, but who at the same time, in the midst of passion, mobilizes the strength to articulate what is happening to him and to oppose it knowingly. When Benjamin, in an inspired essay, said of the early surrealists that "the loosening of the self in intoxication . . . [is] precisely the productive, living experience that allowed them to escape the spell of intoxication," he characterized in particular his own experience with hashish (*One-Way Street,* 227). Benjamin used the drug at infrequent intervals during the twenties and early thirties, and so far as we can judge from his notes, usually under conditions of controlled experiment in the presence of friends—the doctors Joël and Fränkel, both notable specialists in Berlin, as well as Benjamin's philosophical kindred spirit, Ernst Bloch. Less often, apparently, did he use them in the Baudelairean isolation of one concerned with nothing else but affording himself artificial paradises and allowing himself to be taken into the "secret fraternity of initiates," as it is expressed in the "Account of a Hashish Trance."[2] Yet to view the experiments, the object of these protocols and notes, as "heroic" events of the type in which the scientist performs an experiment upon himself, voluntarily laying his life and health at the altar of progress, would be to overlook what is characteristic about them. Benjamin's experiments with hashish do take place within the intellectual dimension, but without such dubious scientific pathos; and as little as they were aimed at an irrational flight from intellectualization, they took place within the realm of "illumination" that Benjamin called "profane," yielded by narcotic illumination (*One-Way Street,* 236f.) Benjamin's experiments correspond quite precisely to the specific cognitive intentions articulated in his most developed philosophical texts, intentions that would find expression above all in the extraordinary *Passagen-Werk,* whose prospecting forays, with their lightning-like illumination of things, bringing bits and pieces to the surface, have much in common with what Benjamin set down in the notes on intoxication and the experimental protocols, formulated as they are as discontinuous, utterly concise, and at the same time painfully incisive fragments. The escapist narcotic practices that have recently become commonplace scarcely have a spokesperson in Benjamin. There is no false, moralizing self-deception in his insight into "how deeply certain powers of intoxication are committed to Reason and its struggle for freedom."[3] Benjamin accurately saw how in the epoch of the decline and self-destruction of bourgeois society, both "the more common productive forces of nature as well as" the "more remote" forces—the powers of ecstasy—are "perverted and spoilt."[4] These forces drive the Subject back into himself altogether, and seal the self-alienation, the deformation that industrial production processes wreak upon people and things. In the pre-fascist and fascist eras, Benjamin was able to turn such deformation into a medium of experience, including self-enlightenment about the character of intoxication. Like the micrological explorations that typify his philosophizing as a whole, his experiences of intoxication bring to light surprising finds.

2

What distinguishes Benjamin's observations from most contemporary ones is their penetrative force and their unique character. They never remain at the level of simply noting the flood of images, which those who consume the drug today choose to describe with the unfortunate stereotype of loss of self or—even more unfortunately, because it betrays an affinity with psycho-technical manipulation—who promote rather than characterize, with terms such as consciousness-expanding or increased sensitivity. The so-called increase in sensitivity (*Sensibilierung*) is not an end in itself but a medium: Benjamin used it as a lever, which he drove into the most brittle points of the whole structure, which cultural petrification had long since made out of the apperceptive capacity, out of the interpenetration of senses and intellect, of Subject and Object. In the contours of the broken pieces Benjamin then reads the striving of Subject and Object toward one another and determines the deformation effected by cultural pressures. Benjamin was able to articulate the one (the Subject) as delicately as he did the other (the Object), precisely tracing the contours of the fissures and the shattered. In each case the word about the object was coaxed from the object itself. Benjamin wrote in fact exactly as he once, entranced, indicated he wished to do: so that what was written "was drawn from the things themselves as wine from grapes" (VI:586). He did not leave things at intoxicated, ecstatic imaginings, as if they sprang from nature: they were to "make possible . . . a pure, filtered, intellectual yield" (VI:587). This filtrate is none other than the concentrated thing itself, and it is not without the person who knows how to bring it to its own essence. In this way Benjamin offers the essence of the experience of intoxication, and at the same time something more; namely, that which forms the content of this experience and upon which light falls beyond the illumination of intoxication itself: the experience of sobriety and of thinking, which reveals itself as "eminently narcotic," as well as that which is apparently the most severely opposed to intoxication, the monad-like and assured self, "that most frightful drug" of all (*One-Way Street*, 237). "What one writes down the following day is more than an enumeration of rapid, successive impressions. During the night, the trance cuts itself off from everyday reality, with fine, prismatic edges; it forms a kind of figure," it shrivels up and leaves behind "the form of a flower" (*One-Way Street*, 220). It was for the sake of such figures, in which experience is precipitated, that Benjamin gave himself to intoxication. If the person who cheats himself of such yields, remaining trapped within the experimentally contrived trance and within bare facticity, can be called *intoxication's positivist*, then Benjamin is its *dialectical theoretician*, who, as Hegel put it, must be "inside things" in order to transcend them.

Without doubt the experience of intoxication is related to that speculation, which pulls down the barriers between Subject and Object and which forces the coalescence of thing- and I-fixations within the whole. Narcotic intoxication has long been used—or at least has created a hallucinatory and imaginary

remedy—against physical pain and against the locking-in of the
Subject behind the petrifying imperatives imposed by the func-
tionalism of caste and division of labor. In the same way speculative thought has been available to oppose instrumental reason
and has sought to heal the suffering the latter has caused in
Nature and the Subject. In the speculative reconciliation of
Subject and Object, the healing should be complete: but that
offered by means of the concept is as idealist and imaginary as
the redemption by means of drugs in intoxication. In the materialist dialectic, however, speculative thinking becomes sober.
In a not dissimilar way, narcotic intoxication "comes to its
senses" in the form of the "profane illumination" that Benjamin tested in his own experiments—that "materialist, anthropological inspiration, to which hashish, opium, or whatever
else can provide a propaedeutics" (*One-Way Street*, 227). They
can do this because they mimetically achieve contact with objects and things. The materialist dialectic—originally in the
form of the critique of political economy—penetrates the
fetishism of the object as "thing" world (*Dinglichkeit*), the existential "world" of projective objectification. This is the source of
that "materialist inspiration" which grasps that magical essence
of the world of things which has kept both subject and objects
under its spell. But just as the spear heals the wound that it has
made, it is profane, narcotic illumination that offers a vision of
profanity and stirs within it the slumbering potential that would
not let it remain debased profanity.

3

Benjamin knew that what led him to seek preliminary schooling
in profane illumination was not escapism, not the "subaltern
wish" to "escape from melancholy" as he has the narrator express it in the Myslowitz story (a story into which, in the manner
of E. T. A. Hoffmann, Benjamin transformed his own drug
experiments). He used drugs, as for instance in Marseilles (the
setting of that story), in order "to duck under that magic hand
with which the city had taken me gently by the scruff of the
neck" (IV:732). It is through the guidance of this hand that the
city first reveals its true physiognomy to the compliant, teaches

him to see what it contains, differently than, for example, someone who—insensitive like the Sunday hunter—strides through Nature, vaingloriously, with resounding, stomping feet, only to see it flee before him. To the adept, things begin to speak, because the intoxicant has made him "tender" and courteous toward them and because all "repulsion disappears" (*One-Way Street*, 216, 218) and with it that idiosyncratic attitude—achieved at great cost via the hardening of libidinal and mimetic impulses into the rational authority of the ego— toward material surroundings degraded to dirt and ugliness.

The disencumbering imagination of intoxication (*lösende Rausch-Imagination*) expands the banal perceptual world (*Merkwelt*) into "absolutely regal" space and time in which, for the hashish eater, "eternity" itself would not be too long. "Against the background . . . of absolute duration and immeasurable space, a wonderful, beatific humor dwells all the more fondly on the contingencies" of that perceptual world (*One-Way Street*, 216), which lose the instrumental- and sign-character to which their essence as objects has been reduced, frozen, by a purposive-rational perspective. The "immense sensitivity evinced by hashish" brings about the drawing close to the essence of objects, the same submission to the material that a materialist anthropology grasps as the constitutively human element of the Passion, and which threatens precisely to turn sensibility into suffering when the communication between objects, things, and subjectivity—whether it be articulated mystically, narcotically, or the unintoxicated experience of deformation—is not understood (VI:589).

He who enjoys profane illumination stands in an extraterritorial relation to the world of sobriety, which despises him. Not because he somehow floats high above the world of sobriety but because he is deeply submerged in it and keeps company with those things that are as suspicious and disreputable to the sober—who keep both people and things at a distance— as every association with what is discarded, despised, and oppressed is for the bourgeois. It is this indignation of the sober that provides the foundation of the grand union of all profane *illuminati:* the readers and thinkers, the opium eaters, those who indulge their talent for waiting or strolling, for dreaming or ecstasy or intoxication, the *poètes maudits*. Their sense of being misunderstood, the desperation to which they are pushed by the sober, is the reverse side of their accord with everything despised and damaged. Those in league with reality, in the absence of profane illumination, are right to suspect the secret presence of powers of insurrection, the revolt of everything deformed wishing to regain its unmutilated form. Whosoever is tenderly "against things" and—as esoteric poets have put it—"especially against words" (VI:598) stands for humanized nature and thereby also for naturalized and whole people, before whom those who have become accustomed to the false and the denatured and inhuman must fear the worst: namely, the turnaround of things.

Benjamin made quite explicit the affinity of the imaginative production in intoxication to artistic production. It is not simply that the observer of these experiments is able to preserve something of the verbal chemistry of someone who speaks from within a trance. "The hashish trance undergoes a kind of evaporation of the imagination into verbal aromas in which the actual imaginative substance in the word . . . is completely vaporized" (VI:598). At the same time this becomes transposed into the aroma of the *name* like the words in a poem by Mallarmé, liberated from their coinage, their mere sign-character. Characteristically, Benjamin himself formulated the relationship—but also the specific difference—in his own protocol of the Marseilles trance: he recognized in the "riddle of the ecstasy of trance" the joy of "unraveling a ball of thread," and he identifies both that joy and the joy of trance with "the joy of creation." The subterranean scheme linking all three proves to be the Ariadne motif of the purposeful Theseus, who finds his way through the Minoan labyrinth. "We proceed," in the labyrinth of trance as in the world of creativity, "forward: but in doing so we not only discover the twists and turns of the cave, but we also enjoy this pleasure of discovery against the background of the other, rhythmical bliss of unraveling the ball. Such an assurance in the artfully wound skein which we unwind, is that not the joy of all productivity, at least in its prosaic form? And under the influence of hashish we are enraptured prose beings of the highest order. *De la poésie lyrique*—

pas pour un sou" (*One-Way Street,* 220). Hashish, and the patient-delighting untangling process that knows deep down that it remains on the right track, grants that which lyric poetry only strives after, what it must appeal to; and the fact that the latter, by contrast, withholds something makes the difference here. To see the correspondence between the "work of intoxication," which is precisely analogous to dreamwork, and Theseus's escape from the labyrinth rather than to the tale of Daedalus and Icarus reveals a genuine materialist inspiration. For Daedalus's upward swing resembles that of idealism itself. Daedalus, who lands happily in Sicily, offers an allegory of idealism's triumph, of which the lyric poem also typically partakes. Icarus, who plunges into the sea, provides an image of idealism's failure. It is proof of the profundity of Benjamin's meditative experience that it does not mistake the pleasures of intoxication or creativity for mere effusiveness, the hollow flight toward the sun in the manner of the idealist cult of the creative genius or of Art Nouveau, whose Solness figures tumble like Icarus from the dizzy heights.

In an illuminating note, Jöel, the observer during another experiment, sketches the peculiar intertwining of idealist and materialist intention: viz., that expression and concept always precede the matter itself; the profound dissatisfaction with all forms of articulation when the innermost essence of the matter eludes their grasp, only to give itself freely and unexpectedly in peripheral matters, as if taking pity on this resignation of expression as long as it openly admits the fact and does not draw from this failure in expression the apparent virtue of rigid and aggressive categorization:

For the hashish trance, it is an occurrence both familiar and characteristic that speech is bound up with a form of resignation, that the person intoxicated has already forgone expressing what truly moves him, and that he makes an effort to express rather something trivial, unserious in place of the authentic but inexpressible . . . that—this is most remarkable and most in need of explanation—the . . . to some extent truncated utterance may be much more remarkable and profound than anything that might correspond with what was "meant." (VI:601)

This remark characterizes faithfully the well-entrenched mechanism of traditional theory construction, the expectation and inevitable resignation of the predominant attitude of knowledge, which always dogmatically presupposes the dichotomy of the authentic and the inauthentic rather than securing the dialectic of essence and appearance by giving itself over to the Object (*Sache*) and making the cognitive subject (*Erkenntnissubjekt*) into the mouthpiece through which it may speak. This well-entrenched mechanism reproduces itself in intoxication, which on the one hand acknowledges its idealist character by doing so, but on the other hand, through a mimetic loosening (*Lockung*) materialistically flips it over, so to speak, and allows that which is articulated in the experience of intoxication, that "truncated utterance," the inconsequential and accidental, to appear as the—fundamentally not intended—more profound and actually more substantial. "Life is not light, but the refracted color" (*Faust II*, Act 1, scene 1). In scraps (*Abhub*) there glimmers darkly the Absolute—that Other which, as Adorno said, appears in "consummate negativity" as the mirror image of script.[5] If Benjamin could say philosophically that the eternal is rather the ruffle on a dress than any asserted and dubious Primary, Transcendental, Original, then the experience of intoxication confirms just that, when in it the sphere of the penny-dreadful coalesces with that of "the most profound theological" intentions.[6] The Absolute appears sunken deep into profanity. "The profoundest truths . . . possess a force powerful enough . . . to mirror themselves in their own way even in the irresponsible dreamer" (VI:565f.), to *reflect* themselves in the manner of the dialectic of Essence and Appearance, in which the former is hidden in the latter and in the latter the inadequacy of being mere appearance points to that essence which it wishes to be. Benjamin construed this dialectic as a dialectic at a standstill; he inwardly balked at being borne over the fissures in the petrified antagonisms of modernity by any mechanism of dialectical progression. This is the reason for his exercise (in the face of a problematic progressivism) of absorption (*Versenkung*), stationary concentration, and the anachronistic practice of illumination, such as in the experience of intoxication, with its retarding, regressive effect. But by this very insistence on the crystalline figure, this penetration of the point, this working away at the frozen "image," the petrified structure becomes possessed of a dynamism, of a swarming chaos under the micrological gaze, which deciphers what has been congealed as a part of the process, which it had not posited dogmatically at the outset and which it least of all attributes to blind social dynamism.

4

Immersion in things material is not the same thing as a cult of materiality, but rather its disenchantment. "Thought tackles the thing as if it wanted to change itself into touching, tasting and smelling. Through such secondary sensuousness," Benjamin hopes "to penetrate down to the veins of gold that no classificatory procedure can reach, but without succumbing to the contingency of blind intuition."[7] Benjamin extended such empiricism to include experiments in intoxication. Tasting, touching, and smelling are joined by seeing. Visual touching of the narcotically illuminated image may seem an intoxicated and blind intuition but is in fact discerning clear-sightedness, in which the shining *surface* (the literal aura) and the overprecisely drawn *façade* (the ornament) become the truth about what lies beneath. The secret fetishism of material things is seldom experienced more distinctly than in the efforts of Benjamin's thought, which his practice of illumination means to support, or to supply with luminous power—similar to the way certain surgical probes are equipped with a light source. "There is no more lasting legitimation of *crock* than the realization that with its help one can penetrate at once into that hidden, generally most inaccessible world of surfaces represented by the ornament" (VI:603). The ornament becomes the paradigm of the structural, coagulated in thing-ness (*Dinglichkeit überhaupt*). Its study throws light on how this coagulation occurs: via *reification*. Benjamin pointedly states what happens during this study. "The smoker of opium or eater of hashish experiences the power of a gaze that can take in a hundred places from a single spot" (VI:607). This is penetration not of the core, but of its shell, the careful dissection of which is actually the properly understood core. This observation is as self-evident as it is paradoxical: "I was . . . less submerged in thought, but more deeply inside" (VI:650)—a succinct formula for profane enlightenment. The process of reification forms a crust over the life of multivalent thing-ness. This multivalency becomes understandable in the "multiple meanings of the ornament" and in the "archetypal phenomenon" of "manifold interpretability" (VI:603f.). This does not imply perspectivism of one's viewpoint, that is, what subjective arbitrariness and empathy impose on things, but the objective "multitude of aspects, contents, and meanings" itself, which resides in all things (VI:604). "I became deeply absorbed in the cobblestones in front of me. . . . It is often said: stones instead of bread. Now these stones *were* the bread of my imagination, which was suddenly seized by a ravenous hunger to taste what is the same in all places and countries" (*One-Way Street,* 220f.)—the ever-the-same and unresolved sameness of existing reality, above which the veils of phantasmagoria flutter back and forth, through which the ever-the-same itself seems to move, to flutter, to "proceed." Phantasmagoria are ideological stylizations of reality mistaken for reality itself. They are that *intoxication of sobriety,* that idealism of construction, which persistently misunderstands its constitutive generation within the constituted, which takes the constituted to be the world as such, and which accuses it of the intoxication of profane illumination. However, it is precisely such profane illumination that becomes aware of the difference between the generation of phantasmagoria and generation of imagination, which "loosens and lures the things from their familiar context," a context phantasmagorically constituted and stylized (VI:564). Narcotic trance exposes the material nature of real things, the constitutive schematism that forms them and from which they want to withdraw. Schematizing instrumental reality is denounced as intoxication. The theme of aura, with which Benjamin deals in extremely impressive trance-variations, connects subtly and seamlessly with Benjamin's theoretical reflections on the phenomenon of aura.

The true aura is "the ornament." It appears "in all things" and "not just in certain things as people think." Phantasmagorical constitution of the object does not penetrate that stylized or ornamental aspect which the aura confers on everything it has constitutively transformed. Instead, it pushes the aura toward the sphere of the illusory, in which "appearance" is expressly produced, by division of labor, artistic-artificially. The auratic shimmer, for which it is commonly taken, represents reification again reified, an intensification of universal fetishistic deception, which is inexorably bound up with the entire constitutive production process. This deception is noted by the gaze of profane illumination, which preserves the aura in every object but which sees through the *auratic* as *reification of the thing*, seizing that stylization or "ornamental enclosure in which the object or character is firmly placed, as if in a lined case" (VI:588). This is why the loss of aura, which Benjamin anticipated in his essay on reproducibility, may not necessarily mean loss of object. Benjamin's work is suffused with the idea that at least enlightened, materialistic, artistic production releases the essence enclosed in this case. This is his metaphor for the stratum beneath the artificial crust, for the commodity character. The case, which signifies it metaphorically, is itself a thing produced and joins the reification of aura, its contours as commodity, which encircle the object, just as formerly the firm lines joined to produce the *Gestalt* (Greek: *eidos*). This is philosophy's hypostasized "form," which long before the capitalist definition of object and man as having exchange values and before the delineation of "Mine" and "Thine" created and transfigured the reified character of the object. But where the artificial aspect comes out of what was really meant to be eternal nature, as in the late Vincent van Gogh, "where the aura is painted as part of every object" (VI:588), with pastiness and drastically emphasized ornamentation intruding almost embarrassingly, in which the objects vibrate and petrify simultaneously: *there* aura is disavowed, there the representation, which disparages the reified vogue, is derided as mannered and insane. The world is artificial in a way that it should not be. This is expressed by the inspiration of both art and intoxication. The "boxed condition" that the narcotic knows, "the lonely chamber" in which man locks away "the images" (VI:596)—these threateningly transmuted products of his own making—reveal the truth about the binnacle (*Gehäuse*) of the world: the transcendental projection

room, in which both the projecting subject and objective pro-
jecta are spellbound. The entranced person looks at things as if
"through glass" (VI:564). They thereby become vitreous and
luminescent themselves, like the panes of the *laterna magica*.
However, this glassy and petrified character denounces natural
objects as themselves artificial and dead. Conversely, the unerr-
ing feeling produced by the ecstatic illumination knows about
these "dead and present objects," that they can "evoke a longing" comparable only to "looking at a person whom one loves"
(VI:607).

If consciousness of reification betrays itself with the cadaveric
rigidity of things present, if it mistakes the latter's mechanical
reflexes for motions of life, then the longing(s) of the suffering
illuminati pull one toward that life, which lives on in the innermost part of the extinguished and dead, and pull one toward
the object underneath the reification, which, like someone un-
loved, awaits the redemption of love. Death represents only
sleep continued under a spell and "every image . . . a sleep of its
own" (VI:616). This is being said about things unredeemed,
which have yet to open their eyes, just like fairy-tale figures
sleeping under the magic spell. Images, representatives for objects trapped under a crust of reification, are released from a
rigidity by the "*open sesame!*" of profane illumination, similar to
the Prince's awakening of Sleeping Beauty by counter-magic.
When Benjamin writes "Important thoughts have to be put to
sleep for a long time" (VI:602), he, unfathomably, means both:
first, the sleep of the world, its existing content as dream production, which is not meant to be touched by enlightenment;
second, the healing subsiding (*Einschlafen*) of instrumental rationality, of the controlling ego in intoxication, which opens up
its eyes while dreaming about itself, which may produce the
relevant "important thought," because while asleep it can speak
itself rather than be spoken of by controlling awakeness, which
in turn only disfigures self-enlightenment speaking (for) itself.

5

When the experience of intoxication helps to gain insight into
the essence of reality (*Dinglichkeit*) and the monstrosity of its

reification, it sheds light above all onto the subject himself entangled herein. Such light is perhaps even more difficult to
bear than the light which narcotic illumination casts on the
object. This is so because the intoxicated ego reveals the "Real
Ego" as truncated. The discontinuity in the allegedly homogenous core of personality is clearly shown once the Real Ego
becomes loosened by ecstasy. What is revealed is the thorough-
going ambiguity and ambivalence of the characteristic identity
features of the Real Ego. In particular, egotism and sociality
expose their inner dialectic. Doubt is cast on the social character
of personality, which is founded equally on the constituents of
"I" and "Thou." The relationship of "Thou" unveils itself during intoxication as a response to the fear of being left alone,
which is something the truncated "I" (Ego) cannot cope with.
At the same time, the Ego diminished in this way is the more
touchy and selfish and needs the "presence of others"—who
are meant to protect it—"as delicately moving relief figures
near the pedestal of one's own throne" (VI:562). The primeval
image of the throne, which flashes up during intoxication,
denounces self-absorption as despotism that denatures the
longed-for others to mere pedestal figures. The participants
lose "their individuality" and are present "as it were, only
generically." The experience of intoxication sharply registers
the *heteronomy* of this generic character: it is "something servile
and slavish" (VI:575) in the others. The usefulness of "Thou"
betrays its double meaning: first, the meaning of the thing-ness
of the Ego and, second, the meaning of the benevolent tolera-
tion, which can only be granted to the Ego by a fellow Ego. But
due to the same ambivalence of self-absorption, the fellow Ego
collides with the first Ego. The alleged harmony of all turns out
to be "bad simultaneity" of all, and disharmony "of the need to
be alone and the need to stay together with others" (VI:562).
This is reminiscent of Kant's concept of unsociable sociability
and Schopenhauer's parable of the hedgehogs. Intoxication,
contrary to the common view that it brings about a Dionysian
union, marks the misanthropic aspect of sociability, which in
turn results from boundless disappointment that the others are
not human beings after all. Yet this disappointment appears
closely associated with the "boundless benevolence," which

from the outset and automatically "with immeasurable pleasure" believes the others capable of everything. Solidarity of
intoxication mirrors the humane communion of all with all on
the basis of misanthropy. As Schopenhauer foresaw, it covers
up and at the same time confirms a boundless egotism. Boundless benevolence loves the other person as silent. This implies
that it hates him as soon as he speaks, as Ego makes claims
against another Ego: "he disappoints us painfully by his stray-
ing from the greatest object of all attention: we ourselves"
(VI:564). If egotism is experienced during a trance as a "cave"
and communication is experienced as fear of being dragged
out of the cave (VI:561), then in intoxication the image expresses only the monadological atomization of the subject in
real society, a subject who must look neither left nor right if it
wants to preserve itself. That the encapsulated self loses the
selfdom it set out to preserve is precisely what the experience of
intoxication records, which through the narcotically prepared
delusion becomes aware of the delusion, to which the subject of
self-preservation in mass society gravitates, though isolated
from himself as well as from others. It is important to insert a
reminder at this juncture that only the subject's readiness to
engage in narcotic experimentation, only his determination to
heighten concentration, impels the narcotic delusion of both
the subjectively and the objectively delusory. The common escape into narcotic delusion *without* this determination does not
penetrate delusion but confirms it, which explains "the dangerous" aspect of this form of profane illumination (*One-Way
Street*, 227). This escapism acquiesces to substitutive practices,
which—like ideology as a whole in late capitalism—have nothing to substitute but continue only to burn out the spent
(*ausgebrannt*) subject of alienation. Only with the *intoxicated
immersion in intoxication*—a paradoxical model of theoretical insistence—does the deceptive become apparent, as well as the
dissolving, the dissociation of the subject and its modes of behavior, which characterizes the frightening anthropomorphosis
of the subject of self-preservation. "The objectification (*Entäus-
serung*) of personality . . . encourages either an expansion of
partiality, such as one might ascribe to a divinity, or a kind of
impartiality typical perhaps of an animal" (VI:578). This obser-

vation of the experimenting person fits perfectly the participation of the ego-less Ego, which becomes increasingly abstract and relationless to the extent to which it participates in everything. This is the attitude of the indifferent spectator who, idolizing his own passivity together with his claim of absolute obedience, stylized the Ego to an image of a cold and apathetic God as spectator in the world theater, who only pulls the strings of marionettes and who is accompanied by soul-destroying apathy. Correspondingly, the intoxicated ego loses all distinction between "meaning and meaninglessness, between important and banal" (VI:578), just like the subject of statistical averages, of the process that transformed people into the disposable commodities of the labor market, thereby depriving them of their capacity to resist and to distinguish. During the experience of intoxication the intermittently surfacing consciousness of doubt signals the universal relativism within the social system. Here, with the disintegration of everything substantial in one functional entity, the old *scepsis* becomes itself totalitarian. But the perception denied to the social subject, just because he is reduced to functions and to functioning, returns in a flash to the narcotically and theoretically inspired person. He experiences in scepticism that negative moment that prevents scepticism from becoming total and that Hegel called the "self-completing scepsis." He also experiences in relativism the particular negation that prevents dialectics from dissolving into everything and nothing. While the distinction between important and unimportant becomes irrelevant to the alienated subject, his feigned indifference mirrors the "value-free" neutrality toward the whole (from smoothly polished "Being" to deformation and murder); the sensitized subject suffers painfully its relativity. "Part and opposite," "meaning and meaninglessness" present themselves to this subject with the same sharpness, but with painful distinction (VI:578). The object itself claims to be what it is, thereby protesting against abstract subsumption and pleading in favor of a substantial pluralism (and not an indifferent pluralism itself devoid of substance). The right of the object itself is illustrated by an expression quoted in a protocol of intoxication: "It is correct what you are saying, but I am right" (VI:579).

What seems at first like the unremarkable joke of someone who in the pluralism of competitors concedes compromisingly to the viewpoint of a competitor, a potentially mortal enemy, by underlining his own, is in the actual experience of intoxication (as in the theoretical-critical experience) an expression of that indispensable seriousness which is irreconcilable with what once was and which brought form to itself. Only the viewpoint that the irreconcilable is subterraneously mediated and emerges from *one* process in implacable multitude can do justice to this. In this way, to the sensitized (person) "affinities and identities" become obvious "in a deeper sphere" (VI:579). This is similar to contemplative experience of *coincidenta oppositorum* but is distinguishable from this by the "delightful feeling of continuity" (VI:579) that can be granted only by mimetic contact within materialistic inspiration. The profanely illuminated fantasy ravenously wants to taste the same in all places and countries, with the mute force of matter, with which it accommodates itself. This force can break through national and rational confines that artificially isolate fantasy but that cannot impede the force with which it is driven out of itself.

"Still the same world—and yet one has patience" (VI:617). Thus speaks profane illumination, which underneath the crust of the new world can feel the movement of the old, invariably still unreleased, truly new world. This patience resembles that ancient patience which awaits a birth, which trusts in the fact that the new is predeveloped to a sufficient degree in the womb of the old to survive the act of birth. To this patience "doing" would be "means for dreaming," whereas "contemplation" represents a means "to stay awake" (VI:616). Reflex-like praxis—this implies—marks the escape route, which leads away from the course of events; but what is reflected can intervene, like the witness awaiting a birth, who mimetically corresponds with what will be born.

Translated by Lloyd Spencer, Stephan Jost, and Gary Smith

Notes

* Edited by Tillman Rexroth (Frankfurt a.M.: Suhrkamp, 1972).

† Walter Benjamin/Gershom Scholem, *Briefwechsel 1933–1940* (Frankfurt a.M.: Suhrkamp, 1980), Letter 4.

1. According to Gershom Scholem's reliable report, Benjamin intended to write a book on aspects of intoxication, primarily about the historical-philosophical and speculative features. He aimed to penetrate what he had repeatedly thematized—with theological as well as materialistic profundity—as "illumination" and "profane illumination," as "rapture" or "trance" (*Entrückung*) and "immersion" (*Versenkung*). Regardless of the fact that the book remained only a plan, the reflections arising in the force field of his idea, and his notes and records, exhibit the reconditeness of Benjamin's intentions. Cf. *Briefe*, 556.

2. "Myslowitz-Braunschweig-Marseille," IV:729–37; cf. 732.

3. Unpublished letter to Max Horkheimer, Paris, February 7, 1938.

4. Ibid.

5. Theodor W. Adorno, *Minima Moralia*, trans. E. F. N. Jephcott (London: New Left Books, 1974), 247.

6. Cf. Rolf Tiedemann, *Studien zur Philosophie Walter Benjamins* (Frankfurt a.M.: Europäische Verlagsanstalt, 1965), 130

7. Cf. Theodor W. Adorno, "A Portrait of Walter Benjamin," in *Prisms* (Cambridge, MA: MIT Press, 1982), 240.

his intuitions about the meaning of the beautiful, and about the Luciferian depth of the "appearance" in which the beautiful conceals and reveals itself. Along the same line is the small piece of an autobiographical nature, about himself and his angel, to which I wish to direct attention here. It represents a depiction of Benjamin's self—disquieting, to be sure—so important to him that on two consecutive days he wrote it down in two versions. At such it seems to me illuminating and precious, even though it is admittedly very much in need of a commentary.

2

This piece, with a title that seems truly enigmatic, "Agesilaus Santander," is in a notebook of Walter Benjamin's that is to be found among his literary remains in Frankfurt, which after Theodor Adorno's death are under the control of a panel constituted to assume such responsibility. This notebook contains writings from the years 1931 and 1933, in which his most diverse observations, Marxist and wholly incompatible with Marxism, are intermingled. Thus it contains (pp. 15–16) "Reflections on Broadcasting" and (pp. 25–27), under the caption "Art for the People—Art for the Connoisseur," the summary of a discussion held in the autumn of 1931 with Willy Haas, the editor of the *Literarische Welt*, in which Benjamin, in Marxist terms, squarely defends the thesis that art is meant for connoisseurs of art. On pages 31–35 there follows a sketch, "Doctrine of Similarity,"[6] written during the spring of 1933 on the island of Ibiza after his flightlike departure from Berlin in March, which contains a theory of occult phenomena of which he sent me an abridged version (omitting essential material); only the latter has previously appeared in his *Schriften* (I:507–10). Afterward follows, on pages 37–39, the "Agesilaus Santander" in a shorter form (p. 39) dated Ibiza, August 12, 1933, and in a somewhat longer and final version (pp. 37–38) dated the following day. From April to October of 1933 Benjamin lived on Ibiza (in San Antonio), where he had first taken up residence from May to the middle of July 1932, a period from which the first pages of the notebook "Notes on the *Jugendstil*" possibly stemmed.

The circumstances under which the piece originated are not known. One may, however, raise the question posed to me by Peter Szondi during a discussion I had with him about the piece, whether "Agesilaus Santander" might not be the product of a fever delirium. According to Jean Selz (this volume, page 364), Benjamin had malaria in the summer of 1933. He indicates no exact dates, only that Benjamin left Ibiza in October. Opposed to this, to be sure, is the indication of Benjamin himself, who in a later application to a French administrative office—obviously in connection with his planned naturalization or extended residence permit in France—gave the dates and duration of his stays. We possess a copy of this application, according to which he left Ibiza on September 25, 1933. From there he jumps over to October 6 and indicates a Paris address for this date. According to a letter to me of October 16, 1933, from Paris, we know that he arrived in Paris seriously ill and that toward the end in Ibiza he had been "generally no longer healthy," and that the day of his departure from there "coincided with the first of a series of highest fever attacks." After his arrival in Paris, malaria had been diagnosed. Could he perhaps have already suffered from this malaria on August 12 and 13, six weeks before his departure? In his letter to me of July 31, 1933, in which he reports about the composition of the important piece, "Loggien" in *Berliner Kindheit*, he tells me that he had been ill for about two weeks. On the other hand, one finds there the passage, "The great heat has begun here. The Spaniards, who know its effects, speak of 'August madness' as a completely common thing. It gives me much pleasure to follow its onset among the foreigners." Obviously, then, he himself had not yet at this time felt its appearance. Nevertheless, one cannot exclude a possible connection between the origin of the piece and a first, still relatively slight, attack of malaria, however hypothetical this must remain. In any case, Selz in his recollections drew the indication from his later knowledge of the diagnosis of Benjamin's malaria, about which he learned only in Paris after Benjamin's return and thus provides no certain proof that the latter really had malaria as early as August. The whole problem carries little weight, I am convinced, for the understanding of the text, for the latter's construction and world of images have an immanent logic that does not differ from his usage in many other writings.

In what follows I reproduce the text of both versions of "Agesilaus Santander."

First Version

When I was born the thought came to my parents that I might perhaps become a writer. Then it would be good if not everybody noticed at once that I was a Jew: that is why they added to the name I was called two very unusual ones. I do not wish to divulge them. Suffice it to say that forty years ago parents could with difficulty see farther ahead. What they held to be a remote possibility has come true. But their precautions, meant to counter fate, were rendered without force by the one most concerned. Instead of making public the two provident names by his writings he locked them within himself. He watched over them as once the Jews did over the secret name they gave to each of their children. The latter did not come to know it before the day of their attainment of maturity. Since, however, that can occur more than once in life, and perhaps, too, not every secret name remains always the same and untransfigured, its transfiguration might reveal itself on the occasion of a new maturity. It does not, therefore, remain any the less the name that contains in itself all the life forces, and by which the latter can be summoned forth and guarded against the unauthorized.

Yet this name is in no way an enrichment of him who bears it. It takes away much from him, but above all the gift of appearing wholly as he was of old. In the room I last occupied, the latter, before he stepped out of the old name, armored and encased, into the light, put up his picture at my place: New Angel. The *kabbalah* relates that in every instant God creates an immense number of new angels whose only purpose is, before they dissolve into naught, to sing His praise before His throne for a moment. Mine was interrupted in doing so; his features had nothing about them resembling the human. As for the rest, he made me pay for having disturbed him at his work. For in taking advantage of the circumstance that I came into the world under the sign of Saturn—the planet of slow rotation, the star of hesitation and delay—he sent his feminine form, after the masculine reproduced in the picture, by way of the longest, most fatal detour, even though both were so very much adjacent to each other.

He did not, perhaps, know that thereby he brought to the fore the strength of him whom he accosted. For nothing can overcome my patience. Its wings resemble those of the angel in that very few pushes are enough for them to preserve themselves immovably in the face of her whom my patience is resolved to await. But it, which has claws like the angel and knife-sharp wings, does not look as though it threatens to pounce on her whom it has sighted. It learns from the angel how he encompasses his partner in his view, but then yields by fits and starts, and incessantly. He pulls him along on that flight[7] into a future from which he has advanced. He hopes for nothing new from the latter except the view of the person he keeps facing.

So I journeyed with you, no sooner than I had seen you for the first time, back from whence I came.

Ibiza, August 12, 1933

Second, final version

When I was born the thought came to my parents that I might perhaps become a writer. Then it would be good if not everybody noticed at once that I was a Jew. That is why besides the name I was called they added two further, exceptional ones, from which one could see neither that a Jew bore them nor that they belonged to him as first names. Forty years ago no parental couple could prove itself more far-seeing. What it held to be only a remote possibility has come true. It is only that the precautions by which they meant to counter fate were set aside by the one most concerned. That is to say that instead of making it public by the writings he produced, he proceeded with regard to it as did the Jews with the additional name of their children, which remains secret. Indeed, they only communicate it to them when they reach maturity. Since, however, this maturity can occur more than once in life, and the secret name may remain the same and untransfigured only to the pious one, its change might reveal itself all at once with a new maturity. Thus with me. It therefore remains no less the name which joins the life forces in strictest union and which is to be guarded against the unauthorized.

Yet in no way is this name an enrichment of the one it names. On the contrary, much of his image falls away when that name becomes audible. He loses above all the gift of appearing anthropomorphous. In the room I occupied in Berlin the latter, before he stepped out of my name, armored and encased, into the light, put up his picture on the wall: New Angel. The *kabbalah* relates that in every instant God creates an immense number of new angels, all of whom only have the purpose, before they dissolve into naught, of singing the praise of God before His throne for a moment. The new angel passed himself off as one of these before he was prepared to name himself. I only fear that I took him away from his hymn unduly long. As for the rest, he made me pay for that. For in taking advantage of the circumstance that I came into the world under the sign of Saturn—the star of the slowest revolution, the planet of detours and delays—he sent his feminine form after the masculine one reproduced in the picture by way of the longest, most fatal detour, even though both happened to be— only they did not know each other—most intimately adjacent to each other.

He did not, perhaps, know that the strength of him whom he thus wanted to accost could show itself best in this way: namely by waiting. Where this man chanced upon a woman who captivated him, he was at once resolved to lurk on her path of life and to wait until sick, aged, in tattered clothes, she fell into his hands. In short, nothing could enfeeble the patience of the man. And its wings resembled the wings of the angel[8] in that very few pushes were enough to preserve themselves long, immovably in the face of that which he was resolved no longer to leave alone.

The angel, however, resembles all from which I have had to part: persons and above all things. In the things I no longer have, he resides. He makes them transparent, and behind all of them there appears to me the one for whom they are intended. That is why nobody can surpass me in giving gifts. Indeed, perhaps the angel was attracted by a gift giver who goes away empty-handed. For he himself, too, who has claws and pointed, indeed knife-sharp wings[,] does not look as though he would pounce on the one who was sighted. He fixes his eyes on him firmly—a long time, then yields by fits and starts but incessantly. Why? In order to pull him along with himself on that way into the future on which he came and which he knows so well that he traverses it without turning around and letting the one he has chosen out of view. He wants happiness: the conflict in which lies the ecstasy of the unique,[9] ["once only"] new, as yet unlived with that[10] bliss of the "once more," the having again, the lived. That is why he can hope for the new on no way except on the way of the return home, when he takes a new human being along with him. Just as I, no sooner than I had seen you, journeyed back with you, from whence I came.[11]

Ibiza, August 13, 1933

3

Before I undertake to explain this thoroughly hermetic text, something must be said about the picture central to it, *Angelus Novus* by Paul Klee. That picture was painted by Klee in 1920 in Munich and carries the signature "1920/32." From 1919 to the end of his life, the work of Klee is interspersed with pictures and drawings of angels on some fifty sheets, in large part from the last years of his life. As his son Felix Klee wrote in a letter of

Paul Klee, *Angelus Novus*

March 1972, "it enticed Paul Klee to render the messenger of the gods—often even in human tragicomedy." Thus there happens to exist a picture *Engel bringt das Gewünschte* with the signature "1920/91" in which the angel seems rather like a waiter or waitress serving the order wished for by Klee. In the works and portfolios about Klee a whole number of such angels is to be found, above all from his later years, as, for example, in the two books by Will Grohmann, *Paul Klee* (1954) and *Paul Klee—Handzeichnungen (Sketches)* (1959). Since, as far as is known, no remarks by Klee himself are to be found about these angels, no reason exists in connection with what is to be considered here for going more closely into the sentences which Grohmann in 1954 (pp. 348–50) dedicated to this theme in Klee. There he attempts to place the angels closer to those of Rilke's "Duino Elegies" which, according to Grohmann, "like Klee's angels, live in the great unity embracing life and death and see in the invisible a higher order of reality" (p. 348). For an analysis of the significance and position possessed by Klee's picture *Angelus Novus* in Benjamin's life and thought, these (rather doubtful) pronouncements are not relevant, since Benjamin's contemplation of the picture was nourished by completely different motives, as will presently be shown.

Klee's picture was exhibited in May and June of 1920 in the great Klee Exhibition of the Hans Goltz gallery in Munich; in the latter's catalog, which appeared as a "special Paul Klee issue" of the periodical *Der Ararat,* it is listed on page 24 as number 245 but not reproduced. It is a relatively small watercolor, which was first reproduced at page length opposite page 128 in Wilhelm Hausenstein's book, *Kairuan oder eine Geschichte vom Maler Klee* (Munich: Kurt Wolff, 1921). Hausenstein, who lived in Munich, could have seen the picture while it was still in Klee's studio or at the Goltz gallery. It was later reproduced again—obviously from Hausenstein's book—in the monograph *Paul Klee* by Carola Giedion-Welcker (Stuttgart: Hatje, 1954), on page 184. At the time Benjamin was not in Munich, but he might have seen it at a small Klee Exhibition which took place in April 1921 in Berlin somewhere on the Kurfürstendamm, and which he mentioned as a special attraction in a letter to me of April 11, 1921 (*Briefe*, 262). I do not, however, even know whether the picture was actually exhibited there.

In any case it was returned to Goltz, for Benjamin obtained it in Munich, when he visited me there in the end of May and the beginning of June 1921. He brought me the picture with the request to keep it for him until he once more would have a permanent lodging in Berlin, where great personal difficulties had arisen in his life. Until the middle of November 1921 the *Angelus Novus* hung in the residence—first Türkenstrasse 98, later Gabelsbergerstrasse 51—I shared with my subsequent first wife, Elsa Burchardt, in whose room it was hanging, a fact to which Benjamin referred in several letters. On November 27, 1921, he had already received the picture in Berlin, where I had sent it to him according to his wish (*Briefe*, 282). Until his divorce it hung in the study of his residence at Delbrückstrasse 23, over the sofa, and later in his last residence of Prinzregentenstrasse 66. In the Hitler era a female acquaintance brought the picture to him in Paris around 1935. At the time of my visit in February 1938 it was again hanging in his large room at 10 rue Dombasle. When, in June 1940, he fled from Paris and stored his papers in two suitcases—which Georges Bataille (connected with Benjamin through the Collège de Sociologie, founded by Bataille) temporarily kept hidden in the Bibliothèque Nationale—Benjamin cut the picture out of the frame and stuffed it into one of the suitcases. And so after the war it made its way to Adorno in America and later in Frankfurt. Benjamin always considered the picture his most important possession, even though he obtained another picture by Klee in the preceding year, namely *Vorführung des Wunders*, but one I have never seen. When at the end of July 1932 he wanted to take his own life and wrote a testament, he designated it as the special personal gift he bequeathed me.

Klee's picture fascinated him most highly from the very first moment on and for twenty years played a significant role in his considerations, as Friedrich Podszus said in his biographical sketch about Benjamin, using a formulation expressed by me in the course of a conversation (*Illuminationen*, 441): as a picture for meditation and as a memento of a spiritual vocation. To be sure, the *Angelus Novus* also represented something else for

him: an allegory in the sense of the dialectical tension uncovered in allegories by Benjamin in his book about tragic
drama. In his conversations as well as in his writings, he frequently had occasion to speak of the picture. When he obtained
it we had talks about Jewish angelology, especially of the talmudic and kabbalistic kind, since at that time I was just writing
a piece about the lyric of the *kabbalah,* in which I gave a detailed
account of the hymns of the angels in the representations of the
Jewish mystics.[12] From my own long contemplation of the picture also stems the poem "Gruss vom Angelus," which I dedicated to Benjamin on his birthday on July 15, 1921, and which I
published in the notes to the collection of his letters (*Briefe*:
269).

In Benjamin's letters, the picture is first mentioned in a post-
card of June 16, 1921, which he and his wife Dora jointly wrote
me from Breitenstein on the Semmering, when the picture was
already on my wall. There the *Angelus Novus* is designated by
his wife as the "newly created protector of the *kabbalah,*" and
Benjamin himself indulged in humorous intimations in the
form of quotations from nonexistent periodicals. In the *Zen-
tralblatt für Angelologie* he pretended to have read: "Under the
influence of the Turkish climate the heavenly *Klee*-leaf has
added three new leaves. It is henceforth reckoned among the
species of the four-leaved (*lucerna fortunata*). We will keep our
subscribers informed about the further development of the
magic plant." In contradiction to this, he simultaneously quotes
Privatnachricht des Zentralorgans für Bücherlein (Private Report of
the Central Organ for Little Books): "The dear little demonology does not agree with the Angelus. He requests the removal
of the same to Berlin. Signed: Dr. Delbrück." The heavenly
Klee-leaf was, naturally, the picture by Klee hanging in the
Türkenstrasse, and the three new leaves referred to me, Elsa
Burchardt, and his friend Ernst Schoen, who was then visiting
with us in the Türkenstrasse. That at the time Benjamin did not
yet connect any Satanic-Luciferian thoughts with the picture
follows from his remark about the "little demonology" the
angel could hardly bear. This little demonology was a booklet
without title and text, consisting only of the reproductions and
symbols ("characters") of demons, in reality the *Tafelband* to *Dr.*

Fausts Höllenzwang, which had been published about 1840 in Stuttgart by lithography. The little book was originally in the possession of Benjamin,[13] who gave it to me as a gift in the latter half of April 1921, in gratitude for my intervention in a matter touching his life deeply; at that time he also suggested we adopt the familiar form of address "Du" instead of "Sie." I still have the book.

Benjamin frequently made use of the signature "Dr. Delbrück" in humorous or satiric communications; in doing so he alluded to the house of his parents at 23 Delbrückstrasse in Berlin-Grunewald. In the letters to me from the year 1921, he made several further references to the *Angelus Novus,* in whose name he held forth or thanked me about various matters. On August 4, 1921, when he accepted the offer of the Heidelberg publisher Richard Weissbach to edit a periodical for him and notified me of it (*Briefe,* 271), he had already decided to call it *Angelus Novus.* For the periodical, as he expressed himself in its prospectus (all that was to reach the printing stage), was from the beginning to have in common with the angel the ephemeral character of the latter. This ephemeral quality seemed to Benjamin the just price it had to exact for its striving after what Benjamin understood as true actuality: "Why according to a talmudic legend even the angels—new ones each moment in innumerable bands—are created so that, after they have sung their hymn before God, they cease and dissolve into the naught. Let the name of the periodical signify that such actuality as is alone true should devolve upon it" (II:246). Klee's picture itself is not mentioned here.

In the course of the years, Benjamin associated very diverse conceptions with the angel, whom he apostrophized in the text reproduced above. In an (unprinted) letter of November 18, 1927, shortly after my return from Europe to Jerusalem, he referred to my poem to the *Angelus* in a rather cheerful connection—in relation to the "University of Muri," invented by us, from whose *Akten* at that time I had had my brothers in Berlin, who were printers, print, with his active intercession, a *Philosophical Alphabet* which was dedicated to Benjamin and presented itself as the "official didactic poem of the Central and State University of Muri." Here he called my poem "the poem to the guardian angel of the university." The guardian angel of the *kabbalah* from the year 1921 has become the guardian angel of the University of Muri, in whose *Akten* a "philosopher" and a "kabbalist"—who in a traditional sense were neither a philosopher nor a kabbalist—made the traditional university and its scholars the object of their derision. The angel, not yet sunk in melancholy as he was later to be, still speaks to both of us, joined in a common cause. One "lays him down on twigs of roses [*Rosenzweigen*]," which is to say he still finds in Franz Rosenzweig's Jewish-philosophical work an abode where he can tarry.

The angel whom Paul Klee evoked in his picture was certainly enigmatic—though enigmatic in a completely different way than, say, the angel of the "Duino Elegies" and other poems, in whom, after all, the Jewish element of the messenger who transmits a message is altogether lost. In Hebrew, after all, the word for "angel" is identical with that for "messenger" (*malakh*). Everlasting angels like, say, the archangels or Satan, seen as the fallen angel of the Jewish and Christian tradition, were evidently less important for Benjamin than the talmudic theme of the formation and disappearance of angels before God, of whom it is said in a kabbalistic book that they "pass away as the spark on the coals." To this, however, was added for Benjamin the further conception of Jewish tradition of the personal angel of each human being who represents the latter's secret self and whose name nevertheless remains hidden from him. In angelic shape, but in part also in the form of his secret name, the heavenly self of a human being (like everything else created) is woven into a curtain hanging before the throne of God. This angel, to be sure, can also enter into opposition to, and a relation of strong tension with, the earthly creature to whom he is attached, as is reflected in Benjamin's assertions in the "Agesilaus Santander." In August 1927, when Benjamin and I spent an extended period of time together in Paris, I had just published a Hebrew work of research containing, among other things, detailed texts on the angelology and demonology of the kabbalists of the thirteenth century, and I told him about these.

The Luciferian element, however, entered Benjamin's meditations on Klee's picture not directly from the Jewish tradition, but rather from the occupation with Baudelaire that fascinated him for so many years. The Luciferian element of the beauty of the Satanic, stemming from this side of Benjamin's interests, comes out often enough in his writings and notes. His recently published notes on hashish referred, in a record of a hashish-impression of January 15, 1928, to a "Satanic-phase" he went through during this intoxication: "My smile assumed Satanic features: though more the expression of Satanic knowing, Satanic contentment, Satanic serenity than that of Satanic destructive activity."[14] However, while the "indescribably beautiful face" of a human being can appear as "Satanic features— with a half-suppressed smile" about 1932 in Benjamin's partly unpublished "Selbstbildnisse des Träumenden," the anthropomorphous nature of Klee's angel, now changing into the Luciferian, is no longer present when one (perhaps two) years later he wrote the piece concerning us here. But the theme of the message transmitted by the angel has not disappeared. Its content, to be sure, changes along with Benjamin's conceptions. Does he bring news from Above? News about the Self of him who views him and about his fate? Or perhaps news about what is occurring in the world of history, as it finally appeared to Benjamin, when he recognized the angel of history in the *Angelus Novus*? The following considerations will provide more exact information about this.

4

When Benjamin wrote this piece on Ibiza, his situation was that of the refugee who in every sense leads an existence on the brink of desperation. Three weeks earlier, he had written me on July 24, 1933, that he had lowered his necessities of life to a "minimum that could hardly be lowered any further." His capacity to concentrate on spiritual matters was of an almost miraculous intensity precisely in such situations. A relative of his quoted to me from a lost letter from him during such a condition an unforgettable sentence she had retained verbatim: "I gather flowers on the brink of subsistence." The review of his life occupied him most deeply during these months. Out of it also arose the new meditation about the angel that is set down here—when the picture itself was no longer with him but present only in his imagination. The latter allied itself with the review of his life as writer, as Jew, and as unrequited lover. That in so desperate a situation he nevertheless decided to write an observation which for all its melancholy is harmonious and does not totally slip into the hopeless, an observation establishing a certain equilibrium of the impulses moving his life— this permits a glance at the forces which then and for so long after prevented his self-destruction and which he summarized by the image of patience, for which he here praises himself with such overwhelming justification.

The following explanation is based on the text of the second, final version, but the important variations of the first one are taken into consideration.

Benjamin proceeds from the fiction that at his birth his parents gave him, besides the name Walter, two additional and thoroughly peculiar names, so that he might if necessary use them as a literary pseudonym without directly being recognized as a Jew, as was inevitable in case of the employment of the name Walter Benjamin. (In Germany, "Benjamin" would invariably be a Jewish name.) To be sure, by, as it were, anticipating his relation to his angel—even if only in Benjamin's imagination—his parents expressed more than they could have guessed. For what conceals itself behind the enigmatic name of the Spartan king Agesilaus and the city of northern Spain, Santander?[15] Nothing other than a significant anagram. Benjamin's taste for anagrams accompanied him through his whole life. It was one of his main pleasures to make up anagrams. In several of his essays he used the anagram Anni M. Bie instead of the name Benjamin. A whole page on which he had written anagrams in his own hand is to be found among his posthumous papers in Frankfurt. In his book on tragic drama he wrote that in anagrams "the word, the syllable, and the sound, strut around, emancipated from every handed-down association with meaning, as a thing that may be exploited allegorically" (I:381), whereby he defined as much the inclination of baroque writers for anagrams as his own inclination.

Jean Selz also most clearly observed this same feature about him. "Sometimes he also investigated and considered a word from all sides and in so doing often discovered in its individual syllables an unexpected meaning" (cf. this volume, p. 357). And Selz observed this feature precisely on Ibiza, where the present piece was written. And what he says here about the syllables of a word holds as much for the combination of individual letters in the words that make up the anagrams.

Agesilaus Santander is, sealed as it were with a superfluous "i," an anagram of The Angel Satan (*Der Angelus Satanas*). Such an Angel-Satan is spoken of not only in Hebrew texts as, for example, the Midrash Rabba for Exodus, Section 20, paragraph 10, but also in New Testament texts, where, in Paul's Second Letter to the Corinthians 12:7, there is talk of the *Angelos Satanas*, who is identical with the fallen, rebellious Lucifer.

Benjamin, who published his own writings under his civil name, made no use, as he says, of this name; he "proceeded . . . as did the Jews with the additional name of their children, which remains secret" and which they reveal to them only when they reach maturity. This is an allusion to the Hebrew name which every male Jewish child receives at circumcision and which is used instead of the usual civil first name in religious documents and synagogue services. In fact this name is "secret" only insofar as no use is made of it by assimilated Jews, even though their children after the completion of the thirteenth year of life—when, according to Jewish law, they reach maturity—are called up by this name for the first time in order to read from the Torah in the synagogue (*bar mitzvah*). Among Jews this "reaching of maturity" means only that they are now obligated under their own responsibility to keep the commandments of the Torah, and that for purposes of public prayer, requiring at least ten "mature" participants, they are among those counted. Indeed, on this solemn occasion, the father pronounces a—to say the least—peculiarly sober blessing: "Praised be [He] who has removed my responsibility for this one here [*sic!*]."

Benjamin transposes this conception further into the mystical. Maturity, which for the Jewish tradition has an only marginal sexual character, is now related to the awakening of love, which can occur more than once in life, namely with each real new love. For the pious man, which is to say the man true to the Law, his "secret name" remains "perhaps" unchanged throughout his life, because apart from the marriage sanctified by the Law he knows no renewed sexuality in reference to other women. For him, by contrast, who like Walter Benjamin does not count himself among the pious, the change of his name can reveal itself all at once with a new reaching of maturity, which is to say with a new love. "Thus with me"—with a new, passionate love there was revealed to him, in place of the name Agesilaus, allegedly given to him by his parents, the new name which is hidden in the old one as an anagram. To the formula employed here, "Thus with me" (*So mir*), there corresponds, at the end of this sketch in the final version, the phrase "Just as I," obviously referring to the same event in his life.

But even in the new transformation of the old name it retains its magic character. It is the name Angelus Satanas, which joins together the angelic and demonic forces of life in the most intimate union, indeed one by which (in the first version) those forces are even summoned forth. Like every truly secret magic name, it may not be trusted or disclosed to unauthorized ones. No wonder that in this sketch, too, Benjamin does not make it public undisguised. To be sure, here a part is also played by the association with the words Benjamin wrote at the end of *One-Way Street* (1927) in a no less mystically inspired sentence about the teaching of antiquity, one closely connected with his notes "On the Mimetic Faculty," which were written in the spring of 1933. In his book *One-Way Street* (in the piece "To the Planetarium") he does not, it is true, speak of the bond of the life forces in the magic name, but of the future which will belong alone to those who "live from the forces of the cosmos," in other words just those in whom the cosmic forces of life are tied together most intimately—even though not as in the case of Agesilaus Santander in a name, but in the intoxication of cosmic experience that the human being of antiquity possessed and that Benjamin still sought to rescue for the expected seizure of power by the proletariat—more in the spirit of Blanqui than of Marx.

From this point Benjamin's piece turns to the angel and the

latter's association with his own, obviously secret, name. For this name is for Benjamin no enrichment of him who bears it, as is clearly stated in the first version. Unexpectedly the human person of Benjamin now changes into the angelic-Luciferian nature of the angel in the picture by Paul Klee, a nature connected so unfathomably deeply and indeed magically with his own. The first version still states, unambiguously referring to the name Agesilaus Santander as Benjamin's name, that the new name, which he discovered in it due to a new situation of life, takes away much from him, above all the gift of perseverance by virtue of which he was able "to appear wholly as he was of old." Somehow he is no longer identical with himself. In the final version, however, the talk turns to the *picture of this new name*, which was revealed to him. Everything said here about this picture must, in connection with what follows, be referred to the picture by Klee.

Now if this picture is called *Angelus Novus,* whereby its proper name—which is to say the one it should have according to Benjamin—"becomes audible," then at the same time it loses much. While in the first version Benjamin's secret name took from him the gift of being himself, of seeming wholly as of old; the picture of this name, the Luciferian angel, loses the gift of appearing anthropomorphic, as is said in the final version. Here Benjamin transcends the old angelological tradition according to which the angel of a person preserves the latter's pure, archetypal form (*Gestalt*) and thereby becomes anthropomorphic. The next sentence deals with the transformation of the name Agesilaus Santander, the "old name" as it is called in the first version, into the name Angelus Satanas, which comes to light out of it, "armored and encased," through a permutation of the letters. For Benjamin the name projects itself on a picture, instead of the customary view, according to which a picture is approximately circumscribed by a name. This picture, however, does not call itself *Angelus Satanas,* though it is that, but rather: new angel. The second version makes precisely clear that this was not the true name in Benjamin's sense. For the angel passed himself off as a new one belonging to those whose only function consists of a hymn before the throne of God, "before he was prepared to name himself." On the picture in Benjamin's room he did not name himself, but Benjamin knew with whom he was dealing. The description "armored and encased" refers to the way of the depiction of the angel in the picture. Benjamin interrupted the angel from the singing of his hymn, or else, in that in Klee's picture he confined him for years in his room, he took him away "unduly long" from the chanting of his hymn, as the second version says.

The following is intelligible only if one takes into consideration the situation in which, as Benjamin sees it here, the new name, upon the reaching of a new maturity, stepped out of the old name and at the same time settled down in the picture by Paul Klee in his room. Benjamin's marriage from 1917 to April 1921 proceeded unimpaired, unaffected by other experiences of love, in spite of many other difficulties. It came to a destructive crisis in the spring of 1921, one full of consequences for his life, when on seeing Jula Cohn again in Berlin he developed a passionate inclination for her. She was a young artist and sister of a friend of his youth, a woman to whom he was tied only by a casual friendship between 1912 and 1917 and whom he had not seen again since then. This love remained unrequited, but for years it constituted the discreet center of his life. When he obtained the Klee picture he was in the throes of his love, through which also, as he sees it in these pieces, his new secret name was revealed to him, transmitted by Klee's picture.

Benjamin was born under the sign of Saturn, as he expressly testifies only here in all the writings of his known to me. Thus the angel, to whom astrological characterology was no less familiar than to the author of *The Origin of German Trauerspiel* and to his melancholy nature, could make him pay for the disturbance of his heavenly and hymnal performance.[16] For after he had appeared to Benjamin in masculine form in the picture by Paul Klee, he sent him, as if to square his account with Benjamin, his feminine form in the earthly appearance of the beloved woman; not, to be sure, in the direct fulfillment of a great love, but rather "by way of the longest, most fatal detour," which is probably an allusion to the difficult, and for Benjamin fatal, situation into which this relationship, remaining essentially unconsummated, had brought him. One could perhaps also interpret the sentence to mean that the detour refers to the time from 1914—when he met the girl, indeed extraordinarily beautiful—to 1921 during which his life made long, and for him fatal, detours, as for example his first engagement in 1914 and his marriage, which in retrospect, at least during certain periods, he experienced as fatal to himself. This interpretation corresponds with the sentence about Saturn as "the planet of detours and delays": he became conscious of his love only after great delay.

What does not seem transparent is the concluding remark of this sentence to the effect that the angel and his feminine form in the figure of the beloved did not know each other though they had once been most intimately adjacent to each other. In the same year in which the Angelus appeared in his life, there also appeared almost at the same time this woman in the center of his life, although they did not see each other in spite of this "adjacency": when she was in Berlin, the Angelus was not yet there—if, that is, he was not to be seen in the above-mentioned Klee exhibition which Benjamin visited at the time. And later, when he had obtained the picture, she was in Heidelberg, her residence at the time. When in the late summer of 1921 she was in Berlin, where I made her acquaintance, the picture was still hanging in my place in Munich. However, the sentence about adjacency could also refer to the fact that before Klee's picture itself had been painted in Munich, Jula Cohn, who was a sculptress, had her studio in Munich at the time Benjamin studied there from autumn 1915 to 1916.

Benjamin's virtue of patient awaiting, which is exhibited by the Saturnian features of hesitation, the slowest revolutions and decisions, is, as he now says, his strength. The angel, in this a genuine Satanas, wanted to destroy Benjamin through his "feminine form" and the love for her—in the first version the text says "accosted" him; the second version speaks of the fact that he "wanted to accost" him in this manner—but in the history of this love the angel first really demonstrated Benjamin's strength. For when he ran into a woman who cast her spell on him, he was resolved (the first version is silent about this) to assert the fulfillment of this love by "lying in wait" on the life path of this woman, until at last, "sick, aged, in tattered clothes" she would fall to his lot. The general formulation of the sentence (in the second version) possibly includes a number of women who cast this spell over him and could refer to both of the women who played a role in Benjamin's life after the crisis of his marriage: to the "feminine form" of the angel in the person of Jula Cohn and to Asja Lacis, who had great influence on his life from 1924 to 1930, especially on his political turning to revolutionary thinking, but over whom he could cast his spell as little as he could over his earlier (and partly concurrent) great love. He lay in wait on the life path of both women, but above all, when he wrote the piece under consideration, still on that of Jula Cohn, from whom he did not wish to leave off, although in 1929–30 he divorced his wife for Asja Lacis, without this divorce then leading to marriage or closer ties with her. When he wrote this piece in 1933, she had already been back in Russia for three years, and he never saw her again, while during these years Jula Cohn, married and the mother of a child, lived in Berlin and at the time also made a wooden bust of him—lost in the chaos of war—of which I possess two photographs. The expectation to which he gives expression in the sketch was not fulfilled. But Benjamin had the right to say of himself, "Nothing could enfeeble the patience of the man." Benjamin was the most patient human being I ever came to know, and the decisiveness and radicalism of his thinking stood in vehement contrast to his infinitely patient and only very slowly opening nature. And to deal with Benjamin one had to have the greatest patience oneself. Only very patient people could gain deeper contact with him.[17]

Thus in the following sentences he praises the wings of his patience, which resemble the wings of the angel that are open in Klee's picture, in that they maintain themselves with a minimum of exertion in the presence of the beloved one for whom he waits. The reason Benjamin passed from the unequivocal formulation of the first version, referring to the person of the beloved, to the more equivocal formulation of the second version is probably connected with the clearer specification of the figure of the angel in the latter. For the final formulation contains not only the possible Preference to the presence or countenance of the beloved one—whom he was

resolved never to leave even though he did not possess her—
but also an assertion about the angel himself, who maintains
himself in the presence of Benjamin, onto whom he casts his
wide-open eyes, whose glance never seems to become empty,
and whom as the person chosen by him he was resolved never
to leave. From a statement about the wings of patience, the
second version goes on to a statement that refers more precisely
to the wings of the angel, who, after he has once descended
from heaven, holds him, as his Angelus Satanas, under his sway
for years, indeed in some way until the end. This passing from
the patience of Benjamin to the angel himself is also carried
through in the further sentences of both versions. In both versions the Satanic character of the angel is emphasized by the
metaphor of his claws and knife-sharp wings, which could find
support in the depiction of Klee's picture. No angel, but only
Satan, possesses claws and talons, as is, for example, expressed
in the widespread notion that on the Sabbath witches kiss the
"clawed hands" of Satan.[18]

In the first version, Benjamin speaks further of his patience,
which, though it conceals a secret sharpness in itself, nevertheless makes no arrangements actively to pounce "on her
whom it has sighted," which is to say the beloved. Instead, it
learns from the angel, who likewise encompasses his partner in
his view, though he does not accost him, but rather yields and
thereby pulls him along, as Benjamin here interprets Klee's
picture. From here on the first version at once goes on to the
conclusion. The second version is, by way of contrast, decisively
different and more detailed. In a wholly new turn of Benjamin's view, the angel no longer resembles that which Benjamin
has or is, but rather all that from which in his current state he
has had to part, what he no longer has. He mentions not only
the people from whom he has had to part, but also the things
that meant something to him, especially emphasizing the latter.
As a refugee at the beginning of a new turn of his life he is
removed from those who were close to him. At a distance they
take on something of the angel, who, after all, is also no longer
with him.

But more: it was precisely in the things he possessed in his
room in Berlin and toward which he had attuned a deep con-

templative relation that the angel had settled. By entering into these objects he made them transparent, and behind the surface of these things, which he remembers with a lively imagination, Benjamin sees the person for whom they were destined. This sentence finds its explanation in Benjamin's testament of July 27, 1932, written by him only one year earlier, in which he enumerated those objects which meant much to him and bequeathed one to each of his male and female friends. Thus he sees himself as a gift giver into whose gifts the angel has wandered. This pleasure in giving often occupied Benjamin as a predominant feature of his character, and whoever knew him, knows how right he was. In the *Berlin Chronicle*, which was also written on Ibiza, but a year earlier, he speaks of it as one of two features he has inherited from his maternal grandmother (Hedwig Schoenflies): "my delight in giving presents and my love of travel" (cf. *Reflections,* 40). The angel himself—so he sees it now—was perhaps allured by a "gift giver who goes away empty-handed," who had to part from everything that was near to him.

The turn of the phrase about the gift giver who goes away empty-handed reminds one of the conclusion of the book on tragic drama (p. 233) that quotes the famous verse from Psalm 126:6 in a paraphrase by one of the baroque writers: "With weeping we strewed the seed into the fallow land/and went away in grief." Whereupon Benjamin then notes, "Empty-handed does allegory go away." Just like the melancholy view that discovers in things the infinite depth of allegories, without however being able to complete the step over the transitory into the religious sphere and therefore at long last goes away empty-handed, because here salvation can fall to one's lot only by way of a miracle; so does it also happen to the gift giver, who goes away empty-handed, who never attains to the beloved whom he has given great portions of his creative power as a gift, even though in his imagination he had realized the deepest community with her, of which the conclusion of the piece is to speak.

Before this, however, Benjamin's consideration becomes engrossed once again in the form and nature of the angel, who, before he took up residence in the vanished things, used to confront him daily. Reference has already been made to the difference between the two versions, in which an assertion about Benjamin's patience is transformed into one about the angel himself. For now it is the angel who, though he possesses claws and knife-sharp wings for attack, does not look as if he is about to "pounce on the one who has sighted." It is difficult to decide whether in this dependent clause the word "him" (*ihn*) has been omitted due to Benjamin's neglect or whether it remains meaningful even without this supplement. I incline toward the first conception. While in the first version it is the beloved whom Benjamin's patience keeps in his field of vision, it is now Benjamin himself who has sighted the angel who was allured by him. Even though the angel would have reason enough to pounce on Benjamin who, after all, interrupted his hymn, he proceeds completely differently. He grasps him who has attained a vision of him, who lets himself be tied eye to eye, firmly in his own eye. Then, however, after he has tarried long with Benjamin, he withdraws inexorably. He does so because it corresponds to his being, only now really disclosed to Benjamin. He takes with him the human being who encounters him or whom he encounters, for whom he perhaps has a message— not wholly in vain is the head of the angel in Klee's picture there, where curls are to be expected, encircled by scrolls of writing on which his message may have been inscribed.

The following sentences now disclose the nature of the angel. In the first version it still says that he pulls along his partner in the flight into a future "from which he has advanced." He knew the latter for it was his origin, and so he can hope for nothing new from it except the view of the person he keeps facing. He has been pushed forward from the future and goes back into it. This is wholly in the sense of the verse Karl Kraus put into the mouth of God in his poem "The Dying Man" (*Der Sterbende Mensch*): "You remained at the origin. Origin is the goal." (*Du bliebst am Ursprung. Ursprung ist das Ziel.*)[19] This verse was well known to Benjamin and he quoted it in an important passage, to be discussed below, in his last piece, which is intimately connected with the one we are considering.

In the final version there is, to be sure, more cautious talk of "that way into the future on which he came." Did he also come from the future? It is not directly said here but seems implied by the continuation. For how else should he know this way so well "that he traverses it without turning around and letting the one he has chosen"—that is to say Walter Benjamin himself— "out of view." Also pointing to this is the talk of the way of the return home, which is precisely the way into the future. Holding him in his sway, he pulls his human partner along with him and therewith makes him a participant in what the angel really wants: happiness, even though in this regard he perhaps has as little success as Benjamin himself, to whose life happiness was denied, unless it is meant in the one sense here defined and whose dialectical character corresponded to Benjamin's deepest intention.

The association of the angel with happiness was first derived from my poem about the picture by Klee in which the angel says resignedly:

My wing is ready for a flight,
I'm all for turning back;
For, even staying timeless time,
I'd have but little luck.

(Mein Flügel ist zum Schwung bereit
Ich kehrte gern zurück
Denn blieb' ich auch lebendige Zeit
Ich hätte wenig Glück.)

The happiness of which my poem spoke referred, to be sure, to the success of his mission, of which he expected little. For Benjamin, however, this happiness, as the angel wishes it, has a wholly new meaning. It refers, amazingly enough, to "the conflict in which lies the ecstasy of the unique ('once only'), new, as yet unlived, with that bliss of the 'once more,' the having again, the lived."

The paradox of this formulation is evident. In contrast to the familiar formula, "once and never again," happiness is based on the conflict between the "once only" and the "yet again." For in this sentence the unique, the "once only," is precisely *not* that which one has lived through, the now of "lived time," as the French expression *le temps vécu* expresses it, but rather the wholly new and as yet unlived. In contrast to it stands the "once more," directed to that which is capable of repetition, to repetition of that which one has already lived through.[20] In leaping out of the familiar formula, Benjamin describes the melancholy happiness of the dialectician. Thus, too, there probably corresponds to the angel's way into the future of the as yet unlived and the new, an expectation of happiness that can only be fulfilled on the way of the return home, that once again traverses what one has already lived through. And the new, which he can only hope for on the way of the return home, consists only in taking along a new person to his origin. In the first version this newness was formulated even more reticently. There the new was not the taking along of a new person on the way of the return home, but only the *view* of the person to whom the angel turns his eyes, and which is the only one he can hope for from the future from which he came. In the final version, the way of the return home is no longer the flight into the Utopian future, which, rather, has disappeared here.

Standing over against these delimitations of happiness—which certainly say much about the angel but also something about the nature of Walter Benjamin's expectations of happiness—is the enigmatically ambiguous formulation of the concluding sentence, which poses the question: is the addressee of this sentence the angel or the beloved? Did Benjamin, when he first saw the angel and when Klee's picture affected him like a revelation of his own angel, journey back with the latter into the future that was his origin? Or does he address the beloved, whom he puts in a position parallel to the angel? As if he wanted, as it were, to say: When I for the first time really, that is to say lovingly, perceived you, I took you along to the place from which I came. I consider this second interpretation of the sentence to be the correct one. The "Just as I, no sooner than I had seen you" by which the concluding sentence is introduced, seems to me clearly to refer to the same situation discussed in this version after being introduced by the sentence "Thus with me."

I would paraphrase as follows: Just as with me, Walter Benjamin, the transformation of my secret name was revealed all at once in the moment of the "new maturity," the awakening of love, so I also journeyed, after scarcely having truly seen you for the first time "back with you from whence I came," which is to say: I took you, the beloved, along on the way from the origin into the future, or, however, on the way into this origin itself, in which I felt at one with you. Just as the angel takes along a new person on the way of the return home, so also did I take you along, when you appeared to me anew, on my way to the origin. Of what, precisely, this origin from whence he came consisted—this remains unsaid. Is it the future of happiness, which in the sense of the happiness desired by the angel, he hoped to enjoy with her, even though he did not achieve it, or is it an origin in another area, lying beyond the erotic sphere? I do not dare to decide between these possibilities. In any case the turn of the phrase "saw you for the first time" cannot at all refer to Benjamin's first encounter with Jula Cohn, whom after all he had in no way seen for the first time in 1921, when the angel appeared to him and he himself was transformed in love along with him. It seems to me that the context also precludes referring the sentence to Asja Lacis, whom he did not see at all until 1924.

In his encounter with the angel, Benjamin, in accordance with this piece, undergoes an illumination about himself. Benjamin expressed himself about the character of such an illumination in an essay on surrealism written in 1928 (published in the *Literarische Welt* in the beginning of 1929), employing a formulation the equivocality of which may have escaped some of his more recent readers. He speaks there about occult experiences and phantasmagoria:

All serious research into occult, surrealistic phantasmagoric gifts and phenomena has as its presupposition a dialectical interweaving which a romantic mind will never appropriate. . . . Rather we penetrate the mystery only to the extent that we rediscover it in daily life. . . . The most passionate investigation of telepathic phenomena, for example, will not teach one half as much about reading (which is an eminently telepathic procedure) as the profane illumination of reading will about telepathic phenomena. Or: the most passionate investigation of a hashish intoxication will not teach one half as much about thinking (which is an eminent narcotic) as the profane illumination of thinking will about hashish intoxication. The reader, the thinking one, the waiting one, the *flâneur* are as much types of the illuminated as are the opium-eater, the dreamer, the drunken one. Not to speak of that most fearful drug—ourselves—which we take in solitude. (*Reflections*, 189f.)

According to Benjamin's sentence about the profane illumination of the reader and other types, out of the experience of daily life—if one would only get to the bottom of it—there leaps the mystical experience, the occult event still hidden in it. Reading is for him an occult event, although the philosophers do not like to admit this. For "profane illumination" is nevertheless still illumination and nothing else. The experience of the reader, the thinker, or the *flâneur* already contains everything that the so-called mystical experience contains, and does not first have to be forced into the latter. But in contradistinction to the materialistic conception of such experience, which causes mystical or occult experience to disappear, the latter is still present precisely there (in everyday experience).[21] In the phantasmagoria of his imagination, the picture of the *Angelus Novus* becomes for Benjamin a picture of his angel as the occult reality of his self.

5

It has been shown how in 1933 Benjamin understood the picture *Angelus Novus* in a deeply personal manner. But already in 1931 a perspective of Klee's picture had opened up to him, in which, in addition to the personal-mystical conception of the angel depicted above, a historical one first asks to be heard. Here, too, the angel appears in a prominent place, at the end of the great essay on Karl Kraus, in which almost for the first time in Benjamin's writings a Marxist way of thinking seeks to make its way alongside one based on the philosophy of language and metaphysics. Just at the end of his considerations—guided by such inspiration—of the social function of Karl Kraus, he comes to speak again of the *Angelus Novus*, in whom he once more recognizes the mission of Karl Kraus:

One must rather have followed the architect Adolf Loos in his battle with the dragon "ornamentation,"[22] one must have absorbed the Esperanto of the stellar creatures abounding in Scheerbart's stories, or have sighted Klee's *New Angel*, who would rather free human beings by taking from them than make them happy by giving to them, in order to grasp a humanity which confirms itself by destruction.

Seen that way, the emancipation that is perhaps hidden in the mission of the angel stands in opposition to happiness—an emancipation somewhat remote from the Revolution's auguries of happiness. Because of this, too, the humanity of justice, which is Karl Kraus's strictest feature, is destructive. The demon contained in Karl Kraus has been conquered by the angel:

Not purity and not sacrifice have become the master of the demon; where, however, origin and destruction find each other, it is all over with his dominion. His conqueror stands before him as a creature made out of child and cannibal, not a new man; an inhuman creature, a new angel. Perhaps one of those who, according to the Talmud, are created anew each moment in innumerable hosts, in order—after they have lifted up their voice before God—to cease and to vanish into nought. Lamenting, accusing, or jubilating? No matter—the ephemeral work of Kraus is an imitation of this quickly vanishing voice. Angelus—that is the messenger of the old etchings. (*Reflections*, 272f.)

Before Benjamin dared to put his own confrontation with the angel down on paper, when he himself, almost hopeless like the angel, sat on Ibiza and had had to separate himself from everything that was part of him, he had already recognized the "perfect nature" of Karl Kraus—if I may use the expression of the old masters of hermetics—in the form of the angel (an inhuman angel as also in "Agesilaus Santander"). He, who undertook language's revenge on its destroyers, the press, is still one of the angels of the talmudic legend. It is no longer certain whether this angel recites a hymn, a song of jubilation, before God, for he would rather recite lamentations or accuse the destroyers of language, true to his hidden Satanic nature; indeed, in Hebrew the word *Satan* has the meaning of "accuser." But as in the announcement of the periodical *Angelus Novus*, the truly actual is the ephemeral, and therefore the work of Karl Kraus imitates that quickly vanishing voice of the angel which has remained from the Jewish conception.

The final form which the angel assumed for Benjamin emerged from a new connection between these two views in the essay of 1931 and the sketch about himself of 1933. In the beginning of 1940, after his release from the camp in which, like almost all of the refugees from Hitler's Germany, he had been interned after the outbreak of the war, Benjamin wrote those theses "On the Concept of History" in which he accomplished his awakening from the shock of the Hitler-Stalin pact. As a reply to this pact, he read them at this time to the writer Soma Morgenstern, an old acquaintance and companion in misfortune. They are as much a discussion of social democracy, as they constitute a metaphysical justification of a "historical materialism," which owes more to theology—to which it so emphatically refers—than could be stomached by its current "Marxist" readers. These, after all, as their writings prove abundantly, feel themselves completely capable, like Marx himself, of managing even today without theology, and therefore in their interpretations they must emasculate the relevant passages in Benjamin. With good reason did an open-minded reader like Jürgen Habermas describe these theses, and precisely the one that will concern us here, as "one of the most moving testimonies of the Jewish spirit."[23] For Benjamin, at the end of his life, historical materialism is no longer anything but a "puppet" that can win the historical game only by taking into its service the hidden mastery of theology, "which today, as we know, is wizened and has to keep out of sight." It did not, to be sure, remain all that invisible in these theses, in which frequently nothing remains of historical materialism except the term itself.[24]

Following the above cited verse from my poem of 1921, which serves as a motto, one reads in the ninth of these theses:

There is a painting by Klee called *Angelus Novus*. It shows an angel looking as though he is about to move away from something he is fixedly contemplating. His eyes are staring, his mouth is open, his wings are spread. This is how the angel of history must look. His face is turned toward the past. Where we perceive a chain of events, he sees one single catastrophe that keeps piling wreckage on wreckage and hurls it in front of his feet. The angel would like to stay, awaken the dead, and make whole what has been smashed. But a storm is blowing from Paradise; it has got caught in his wings with such violence that the angel can no longer close them. This storm irresistibly propels him into the future to which his back is turned, while the pile of debris before him grows skyward. This storm is what we call progress. (*Illuminations*, 259f.)

Here, then, Benjamin's personal angel, who stands between past and future and causes him to journey back "from whence I came," has turned into the angel of history, in a new interpretation of Klee's picture. He stares into the past, from which he is removing himself or just about to remove himself, but he turns his back to the future into which a storm from Paradise is driving him. This storm from Paradise blows into his wings and prevents him from closing them and tarrying. So he proceeds along like a herald before this storm, which in profane language is called progress. He announces the future from which he came, but his countenance is turned toward the past. The new turn of phrase in the conception of the angel's mission quotes almost verbatim the old text he had in front of him in his notebooks, at the time of writing. Whereas in Agesilaus Santander there stood the concrete human being Walter Benjamin, whom the angel drew along with him, or after him, into the future out of which he had been thrust, there now stands man as a general essence, as bearer of the historical process. But if before it was the *patience* of the lover who waits, it is now the *storm* from Paradise that drives him into the future, though he does not so much as turn around his countenance.

The antithesis in the transformation of the sentences from patience to storm, which all the more casts light on Benjamin's changed conception, is a striking one. But what is more, Paradise is at once the origin and the primal past of man as well as the utopian image of the future of his redemption—a conception of the historical process that is really cyclical rather than dialectical. "Origin is the goal"—even at this time, and not for nothing, does this sentence by Kraus stand as motto over the fourteenth thesis. Even in the earlier sketch the angel yields and withdraws back into the future "incessantly" or "inexorably." Why incessantly? The reasons are given only in the theses, in which the storm prevents him from tarrying and drives him on. What is really deeply moving and melancholy in this new image of the angel is that he walks into a future into which he does not look at all and will never look, so long as he, as the angel of history, fulfills his sole and singular mission.

This angel no longer sings any hymns. Indeed, it is more

than doubtful whether he will fulfill his angelic mission at all. That is connected with Benjamin's conception of the past in this thesis. That which appears as history and past to the human observer—I should say to the undialectical philosopher of history—the angel sees as one great catastrophe, which in a pernicious eruption incessantly "keeps piling wreckage on wreckage" and hurls it at the feet of the angel. He knows of his task: he would really like to "awaken the dead and make whole what has been smashed." In this sentence two themes come together that were well known to Benjamin, a theme from the Christian baroque and another one from Jewish mysticism. It is already said in *The Origin of German Trauerspiel* that for the baroque writers of allegory history was not a process in which eternal life takes shape, but rather a "process of incessant decay." The baroque dismemberment, of which there is so much talk in the book on tragic drama and which the angel of this thesis takes up again when he wishes "to make whole what has been smashed," is connected with the melancholy gaze at the past of history. The process of decay has turned into the one great catastrophe which brings the past before the angel's eyes only as a pile of debris. At the same time, however, Benjamin's meaning includes the kabbalistic concept of *tikkun,* the messianic restoration and repair which mends and restores the original being of things, and of history as well, after they have been smashed and corrupted by the "breaking of the vessels."[25] To be sure, for the Lurianic *kabbalah* the awaking of the dead and the joining together and restoring of what has been smashed and broken is the task not of an angel but of the Messiah. Everything historical, unredeemed, has according to its nature a fragmentary character.

The angel of history, however, as Benjamin sees him here, fails in this task, which can be fulfilled, in the last thesis of this sequence, only by the Messiah, who might enter through the "strait gate" of every fulfilled second of historical time, as Benjamin says in an exposition concerning the relationship of the Jews to time and the future. What prevents the angel from such a completion of his mission? Precisely that storm from Paradise, which does not permit him to tarry, but also the unredeemed past itself, which as a pile of debris grows skyward before him.[26]

That he can overcome this pile of debris or go so far as to join it together in a Utopian or redeemed unity, of this nothing is said. It is precisely "progress" which causes the real *tikkun* of redemption to turn into an ever more threatening and insoluble problem. The solution of that problem, then, in the language of theology, lies with the Messiah; in the language of historical materialism, however, for the sake of which Benjamin annexes theology, it consists of the dialectical leap "in the open air of history," of the revolution which for Benjamin is "a tiger's leap into the past," as is said in the fourteenth of these theses.

The angel of history is, then, basically a melancholy figure, wrecked by the immanence of history, because the latter can only be overcome by a leap that does not save the past of history in an "eternal image," but rather in a leap leading out of the historical continuum into the "time of now," whether the latter is revolutionary or messianic. It is a matter of dispute whether one can speak here—as I am rather inclined to do—of a melancholy, indeed desperate, view of history for which the hope that the latter might be burst asunder, by an act like redemption or revolution, continues to have about it something of that leap into transcendence which these theses seem to deny but which is even then implied in their materialistic formulations as their secret core. To be sure, with what one is accustomed to call historical materialism, this angel of the last datable writing by Benjamin has left in common only the ironic relation of the *termini technici,* which, however, signify the opposite of what a more robust, less mystical materialist than Walter Benjamin would like to understand by them.

Benjamin divided up the function of the Messiah as crystalized by the view of history of Judaism: into that of the angel who must fail in his task, and that of the Messiah who can accomplish it. In this division, if one keeps in mind the writings of ten years discussed here, the angel itself has become, *sit venia verbo,* "transfunctioned." But his image has remained a "dialectical image" in the sense of Benjamin's usage of this concept. This concept first appears in his work in a connection not yet estranged by Marxism.[27] Later he says of it what certainly holds good of his interpretation of Klee's angel: "The dialectical image is a flashing one . . . an image flashing in the Now of

Knowability." In it the "salvation of what has been is accomplished"—and only in it.[28]

The reality of the messenger from the world of Paradise who is incapable of accomplishing his mission is dialectically burst asunder by the storm wind blowing from Paradise. I would interpret it this way: by a history and its dynamic determined by Utopia and not, say, the means of production. As angel of history he really has nothing to hope for from his efforts in its behalf, nothing other than what became of the angel in "Agesilaus Santander," who "can hope for the new on no way" except on the way of the return home on which, because of an encounter with a new human being, the human being Walter Benjamin, he takes the latter along with him.

If one may speak of Walter Benjamin's genius, then it was concentrated in this angel. In the latter's saturnine light Benjamin's life itself ran its course, also consisting only of "small-scale victories" and "large-scale defeats," as he described it from a deeply melancholy point of view in a letter which he addressed to me on July 26, 1932, one day before his intended, but at the time not executed, suicide.[29]

Translated by Werner Dannhauser

Notes

1. C. Z. von Manteuffel, *Neue Zürcher Zeitung*, December 13, 1970, in the supplement *Literatur und Kunst*, p. 53.

2. *Deutsche Zeitung–Christ and Welt*, September 10, 1971, p. 11.

3. Walter Benjamin, *Briefe*, 659. Noteworthy is the parallel formulation in an (unprinted) letter to Alfred Cohn of May 1935, where the talk is of the "beneficial process of recasting, in which the whole, originally directly metaphysically organized mass of thought [of *Pariser Passagen*] has been transferred into an aggregate condition [*sic*] more suitable to present existence."

4. Dietrich Böhler, *Neue Rundschau*, 78 (1967): 666.

5. See Scholem, *On Jews and Judaism in Crisis*, trans. Werner Dannhauser (New York: Schocken, 1976), 172–97.

6. In English as "Doctrine of the Similar," trans. Knut Tarnowski, *New German Critique* 17 (Spring 1979): 65–69.

7. Benjamin had first written "journey" (*Fahrt*), then changed it to "flight" (*Flucht*) and written the world "flight" under it once more.

8. First Benjamin wrote "those of the angel," and crossed it out.

9. First only "in that the 'once only,' new, as yet unlived with it"; then improved as in the text.

10. "That" (*jener*)—instead of the crossed out, preceding "that" (*dem*).

11. First "journeyed back from whence"; then crossed out and newly written "journeyed back with you from whence."

12. This essay, a critique of a book by M. Wiener, *Lyrik der Kabbala* (Vienna and Leipzig, 1920) appeared in the monthly periodical edited by Buber, *Der Jude* 6 (Autumn 1921): 55–68; concerning the hymns, see especially 60–61.

13. Hugo Ball described this copy in his journal (*Flucht aus der Zeit* [Lucerne: Vita Nova, 1927], 243) after his visit with Benjamin on March 3, 1919: "A kabbalistic book on magic with demonological illustrations. Devils who bring to view an intentional banality in order to conceal that they are devils. Plump chubby-faced wenches who trail off into a lizard's body. Offspring of the fiery sphere, of a fat obtusiveness. . . . Banality corpulent and strapping, accentuated in order to mislead."

14. Walter Benjamin, *Über Haschisch, Novellistisches. Berichte. Materialien,* ed. Tillman Rexroth; introduction by Hermann Schweppenhäuser (Frankfurt a.M.: Suhrkamp, 1972), sentence 69.

15. A young scholar who became familiar with Benjamin's sketch in connection with a lecture by me pointed out the possibility that Benjamin was stimulated to the use of this name by a passage in Karl Marx's *The Eighteenth Brumaire of Louis Napoleon,* where a famous ancient anecdote about King Agesilaus is quoted; cf. the edition in volume 8 of the *Werke* of Karl Marx and Friedrich Engels (Berlin, 1960), 175 and 623. This conjecture is, however, unacceptable, for while Benjamin had read just this writing by Marx (of whom he otherwise read very little), he did so only in June 1938, during his last visit with Brecht in Skovsbostrand. This follows from Benjamin's carefully kept list of books read by him, the main part of which has been preserved, and on which the book by Marx is listed as number 1649. Before 1933, Benjamin had completely read only one writing by Marx at all, namely in 1928 the book *Class Struggles in France,* number 1074 of his list.

16. One may perhaps point to an almost obtrusive parallel between Benjamin's relation to the angel and a Jewish tradition about Jacob's battle with the angel in Genesis 32:27. Here, too, the tradition of the Talmud and the Midrash fluctuates about whether the angel with whom Jacob wrestled at the break of day was an angel of light or perhaps Samael, the name of Satan or Lucifer in the Jewish tradition. The "man" who, according to the text of the Bible, wrestled with Jacob and at the break of day said to him, "Let me go, for the dawn is coming," supposedly said to him, according to one version of the Jewish legend: "I am an angel and since I have been created the time has until now not come for me to say my hymn [before God], but just now the hour for the singing has come." And just as Benjamin's angel makes him suffer for having prevented him from the singing of his hymn, by detaining him in his room, so also does the angel of the biblical narrative, and the legend spun out of it, exact suffering for the delay of his hymn by dislocating Jacob's hip joint. In the Midrash (Genesis Rabba 78:1) an opinion is expressly brought up that Jacob's angel is among those "new angels" ever and again

created anew, whose task is limited to the singing of hymns. Just as Benjamin in his encounter with the angel transfigured his own name Agesilaus Santander to a new secret name, so too does Jacob, according to the biblical narrative, change his own name in his battle with the angel and is from then on called Israel. And in the Jewish legend, too, the angel refuses, upon Jacob's question, to give his own name: "I do not know into what name I will transfigure myself"—completely like Angelus Novus's not wishing to give his real name to Benjamin.

17. Even during his internment in the stadium near Paris and in Nevers in the autumn of 1939, Benjamin made an indelible impression on people who came into closer contact with him at the time, by his infinite and stoic patience, which he demonstrated without any ostentation whatever and under the most difficult conditions. This has been made grippingly clear to me only recently by the oral descriptions I owe to Moshe Max Aron, who lived closely together with Benjamin during Benjamin's whole stay in the camp from September 1 to the middle of November 1939.

18. As, for example, it is mentioned in Hölty's *Hexenlied*. See *Gedichte* by Ludwig Heinrich Hölty (Hamburg: C. E. Bohn, 1783), 143. The claws of Satan are a common metaphor in the Christian tradition.

19. Karl Kraus, *Worte in Versen* I (1916), 67. Cf. also Werner Kraft "Die Idee des Ursprungs bei Karl Kraus," *Süddeutsche Zeitung*, July 25, 1971.

20. Here, then, already five years before Benjamin's paper on Baudelaire, in the picture of *Angelus Novus*, the opposition, the "dialectic between the new and the ever-same" is addressed or sighted, the opposition with which the third part of his planned book on Baudelaire was to find its conclusion and crown, as he wrote to Adorno (*Briefe*, 793). A basic theme of Benjamin's thinking is here still enclosed in mystical form. To be sure, already in 1929, in a polemically skilled opposition to "experience" (*Erlebnis*) he had formulated: "Experience [*Erlebnis*] wants the unique, and sensation, practical experience [*Erfahrung*], that which is ever the same" (III: 198).

21. This interpretation of the sentence contradicts the one by K. H. Bohrer, *Die gefährdete Phantasie oder Surrealismus und Terror* (Frankfurt a.M.: Suhrkamp, 1970), 44.

22. An allusion to the essay by Loos, "Ornament und Verbrechen," 1907.

23. Habermas, *Philosophical-Political Profiles* (Cambridge, MA: MIT Press, 1983), 34.

24. In 1940, his conception of the significance of theology had not deviated essentially from the one advocated in 1928, in which, in a sketch in memory of a hashish "trip," he still found the "deepest truths" in the sphere of the theological (*Über Haschisch*, 75).

25. On this concept, with which Benjamin was familiar from conversations with me as well as from F. J. Molitor's work, *Philosophie der Geschichte*, cf. my exposition in *Major Trends in Jewish Mysticism* (1961), 268–74. Benjamin also knew my presentation of these thoughts appearing in 1932 in the article "Kabbala" in the (German) *Encyclopaedia Judaica*, vol. IX, columns 693–98.

26. Hannah Arendt says of the situation of the angel: "The angel of history observes the field of debris of the wholly unparadisical past, but the storm of progress blows him backwards into the future." (See her Introduction to *Illuminations*, 12–13. That book contains a translation of "Theses on the Philosophy of History" by Harry Zohn, pp. 253–64, from which the passages quoted in this essay have been adapted). But precisely in the "Agesilaus Santander," which was unknown to Hannah Arendt, the angel in fact retreats into the future, as there is no mention yet made of progress. She further

remarks on the above-quoted sentence: "that a dialectically sensible, rationally inter-pretable process could present itself to such eyes—that is out of the question." But is that right? Certainly not an unequivocal process, but why not a dialectically sensible one? The immanent logic of Benjamin's conception, as I have attempted to present it here, seems to me sensible in spite of the paradox inherent in it.

27. Cf. the piece "Nach der Vollendung," IV:438.

28. Cf. Benjamin, "Central Park," trans. Lloyd Spencer, *New German Critique* 34 (Winter 1985): 49.

29. Benjamin/Scholem, *Briefwechsel 1933–1940,* Letter 4.

Walter Benjamin: Consciousness-Raising or Rescuing Critique

Jürgen Habermas

In 1972 Jürgen Habermas was asked by his publisher to deliver one of the main addresses at a colloquium "on the occasion of Walter Benjamin's 80th birthday." The gathering also marked the appearance of the first volumes of Benjamin's collected papers. Habermas was already the most prestigious figure in the postwar generation of the Institut für Sozialforschung, having produced virtually a book every year since his Structural Transformation of the Public Sphere *appeared a decade earlier. Most of those works were closely tied to the critical-theoretical concerns of the period's left-intellectual trendsetters, and Habermas's discussion of Benjamin's writings and his choice of themes are consciously situated in this context. One should not forget the importance of Benjamin for the German student protesters; and though Habermas held Benjamin's writings in high esteem, he was at odds with the students' view: a secondary strategy of his lecture seems to be to demonstrate that Benjamin's thought is ultimately anti-instrumental and bereft of implications for political action.*

Those familiar with Habermas's recent writings—and their not infrequent references to Benjamin—might be surprised to learn that before 1972 Benjamin received practically no mention in his works. By that time, however, Habermas's interests were turning to the philosophy of language, and this turn provided a productive backdrop for his first published encounter with Benjamin's thought. He recognized that unraveling Benjamin's theory of experience necessitated first finding a key to Benjamin's philosophy of language. Habermas sees this key in the theory of mimetic ability, of which he gives a brief anthropological account. All this aims not only to unpack Benjamin's notion of rettende *critique, but also to detail the divergences of this notion from ideology critique. These two points constitute Habermas's most substantial contribution to understanding Benjamin's method.*

Benjamin is relevant even in the trivial sense: In relation to him there is today a division of opinion. The battle lines drawn in the brief period since the appearance of his collected works[1] and their almost eruptive influence in Germany were presaged in his biography. The constellation of Scholem, Adorno, and Brecht, a youthful dependence on the school reformer Gustav Wyneken, and later closer relations with the surrealists were decisive for Benjamin's life history. Scholem, his most intimate friend and mentor, is today represented by Scholem the unpolemical, sovereign, and totally inflexible advocate of the dimension in Benjamin that was captivated with the traditions of Jewish mysticism.[2] Adorno, Benjamin's heir, partner, and forerunner all in one person, not only introduced the first wave of the posthumous reception of Benjamin but also put his lasting imprint on it.[3] After the death of Peter Szondi[4] (who doubtless would have stood here today in my place), Adorno's place was taken mainly by Benjamin's editors, Tiedemann and Schweppenhäuser.[5] Brecht, who must have served as a kind of reality principle for Benjamin, brought Benjamin around to breaking with his esotericism of style and thought. In Brecht's wake, the Marxist theoreticians of art Hildegard Brenner, Helmuth Lethen, and Michael Scharang[6] put Benjamin's late work into the perspective of the class struggle. Wyneken, whom Benjamin (who was active in the Free School Community or *Freie Schulgemeinde*) repudiated as a model while still a student,[7] signalizes ties and impulses that continue on; the youthful conservative in Benjamin has found an intelligent and valiant apologist in Hannah Arendt,[8] who would protect the suggestible, vulnerable aesthete, collector, and private scholar against the ideological claims of his Marxist and Zionist friends. Finally Benjamin's proximity to surrealism has again been brought to our attention with the second wave of the Benjamin reception that took its impetus from the student revolt; the works by Bohrer and Bürger, among others, document this.[9]

Between these fronts there is emerging a Benjamin philology that relates to its subject in a scholarly fashion and respectably gives notice to the incautious that this is no longer an unexplored terrain.[10] In relation to the factional disputes that have nearly splintered the image of Benjamin, this academic treatment furnishes a corrective, if anything, but surely not an alternative. Moreover, the competing interpretations have not been simply tacked on. It was not mere mystery-mongering that led Benjamin, as Adorno reports, to keep his friends apart from one another. Only as a surrealistic scene could one imagine, say, Scholem, Adorno, and Brecht sitting around a table for a peaceful symposium, with Breton and Aragon crouching nearby, while Wyneken stands by the door, all gathered for a debate on Bloch's *Spirit of Utopia* or even Klages's *Geist als Widersacher der Seele*. Benjamin's intellectual existence had so much of the surreal about it that one should not confront it with facile demands for consistency. Benjamin brought together motifs that ordinarily run at cross purposes, but he did not actually unite them, and had he united them he would have done so in as many unities as there are moments in which the interested gaze of succeeding interpreters breaks through the crust and penetrates to where the stones still have life in them. Benjamin belongs to those authors on whom it is not possible to gain a purchase, whose work is destined for disparate effective histories; we encounter these authors only in the sudden flash of "relevance" with which a thought achieves dominance for brief seconds of history. Benjamin was accustomed to explaining the nature of relevance in terms of a Talmudic legend according to which "the angels—new ones each moment in countless hosts— are created so that, after they have sung their hymn before God, they cease to exist and pass away into nothingness" (II:246).

I would like to start from a statement Benjamin once turned against the procedure of cultural history: "It [cultural history] may well increase the burden of treasures that is piled on humanity's back. But it does not give mankind the strength to shake it off, so as to get its hands on it" (*One-Way Street*, 361). Benjamin sees the task of criticism precisely in this. He deals with the documents of culture (which are at the same time those of barbarism) not from the historicist viewpoint of stored-up cultural goods but from the critical viewpoint (as he so obstinately expresses it) of the decline of culture into "goods that can become an object of possession for humanity" (*One-Way*

Street, 360). Benjamin says nothing, of course, about the "overcoming of culture" (*Aufhebung der Kultur*).

1

Herbert Marcuse speaks of the overcoming of culture in a 1937 essay, "The Affirmative Character of Culture."[11] As regards classical bourgeois art, he criticizes the two-sidedness of a world of beautiful illusion that has been established autonomously, beyond the struggle of bourgeois competition and social labor. This autonomy is illusory because art permits the claims to happiness by individuals to hold good only in the realm of fiction and casts a veil over the unhappiness of day-to-day reality. At the same time there is something true about the autonomy of art because the ideal of the beautiful also brings to expression the longing for a happier life, for the humanity, friendliness, and solidarity withheld from the everyday, and hence it transcends the status quo:

Affirmative culture was the historical form in which were preserved those human wants which surpassed the material reproduction of existence. To that extent, what is true of the form of social reality to which it belonged holds for it as well: Right is on its side. Certainly, it exonerated 'external relationships' from responsibility for the 'vocation of humanity,' thus stabilizing their injustice. But it also held up to them the image of a better order as a task. (*Negations*, 120)

In relation to this art, Marcuse makes good the claim of ideology critique to take at its word the truth that is articulated in bourgeois ideals but has been reserved to the sphere of the beautiful illusion—that is, to overcome art as a sphere split off from reality.

If the beautiful illusion is the medium in which bourgeois society actually expresses its own ideals but at the same time hides the fact that they are held in suspense, then the practice of ideology critique on art leads to the demands that autonomous art be overcome and that culture in general be reintegrated into the material processes of life. The revolutionizing of bourgeois conditions of life amounts to the overcoming of culture: "To the extent that culture has transmuted fulfillable, but factually unfulfilled, longings and instincts, it will lose its object. . . . Beauty will find a new embodiment when it no longer is represented as real illusion but, instead, expresses reality and joy in reality" (*Negations*, 130ff.).

In the face of the mass art of fascism, Marcuse could not have been deceived about the possibility of a false overcoming of culture. Against it he held up another kind of politicization of art, which thirty years later seemed to assume concrete shape for a moment in the flower-garlanded barricades of the Paris students. In his *Essay on Liberation*[12] Marcuse interpreted the surrealist praxis of the youth revolt as the overcoming of art with which art passes over into life.

A year before Marcuse's essay on the affirmative character of culture, Benjamin's treatise "The Work of Art in the Age of Mechanical Reproduction" had appeared in the same journal, *Zeitschrift für Sozialforschung*. It seems as if Marcuse only recast Benjamin's more subtle observations in terms of the critique of ideology. The theme is once again the overcoming of autonomous art. The profane cult of beauty first developed in the Renaissance and remained valid for three hundred years (*Illuminations*, 226). In the measure that art becomes dissociated from its cultic basis, the illusion of its autonomy disappears (*Illuminations*, 228). Benjamin grounds his thesis that "art has escaped from the realm of 'beautiful illusion' " by pointing to the altered status of the work of art and to its altered mode of reception.

With the destruction of the aura, the innermost symbolic structure of the work of art is shifted in such a way that the sphere removed from the material processes of life and counterbalancing them falls apart. The work of art withdraws its ambivalent claim to superior authenticity and inviolability. It sacrifices both historical witness and cultic trappings to the art spectator. Already in 1927 Benjamin noted that "what we used to call art starts only 2 meters away from the body" (II:622). The trivialized work of art gains its value for exhibition at the cost of its cultural value.[13]

To the altered structure of the work of art corresponds a changed organization of the perception and reception of art. As autonomous, art is set up for individual enjoyment; after the loss of its aura it is geared to reception by the masses.

Benjamin contrasts the contemplation of the isolated, art-viewing individual with the diffusion of art within a collective, stimulated by its appeal. "In the degeneration of the bourgeoisie, meditation became a school for asocial behavior; it was countered by diversion as a variety of social behavior" (*Illuminations*, 240). Moreover, in this collective reception Benjamin sees an enjoyment of art that is at once instructive and critical.

I believe I can distill from these not completely consistent utterances the notion of a mode of reception that Benjamin acquired from the reactions of a relaxed, and yet mentally alert, film-viewing public:

Let us compare the screen on which a film unfolds with the canvas of a painting. The painting invites the viewer to contemplation; before it the viewer can abandon himself to his own flow of associations. Before the movie frame, he cannot do so. . . . In fact, when a person views these constantly changing (film) images, his stream of associations is immediately disrupted. This constitutes the shock effect of the film, which like all shock effects needs to be parried by a heightened presence of mind. Because of its technical structure, the film has liberated the physical shock effect from the moral cushioning in which Dadaism had, as it were, held it. (*Illuminations*, 240)

In a succession of discrete shocks, the art work deprived of its aura releases experiences that used to be enclosed within an esoteric style. In the mentally alert elaboration of this shock Benjamin notices the exoteric dissolution of a cultic spell that bourgeois culture inflicts on the solitary spectator in virtue of its affirmative character.

Benjamin conceives the functional transformation of art, which takes place the moment the work of art is freed "from its parasitic dependence on ritual," as the politicizing of art. "Instead of being based on ritual, it begins to be based on another practice—politics" (*Illuminations*, 226). In the claim of fascist mass art to be political, Benjamin, like Marcuse, sees the risk in the overcoming of autonomous art. Nazi propaganda art carries out the liquidation of art as pertaining to an autonomous realm, but behind the veil of politicization it really serves the aestheticizing of naked political violence. It replaces the degraded cult value of bourgeois art with a manipulatively produced one. The cultic spell is broken only to be revived synthetically; mass reception becomes mass suggestion.[14]

Benjamin's theory of art appears to develop a notion of culture proper to the critique of ideology, which Marcuse will take up a year later; however, the parallels are deceptive. I note four essential differences:

• Marcuse deals with the exemplary forms of bourgeois art in accord with ideology critique, inasmuch as he fastens on the contradiction between the ideal and the real. From this critique results an overcoming of autonomous art only as the consequence of an idea. In contrast, Benjamin does not raise critical demands against a culture still unshaken in its substance. Instead, he describes the factual process of the disintegration of the aura, upon which bourgeois art grounds the illusion of its autonomy. He proceeds descriptively. He observes a functional change in art, which Marcuse only anticipates for the moment in which the conditions of life are revolutionized.

• It is thus striking that Marcuse, like most other proponents of idealist aesthetics, limits himself to the periods acknowledged within bourgeois consciousness as classical. He is oriented toward a notion of artistic beauty taken from the symbolic forms within which essence comes to appearance. The classic works of art (in literature this means especially the novel and the bourgeois tragic drama) are suitable objects for a critique of ideology precisely because of their affirmative character, just as in the realm of political philosophy rational natural right is suitable on account of its affirmative character. Benjamin's interest, however, is in the nonaffirmative forms of art. In his investigation of the baroque tragic drama he found in the allegorical a concept that contrasted with the individual totality of the transfigurative work of art.[15] Allegory, which expresses the experience of the passionate, the oppressed, the unreconciled, and the failed (that is, the negative), runs counter to a symbolic art that prefigures and aims for positive happiness, freedom, reconciliation, and fulfillment. Whereas the latter needs ideology critique for decodifying and overcoming, the former is itself suggestive of critique: "What has survived is the extraordinary detail of the allegorical references: an object of knowledge whose haunt lies amid the consciously constructed ruins. Criticism is the mortification of the works. This is cultivated by the essence of such production more readily than by any other" (*Trauerspiel*, 182).

• In this connection, it is furthermore remarkable that Marcuse spares the transformation of bourgeois art by the avant-garde from the direct grasp of ideology critique, whereas Benjamin shows the process of the elimination of autonomous art within the history of modernity. Benjamin, who regards the emergence of the metropolitan masses as a "matrix from which all traditional behavior toward works of art emerges rejuvenated" (*Illuminations*, 241), uncovers a point of contact with this phenomenon precisely in the works that seem to be hermetically closed off from it: "The masses are so interiorized by Baudelaire that one searches in vain for clarification of them by him" ("On Some Motifs in Baudelaire," *Illuminations*, 157–202). [For this reason Benjamin opposes the superficial understanding of *l'art pour l'art*: "This is the moment to embark on a work that would illuminate as no other the crisis of the arts that we are witnessing: a history of esoteric poetry. . . . On its last page one would have to find the x-ray image of surrealism" (*Reflections*, 184)]. Benjamin pursues the traces of modernity because they lead to the point where "the realm of poetry is exploded from within" (*Reflections*, 178). The insight into the necessity for overcoming autonomous art arises from the reconstruction of what avant-garde art exposes about bourgeois art in transforming it.

• Finally, the decisive difference with Marcuse lies in Benjamin's conceiving the dissolution of autonomous art as the result of an upheaval in techniques of reproduction. In a comparison of the functions of painting and photography, Benjamin demonstrates in exemplary fashion the consequences of new techniques moving to the fore in the nineteenth century. In contrast with the traditional printing methods of pouring, casting, woodcarving, engraving, and lithography, these techniques represent a new developmental stage that may be comparable to the invention of the printing press. In his own day Benjamin could observe a development in phonograph records, films, and radio, which was accelerated by electronic media. The techniques of reproduction impinge on the internal structure of works of art. The work sacrifices its spatio-temporal individuality, on the one hand, but on the other hand it purchases more documentary authenticity. The temporal structure of ephemerality and repeatability, which replaces the uniqueness and duration typical of the temporal structure of the autonomous work of art, destroys the aura, "the unique appearance of a distance," and sharpens a "sense for sameness in the world" (*Illuminations*, 224ff.). Things stripped of their aura move nearer the masses, as well, because the technical medium intervening between the selective organs of sense and the object copies the object more exactly and realistically. The authenticity of the subject matter, of course, requires the constructive use of means for realistic replication, that is, montage and literary interpretation (the inscription of photographs).[16]

2

As these differences make clear, Benjamin does not let himself be guided by the concept of art based on ideology critique. With the dissolution of autonomous art, he has something else in mind than does Marcuse with his demand for the overcoming of culture. Whereas Marcuse confronts ideal and reality and highlights the unconscious content of bourgeois art that legitimates bourgeois reality while unintentionally denouncing it, Benjamin's analysis forsakes the form of self-reflection. Whereas Marcuse (by analytically disintegrating an objective illusion) would like to prepare the way for a transformation of the thus unmasked material relationships of life and to initiate an overcoming of the culture within which these relationships of life are stabilized, Benjamin cannot see his task to be an attack on an art that is already caught up in a process of dissolution. His art criticism behaves conservatively toward its objects, whether he is dealing with baroque tragic drama, with Goethe's *Elective Affinities*, with Baudelaire's *Fleurs du mal*, or with the Soviet films of the early 1920s. It aims, to be sure, at the "mortification of the works" (*Trauerspiel*, 182), but the critique practices this mortification of the art work only to transpose what is worth knowing from the medium of the beautiful into that of the true and thereby to rescue it.

Benjamin's peculiar conception of history explains the impulse toward rescuing[17]: There reigns in history a mystical causality of the sort that "a secret agreement (comes about) between past generations and ours." "Like every generation that preceded us, we have been endowed with a *weak* messianic power, a power on which the past has a claim" ("Theses on the Philosophy of History," *Illuminations*, 256). This claim can only be redeemed by an ever-renewed critical exertion of historical vision toward a past in need of redemption; this effort is conservative in an eminent sense, for "every image of the past that is not recognized by the present as one of its own concerns threatens to disappear irretrievably" (*Illuminations*, 257). If this claim is not met, then danger threatens "both for the continuance of the tradition and for its recipients."[18]

For Benjamin the continuum of history consists in the permanence of the unbearable and progress is the eternal return of catastrophe: "The concept of progress is to be founded within the idea of catastrophe." Benjamin notes in a draft of his work on Baudelaire that "the fact that 'everything just keeps on going' is the catastrophe." This is why "rescuing" has to cling "to the little crack within the catastrophe."[19] The concept of a present in which time stops and comes to rest belongs to Benjamin's oldest insights. In the "Theses on the Philosophy of History," written shortly before his death, the following statement is central: "History is the object of a construction whose site forms not homogeneous and empty time but time filled by the 'presence of the now' (*Jetztzeit; nunc stans*). Thus, to Robespierre ancient Rome was a past charged with the time of the now, which he blasted out of the continuum of history" (*Illuminations*, 263). One of Benjamin's earliest essays, "The Life of the Students," starts off in a similar sense:

There is an apprehension of history that, trusting in the endlessness of time, discriminates only the different tempos of humans and epochs, which roll rapidly or slowly along the highway of progress. . . . The following treatment, on the contrary, is concerned with a distinct condition in which history rests as if gathered into one burning point, as has always been the case with the utopian images of thinkers. The elements of the final condition do not lie evident as shapeless, progressive tendencies, but are embedded in *any* present time as the most imperiled, scorned, and derided creations and ideas. (II:75)

To be sure, the interpretation of the rescuing intervention into the past has shifted since the doctrine of ideas presented in Benjamin's book on baroque tragic drama. The retrospective gaze was then supposed to gather the phenomenon rescued, inasmuch as it escaped processes of becoming and passing away, into the fold of the world of ideas; with its entry into the sphere of the eternal, the primordial event was supposed to shed its pre- and post-history (now become virtual) like a curtain of natural history (*Trauerspiel*, 45–47). This constellation of natural history and eternity later gives way to the constellation of history and the time of the now; the messianic cessation of the event takes over the place of the origin.[20] But the enemy that threatens the dead as much as the living when rescuing critique is missing and forgetting takes its place remained one and the same: the dominance of mythic fate. Myth is the mark of a human race hopelessly deprived of its vocation to a good and just life and exiled into the cycle of sheer reproduction and survival.[21] The mythic fate can be brought to a standstill only for a transitory moment. The fragments of experience that have been wrung at such moments from fate (from the continuum of empty time) for the relevance of the time of the now shape the duration of the endangered tradition. The history of art belongs to this tradition. Tiedemann quotes from the Paris Arcades project the following passage:

In every true work of art there is a place where a cool breeze like that of the approaching dawn breathes on whoever puts himself there. It follows from this that art, which was often enough regarded as refractory toward any relationship with progress, can serve its *authentic* distinctiveness. Progress is at home not in the continuity of the flow of time, but in its interferences: wherever something genuinely new makes itself felt for the first time with the sobriety of dawn. (Tiedemann, *Studien*, 103ff.)

Benjamin's partially carried out plan for a primal history of modernity also belongs in this context. Baudelaire became central for Benjamin because his poetry brings to light "the new within the always-the-same, and the always-the-same within the new" (I:673).

Within the headlong processes of antiquation, which understands and misunderstands itself as progress, Benjamin's critique uncovers the coincidence of time immemorial. It identifies within the modernization of forms of life propelled by the forces of production a mythological compulsion toward repetition which is just as pervasive under capitalism—the always-the-same within the new. However, in doing this, Benjamin's aims—and in this it is distinguished from critique of ideology—at rescuing a past charged with the *Jetztzeit*. It ascertains the moments in which the artistic sensibility puts a stop to fate draped as progress and enciphers the utopian experience in a dialectical image—the new within the always-the-same. The reversal of modernity into primal history has an ambiguous meaning for Benjamin. Myth belongs to primordial history, as does the content of the images. These alone can be broken away from myth. They have to be revived in another, as it were, awaited present and brought to "readability" for the sake of being preserved as tradition for authentic progress.[22] Benjamin's antievolutionary conception of history, in accord with which the *Jetztzeit* runs perpendicular to the continuum of natural history, is not rendered utterly blind toward steps forward in the emancipation of the human race. However, it judges with a profound pessimism the chances that the punctual breakthroughs that undermine the always-the-same will combine into a tradition and not be forgotten.

Benjamin is acquainted with a continuity that, in its linear progress, breaks through the cycle of natural history and thereby menaces the lastingness of tradition. This is the continuity of demystification, whose final stage Benjamin diagnoses as the loss of aura:

In prehistoric times, because of the absolute emphasis on its cult value, the work of art was an instrument of magic. Only later did it come to be recognized as a work of art. In the same way today, because of the absolute emphasis on its exhibition value, the work of art becomes a structure with entirely new functions, among which the one we are conscious of, the artistic function, later may be recognized as incidental. (*Illuminations*, 227)

Benjamin does not explain this deritualization of art, yet it has to be understood as part of the world-historical process of rationalization that the developmental surge of the forces of production causes in social forms of life through revolutionizing the mode of production. Max Weber uses the term *disenchantment* too. Autonomous art became established only to the degree that, with the rise of civil society, the economic and political system was uncoupled from the cultural system and traditionalistic world views were undermined by the basic ideology of fair exchange, thus freeing the arts from the context of ritual.[23] In the first place, art owes to its commodity character its liberation for the private enjoyment of the bourgeois reading, theater-going, exhibition-going, and concert-going public that was coming into being in the seventeenth and eighteenth centuries.[24] The advance of the process to which art owes its autonomy leads to its liquidation as well. In the nineteenth century the public made up of bourgeois private persons gave way to the laboring populace of large urban collectives. Thus, Benjamin concentrates on Paris as the large city *par excellence*. He also concentrates on mass art, since "photography and the film provide the most suitable means" to recognize the deritualization of art" (*Illuminations*, 227).

3

On no point did Adorno contradict Benjamin as vigorously as on this one. He regarded the mass art emerging with the new techniques of reproduction as a degeneration of art. The market that first made possible the autonomy of bourgeois art permitted the rise of a culture industry that penetrates the pores of the work of art itself and, along with art's commodity character, imposes on the spectator the attitudes of a consumer. Adorno first developed this critique in 1938, using jazz as an example, in his essay "On the Fetish-Character in Music and the Regression of Listening."[25] He summarized and generalized the criticism—since carried out with regard to a number of different objects—in his posthumous volume *Aesthetic Theory* under the title "Desubstantialization of Art" (*Entkunstung der Kunst*):

Of the autonomy of works of art, which incites the wrath of the consumer of culture when he realizes that he is taken for something better than he thinks he is, of that autonomy nothing is left but the fetish character of commodities. . . . If art is viewed as a clean slate for subjective projections, it loses its distinctive character. The two extreme forms of *Entkunstung* of art, therefore, are reification—art viewed as a thing among things—and psychologism—art viewed as a vehicle for the psychology of the viewer. The reified works of art, which have ceased to speak, are made to say the things the viewer wants them to say and which are the stereotyped echo of himself.[26]

The ingredient of historical experience in this critique of the culture industry is disappointment, not so much about the history of the decline of art, religion, and philosophy as about the history of the parodies of their overcoming. The constellation of bourgeois culture in the age of its classical development was, to put it rather roughly, characterized by the dissolution of traditional images of the world, first by the retreat of religion into the sphere of privatized faith, then by the alliance of empiricist and rationalist philosophy with the new physics, and finally by an art which, having become autonomous, took up the complementary positions on behalf of the victims of bourgeois rationalization. Art was the preserve for a satisfaction, be it only virtual, of those needs that became, so to speak, illegal within the material processes of life in bourgeois society: the need for a mimetic relation with external nature and the nature of one's own body, the need for life together in solidarity, and, in general, the need for the happiness of a communicative experience removed from the imperatives of purposive rationality and leaving room for fantasy and spontaneous behavior. This constellation of bourgeois culture was by no means stable; it lasted, as did liberalism itself, only a moment; then it fell prey to the dialectic of the enlightenment (or, rather, to capitalism as its irresistible vehicle).

Hegel already announced the loss of aura in his *Lectures on Aesthetics*.[27] In conceiving art and religion as restricted forms of absolute knowledge which philosophy as the free thinking of the absolute spirit penetrates, he set in motion the dialectic of a "sublation" (*Aufhebung*), which immediately transcended the limits of the Hegelian logic. Hegel's disciples achieved secular

Jürgen Habermas

critiques of religion and then philosophy in order finally to allow the sublation of philosophy and its realization to come to term in the overcoming of political violence; this was the hour when Marxist ideology critique was born. What in the Hegelian construction was still veiled now came into the foreground: the special status assumed by art among the figures of the absolute spirit to the extent that it did not (like religion once it became subjectivized and philosophy once it became scientific) take over tasks in the economic and political system, but gathered residual needs that could not be satisfied in the "system of needs." Consequently, the sphere of art was spared from ideology critique right down to our century. When it finally fell subject to ideology critique, the ironic overcoming of religion and philosophy already stood in full view.

Today not even religion is a private matter, but with the atheism of the masses the utopian contents of the tradition have gone under as well. Philosophy has been stripped of its metaphysical claim, but within the dominant scientism even the constructions before which a wretched reality was supposed to justify itself have disintegrated. In the meantime, even a "sublation" of science is at hand. This destroys the illusion of autonomy, but less for the sake of discursively guiding the scientific system than for the sake of functionalizing it for unreflected interests.[28] Adorno's critique of a false elimination of art should also be seen in this context; it does destroy the aura, but along with the dominative organization of the work of art it liquidates its truth at the same time.

Disappointment with false overcoming, whether of religion, philosophy, or art, can evoke a reaction of restraint, if not of hesitancy, of the sort that one would rather be mistrustful of absolute spirit's becoming practical than consent to its liquidation. Connected with this is an option for the esoteric rescue of moments of truth. This distinguishes Adorno from Benjamin, who insists that the true moments of the tradition will be rescued for the messianic future either exoterically or not at all. In opposition to the false overcoming of religion, Adorno—like Benjamin an atheist, if not in the same way—proposes bringing in utopian contents as the ferment for an uncompromisingly critical thought, but precisely not in the form of a universalized profane illumination. In opposition to the false overcoming of philosophy, Adorno—an antipositivist, like Benjamin—proposes bringing a transcendent impetus into a critique that is in a certain way self-sufficient, but does not penetrate into the positive sciences in order to become universal in the form of a self-reflection of the sciences. In opposition to the false overcoming of autonomous art, Adorno presents Kafka and Schoenberg, the hermetic dimension of modernity, but precisely not the mass art that makes the auratically encapsulated experience public. After reading the manuscript of Benjamin's essay on the work of art, Adorno (in a letter dated March 18, 1936) objects to Benjamin that "the center of the autonomous work of art does not itself belong on the side of myth." He continues:

Dialectical though your essay may be, it is not so in the case of the autonomous work of art itself; it disregards the elementary experience which becomes more evident to me every day in my own musical experience—that precisely the utmost consistency in the pursuit of the technical laws of autonomous art changes this art and, instead of rendering it into a taboo or a fetish, brings it close to the state of freedom, of something that can consciously be produced and made. (*Aesthetics and Politics*, 121f.)

After the destruction of the aura, only the formalist work of art, inaccessible to the masses, resists the pressures toward assimilation to the needs and attitudes of the consumer as determined by the market.

Adorno follows a strategy of hibernation, the obvious weakness of which lies in its defensive character. Interestingly, Adorno's thesis can be documented with examples from literature and music only insofar as these remain dependent on techniques of reproduction that prescribe isolated reading and contemplative listening (the royal road of bourgeois individuation). In contrast, for arts received collectively—architecture, theater, painting—just as for popular literature and music, which have become dependent on electronic media, there are indications of a development that points beyond mere culture industry and does not *a fortiori* invalidate Benjamin's hope for a generalized profane illumination.

Of course, the deritualization of art has an ambiguous meaning for Benjamin too. It is as if Benjamin were afraid of myth's being eradicated without any intervening liberation—as if myth would have to be given up as beaten, but its content could be preserved for transposition into tradition, in order to triumph even in defeat. Now that myth is wearing the robes of progress, the images that tradition can find only within the innermost recesses of myth are in danger of toppling over and being forever lost to rescuing criticism. The myth nesting within modernity, which is expressed in positivism's faith in progress, is the enemy against which Benjamin sets the entire pathos of rescuing. Far from being a guarantee of liberation, deritualization menaces us with a specific loss of experience.

4

Benjamin was always ambivalent about the loss of aura.[29] In the aura of a work of art is enclosed the historical experience of a past *Jetztzeit* in need of revitalization; the undialectical destruction of aura would be a loss of that experience. When Benjamin, as a student, still trusted himself to sketch "The Program of Coming Philosophy" (II:159), the notion of an unmutilated experience already stood at the center of his reflections. At that time, Benjamin polemicized against "experience reduced to point zero, the minimum of significance," against the experience of physical objects with respect to which Kant had paradigmatically oriented his attempt at an analysis of the conditions of possible experience. Against this, Benjamin defended the more complex modes of experience of people living close to nature, madmen, seers, and artists. At that time he still had hopes of restoring a systematic continuum of experience through metaphysics. Later he assigned this task to art criticism, supposing that *it* would transpose the beautiful into the medium of the true, by which transposition "truth is not an unveiling, which annihilates the mystery, but a revelation and a manifestation that does it justice" (*Trauerspiel*, 31). The concept of aura ultimately takes the place of the beautiful illusion as the necessary outer covering, which, as it disintegrates, reveals the mystery of complex experience:

Experience of the aura thus rests on the transposition of a response common in human relationships to the relationship between the inanimate or natural object and human beings. The person whom we look at, or who feels he is being looked at, looks at us in turn. To perceive the aura of a phenomenon means to invest it with the capacity to look at us in turn. (*Illuminations*, 190)

The auratic appearance can occur only in the intersubjective relationship of the I with its counterpart, the alter ego. Wherever nature gets so "invested" that it opens its eyes to look at us in return, the object is transformed into a counterpart. Universal animation of nature is the sign of magical world views in which the split between the sphere of the objectified, over which we have manipulative disposal, and the realm of the intersubjective, in which we encounter one another communicatively, has not yet been achieved. Instead, the world is organized according to analogies and correspondences for which totemistic classifications supply an example. A subjectivistic remainder of the perception of such correspondences are the synaesthetic associations.[30]

In the light of the appearance of aura, Benjamin develops the emphatic notion of an experience that needs to be critically conserved and appropriated if the messianic promise of happiness is ever to be redeemed. On the other hand, he also treats the loss of aura in a positive way. This ambiguity is also expressed in Benjamin's emphasis on just those achievements in autonomous art that are also distinctive of the deritualized work of art. Art fully stripped of the cultic element—and surrealist art, whose proponents have once again taken up Baudelaire's notion of *correspondances*, is exemplary in this regard— has the same aim as autonomous art, namely to experience objects within the network of rediscovered correspondences as a counterpart that makes one happy:

The *correspondances* constitute the court of judgment before which the object of art is found to be one that forms a faithfully reproduced image—which, to be sure, makes it entirely problematic. If one attempted to reproduce even this aporia in the material of language, one would define beauty as the object of experience in the state of resemblance. (*Illuminations*, 201)

The ambiguity can be resolved only if we separate the cultic moment in the notion of the auratic appearance from the universal moments. With the overcoming of autonomous art and the collapse of aura, the esoteric access to the work of art and its cultic distance from the viewer disappear. Hence, the contemplation characteristic of the solitary enjoyment of art disappears too. However, the experience released by the shattered shell of aura, namely the transformation of the object into a counterpart, was already contained in the experience of aura as well. A field of surprising correspondences between animate and inanimate nature is thereby opened up wherein things, too, encounter us in the structure of vulnerable intersubjectivity. In such structures, the essence that appears escapes the grasp after immediacy without any distance at all; the proximity of the other refracted in the distance is the signature of a possible fulfillment and a mutual happiness.[31] Benjamin's intention aims at a condition in which the esoteric experiences of happiness have become public and universal, for only in a context of communication into which nature is integrated in a brotherly fashion, as if it were set upright once again, can human subjects open up their eyes to look in return.

The deritualization of art conceals the risk that the work of art also sacrifices the experiential content along with its aura and becomes trivial. On the other hand, the collapse of aura opens up the chance of universalizing and stabilizing the experience of happiness. The absence of a protective shell around a happiness that has become exoteric and has dispensed with auratic refraction grounds an affinity with the experience of the mystic, who in the experience of rapture is more interested in the actuality of the nearness and sensible presence of God than in God himself. Only the mystic closes his eyes and is solitary; his experience as well as its transmission is esoteric. Exactly this moment separates the experience of happiness that Benjamin's rescuing critique validates from religious experience. Benjamin therefore calls *profane* the illumination he elucidates in terms of the effect of surrealistic works that are no longer art in the sense of autonomous works but manifestation, slogan, document, bluff, and counterfeit. Such works bring us to the awareness that "we penetrate the mystery only to the degree that we recognize in it the everyday world, by virtue of a dialectical optic that knows the everyday as impenetrable, the impenetrable as everyday" (*Reflections*, 190). This experience is profane because it is exoteric.[32]

No interpretation—however insistent in wrestling for the soul of a friend, as is Scholem's contribution to the volume *Zur Aktualität Walter Benjamins*[33]—can dismiss Benjamin's break with esotericism. In the face of the rise of fascism, political insight forced Benjamin to break with that esotericism of the true for which the young Benjamin had reserved the dogmatic concept of doctrine.[34] Benjamin once wrote to Adorno that "speculation sets out upon its necessarily bold flight with some prospect of success only if, instead of donning the waxen wings of esotericism, it sees its source of power in construction alone" (*Aesthetics and Politics*, 136). Benjamin turned against the esotericism of fulfillment and happiness just as decisively. His intention—and this sounds like a repudiation of Scholem—is "the true, creative *overcoming* of religious illumination . . . a *profane* illumination, a materialist, anthropological inspiration" (*Reflections*, 179), for which solitary ecstasy could at most serve as a primer.

If we look back at Benjamin's thesis about the overcoming of autonomous art from this point, we see why it cannot be a thesis of ideology critique: Benjamin's theory of art is a theory of experience (but not of the experience of reflection).[35] In the forms of profane illumination, the experience of aura has burst the protective auratic shell and become exoteric. It does not derive from an analysis that sheds light on what has been suppressed and sets free what has been repressed. It is gained in a manner other than reflection would be capable of, namely by taking up again a semantics that is pried piece by piece from the interior of myth and released messianically (that is, for purposes of emancipation) into works of great art at the same time as it is preserved. What is unexplainable in this conception is the peculiar undertow that must be stemmed by rescuing critique: Without its permanent exertion, it seems, the transmitted testimony of punctual liberations from myth and the semantic contents wrung from it would have to fall into a void; the contents of tradition would fall victim to forgetfulness without leaving a trace. Why? Benjamin is obviously of the opinion that meaning was not a good capable of being increased, and that experiences of an unimpaired interchange with nature, with other people, and with one's self cannot be engendered at will. Benjamin thought instead that the semantic potential on which human beings draw in order to invest the world with meaning and make it accessible to experience was first deposited in myth and needs to be released from it, and that this potential cannot be expanded but only transformed. Benjamin was afraid that semantic energies might escape during this transformation and be lost to humanity. His linguistic philosophy affords a foothold for this perspective of decline and fall; the theory of experience is founded in it.[36]

5

Throughout his life, Benjamin adhered to a mimetic theory of language. Even in the later works he comes back to the onomatopoetic character of single words and even of language as a whole. It is unimaginable to him that words are related to reality accidentally. Benjamin conceives words as names. In giving names to things, however, we can either hit their essence or miss the mark; naming is a kind of translation of the nameless into names, a translation from the incomplete language of nature into the language of humans. Benjamin did not consider the special property of language to lie in its syntactical organization (in which he had no interest) or in its representational function (which he regarded as subordinate to its expressive function[37]). It is not the specifically human properties of language that interest Benjamin but the function that links it with animal languages. Expressive speech, he thinks, is only one form of the animal instinct that is manifested in expressive movements. Benjamin brings this together with the mimetic capacity to perceive and reproduce similarities. An example is dance, in which expression and mimesis are fused. He cites a statement by Mallarmé: "The dancer is not a woman but a metaphor that can bring to expression an aspect of the elementary forms of our existence: a sword, a drinking cup, a flower, or anything else" (III:478). The primordial mimesis is the representation of correspondences in images: "As is known, the sphere of life that formerly seemed to be governed by the law of similarity was comprehensive; it ruled both microcosm and macrocosm. But these natural correspondences acquire their real importance only if we recognize that they serve without exception to stimulate and awaken the mimetic capacity in the human being that responds to them" (*Reflections*, 333). Whatever is expressed in linguistic physiognomy or in expressive gestures generally is not a mere subjective state but, by way of this, the as-yet-uninterrupted connection of the human organism with surrounding nature; expressive movements are systematically linked with the qualities of the environment that evoke them. As adventurous as this mimetic theory of language sounds, Benjamin is correct in supposing that the oldest semantic stratum is that of expression. The expressive richness of the language of primates is well researched, and, according to Ploog, "to the extent that language is entoned emotional expression, there is no basic difference from the vocal expressive capacity of the nonhuman family of primates."[38]

One might speculate that a semantic basis from the subhuman forms of communication entered into human language and represents a potential in meanings that is incapable of being increased and with which humans interpret the world in light of their needs and thereby engender a network of correspondences. Be that as it may, Benjamin counts on such a mimetic capacity with which the species on the verge of becoming human was equipped before it entered upon the process of reproducing itself. It is one of Benjamin's fundamental (non-Marxist) convictions that meaning is not produced by labor, as value is, but can at most be transformed in dependence upon the process of production.[39] The historically changing interpretation of needs feeds from a potential with which the species has to economize, because although we can indeed transform it we cannot enrich it:

It must be borne in mind that neither mimetic powers nor mimetic objects or referents (which, one could add, have stored away in them something of the releasing qualities of whatever is compelling and pregnant) remain the same in the course of thousands of years.

Rather, we must suppose that the gift of producing similarities (for example, in dances, whose oldest function was this), and therefore also the gift of recognizing them, have changed with historical development. The direction of this change seems definable as the increasing decay of the mimetic faculty. (*Reflections*, 333ff.)

This process has an ambiguous significance.

In the mimetic capacity, Benjamin sees not only the source of the wealth of meaning that human needs, released in the socio-cultural form of life, pour out in language over a world that is thereby humanized. He also sees in the gift of perceiving similarities the rudimentary form of the once-violent compulsion to become similar, to be forced into adaptation—the animal legacy. To this extent, the mimetic capacity is also the signature of a primordial dependence on the violent forces of nature; it is expressed in magical practices, lives on in the primal anxiety of animistic world views, and is preserved in myth. The vocation of the human species, then, is to liquidate that dependence without sealing off the powers of mimesis and the streams of semantic energies, for that would be to lose the poetic capacity to interpret the world in the light of human needs. This is the profane content of the messianic promise. Benjamin has conceived the history of art, from the cultic to the postauratic, as the history of the attempts to represent in images these insensible similarities or correspondences but at the same time to loose the spell that once rested on this mimesis. Benjamin called these attempts divine, because they break myth while preserving and setting free its richness.

If we follow Benjamin this far, the question arises what is the source of those divine forces that at once preserve and liberate. Even the critique whose conservative-revolutionary power Benjamin counts on has to be directed retrospectively toward past *Jetztzeiten*; it lights on structures in which contents recovered from the myth (that is, documents of past deeds of liberation) have been deposited. Who produces these documents? Who are their authors? Benjamin obviously did not want to rely, in an idealist way, on an underivable illumination of great authors, and thus on an utterly nonsecular source. Indeed he was close enough to the idealist answer to the question, for a theory of experience grounded in a mimetic theory of language permits no other response. Benjamin's political insights stood opposed to this, however. Benjamin, who uncovered the pre-historic world by way of Bachofen, knew Schuler, studied and appreciated Klages, and corresponded with Carl Schmitt—this Benjamin, as a Jewish intellectual in the Berlin of the 1920s could still not ignore where his (and our) enemies stood. This awareness compelled him to a materialist response.

This is the background to Benjamin's reception of historical materialism, which he naturally had to unite with the messianic conception of history developed on the model of rescuing critique. This domesticated historical materialism was supposed to supply an answer to the open question about the subject of the history of art and culture, an answer at once materialist and yet compatible with Benjamin's own theory of experience. To have thought he had achieved this was Benjamin's mistake and the wish of his Marxist friends.

Ideology critique's concept of culture has the advantage of introducing the cultural tradition methodologically as a part of social evolution and making it accessible to a materialist explanation. Benjamin went behind this concept, because the kind of critique that appropriates the history of art under the aspects of rescuing the messianic moments and preserving an endangered semantic potential has to comprehend itself not as reflection of a process of self-formation but as identification and *re-trieval* of emphatic experiences and utopian contents. Benjamin also conceived the philosophy of history as a theory of experience.[40] Within this framework, however, a materialist explanation of the history of art—which Benjamin, for political reasons, does not want to give up—is not possible in any direct way. That is why he tries to integrate this doctrine with basic assumptions of historical materialism. He announces his intention in the first of his "Theses on the Philosophy of History": The hunchbacked dwarf theology is supposed to take the puppet historical materialism into its service. This attempt must fail, because the materialist theory of social development cannot simply be fitted into the anarchical conception of the *Jetztzeiten* that intermittently break through fate as if from above. Historical materialism, which reckons on progressive steps not only in the dimension of productive forces but in that of domination as well, cannot be covered over with an anti-evolutionary conception of history as with a monk's cowl. My thesis is that Benjamin did not succeed in his intention of uniting enlightenment and mysticism because the theologian in him could not bring himself to make the messianic theory of experience serviceable for historical materialism. That much, I believe, has to be conceded in Scholem's favor.

I would like now to take up two difficulties: the odd adaptation of Marxian critique of ideology and the idea of a politicized art.

6

In 1935, at the behest of the Institute for Social Research, Benjamin prepared an exposé in which he presented for the first time some motifs of the Paris Arcades project ("Paris, Capital of the Nineteenth Century"). Looking back on the lengthy history of its genesis, Benjamin writes in a letter to Adorno about a process of recasting that "has brought the entire mass of thought, which was metaphysically motivated at the start, to a state in which the universe of dialectical images has been secured against the objections provoked by metaphysics" (*Briefe*, 664). By this he is referring to "the new and incisive sociological perspectives that provide a secure framework for the span of interpretation" (*Briefe*, 665). Adorno's response to this exposé and his critique of the first study on Baudelaire that Benjamin offered the *Zeitschrift für Sozialforschung* three years later reflect very exactly the way Benjamin makes original use of Marxist categories—and in terms of both what Adorno understands and what he misunderstands.[41] Adorno's impression is that Benjamin does violence to himself in the Arcades project in order to pay tribute to Marxism, and that this turns out for the good of neither. He warns against a procedure that "gives to conspicuous individual features from the realm of the superstructure a 'materialist' turn by relating them, without mediation and perhaps even causally, to corresponding features of the base" (*Aesthetics and Politics*, 129). He refers particularly to the merely metaphorical use of the category of commodity fetishism, concerning which Benjamin had announced in a letter to Scholem that it stood at the center of the new work in the same way the concept of the tragic drama stood at the center of his book about the baroque. Adorno lances the superficially materialist tendency to relate the "contents of Baudelaire's work immediately to adjacent features in the social history of his time, and, as much as possible, to those of an economic kind" (*Aesthetics and Politics*, 128). In doing so, Benjamin gives Adorno the impression of a swimmer "who, covered with great goose pimples, plunges into cold water" (ibid.). This sharp-sighted judgment, which loses none of its trenchancy even when Adorno's rivalry with Brecht is taken into account, still contrasts oddly with the unintelligent insistence that his friend might wish to make good the "omitted theory" and the "lacking interpretation" so that the dialectical mediation between cultural properties and the overall social process would become visible. Adorno never noticeably hesitated to attribute to Benjamin the precise intention of ideology critique that he followed in his own work, and in this he was wrong. This error is shown in exemplary fashion by the objections that were supposed to have moved Benjamin to revise the notion of dialectical image that was central to his theory of experience so that "a purification of the theory itself might be achieved" (*Aesthetics and Politics*, 111). Adorno does not see how legitimate it is to want to carry out the project for a primary history of modernity—which aims at decodifying a semantics that has been buried and is threatened with forgetfulness—by hermeneutical means, through the interpretation of dialectical images. For Benjamin, imaginal fantasies of the primal past are set loose under the impulse of the new, in which the continuity of the always the same is carried on; they "mingle with the new to give birth to utopias" (*Reflections*, 148).

Benjamin's exposé speaks of the collective unconscious as the storehouse of experiences. Adorno is rightly put off by this use of language; however, he is quite incorrect in thinking that disenchantment of the dialectical image has to lead back to an unbroken mythic thinking, for the archaic dimension of modernity—in which Adorno would see Hell instead of the golden age—contains just the potentialities for experience that point the way to the utopian condition of a liberated society. The model is the French Revolution's recourse to Roman antiquity. Here Benjamin uses a comparison with the realization of dream elements upon waking, which was developed into a technique in surrealism and which Benjamin misleadingly calls a classic instance of dialectical thinking. Adorno takes Benjamin too literally here. Transposing the dialectical image into consciousness as a dream seems to him to be naked subjectivism. The fetish character of commodities, he contends against Benjamin, is no mere fact of consciousness but is dialectical in the eminent sense that it produces consciousness—archaic images—within alienated bourgeois individuals. However, Benjamin has no need to take up this claim of ideology critique; he does not want to reach behind the formations of consciousness to the objectivity of an evaluation process by means of which the commodity as fetish gains power over the consciousness of individuals. Benjamin wants and needs to investigate only "the mode of apprehension of the fetish character in the collective consciousness," because dialectical images are phenomena of consciousness and not (as Adorno thought) transposed into consciousness.

Of course, Benjamin also deceived himself about the difference between his manner of proceeding and the Marxist critique of ideology. In the manuscripts for the Arcades project he once put it as follows:

> If the base determines the superstructure to a certain extent in regard to the material for thought and experience, and if this determination is, however, not that of a simple mirroring, how then is it to be characterized, quite apart from its causal origin (!)? As its expression. The superstructure is the expression of the base. The economic conditions under which the society exists come to expression in the superstructure. (Quoted in Tiedemann, *Studien,* 106)

Expression is a category of Benjamin's theory of experience; it is related to those insensible correspondences between animate and inanimate nature upon which the physiognomical gaze of the child and of the artist rests. Expression, for Benjamin, is a semantic category that is more akin to what Kassner or even Klages intended than to the base-superstructure theorem. The same misunderstanding is shown in relation to the critique of ideology as practiced by Adorno, when Benjamin remarks about chapters of his later book on Wagner that "*one* tendency of this work interested (me) in particular: situating the physiognomical immediately, almost without psychological mediation, within the social realm" (*Briefe*, 741). In fact Benjamin did not have psychology in mind, but neither was he concerned with a critique of necessarily false consciousness. His criticism was concerned with doing justice to the collective fantasy images deposited in the expressive qualities of daily life as well as in literature and art. These images arise from the secret communication between the oldest semantic potentials of human needs and the conditions of life generated by capitalism.

In their correspondence concerning the Arcades project, Adorno appeals to the goal "for the sake of which you sacrifice theology" (*Aesthetics and Politics*, 111). Benjamin had surely made this sacrifice, inasmuch as he now accepted mystical illumination only as profane (i.e., universalizable) exoteric experience. However, Adorno, who in comparison with Benjamin was certainly the better Marxist, did not see that his friend was never prepared to give up the theological heritage, inasmuch as he always kept his mimetic theory of language, his messianic theory of history, and his conservative-revolutionary understanding of criticism immune against objections from historical materialism (to the degree that this puppet could not simply be brought under his direction). This can also be seen in Benjamin's assent to the instrumental politicization of art, where he confessed to being an engaged Communist. I understand this assent, which becomes clearest in the lecture "The Author as Producer" (*Reflections*, 220–38), as a perplexity resulting from the fact that an immanent relation to political praxis is by no means to be gained from rescuing critique, as it is from consciousness-raising critique.

When it uncovers within apparently universal interests the particular interest of the ruling class, ideology critique is a political force. Insofar as it shakes the normative structures that hold the consciousness of the oppressed captive and comes to term in political action, ideology critique aims to dismantle the structural violence invested in institutions. It is oriented toward the participatory eradication of the violence thus set loose. Structural violence can also be released preventatively or reactively from above; then it has the form of a fascist partial mobilization of the masses, who do not eradicate the violence unleashed but "act it out" in a diffuse manner.

I have shown that there is no room in this relational frame of reference of ideology critique for the type of critique developed by Benjamin. A critique that sets out to rescue semantic potential with a leap into past *Jetztzeiten* has a highly mediated position relative to political praxis. On this, Benjamin did not manage to achieve sufficient clarity.

In the early essay "Toward a Critique of Violence," Benjamin differentiates law-making violence from law-keeping violence. The latter is the legitimate violence exercised by the organs of the state; the former is the structural violence set loose in war and civil strife, which is present latently in all institutions.[42] Law-making violence, unlike law-keeping violence, does not have an instrumental character; instead it "manifests itself." And, to be sure, the structural violence embodied in interpretations and institutions is manifested in the sphere that Benjamin, like Hegel, reserves for destiny or fate (the fates of wars and families). Of course, changes in the sphere of natural history change nothing: "A gaze directed only at what is close at hand can perceive at most a dialectical rising and falling in the law-making and law-preserving formations of violence. . . . This lasts until either new forces or those suppressed earlier triumph over the hitherto law-making violence and thus found a new law, which is destined in turn to decay" (*Reflections*, 300). Here again we meet Benjamin's conception of fate, which affirms a natural historical continuum of the always-the-same and excludes cumulative changes in the structures of domination.

This is where the figure of rescuing critique sets in. Benjamin then shapes the concept of revolutionary violence in accord with this figure; he invests with all the insignia of praxis the act of interpretation that extracts from the past work of art the punctual breakthrough from the continuum of natural history and makes it relevant for the present. This is then the "pure" or "divine" violence that aims at "breaking the cycle under the spell of mythical forms of law" (ibid.). Benjamin conceptualizes the "pure" violence in the framework of his theory of experience; hence, he has to divest it of the attributes of purposive rational action: Revolutionary violence, like mythical violence, manifests itself—it is the "highest manifestation of unalloyed violence in humans" (ibid.). In a consistent way, Benjamin refers to Sorel's myth of the general strike and to an anarchistic praxis characterized by the way it bans the instrumental character of action from the realm of political praxis and negates purposive rationality in favor of a "politics of pure means": "The violence (of such a praxis) may be assessed no more from its effects than from its goals, but only from the law of its means" (*Reflections*, 292).

That was in 1920. Nine years later Benjamin wrote his famous essay on the surrealist movement, in which Baudelaire's idea of an intimate connection between dream and deed had in the meantime gained ascendancy. What Benjamin had conceived as pure violence had, in the surrealist provocation, surprisingly taken shape: In the nonsensical acts of the surrealist, art was translated into expressive activity; the separation between poetic and political action had been overcome. Thus, Benjamin could see in surrealism the confirmation of his theory of art. Nonetheless, the illustrations of pure violence offered by surrealism found in Benjamin an ambivalent spectator. Politics as show, or even poeticizing politics—when Benjamin saw these realizations, he did not want after all to close his mind to the difference in principle between political action and manifestation: "This would mean the complete subordination of the methodical and disciplinary preparation for revolution to a praxis oscillating between training for it and celebrating its imminent onset" (*Reflections*, 199). Encouraged by his contact with Brecht, Benjamin thus parted with his earlier anarchist inclinations; he then regarded the relationship of art and political praxis primarily from the viewpoint of the organizational and propagandistic utility of art for the class struggle. The resolute politicizing of art was a concept that he found ready at hand. He may have had good reasons for taking up his notion, but it did not have a systematic relation to his own theory of art and history. Inasmuch as Benjamin accepted it without any bother, he mutely admitted that an immanent relation to praxis cannot be gained from his theory of experience: The experience of shock is not an action, and profane illumination is not a revolutionary deed.[43]

Benjamin's intention was to "enlist the services" of historical materialism for the theory of experience, but that intention had to lead to an identification of ecstasy and politics that Benjamin could not have wanted. The liberation from cultural tradition of semantic potentials that must not be lost to the messianic condition is not the same as the liberation of political domination from structural violence. Benjamin's relevance does not lie in a theology of revolution.[44] His relevance can be seen if we attempt now, conversely, to "enlist the services" of Benjamin's theory of experience for historical materialism.

7

A dialectical theory of progress, which historical materialism claims to be, is on its guard; what presents itself as progress can quickly show itself to be the perpetuation of what was supposedly overcome. More and more theorems of counter-enlightenment have therefore been incorporated into the dialectic of the enlightenment, and more and more elements of a critique of progress have been incorporated into the theory of progress—all for the sake of an idea of progress that is subtle and relentless enough not to let itself be blinded by the mere illusion of emancipation. Of course, this dialectical theory of progress has to contradict the thesis that emancipation itself mystifies.[45]

In the concept of exploitation that was determinative for Marx's critique, poverty and domination were still one. The development of capitalism has taught us in the meantime to differentiate between hunger and oppression. The deprivations that can be provided against by an increase in the standard of living are different from those that can be helped, not by the growth of social wealth, but by that of freedom. In *Natural Law and Human Dignity* Bloch introduced into the concept of progress distinctions that were made necessary by the success of the forces of production developed under capitalism.[46] The more the possibility grows in developed societies of uniting repression with prosperity (that is, satisfying demands directed to the economic system without necessarily having to redeem the genuinely political exigencies), the more the accent shifts from the elimination of hunger to emancipation.

In the tradition that reaches back to Marx, Benjamin was one of the first to emphasize a *further* moment in the concepts of exploitation and progress: besides hunger and oppression, failure; besides prosperity and liberty, happiness. Benjamin regarded the experience of happiness he named profane illumination as bound up with the rescuing of tradition. The claim to happiness can be made good only if the sources of that semantic potential we need for interpreting the world in the light of our needs are not exhausted. Cultural goods are spoils that the ruling elite carries in its triumphal parade, and so the process of tradition has to be disentangled from myth. The liberation of culture is certainly not possible without the overcoming of the repression anchored in institutions. Yet, for a moment the suspicion cannot help but arise that an emancipation without happiness and lacking in fulfillment might not be just as possible as relative prosperity without the elimination of repression. This question is not without risks; however, on the verge of *posthistoire*, where symbolic structures are exhausted, worn thin, and stripped of their imperative functions, neither is it entirely idle.

Benjamin would not have posed this question. He insisted on a happiness at once most spiritual and most sensual as an experience for the masses. Indeed, he was almost terrified by the prospect of the possibility of the definitive loss of this experience, because, with his gaze fixed on the messianic condition, he observed how progress was successively cheated for the sake of its fulfillment by progress itself. The critique of the Kautskian way of viewing progress is therefore the political context of the theses on the philosophy of history. Even if one does not argue with respect to each of the three dimensions discussed above that progress in the increase of prosperity, the expansion of liberty, and the promotion of happiness does not represent real progress as long as prosperity, liberty, and happiness have not become universal, it still can plausibly be argued with respect to the hierarchy of the three components that prosperity without liberty is not prosperity and that liberty without happiness is not liberty. Benjamin was profoundly imbued by this: We cannot be sure about even partial progress before the Last Judgment. Naturally, Benjamin wove this emphatic insight into his conception of fate, according to which historical changes effect no change unless they are reflected in the orders of happiness: "The order of the profane should be erected upon the idea of happiness" (*Reflections*, 312). In this totalizing perspective, the cumulative development of the productive forces and the directional change of the structures of interaction are wound down into an undifferentiated reproduction of the always-the-same. Before Benjamin's Manichean gaze, progress can be perceived only at the solar prominences of happiness; history spreads out like the orbiting of a dead planet upon which, now and then, lightning flashes down. This forces us to construe the economic and political systems in concepts that would really only be adequate to cultural processes: Within the ubiquity of the context of guilt, evolutions are submerged beyond recognition—evolutions that, for all their questionable partiality, take place not only in the dimensions of the forces of production and of social wealth but even in the dimension in which distinctions are infinitely difficult to make in the face of the weight of repression. (I mean progress, which is certainly precarious and permanently threatened by reversal, in the products of legality if not in the formal structures of morality.) In the melancholy of remembering what has been missed and in conjuring up moments of happiness that are in the process of being extinguished, the historical sense for secular progress is in danger of atrophy. No doubt these advances generate their regressions, but this is where political action starts.

Benjamin's critique of empty progress is directed against a joyless reformism whose sensorium has long since been stunted as regards the difference between an improved reproduction of life and a fulfilled life (or, better, a life that is not a failure). But this criticism becomes sharp only when it succeeds in making this difference visible in connection with the uncontemptible improvements of life. These improvements create no new memories, but they dissolve old and dangerous ones. The step-by-step negations of poverty and even repression are, it has to be conceded, oddly without traces; they make things easier, but they do not fulfill, for only alleviation that was remembered would be a preparatory stage for fulfillment. In the face of this situation, there are in the meantime two overworked positions. The counter-enlightenment based on a pessimistic anthropology would have us realize that utopian images of fulfillment are the life-serving fictions of a finite creature that will never be able to transcend its mere life to reach the good life. On the other side, the dialectical theory of progress is quite sure of its prognosis that successful emancipation also means fulfillment. Benjamin's theory of experience could—if it were not the monk's cowl but the core of historical materialism—oppose to the one position a grounded hope and to the other a prophylactic doubt.

Here we are talking only about the doubt that Benjamin's semantic materialism suggests. Can we preclude the possibility of a meaningless emancipation? In complex societies, emancipation means the participatory transformation of administrative decision structures. Is it possible that one day an emancipated human race could encounter itself within an expanded space of discursive formation of will and yet be robbed of the light in which it is capable of interpreting its life as something good? The revenge of a culture exploited over millennia for the legitimation of domination would then take this form: Right at the moment of overcoming age-old repressions, it would harbor no violence but it would have no content either. Without the influx of those semantic energies with which Benjamin's rescuing critique was concerned, the structures of practical discourse—finally well established—would necessarily become desolate.

Benjamin comes close to wresting the reproach of empty reflection from the counter-enlightenment and appropriating it for a theory of progress. Whoever looks for Benjamin's relevance in this direction is of course open to the objection that emancipatory efforts, in the face of an unshaken political reality, should not be encumbered so lightheartedly with further mortgages, however sublime they might be—first things first. I of course think that a differentiated concept of progress opens a perspective that does not simply obstruct courage but can make political action more sure of hitting its mark, for under historical circumstances that prohibit the thought of revolution and give one reason to expect revolutionary processes of long duration, the idea of the revolution as the process of forming a new subjectivity must also be transformed. Benjamin's conservative-revolutionary hermeneutics, which deciphers the history of culture with a view to rescuing it for the upheaval, may point out one path to take.

A theory of linguistic communication that wanted to bring Benjamin's insights back into a materialist theory of social evolution would need to conceive two of Benjamin's theses together. I am thinking of the assertion that "there is a sphere of human agreement that is nonviolent to the extent that it is wholly inaccessible to violence: the proper sphere of 'mutual understanding,' language" (*Reflections*, 289). And I am thinking of the warning that belongs with this: "pessimism all along the line. Absolutely . . . , but above all mistrust, mistrust, and again mistrust in all reciprocal understanding between classes, between nations, between individuals. And unconditional trust only in I. G. Farben and the peaceful perfection of the Luftwaffe" (*Reflections*, 191).

Notes

1. Walter Benjamin, *Schriften*, 2 vols., ed. T. W. and Gretel Adorno (Frankfurt a.M.: Suhrkamp, 1955).

2. Gershom Scholem, "Walter Benjamin," in Scholem, *On Jews and Judaism in Crisis* (New York: Schocken, 1976). Cf. also Scholem, "Walter Benjamin and His Angel," this volume, and Scholem, *Walter Benjamin und sein Engel*, ed. Rolf Tiedemann (Frankfurt a.M.: Suhrkamp, 1984), the latter being the posthumous collection of his essays about Benjamin.

3. T. W. Adorno, "A Portrait of Walter Benjamin," in Adorno, *Prisms*, trans. Samuel and Shierry Weber (Cambridge, MA: MIT Press, 1982).

4. Peter Szondi, this volume.

5. Cf. Rolf Tiedemann, *Studien zur Philosophie Walter Benjamins* (Frankfurt a.M.: Suhrkamp, 1965); Tiedemann, *Dialektik im Stillstand* (Frankfurt a.M.: Suhrkamp, 1984). Two essays from the latter are published in English: "Historical Materialism or Political Messianism?" *The Philosophical Forum* 15, 1–2 (Fall–Winter 1983–84): 71–104, and "Dialectics at a Standstill: Approaches to the *Passagen-Werk*," this volume; Hermann Schweppenhäuser, "Propaedeutics of Profane Illumination," this volume.

6. H. Brenner, "Die Lesbarkeit der Bilder. Skizzen zum Passegenentwurf," *alternativ* 59–60 (April–June 1968): 48ff.; H. Lethen, "Zur materialistischen Kunsttheorie Benjamins," *alternativ* 56–57 (October–December 1967): 225–32; M. Scharang, *Zur Emanzipation der Kunst* (Neuwied: Luchterhand, 1971).

7. W. Benjamin, *Briefe*, 120ff.

8. H. Arendt, *Benjamin, Brecht. Zwei Essays.* (Munich: Piper, 1971); "Introduction: Walter Benjamin 1892–1940," in *Illuminations*, 1–55.

9. P. Bürger, *Der Französische Surrealismus* (Frankfurt a.m.: Suhrkamp, 1971); K. H. Bohrer, *Die gefährdete Phantasie oder Surrealismus und Terror* (Munich: Rogner & Bernhard, 1970); E. Lenk, *Der springende Narziss* (Munich: Rogner & Bernhard, 1971). Adorno's critique of surrealism may be found in *Noten zur Literatur* I (Frankfurt a.M.: Suhrkamp, 1958), 153–60. Following him is H. M. Enzensberger, "Die Aporien der Avantgarde," in *Einzelheiten* (Frankfurt a.M.: Suhrkamp, 1962). On the status of the secondary literature see W. S. Rubin, "The D-S Expedition," *New York Review of Books* 18 (1972): 9–10.

10. See *Text und Kritik* 31–32 (1971), the issue dedicated to Benjamin, which has essays by B. Lindner, L. Wiesenthal, and P. Krumme and an annotated bibliography (pp. 85ff.) with references to uncompleted dissertations on Benjamin.

11. H. Marcuse, *Kultur und Gesellschaft* I (Frankfurt a.M.: Suhrkamp, 1965), 56–101; English translation: *Negations* (Boston: Beacon Press, 1968), 88–133).

12. H. Marcuse, *An Essay on Liberation* (Boston: Beacon Press, 1969), especially chapter II. Marcuse has developed and also partially modified this perspective in "Art and Revolution," in *Counterrevolution and Revolt* (Boston: Beacon Press, 1972). Cf. G. Rohrmoser, *Herrschaft und Versöhnung. Aesthetik und die Kulturrevolution des Westens* (Freiburg: Rombach, 1972).

13. "Certain Madonnas remain covered nearly all year round; certain sculptures on medieval cathedrals are invisible to the spectator on ground level. With the emancipation of various art practices from ritual go increasing opportunities for the exhibition of their products" (*Illuminations*, 221).

14. "Fascist art is executed not only for the masses but also by the masses. . . . [It] casts the ones performing as well as the recipients under a spell. Under this spell they must appear monumental to themselves, i.e., incapable of well-considered and independent actions. . . . Only in the attitude imposed on them by the spell, so Fascism teaches us, do the masses find their expression" (III:488).

15. "Whereas in the symbol destruction is idealized and the transfigured face of nature is fleetingly revealed in the light of redemption, in allegory the observer is confronted with the *facies hippocratica* of history as a petrified, primordial landscape. . . . This is the heart of the allegorical way of seeing, of the baroque, secular explanation of history as the Passion of the world. Its importance resides solely in the stations of its declines" (*Trauerspiel*, 166).

16. Here, too, Benjamin sees Dadaism as a precursor of the technical arts by other means: "The revolutionary strength of Dadaism lay in testing art for its authenticity. One made still lifes out of tickets, spools of cotton, cigarette butts, and mixed them with pictorial elements. One put a frame around the whole thing. And in his way one showed the public: Look, your picture frame explodes time; the smallest authentic

Jürgen Habermas

fragment of everyday life says more than a painting. Just as a murderer's bloody fingerprint on a page says more than the book's text. Much of this revolutionary content has been rescued and redeemed by passing into photomontage" (*Reflections*, 229).

17. Tiedemann, *Studien*, 103ff.; H. D. Kittsteiner, "Die Geschichtsphilosophischen Thesen," *alternativ* 55–56 (1966): 243–51.

18. The rescuing power of a retrospective criticism is, of course, not to be confused with the empathy and reexperiencing that historicism took over from Romanticism: "With Romanticism begins the hunt for false wealth, for the assimilation of every past, not by a progressive emancipation of the human race in virtue of which it takes its own history into view with even more heightened awareness and constantly gets new angles on it, but by imitation, which ferrets out all the works from all the nations and world epochs that have ever lived" (II:581). On the one hand, this is not a recommendation to apprehend history hermeneutically as a continuum of effective history or to reconstruct it as the self-formative process of the human species. Over against this stands the most profoundly antievolutionary conception of history.

19. "Central Park," *New German Critique* 34 (Winter 1985):50.

20. B. Lindner, "Natur-Geschichte—eine Geschichtsphilosophie und Welterfahrung in Benjamins Schriften," *Text und Kritik* 31–32 (1971), 56.

21. In this sense, enlightened sciences such as systems theory and behaviorist psychology conceive human beings as "mythic" natures.

22. "[I]ndeed this attainment of readability is a distinctive critical point interior to them (i.e., the dialectical images). Each present is determined by those specific images which are synchronic with it: Each now is the now of a distinctive recognizability. In the now the truth is changed with time to the explosion-point" (cited in Tiedemann, *Studien*, 310).

23. "Autonomy" here designates the independence of the works of art in relation to the intentions of employing them, which are extrinsic to art. The autonomy of the *production* of art could already develop earlier, namely in the forms of support connected with patronage.

24. A. Hauser, *Sozialgeschichte der Kunst*, 2 vols. (Munich: Hanser, 1953); J. Habermas, *Strukturwandel der Öffentlichkeit*, fifth edition (Neuwied: Luchterhand, 1971), 46ff.

25. T. W. Adorno, in *Dissonanzen* (Göttingen: Vandenhoeck & Ruprecht, 1969). English translation in *The Essential Frankfurt School Reader*, A. Arato and E. Gebhardt, eds. (New York: Urizen Books, 1977).

26. T. W. Adorno, *Aesthetic Theory*, trans. C. Lenhardt (London: Routledge & Kegan Paul, 1984), 25.

27. "Art in its beginnings still leaves something mysterious, a secret foreboding and a longing. . . . But if the perfect content has been perfectly revealed in artistic shapes, then the more farseeing spirit rejects this objective manifestation and turns back into its inner self. This is the case in our time. We may hope that art will always rise higher and grow to perfection, but the form of art has ceased to be the supreme need of the spirit. No matter how excellent we find the statues of the Greek gods, no matter how we see God the Father, Christ, Mary so estimably and perfectly portrayed, it is no help; we bow

Consciousness-Raising or Rescuing Critique

the knee no longer" (G. W. F. Hegel, *Aesthetics, Lectures on Fine Art* I, trans. T. M. Knox [Oxford: Oxford University Press, 1975], 103).

28. J. Behrmann, G. Böhme, and W. van den Daele put forward this thesis in the manuscript "Alternativen in der Wissenschaft."

29. "For the last time the aura emanates from the early photographs in the fleeting expression of a human face. This is what constitutes their melancholy and incomparable beauty." (*Illuminations*, 228).

30. "The important thing is that the *correspondances* record a concept of experience that includes ritual elements. Only by appropriating these elements was Baudelaire able to fathom the full meaning of the breakdown that he, a modern man, was witnessing. Only in this way was he able to recognize in it the challenge meant for him alone, a challenge he incorporated into the *Fleurs de Mal*" (*Illuminations*, 183). "Baudelaire describes eyes of which one is inclined to say that they have lost their ability to look" (*Illuminations*, 191).

31. On Adorno's speculations about reconciliation with nature, especially those presented in *Minima Moralia*, see my essay "Theodor W. Adorno, Ein philosophierender Intellektueller (1963)," in *Philosophisch-politische Profiles* (Frankfurt a.M.: Suhrkamp, 1971). See also my essay on Adorno in *Philosophical-Political Profiles*, trans. F. G. Lawrence (Cambridge, MA: MIT Press, 1983).

32. This is why Benjamin does not accept private ecstasy or hashish as a model for this experience: "The reader, the thinker, the loiterer, the flâneur, are types of illuminati just as much as the opium eater, the dreamer, the ecstatic. And more profane" (*Reflections*, 190).

33. *Zur Aktualität Walter Benjamin. Aus Anlass des 80. Geburtstages von Walter Benjamin*, S. Unseld, ed. (Frankfurt a.M.: Suhrkamp, 1972). See also Scholem, "Walter Benjamin and His Angel," this volume.

34. "[T]hus the demands on future philosophy can finally be put into words: to fashion a notion of knowledge on the basis of the Kantian system that corresponds to the concept of experience for which the knowledge is doctrine" (II:168).

35. "It would be worth demonstrating that the theory of experience represents the by no means secret center of all Benjamin's conceptions" (P. Krumme, "Zur Konzeption der dialektischen Bilder," *Text und Kritik* 31–32 [1971]: 80, n. 5.

36. Already in the "Program of Coming Philosophy" there is the following suggestion: "A notion of [philosophy] gained through reflection on the linguistic nature of knowledge will create a corresponding notion of experience, which will also comprise areas whose true systematic ordering Kant did not achieve" (II:168). Hamann had already attempted this during Kant's lifetime.

37. "The word must communicate *something* (other than itself). That is really the Fall of the spirit of language. The word as something externally communicating, as it were a parody of the expressly mediate word" (*Reflections*, 327).

38. D. Ploog, "Kommunikation in Affengesellschaften und deren Bedeutung für die Verstandesweisen des Menschen," in *Neue Anthropologie*, vol. 2, ed. H.-G. Gadamer and P. Vogler. On Benjamin's philosophy of language, which has been relatively neglected in the discussion until now, see H. H. Holz, "Prismatisches Denken," in *Über Walter Benjamin* (Frankfurt a.M.: Suhrkamp, 1968), 62–110.

39. The thesis "that meaning, significance, etc.—in a Marxist fashion—gets engendered only by the world-historical labor processes of the human species—in which it produces itself—Benjamin never made his own" (Lindner, "Natur-Geschichte," 55).

40. Among other things, the fourteenth thesis on the philosophy of history proves this. Benjamin is interested in the experiential context of the French Revolution rather than the objective changes to which it led: "The French Revolution understood itself as Rome returned. It cited Rome precisely the way fashion cites a costume of the past" (*Illuminations*, 263).

41. I am referring to two letters from Adorno to Benjamin, dated August 2, 1935, and November 10, 1938 (*Briefe*, 671–83 and 782–90; *Aesthetics and Politics*, 110–20 and 126–35). For Benjamin's answer, see *Briefe*, 790–99; *Aesthetics and Politics*, 134–41. On this whole complicated matter, see Jacob Taubes, "Kultur und Ideologie," in *Spätkapitalismus oder Industriegesellschaft?*, ed. T. W. Adorno (Stuttgart: Enke, 1969).

42. In this context, Benjamin put forth a critique of parliamentarianism that drew Carl Schmitt's admiration: "They [the parliaments] offer the familiar, woeful spectacle because they have not remained conscious of the revolutionary forces to which they owe their existence. Accordingly, in Germany in particular, the last manifestation of such forces bore no fruit for parliaments. They lack the sense that a lawmaking violence is . . . a supposedly nonviolent manner of dealing with political affairs" (*Reflections*, 288).

43. On this see Bohrer, *Die gefährdete Phantasie*, especially 53ff., and B. Lypp, *Ästhetischer Absolutismus und politische Vernunft* (Frankfurt a.M.: Suhrkamp, 1972).

44. See H. Salzinger, "W. Benjamin—Theologe der Revolution," *Kürbiskern* (1969): 629–47.

45. From this perspective, critical theory is viewed as "modern sophistry." See, for example, R. Bubner, "Was ist kritische Theorie?," in *Hermeneutik und Ideologiekritik* (Frankfurt a.M.: Suhrkamp, 1971).

46. "Social utopia aimed at human happiness, natural right, and human dignity. Social utopia portrayed relationships in which the miserable and heavy-laden were no longer to be found; natural right constructed relationships in which the downtrodden and the degraded disappear" (E. Bloch, *Naturrecht und menschliche Würde* [Frankfurt a.M.: Suhrkamp, 1961], 13). See my references in the article on Ernst Bloch in *Philosophical-Political Profiles*, 63–79.

The Ruins of Walter Benjamin

Charles Rosen

The ill-fated translation of Benjamin's Ursprung des deutschen Trauer-spiels *in 1977 could be construed as a holding maneuver in the face of pressing demands to make Benjamin's most important writings available in English. Charles Rosen conveys the situation near the beginning of his review essay: "For those who are interested in Benjamin and who do not read German, the situation is gloomy," and his essay can be read in part as an attempt to compensate for this shortcoming. His reading of* Trauerspiel *takes into account untranslated texts, including "Goethes* Wahlverwandtschaften," *the most important essay still untranslated.*

The paucity of critical writing on Trauerspiel *is itself astonishing, given the resonance today of Benjamin's treatment of allegory and melancholy. Rosen is masterful at elucidating certain central—for some, arcane—features of Benjamin's "radical methodology." In contrast to many other readers, he resists the lure of Benjamin's frequently ornamental injunctions of Plato and Kant. In their stead, Rosen correctly emphasizes the influence of early Romantic aesthetics on Benjamin's otherwise original use of "Idea." Rosen is also refreshingly unsusceptible to the easy identification of Benjamin with his figure of the "bucklichte Männekin."* These elements of Rosen's essay account for the high regard in which it is held in Europe. (It appeared prominently in France's* Critique *and Italy's* Communitá.*)*

1

But Marlow was not typical (if his propensity to spin yarns be excepted), and to him the meaning of an episode was not inside like a kernel but outside, enveloping the tale which brought it out only as a glow brings out a haze, in the likeness of one of these misty halos that sometimes are made visible by the spectral illumination of moonshine.

—Joseph Conrad, *Heart of Darkness*

The reputation of the German philosopher-critic Walter Benjamin is now secure; paradoxically it has been given its firm basis by the disputes among those who believe they have a claim upon him, and by the widely differing interpretations of his work. The history of the dispersal of his papers and their posthumous publication has been determined by these conflicting and disparate claims.

Just before his death in 1940, some of his manuscripts were confiscated by the Gestapo: these have now turned up in East Germany. Many others were preserved through the war at the Bibliothèque Nationale by the surrealist author Georges Bataille. Benjamin's great friend Gershom Scholem, professor of Jewish mysticism in Jerusalem, had many copies; most of the rest came from Theodor Wiesengrund Adorno, one of the founders of the idiosyncratic version of Marxism called the Frankfurt School. Scholem openly disapproves of the Marxist influence on Benjamin; Marxists in turn generally discount, or attempt to ignore, the theological elements always present in his work.

His publisher in the West is the fashionable and respectable left-wing firm of Suhrkamp. The East Germans publish another edition, and accuse the Western editors of denaturing Benjamin's late Marxist thought. The two editions show little divergence.

Benjamin's work has been less an influential force than a quarry: he has been pillaged but not imitated. He provided what seemed most original in Marshall McLuhan's theories and in André Malraux's writing on art. The structuralists—whoever they were (no one answers to that name any more)—have claimed him as their own, but then so have mystics, neo-idealists, liberals, and followers of Bertolt Brecht. Frank Kermode has called him the greatest critic of the century, but Kermode's own work has remained relatively untouched by Benjamin's methods. Benjamin's study of what might be called the post-history or the afterlife of works of literature has spurred the recent interest in the "history of reception" among younger critics in Germany—principally Hans Robert Jauss—but they cannot be said to share his philosophy. Only the late

Peter Szondi, the most distinguished German literary critic since Benjamin's death, has shown a genuine affinity for Benjamin's thought. Most academic work pays him a brief homage, lists his work in the bibliography, and otherwise ignores him.

Plundered without acknowledgment, appropriated without confrontation—his work has met with a degree of misunderstanding that would no doubt have seemed suitable to Benjamin himself, who was thoroughly aware of its esoteric nature. This esoteric quality adds to the work's prestige, protects its aura.

But if Benjamin's reputation is secure, access to his work still remains difficult. A full assessment is impossible while publication remains incomplete. The large essay on Goethe commissioned and rejected by the Moscow Encyclopedia is still unprinted. Most important of all, the book on which Benjamin was working for more than twelve years before his death in 1940, *Paris, Capital of the Nineteenth Century*, has been doled out piecemeal by the German publishers, and most of it has yet to see the light of print. The collected edition of Suhrkamp has reserved this for the last.

For those who are interested in Benjamin and who do not read German, the situation is gloomy. A small selection called *Illuminations* has been available for some time in America, with an introduction by Hannah Arendt. Of the major achievements of Benjamin, it contains only "The Work of Art in the Age of Mechanical Reproduction," the introduction to his translation of Baudelaire, and the essay on the stories of Leskov; from his final, unfinished book, there is a chapter of the section on Baudelaire in the injudicious revision that Benjamin made to satisfy Adorno and his colleagues at the Institute for Social Research (although parts of the original version had already appeared posthumously in Germany before the American selection). A translation of both the original and revised versions of the Baudelaire essays has been issued by New Left Books in Great Britain, but there seems to be no plan for similar publication here.

The most important of Benjamin's literary essays, that on Goethe's *Elective Affinities*, was omitted by Hannah Arendt on the questionable grounds that the polemic in it against Friedrich Gundolf's biography of Goethe would have required too many explanatory notes, since Gundolf is unknown in English-speaking countries. This essay on the *Elective Affinities*, however, may be found in a larger, two-volume French selection, disfigured by a translation of exceptional ugliness and opacity (such admittedly difficult terms to render as *Einfühlung*, empathy, and *Sachgehalt*, material content, appear barbarously as *Intropathie* and *teneur chosale*).

The largest gap has been filled for the English reader—but not for the American: the one book after his doctoral thesis that Benjamin finished, *The Origin of German Tragic Drama (Trauerspiel)*, on German baroque drama. New Left Books has finally issued a translation of this work in England after many years of announcement and postponement. The holders of the American rights are sitting on them, and appear to have no intention of making the British translation of this work available here. However, rumors rise from time to time of a new selection which will excerpt from the baroque drama book only the "Epistemo-Critical Prologue" (*Erkenntniskritische Vorrede*).

This preface is composed with a density so unrelenting that the author himself suggested it should be read at the end of the book instead of the beginning: it sketches a theory of criticism as part of a theory of knowledge, and attempts a reformulation of so many of the fundamental problems of epistemology that Benjamin gaily characterized it in a letter to his friend Gershom Scholem as "an immeasurable *chutzpah*." I cannot imagine why a publisher would suppose this preface to be more interesting to the average reader than the rest of the work, which deals not only with the German baroque drama but extensively with Romantic symbolism, Greek tragedy, the Spanish baroque theater, Shakespeare (above all, the figure of Hamlet), the nature of allegory, and the emblematic concept of melancholy during the Counter Reformation. This book makes more explicit than any other work by Benjamin his critical principles and his idiosyncratic views of art, language, and history.

2

The goal I had proposed to myself is not yet fully realized, but finally I am very close. It is to be considered as the principal critic of German literature. The difficulty is that, for more than fifty years, literary criticism in Germany has no longer been considered as a serious genre. To make oneself a place in criticism means, basically, to re-create it as a genre.

—Walter Benjamin to Gershom Scholem, Paris, January 20, 1930 (written in French), *Briefe,* 505

Benjamin's training was in philosophy, his work in literary criticism. Yet his essays are not often purely literary, or purely philosophical. They map out an important area between the two. The major essays exhibit both criticism and a philosophy of criticism. This tactic was, for Benjamin, a heritage from early Romantic German thought. George Steiner was right to affirm that Benjamin never abandoned the principles of Friedrich Schlegel and Novalis that he expounded in his first thesis, "Der Begriff der Kunstkritik in der deutschen Romantik."[1]

Criticism was central to Schlegel's view of art—at least, the art of his contemporaries. In a well-known opposition that he derived basically from Schiller, he defined modern Romantic art as self-conscious and critical, in contrast to the naïve, immediate, and natural classical art of antiquity. This polarity was eventually to receive strange treatment at Schlegel's hands, including an expansion of Romantic art to include even the plays of Sophocles; but it placed the critical act at the center of the work of art. In 1798 Schlegel introduced the book reviews of the *Athenäum* (which he edited for two years with his brother) by declaring: "Great works of art criticize themselves. The work of criticism is therefore superfluous unless it is itself a work of art as independent of the work it criticizes as that work is independent of the material that went into it." The critical essays of Benjamin aim at this status and this independence.

Placing criticism at the heart of literature (or, for that matter, music and the visual arts) was an inevitable step for the early Romantic generation in Germany, those poets and writers whose youth had coincided with the French Revolution. Their exaltation of the critical process was necessary to their rejection of earlier standards, to their invention of "modernism."

As early as 1770, Herder and Goethe had insisted that a new art should not be judged by rules derived from antiquity; each civilization, each folk, each nation created its own standards. For Schlegel and Novalis this had become true for each artist and even each work of art. It is only from within a work that one could derive the principles by which it was to be judged. Criticism was, therefore, immanent in the work itself. Essentially this was, with one stroke, to turn criticism from an act of judgment into an act of understanding. Although the theoretical problems it provoked are not to be underestimated, this new approach guaranteed both the individuality of the artist and the integrity of the work. But by making works of art incommensurable one with another, it also seemed to destroy the possibility of a history of art.

Benjamin was, in fact, to deny the existence of the history of art for this reason, as well as on other and more complex grounds. He had no taste for Hegel's attempt to restore history to Romantic aesthetics by envisaging the relations among the arts as a historical process, from the supremacy of sculpture in the antique world to the ascendance of music in the Romantic period, and finally to the eventual disappearance of all the arts—or rather their absorption into philosophy. Hegel's system of aesthetics fell into ruins almost within a few years of its erection, but something like his more general conception of history reappeared much later in art history, in 1901, with a book to which Benjamin ascribed the greatest influence on his thought: Alois Riegl's *Spätrömische Kunstindustrie*.

Riegl drew the final consequences from early Romantic aesthetics and from what has been called Hegelian "expressionism"—the view that at any point in history all social institutions and all human activity as well as art, philosophy, and religion are expressions of a certain state in the development of history. Riegl saw that if the criteria for understanding any given style or period in the development of art were to be drawn from within the style itself, then the concept of decadence was not tenable. Each style was an expression of its period, an answer to its needs, a realization of its will. His book was a justification and a validation of what had seemed the least attractive artistic period in Western history—the Western European art of the fourth to the eighth centuries AD—a period which deliberately rejected both the serene beauty of classical art and the lively energy of the unclassical, Hellenistic style. Riegl claimed an expressive value not only for the products of the high arts of painting, architecture, and sculpture, but also for the industrial artifacts and the decorative motifs of the age.

The derivation of Benjamin's work on seventeenth-century German drama from Riegl's *Spätrömische Kunstindustrie* is evident; Benjamin himself acknowledged it as his inspiration. Like the art of the fourth to the eighth centuries, German baroque tragedies were generally considered either a decadent form, a weak and imperfect attempt to imitate classical Greek tragedy, or an immature and unsuccessful attempt to move toward a more modern ideal. In Benjamin's reinterpretation of these works, a surprising and perhaps unconscious adaptation of Riegl may be observed. Where Riegl elucidated the significance of industrial forms (buckles, earrings, spoons, etc.) and the abstract decorative patterns in the late Roman period, Benjamin turned his attention to the structure of figures of speech in German dramatic poetry of the seventeenth century, the use of double titles, the insertion of mottoes into dialogue, and the expressive values in syntactical forms. As long ago as the early 1920s, in fact, Benjamin was studying what Roman Jakobson has since called "the poetry of grammar."

The Origin of German Trauerspiel[2] (or *Tragic Drama*) was intended as Benjamin's *Habilitations* thesis, as the work that would entitle him to a teaching position in a German university. It was turned down by the members of the faculty at the University of Frankfurt, who declared they could not understand a word of it. No doubt. If they had understood it, they would have turned it down anyway. In his work, Benjamin mounted a sustained attack on almost all the forms of criticism and literary study that were practiced in the university—and that are still practiced today.

This put an end to any of Benjamin's hopes for an academic career. It was, moreover, only one of many such incidents. Benjamin regularly and emphatically marked his critical distance from those who otherwise would have, if not given him aid, at least stood out of his way. He estranged the only other group in Germany that could have helped him to a university position, the avant-garde group around Stefan George, by at-

tacking—in his study of the *Elective Affinities*—the biography of
Goethe written by one of their members, Gundolf.

Later, in the 1930s, after he had become a Marxist, Benjamin
deliberately offended the orthodox communists by his rejection
of orthodox communist criticism and his public defense of literary movements then being suppressed in Russia. His attacks on
liberal center-left figures like Tucholsky may have made access
to some of the literary reviews more difficult for him. Finally,
he insisted upon defending the virtues of the traditional
philological methods so that not only did his friends of the
Frankfurt School, now transferred to New York, refuse to publish the original versions of his Baudelaire essays at a crucial
moment in his career, but they were to prevent publication for
more than twenty-five years after his death.

Hannah Arendt, in her sympathetic essay, puts such mishaps
down to monumental bad luck or to bungling on Benjamin's
part. It is difficult to believe, however, that these successive
moves were not necessary to Benjamin's program, to his conception of the work he felt obliged to carry out. Each attack of
Benjamin was a strategic move; no doubt he hoped not to have
to pay too high a price for each, not to suffer so great a loss. He
must, however, have envisaged the possible consequences, realized that the chances of getting the book on the German baroque drama through the examiners were minimal. It is worth
examining the operation of Benjamin's strategy, his successive
attempts to define his own methods against those practiced by
his contemporaries (and still practiced today). By the ruin of his
career he ensured the permanence of his work.

3

"M. Mallarmé, ne pleurez-vous jamais en vers?"
"Ni ne me mouche."

(Mr. Mallarmé, do you never weep in verse?)
"Nor blow my nose.")

The trail of Benjamin's misadventures begins with his first important published work, the essay on Goethe's novella *Elective
Affinities*. It contains an extended polemic against the general

practice of biographical criticism, with Gundolf's biography of Goethe chosen as the exemplary enemy. This long essay by Benjamin (which Hugo von Hofmannsthal, who published it, called "simply incomparable . . . it has made an epoch in my life") proclaims, in an esoteric fashion, his continuation of early Romantic criticism. A study of Goethe's *Wilhelm Meister* had opened Friedrich Schlegel's career as a Romantic critic, and it was the first attempt at giving a critical essay the status of a work of art as independent as the work it criticized. Like Schlegel, Benjamin also claimed to draw all that can be said of the *Elective Affinities* from an examination of the work alone.

This declaration of purism and the sustained polemic against Gundolf was an attempt not to remove Goethe's work from history, but to find the proper relation of the work to the life from which it came and—a point of equal importance to Benjamin—to which it was going. For Benjamin, the significance of the work is not exhausted by the meaning given to it by the author and his contemporaries, and is often not even adequately realized by them. The work is "timeless" in that it is not limited to the moment of its appearance. It transcends history, but this transcendence is only revealed by its projection through history. The transcendence is double: on the one hand the work gradually reveals a meaning accessible without a knowledge of the time in which it arose, and on the other it preserves for posterity some aspect of that time. A symphony of Haydn is meaningful and moving even to those who know little or nothing of Haydn's contemporaries and of his age, and yet it appears to embody that age for us today. The work detaches itself both from the life that produced it and from the specific cultural milieu within which it was conceived; nevertheless, it keeps a sense of that past life as an effect of distance from us. Commentary and criticism are Benjamin's names for the two ways of approaching this double nature of literature. Commentary deals with the sense of the past life evoked by the work; criticism with the way the work detaches itself from that life. Commentary is philological in its method: criticism is philosophical. They are interdependent: without commentary, criticism is self-indulgent revery; without criticism, commentary is frivolous information.

In his essays on Proust, Kafka, and Baudelaire, we find that Benjamin never hesitates to refer from the literary work to the life and back again, but always with a tact that is a sign of his respect for the dignity and integrity of both life and work. Tracing the development of a work in the writer's life was as fascinating to Benjamin as to a professional biographer. What he protested in Gundolf was a form of interpretation which diminishes and restricts the meaning of the work by viewing it as a direct product of the author's life. Unlike an act, a work does not draw its immediate meaning from the life—if it did, the *Elective Affinities* would be unintelligible to a reader ignorant of Goethe's biography. The work is to be understood first of all in a more objective literary, historical, and even philosophical tradition. Underlying Gundolf's approach, Benjamin felt, was a process of sentimental mythmaking, which turned the life of Goethe into a work of art in order to place it into a correspondence with the novella.

Supporting the myth is a tenacious fallacy, which distorts the life even more than the work, the gratuitous hypothesis that what is most profound, most moving in a work must have a corresponding emotional experience of equal power in the author's life. For Benjamin, this inevitably and disastrously misrepresented the imaginative process. The artist transforms his experience, but the experience is not simply a source of emotions and motifs that the artist must accept, nor does the experience impose itself on the work. The artist does not sing his emotions, but actively seeks for "occasions" to make into song. By too simply identifying life and art, the biographer has failed to notice the most essential relationship: the artist shapes his life and his experience to make his art possible.

In Benjamin's essay on Proust, this relationship is given its full weight. A few sentences of Benjamin's mosaic style show the importance he attached to it:

The doctors were powerless in the face of this malady [asthma]; not so the writer, who very systematically placed it in his service. To begin with the most external aspect, he was a perfect stage director of his sickness. . . . This asthma became part of his art—if indeed his art did not create it. Proust's syntax rhythmically and step by step reproduces his fear of suffocating. And his ironic, philosophical, didactic reflections invariably are the deep breath with which he shakes off the weight of memories. On a larger scale, however, the threatening, suffocating crisis was death, which he was constantly aware of, most of all while he was writing.[3]

Work and life here interpret each other literally and metaphorically, and the work is seen more as creating the experience than as helplessly dependent on it. Proust's life, unsentimentalized, retains its dignity, and his art is left free to seek meanings beyond the restricted range of the author's own biography, as the metaphorical cast of Benjamin's style avoids constraint.[4]

The refusal of Benjamin to allow a privileged status to the meaning the work may have had for the author is based both on his idiosyncratic view of history and on his philosophy of language. From the beginning, his criticism was a protest against historicism, the view that the past must be viewed as far as possible through the eyes of the past. The theory that the critic's job is to reconstruct what was in the author's mind at the moment of writing is only a limited and dubious form of historicism—dubious because it reaches most often behind the text for what is essentially unknowable and unverifiable. Basic to Benjamin's philosophy of language was an emphasis on the functions of language other than that of communication—functions that were aesthetic and, above all, contemplative: the biographical interpretation reduces the significance of the literary work to that of voluntary or involuntary communication. Benjamin's philosophy of history and of language is best treated in connection with his next misadventure, the thesis rejected by the University of Frankfurt on German baroque drama.

4

In Shakespeare's historical plays, there is throughout a conflict of the poetic and the unpoetic. The common people appear witty and unruly—when the great appear stiff and melancholy, etc. Low life is generally opposed to high—often tragically, often as parody, often for the sake of the contrast. History, what history meant to the poet, was represented in these plays. History dissolved in speech. Exactly the opposite of real history, and nevertheless history as it should be—prophetic and synchronic.

—Novalis, *Fragments and Studies of 1799–1800*

When Benjamin wrote *The Origin of German Trauerspiel,* between 1919 and 1925, there was already a new interest in Germany in the once-despised literary art of the German seventeenth century. This was in part owing to a revaluation of baroque art strongly influenced by Wölfflin's publications before the turn of the century. In addition, the rediscovery, or the invention, of the literary baroque of Germany was stimulated by expressionism, just as the expressionist painters of the *Blaue Reiter* had made El Greco's cause their own: the exaggeration and the violence of the expressionist poetry and drama of such writers as Georg Trakl and Franz Werfel stimulated an interest (which Benjamin qualified as largely sentimental) in similar manifestations in the works of the seventeenth century. Both styles juxtaposed neologisms and archaisms, delighted in extravagance.

The scholarly treatment of seventeenth-century German literary style before Benjamin remained largely hostile, particularly in its view of the drama, generally condemned as a mistaken, barbarous, and pedantic imitation of Greek tragedy. The plays themselves, by such writers as Andreas Gryphius, Martin Opitz, and Daniel Caspers von Lohenstein, had largely been neglected, were seldom read, and almost never produced. The tentatively positive assessments of these works (by Herbert Cysarz, for example) considered them as primitive but necessary first steps to the classical drama of Goethe and Schiller. It was Benjamin's task to rehabilitate this style for its own sake, to give its own reason for being, and to justify its existence.

In this, as we have seen, he explicitly followed the example of Riegl's rehabilitation of late Roman art: common to both projects was the choice of a period whose art violated the fundamental classical canons of aesthetics, an art that was—to most eyes—neither beautiful nor vital, but awkward and lifeless. If expressionism reinforced Benjamin's project, Riegl's had been helped and no doubt partly inspired by impressionism and post-impressionism. These changes of taste, fashion, or sensibility may account for the urge to rewrite history but not for the grander project of profoundly altering our conception of the nature of history itself. In this, Benjamin was more radical than

Riegl; he explicitly set out to demonstrate a thesis that Riegl had only hinted at, and had held largely in reserve in the back of his mind: that there is no such thing as an independent history of art.

In a curriculum vitae, Benjamin claimed that just as Benedetto Croce had opened a path to the particular concrete work of art by smashing the concept of genre, so his book was intended to clear the way to the work by smashing the doctrine of the independent field of art. As he wrote to a friend while working on the *Trauerspiel* book:

> What occupies me is how works of art are related to historical life. On this point what seems to me certain is that there is no such thing as a history of art. . . . The explorations of the current history of art always end up only as a history of material or history of form, for which works of art serve only as examples, almost as models: of a history of works themselves there is absolutely no question. . . .
>
> Works of art are, in this respect, like philosophical systems, and the so-called "history" of philosophy is either an uninteresting history of dogmas, or a history of problems, in which case it threatens to lose contact with the temporal extension and to change into timeless, intensive *interpretation*. The specific historicity of works of art is of a similar kind, which opens not into the history of art but only into interpretation. In the interpretation there arise connections between works of art which are timeless and yet not without historical importance. The same forces which in the revealed world (that is, in history) become explosive and temporally extensive show themselves in the world of silence as intensive.[5]

Here, with Benjamin's idiosyncratic theological terminology, is a formulation of his task; to relate the work to history while respecting its essential function of stepping out of the historical time and space in which it was produced. The achievement of Benjamin was to have recognized and exploited this tension, to have developed a way of interpreting the historical significance of a work that does not question its suprahistorical integrity.

In *The Origin of German Trauerspiel*, paradoxically, he does this by resurrecting the concept of genre which he praised Croce for smashing, but in a very different sense. Terms like "tragedy" were not, for Benjamin, either a means of classifying various individual works, or a set of norms by which they could be judged. He states his position in a form so provocative that it was evidently designed to make the hackles of the academic world rise:

For these ideas [of "tragedy" and "comedy"] are not at all embodiments of rules; they are themselves entities [or structures], at the very least equal in substance and reality to any and every drama, without being in any way commensurable. They therefore make no claim to embrace a number of given works of literature on the basis of some feature or other common to them. For even if there were no such thing as the pure tragedy or the pure comedy which can be named after them, these ideas can endure.[6]

This appears a straightforward affirmation of Platonic realism, but Benjamin's position, as I shall try to make clear, was a much stranger one.

The Origin of German Trauerspiel is a relatively short book of a little over 200 pages, divided into two parts. The first deals specifically with the *Trauerspiel,* the second with the technique of allegory, intimately related to the drama of the seventeenth century. The *Trauerspiel* is marked off from classical tragedy; the efforts of contemporary baroque theorists to base their discussions on Aristotle are shown as factitious and misleading, an attempt to give dignity and tradition to radically new work. Benjamin distinguishes tragedy from *Trauerspiel* as two totally distinct genres:

Historical life, as it was conceived at that time, is the content, the real object [of the *Trauerspiel*]. In this it is different from tragedy. For the object of the later is not history, but myth, and the tragic stature of the *dramatis personae* does not derive from rank—the absolute monarchy—but from the pre-historic epoch of their existence—the past age of heroes. (62)

Tragedy and *Trauerspiel* are, as genres, bound to time: neither one is possible outside the era in which it originated.

For the seventeenth-century German poet, history was the fall of kings. Benjamin traces in the *Trauerspiel* the relation of the plays to contemporary theories of sovereignty ("The sovereign represents history. He holds the course of history in his hand like a scepter" (65).), as well as to the theological outlook of the German seventeenth century, in particular to the devaluation of everyday life in the Lutheran opposition to the Counter

Reformation (most of the German playwrights were Lutheran). As he writes:

The relationship of Lutheranism to the everyday had always been antinomic. The rigorous morality of its teaching in respect of civic conduct stood in sharp contrast to its renunciation of "good works." By denying the latter any special miraculous spiritual effect, making the soul dependent on grace through faith, and making the secular-political sphere a testing ground for a life which was only indirectly religious, being intended for the demonstration of civic virtues, it did, it is true, instill into the people a strict sense of obedience to duty, but in its great men it produced melancholy. (138)

From this melancholy, foreign to Greek tragedy, springs the grief, the *Trauer* of the *Trauerspiel*.

Politics and theology are reflected in the psychology of the plays:

The antithesis between the power of the ruler and his capacity to rule led to a feature peculiar to the *Trauerspiel* which apparently comes from the nature of the genre but which can be illuminated only against the background of the theory of sovereignty. This is the indecisiveness of the tyrant. The prince, who is responsible for making the decision to proclaim the state of emergency, reveals, at the first opportunity, that he is almost incapable of making a decision. Just as compositions with restful lighting are virtually unknown in mannerist painting, so it is that the theatrical figures of this epoch always appear in the harsh light of their changing resolve. What is conspicuous about them is not so much the sovereignty evident in the stoic turns of phrase, as the sheer arbitrariness of a constantly shifting emotional storm in which the figures of Lohenstein especially sway about like torn and flapping banners. (70–71)

Benjamin follows this with a series of extraordinary examples of vacillations drawn from the plays, moments of crisis in which the hero hesitates in an agony of indecision. In Lohenstein's *Sophonisbe* the hero, about to send Sophonisbe poison to save her from imprisonment by the Romans, cries: "Alas, what terrors weigh upon my tortured heart! Away! Be gone! But no! Stay! Come back! Yes, go! It must be done at last" (71n). Politics and theology together are implicated in the *Trauerspiel*'s conception of history as catastrophe.

The enduring fascination of the downfall of the tyrant is rooted in the conflict between the impotence and depravity of his person, on the one hand, and, on the other, the extent to which the age was convinced of the sacrosanct powers of his role. It was therefore quite impossible to derive an easy moral satisfaction . . . from the tyrant's end. For if the tyrant falls, not simply in his own name, as an individual, but as a ruler and in the name of mankind and history then his fall is played out as a judgment, and the subject too feels himself implicated in the sentence. (72)

The limits of the genre are revealed by the tyrant-drama and the martyr-drama:

In the baroque the tyrant and the martyr are the Janus-head of the monarch. They are the necessary extreme coinings of the princely essence. (69)

The image is that of the royal medal, and the martyr and tyrant imply each other, are the reverse images of the same form.

Benjamin's ideas, conveyed by a deliberately discontinuous mosaic of quotation, observation, and metaphor, are difficult to summarize—or even to translate.[7] What was, as far as I know, without precedent at that time, except for Georg Lukács's analysis of the nineteenth-century novel, was Benjamin's representation of a genre historically—treating the political, theological, and social aspects of the drama as formal elements of the work, examining them exactly as he did the figures of speech, the verse forms, and the grammatical structure of the style. In this way Benjamin avoided both the falsifications of the usual historical approach, which reduces and simplifies the work to signifying something outside itself, and the limitations of formalism, which has blinded itself to some of the most characteristic and representative elements of art.

5

I will! and once more fill a kingdom's throne.
Spain, I'll new mould thee: I will have a chair
Made all of dead men's bones; and the ascents
Shall be the heads of Spaniards set in ranks:
I will have Philip's head, Hurtenzo's head,
Mendoza's head, thy mother's head, and this—
This head, that is so cross, I'll have't.
The scene wants actors; I'll fetch more and clothe it

In rich cothurnal pomp; a tragedy
Ought to be grave: graves this shall beautify.

—Thomas Dekker, *Lust's Dominion, or the Lascivious Queen,* Act V, scene 5

By representing the *Trauerspiel* through its relations to the politics, religion, and philosophy of the society in which it was produced, Benjamin made his work applicable to the contemporary Spanish baroque, and the late Elizabethan and Jacobean dramas. In an early draft of his preface, in fact, Benjamin doubts whether the German *Trauerspiel* can be adequately described without reference to the drama of Shakespeare and Calderón (the English and Spanish *Trauerspiel* we might call them). The power of Benjamin's method may be indicated briefly by extending his observations on theatrical conventions of the time, above all the use of illusion and stage properties.

Theatrical conventions are generally treated as something that the contemporary audience—and we, today, as well—must accept blindly and unquestioningly; the conventions are simply given, and we surrender to them. In a brilliant essay[8] Christopher Ricks protests against the slackness of this view and insists that a convention must be justified, its probability vindicated by the dramatist each time, and that the vindication must come from plot and character. Against his opponents Ricks wins easily, but he stops midway in his considerations of convention. A convention is indeed not simply given, but has its own *raison d'être:* the dramatist uses or abuses the convention. Ricks interprets the use, Benjamin goes one step further to interpret the convention itself.

There is an extreme form of *Trauerspiel,* in which probability has little relevance: the so-called Tragedy of Fate, in which the action moves mechanically and inexorably toward the catastrophe. In this kind of play—for Benjamin the supreme examples are by Calderón—psychological motivation is often deliberately abandoned. Calderón's "whole mastery lies in the extreme exactitude with which, in a play like the Herod-drama, the violent passion is elevated out of the psychological motivation of the action which the modern reader looks for" (133).

This lack of motivation is a sign of man's total subjection to powers which he cannot control or influence, and it brings with it the fatal role of the stage property—the inorganic object which inexorably involves the characters in their doom.

Unmentioned here by Benjamin but clearly relevant is *Othello,* the only great example of the Tragedy of Fate in English. The stage property is the handkerchief, and the psychological motivation that Ricks demands is emphatically refused to Iago:

Othello: Will you, I pray, demand that demy-Divell,
Why he hath thus ensnar'd my Soule and Body.
Iago: Demand me nothing: what you know, you know.

This lack of motivation disconcerts not only critics but Iago himself, who says earlier that he hates the Moor because of a rumor that "twixt my sheets / He's done my Office. I know not if't be true, / But I, for meere suspition in that kinde, / Will do, as if for Surety." Neither he nor Shakespeare seems to believe it much, and no one else ever has either.[9]

In 1692 the critic Thomas Rymer, in a famous attack on *Othello,* made the infamous suggestion that Othello's jealousy would have been better grounded had the handkerchief been a garter. Ricks replies that this

ignores the fact that from one point of view such an item as a garter would be too incriminating, might hint a frame-up. The great thing, the fatal thing, about the handkerchief is precisely that it is a trifle.[10]

Ricks does not appreciate his own insight in the last sentence, because he is, for the moment, too concerned with propriety of motivation—from that point of view Rymer is, after all, surely right, a garter would be more convincing. But it would not be a trifle.

Benjamin's method, extended to Jacobean drama, tells us, as Ricks cannot, why the garter will not do—it would have too much of the life of Desdemona about it, it is not sufficiently neutral, dead. Benjamin is not concerned, like the scholars that Ricks attacks, with merely confirming the existence of a convention, or, like Ricks, only with its use: he wants to force out its meaning.

He therefore enables us to discover something in *Othello* that Ricks does not: that the blindness of Othello's passion, jealousy, is expressed, not motivated, by something as insignificant as the handkerchief. The disparity between the cause of his jealousy and its fury is essential. As Benjamin writes about the German Tragedy of Fate:

For once human life has sunk into the merely natural, even the life of apparently dead objects secures power over it. The effectiveness of the object where guilt has been incurred is a sign of the approach of death. The passionate stirrings of natural life in man—in a word, passion itself—bring the fatal property into action. It is nothing other than the seismographic needle which registers its vibrations. (132)

For Benjamin, the stage property in the Tragedy of Fate, like the absence or presence of psychological motivation, was not merely a convention given to the baroque dramatist, which he could use or abuse: it came to him with ideological strings attached. It had, in short, an inherent expressive function.

The breaking of stage illusion so essential to baroque style was another such convention with an expressive value. It can be understood only in a critical approach as wide as Benjamin's that reinterprets the past from the perspective of a much later period. Put the following remarks of Ricks against Benjamin's treatment of illusion:

The scene in *Othello* (Act 4, scene 1) in which the credulous Othello is snared by Iago into overhearing (and misconstruing) a conversation between Iago and Cassio about Bianca . . . is no more convincing, no less stagey than [a similar scene in *The White Devil* by Webster]; the particular convention presents such difficulties, is so intractable, that even Shakespeare here fails to master it."[11]

"Stagey" is the exact and necessary word; Ricks mistakenly proffers it as a reproach. Benjamin relates the breaking of illusion, the staginess of the *Trauerspiel,* to the effort to express the "play" character of life itself, which has lost its ultimate seriousness in the despair of Counter-Reformation theology.

In the drama the play element was demonstratively emphasized, and transcendence was allowed its final word only in the worldly disguise of a play within a play. The technique is not always obvious as when the stage itself is set up on the stage, or the auditorium is extended onto the stage area. (82)

The scene in *Othello* is such a play within a play, staged by Iago for Othello, who becomes a member of the audience, the only one, in fact, to misunderstand what is being played.

This explicit reference to the stage that Benjamin remarks in the German *Trauerspiel*, moreover, occurs at the moment of crisis of every one of Shakespeare's major tragedies. King Lear, cast out by his daughters into the storm, stages a mock trial with the footstool as Goneril; Cleopatra, preparing for suicide, does so in order not to be dragged in triumph to Rome and see herself played on the stage by a boy; at the death of his wife before his final disaster, Macbeth compares life to a poor player that struts and frets his hour upon the stage; and, perhaps most movingly, Coriolanus, about to order the sack of Rome, sees his wife and mother come to plead with him and says hopelessly:

Like a dull actor now, I have forgot my part,
And I am out, even to a full Disgrace. . . .

The staginess of these references[12] is allegorical: they turn the stage itself into an emblem of illusion. Nowhere is this made more emphatic than in *Richard II*. Forced to abdicate, Richard calls for a looking glass, and begins to quote Marlowe's *Faustus*:

Was this Face the Face
That every day under his household roof
Did keep ten thousand men? Was this the Face
That, like the Sun, did make beholders wink?
Is this the Face that fac'd so many follies
And was at last outfac'd by Bolingbroke?

(each phrase approaching more and more closely to the famous lines on Helen "Is this the face that launch'd a thousand ships?"). This reference to the stage at the climax of the tragedy is not a poet's game, an irrelevant frivolity. Richard with his looking glass, like Hamlet with the skull of Yorick, or Lear judging the footstool, is a figure of allegory, frozen for a moment into an emblematic stiffness. "The shadow of your Sorrow," Bolingbroke says when Richard smashes the looking glass, "hath destroyed the shadow of your Face." The references to the stage, the looking glass, the death's head, are all emblems of illusion and premonitions of death. This is why the catastrophe in Jacobean drama arrives so often as a play within a play, a game of chess, or even a dance.

As Benjamin says, the allegorical technique is central to the view that life is an illusion which, when dissipated, reveals nothing. The essential characteristic of seventeenth-century allegory (the only kind with which Benjamin is basically concerned) is discontinuity, an unresolvable discrepancy between a visual sign or image and its meaning, "a dualism of signification and reality" (194). Allegories are never understood easily and naturally, but decoded: they require effort, which takes time, so sign and meaning are never simultaneous, never fused.

When John Donne, in the famous lines of "A Valediction: forbidding mourning," compares the departing lover and his love that stays behind to "stiff twin compasses" (i.e., the two legs of a drawing compass)—

Thy soule the fixt foot, makes no show
To move, but doth, if the other doe.
And though it in the center sit,
Yet when the other far doth roam,
It leanes, and hearkens after it,
And growes erect, as that comes home.

—the discrepancy between image and meaning is audacious. The inanimate scientific sign of the compass arrests and stiffens the vital meaning and reveals the kinship of such an emblematic figure with the fatal stage property that seems to have a life of its own and brings death. The dead image of the compass controls the living souls of which it is the sign, and the poem, indeed, starts with a scene of death:

As virtuous men passe mildly away,
And whisper to their soules, to goe,
Whilest some of their sad friends doe say
The breath goes now, and some say, no:
So let us melt, and make no noise. . . .

an image both of death and of the act of love which changes— imperceptibly—to the image of absence and love figured by the compass.

Benjamin was by no means the first critic to find allegorical elements in baroque drama, but he was, I think, the first to insist on their importance for the works as a whole, not merely for the occasional detail or character; he did not conceive allegory merely as a survival of an archaic technique within a more developed style. He was also a pioneer—as George Steiner has remarked[13]—in the study of sixteenth- and seventeenth-century emblem books, and the way that their figures appear in the drama. Other English examples of such emblems abound, and it is easy to add to Benjamin's German ones. The Duke in *The Traitor* by James Shirley dies with a series of images drawn from the emblem books on his lips:

For thee, inhuman murderer, expect
My blood shall fly to heaven, and there inflam'd,
Hang a prodigious meteor all thy life,
And when by some as bloody hand as thine
Thy soul is ebbing forth, it shall descend
In flaming drops upon thee: oh, I faint!—
Thou flattering world, farewell! let princes gather
My dust into a glass, and learn to spend
Their hour of state, that's all they have; for when
That's out, Time never turns the glass agen.

This magnificent collection of bric-a-brac—meteor, burning shower of blood, hourglass, all familiar from emblem books—illustrates what Benjamin called the arbitrary grouping of elements within the allegory. He wrote:

It is perfectly clear that this fragmentation in the graphic aspects is a principle of the allegorical approach. In the baroque, especially, the allegorical personification can be seen to give way in favor of the emblems, which mostly offer themselves to view in desolate, sorrowful dispersal. . . . It is as something incomplete and imperfect that the objects stare out from the allegorical structure. (186)

"In allegory the observer is confronted with the pallor of death, the 'Hippocratic countenance' of history as a petrified, primordial landscape," as Benjamin writes (166). Earlier, he observes that the *Trauerspiel* gives us "the transposition of the originally temporal data into a figurative spatial form" (81)—as the Duke's dying speech in *The Traitor* freezes the movement of the sovereign's life into the image of the hourglass.

The allegorical structures of the baroque age are better represented by the German *Trauerspiel* than by its more successful relatives in Spain and England—just because of their greater artistic success: the vitality of Spanish baroque drama comes from its playful brilliance, that of the English from the fusion of comedy with *Trauerspiel*. The elemental power of Shakespeare, as Benjamin says, rendered the equally important allegorical character of the plays almost unrecognizable for Romantic critics. Precisely because such artistic power was denied it, the German *Trauerspiel* can reveal the beauty of the genre and of the allegorical structure that underlies it.

For allegory is not just an artistic technique but also, as Benjamin points out, a corrective to art. By its discontinuity of image and meaning it rejects the false appearance of artistic unity, the fusion of meaning in the symbol, and presents itself as a fragment, a ruin. The German *Trauerspiel*, too, is just such a ruin. It has been eroded by time. The critical action of time is a well-worn cliché: it is time that separates the masterpieces from the second-rate, the great artist from the small fry. For Benjamin, time had a different function: the passage of time not only decided the success of a work, but—more importantly—separated the essential from the inessential in it, distinguished between the elements which were immediately appealing to contemporaries and those which had a more lasting interest. That is why the post-history of a work, the tradition it created, is as indispensable to the critic as its pre-history, its sources and the tradition it came from.

The Origin of German Trauerspiel has an esoteric secret, nowhere stated directly although implied at many points and inescapable from a close reading. Benjamin believed that every work of art in order to retain its essential nature had to become a ruin. This could—and generally does—happen in its history, but it is a potential of all works and discoveries to the critic. Every authentic work of literature, for Benjamin, was a metaphorical embodiment of philosophical ideas. Every critical reading should move toward that moment when the work appears to exist for the sake of the philosophical truth within it: it no longer exists for itself, and it therefore loses its charms. It reaches the condition of the *inexpressive*. As a ruin, the *Trauerspiel* is an allegory of art in general.

The business of the critic, for Benjamin, is not to resuscitate the dead, or to reconstitute the original which now stands before us fragmented, but to understand the work as a ruin, and in so doing paradoxically to awaken the beauty present in it as a ruin. But to achieve this Benjamin had to invent a methodology for criticism, based on an idiosyncratic and esoteric philosophy of language, and a radical theory of knowledge and history.

6

Eine klassische Schrift muss nie ganz verstanden werden können. Aber die, welche gebildet sind und sich bilden, müssen immer mehr draus lernen wollen.

(A classical text must never be completely understandable. But those who are educated and who continue to educate themselves must always wish to learn more from it.)

—Friedrich Schlegel, Lyceum Fragment, number 20

The *Trauerspiel* is an esoteric book. That is surely the immediate reason why first the Department of Germanic Studies and then the Department of Philosophy of Art of the University of Frankfurt rejected this study of seventeenth-century dramatists when it was presented to them as a thesis. The publishers of the English translation have enhanced Benjamin's esotericism by omitting all page numbers from the table of contents, as well as by printing the six separate sections of the book's two parts with no indication of where one stops and the next one starts. The esotericism is deeply rooted in Benjamin's style: even where the book is easy to read—by no means necessarily where it is best— the argument is not made explicit, and the connection between ideas is only suggested, never emphasized.

This is what makes his work resist summary and paraphrase, or even quotation, unless one wrenches his sentences as brutally from their contexts as he tore his quotations from theirs. The difficulty of reading his mosaic of quotations and commentary, which demands a pause for reflection after each sentence, is characteristic of his era, an age of great esoteric literature. The *Trauerspiel* book was finished in 1925; 1921 is the date of Joyce's

Ulysses, 1922 of Eliot's *The Waste Land* and Rilke's *Sonnets to Orpheus*, while Yeats's *A Vision* appeared in 1926. *The Origin of German Trauerspiel* is a masterly work in that tradition.

The esoteric had a more general value for Benjamin: it revealed something about literature in general. Esoteric journalism is a contradiction in terms: literature, however, is permitted to baffle us. Even more, we might say that all literature which lasts, which remains literature and has not become a document, is baffling.

This well-known phenomenon is generally sentimentalized by saying—about simple lyric poems, for example—that they express the inexpressible, or that every great work has a mysterious quality that can never be reached by analysis but only felt by instinct. Such evasions are unnecessary. The mystery arises because literature invokes aspects of language other than that of communication.[14]

Language cannot be reduced to communication even if its other functions sometimes take second place. Among them is an expressive function: swearing to oneself without the benefit of an audience. There is the sheer pleasure in nonsense syllables that children develop early and that adults never lose. And there is the magic formula and the sacred text.

A sacred text can never be simply described as communication except by metaphor. There are questions necessary to communication that we are forbidden to ask of a text whose sacred character we accept: is the speaker mistaken? is he sincere?—or indeed any question designed to test the validity of what is said by an appeal to experience. The sacred text is characterized, in short, by its autonomy. Its meaning is independent of all human contingency; the divine is not contingent.

Since the sixteenth century, if not before, some of the forbidden questions have been asked of Scripture; it has been considered subject to contingency, losing its sacred character. It has become literature, which is not sacred, but which has always tended to usurp the place of religion. Literature—at least ever since Homer—has appropriated and exploited the functions of a sacred text. For an essential part of our experience of them, the texts of literature demand to be taken as objective, as given for contemplation, for meditation, incantation, for a form of understanding that evades intention, author's as well as reader's. Literature aspires not so much to attain as to return to the condition of music, which is, in Romantic mythology, the original form of speech.

These noncommunicative aspects of language exist in everyday usage (the slogan, for example, works partly like a magic formula), but they are either hidden by the overwhelming needs of communication or pushed aside as reprehensibly primitive. A work of literature, however, not only preserves them but would lose all its power without them. That is what Valéry meant by saying that a work of literature lasts just so long as it is able to appear other than as its author conceived it.

The illusion of autonomy enables the work to operate effectively: it stops the reader from taking it simply as a form of communication and so allows the other aspects of language to press forward. The autonomy is an illusion, of course, because a work of literature is subject to history, created by an author, its words and even its form comprehensible only if one starts from a specific culture (even if, in the end, the work is not restricted to that culture). The illusion can neither be simply dispelled nor maintained.

No critic saw this as clearly as Benjamin. The formalist critic respects the autonomy of the work, but rejects whole areas of meaning and thereby impoverishes the form itself. The biographical and historical critic denies the autonomy and freezes the work into a fixed mold of interpretation, limiting its range of meaning as constrictingly as the formalist.

The difficulty, the esoteric quality of Benjamin's writing, arises from his attempt to give full weight to both sides of the dual nature of literature. The insights of critics often come in spite of their systems. In Benjamin's case, I believe, his success is directly related to his radical methodology, a compound of early Romantic aesthetics, Symbolist theory, and much that is wholly new. It is worth examining this system above all in order to see briefly how it applies to criticism in our own day.

Benjamin's sporadic attacks on academic criticism in all its forms are phrased with an intransigence that was to cost him any chance for a position in a German university.[15] It was essential for him decisively to cut off what he was doing from the procedures of most of his contemporaries—and most of ours as well. His arguments have not lost their immediacy.

Where Benjamin's convictions depart most trenchantly from those of other critics is, first, in his attack on what he called "inductive" methods of analysis—that is, his preference for studying the extreme, the exceptional in place of the average, the normative, in the belief that the extremes give the most accurate picture of a style; second, in his insistence on the autonomy of the work of art as opposed to the autonomy of "literature" or "art"; and, above all, in his affirmation that words are not signs, that they only degenerate into signs (that is, into things that arbitrarily stand for something other than themselves—necessary substitutes for what they refer to): or, in idealist terminology, that words degenerate from Ideas into concepts.

This latter point is the most radical, the one in which Benjamin opposes himself to most forms of contemporary philosophy, linguistics, and criticism. The word, for Benjamin, was not a substitute for something else; it had a value of its own, and was the name of an Idea.

In spite of his explicit appeal to the authority of Plato and the implicit references to Kantian terminology, Benjamin's use of "Idea" is in large part original. It derives most immediately from the aesthetics of the early Romantics, above all, that of Schlegel and Novalis. The word names an Idea, the work of art is a metaphor for an Idea. A quotation from the notebooks of Novalis clarifies the notion of "Idea" that Benjamin was drawing upon (in what follows, "novel" (*Roman*) is to be understood as any work of art of some substance—for example, a play by Shakespeare was called a *Roman* around 1800 by these young German critics):

The novel, as such, contains no defined result—it is not the picture or the factual reality of a *proposition (nicht Bild und Faktum eines Satzes)*. It is the graphic carrying-out—the realization—of an Idea. But an Idea cannot be seized by a proposition. An Idea is *an infinite series* of propositions—an *irrational quantity*—*untranslatable* (musical)—incommensurable. (Should not all irrationality be relative?) What can be set down, however, is the law of its development [*Ausführung*, i.e., the rule for deriving the infinite series]—and a novel should be criticized from this standpoint.[16]

The distinction between concept and Idea is partially derived from Kant and is the one still employed by Benjamin: a concept may be defined by a simple sentence, or proposition, an Idea cannot.

This makes an Idea much grander than a concept (which is why I have conserved its initial capital) but not, according to Novalis, vaguer. It is precise and definable, but not as a sign— that is, not as a simple relationship between two sets of words in which the definition may be substituted for the original expression. The definition of an Idea is not an exhaustible process.

Novalis uses the infinite series as a metaphor for the process of describing the Idea. Benjamin accepts the distinction between concept and Idea, and like Novalis he, too, draws philosophy and art together. His description of Ideas, however, is not that of Novalis, and he substitutes very different metaphors: configuration and constellation.

The representation of Ideas takes place through the medium of empirical reality. For Ideas are not represented in themselves, but solely and exclusively as an arrangement of real, concrete elements in the concepts. And indeed as the configuration of these elements. . . . The staff of concepts which serves as the representation of an Idea realizes it as such a configuration. . . . Ideas are to things as constellations are to stars. This means, in the first place, that they are neither their concepts nor their laws. (34, translation altered)

The distinction in Benjamin between concept and Idea may be roughly summarized: the concept defines a class of phenomena, the Idea determines the relation of the phenomena in the different classes to each other. Tragedy as a concept defines a certain number of plays: Tragedy as an Idea figures the relation of these plays to history in the widest sense.

Here we come to the root of Benjamin's attack on the academic history of literature: its reliance on classification. "Tragedy," for example, *as a concept* is ordinarily defined by "induction," that is, taking a large number of examples and then analyzing

what they have in common. This blurs more than it reveals.
When one puts modern

plays by Holz or Halbe alongside dramas by Aeschylus or Euripides,
without so much as asking whether the tragic is a form which can be
realized at all at the present time, or whether it is not a historically
limited form, then, as far as the tragic is concerned, the effect of such
widely divergent material is not one of an overarching conception,
but of sheer incongruity. When facts are amassed in this way . . . , the
less obvious original qualities are soon obscured by the chaos of more
immediately appealing modern ones. (39, translation altered)

So defined, the concept of tragedy gives not the general, but
the average: it is therefore incapable of aiding us to assess the
significance either of the norm itself or of the most characteristic divergences from the norm. Induction can at best help us to
discern the outlines of an Idea, but not to validate it. Indeed,
Benjamin's distinction between *Trauerspiel* and tragedy depends on his refusal to fit the German baroque drama into a
generalized concept of tragedy; in Benjamin's method of describing a genre, no example can be admitted without questioning its right to be there, and this destroys the basis for simple
inductive or statistical definitions.

Benjamin's ponderous idealist terminology (to which I am
probably as allergic as the next man) provokes two fundamental questions to which Benjamin gives by no means the traditional idealist answers—his solutions are indeed already in
many ways close to materialism. The questions are: how are
Ideas to be known? and how are they to be described?

Benjamin starts by denying any form of immediate intuition
or perception, mystical or otherwise, of Ideas. They are not to
be found as data, as given in the phenomenal world. They are
given in language—but in language seen as extending far beyond its function of communication. In Benjamin's own oracular terms:

The Idea is something linguistic, it is that very moment in the essence
of any word in which it becomes a symbol. In empirical understanding, in which the word has disintegrated, it possesses, in addition to its
more or less hidden, symbolic aspect, an obvious, profane meaning. It
is the task of the philosopher to restore, *by representation,* the primacy
of the symbolic character of the word. (36, translation altered, my
italics)

In what follows this—the theory of the word as "name"—we find the principal locus for Benjamin's interest in the Kabbalah and in mysticism; in spite of his refusal of mystical forms of perception, he found much that was congenial to him in mystical writings, particularly those of the seventeenth century. Nevertheless, the little that Benjamin found in the Kabbalah was only what he had already been looking for, and we may say that the words I have set in relief—"by representation"—introduce a new and very different emphasis into mystical theory. The symbolic aspect of the word has not been perceived until its representation has been constructed.[17]

To understand what Benjamin meant by "representation" we must see that his philosophy of language does not derive directly from any mystical source whatever but from Mallarmé and from the linguist and critic Wilhelm von Humboldt.[18] For Humboldt, writing around 1800 at the great moment when comparative linguistics first came into its own, language was less a means of expressing ideas than of discovering them. It was an independent system, a separate world different from the objective world of reality and the subjective world of consciousness: only through language, in fact, do we realize that the subjective and objective worlds are one. On the origin of language (a question discussed by almost every writer of the eighteenth century) Humboldt claimed that language could not come into being element by element but must exist all at once: the use of one word implies the whole system, the structure of the language of which it is only a part.

Benjamin's attack upon the arbitrary sign-character of language is already explicit in Humboldt:

A word is indeed a sign insofar as it is used to signify a thing or a concept, but in the way it is formed and acts it is a particular and independent being—an individual.

Even more in Benjamin's style, we find Humboldt writing:

A word reveals itself as an individual with a nature of its own which bears a resemblance to a work of art insofar as it makes possible an idea beyond all Nature with a form borrowed from Nature.

And finally a point that Benjamin was to appropriate in his essay on translation:

To say '*íppos,* equus and horse is not to say thoroughly and completely the same thing.[19]

Benjamin's version of this is more developed:

The words *Brot* and *pain* [bread] "intend" the same object, but the modes of this intention are not the same. It is owing to these modes that the word *Brot* means something different to a German than the word *pain* to a Frenchman, that for them these words are not interchangeable, that in the end they strive to exclude each other.[20]

By "mode of intention" Benjamin means something more than "connotation": the words *Brot* and *pain* have a range of significance in French and German culture which, when followed to its limits, to the extreme, will mirror the whole civilization and history governed by their languages. The total range of significance, *represented objectively,* and as a structure of its most distant relationships, is the Idea in Benjamin's sense.[21]

The objectivity of the representation, guaranteed by the nature of language, which is a system independent of our subjective intentions, is preserved only by invoking those aspects of language that transcend its use as a tool for communication—its poetic and contemplative functions, and even the ways in which it can transform itself into a sacred text or become petrified as a magic formula.

For Benjamin, the failure to consider these aspects and the attempts to deny their existence and their power account for the weakness of most contemporary criticism and philosophy. It is communication—language used for an individual purpose, the Ideas reduced to concepts—which is subjective. Language is not arbitrary, present at the moment of speaking without reason or justification, but given by tradition and history; it is the repository of experience, including the experience that no one will ever have again. Benjamin had thoroughly absorbed the criticism of Kant by Hamann, the eighteenth-century philosopher of the *Sturm und Drang,* who attacked Kant's "pure reason" as an unwitting attempt to get behind language. Hamann demonstrated that the ideas of philosophy

were embedded in language: even Descartes's project of starting afresh, provisionally wiping away all of experience and
reconstructing it, entailed the absurdity of doing away with
language, which cannot be separated from experience and
tradition.

The objectivity of language, its independence, its momen-
tum, was perhaps stated best by Friedrich Schlegel, when he
said that words generally understood each other better than the
people who used them. The exhibition of this independence,
or, better, its symbolic reconstruction *in* art and *through* history
is the critic's job.

7

Verbindet die Extreme, so habt ihr die wahre Mitte.
(Unite the extremes, then you have the true mean.)

—Friedrich Schlegel, *Ideen,* no. 74

Benjamin's attack upon the contemporary practice of criticism
was deeply rooted in an attempt to reformulate the relations of
literature, philosophy, language, and history. In this he anticipated many of the solutions that were to be offered years later,
and even answered in advance the objections that are now put
forth against positions similar to his. It is evident that Idea, in
his sense, undefinable in any simple way but representable, is
allied to the theory of "open concepts" that has recently developed[22] as well as to Wittgenstein's concept of meaning as a
"family," in which the various meanings of a word are conceived as a loose assemblage. Arthur O. Lovejoy, for example,
in his influential essay of 1948, "On the Discrimination of Romanticism," called attention to the existence of such a family:
the word "romantic" is used with a variety of meanings, some so
far apart as to appear to exclude each other.

Against theories of this kind, however, Benjamin posits the
coherence of relationships among the various meanings of a
word.[23] He retains the openness but insists that the relationships are neither loose nor inchoate. They form a pattern—a
configuration—which it is the business of the critic to recon-

struct. The configuration of "romantic," for example, when applied to landscape, starts in the eighteenth century with the meaning of "picturesque"; by the early nineteenth century it indicates the landscape painting of artists to whom the "picturesque" is anathema—John Constable, Caspar David Friedrich, and many others. To trace the historical pattern of this radical change of meaning in its relation to European culture as a whole is to represent the "romantic" as an Idea in Benjamin's terms, to investigate two of its extremes.

Applied to terms of period style—like "baroque," "romantic," "classic"—Benjamin's philosophy of language and history presupposes the coherence of the period, assumes that the critic may work with the arts, sciences, theology, and politics of a given age and with the assurance he will not find himself with disparate, unrelated strands that he cannot weave together.

The method of weaving, however, is crucial: when, for example, the art historian John Shearman recently related some aspects of sixteenth-century music to his etiolated version of "mannerist" style in painting, the result was not encouraging (particularly as the same tendencies in music could be found centuries before and after). Benjamin had a word for such strategies which his translator renders excellently as "analogy-mongering." Benjamin's method requires the exploration of the most contradictory aspects of a period, an investigation of extremes, not the limitation of the research to the normative aspects. It is not as concepts "which make the similar identical" that Benjamin advised employing terms like "Renaissance" or "baroque," but as Ideas.[24] "When an Idea takes up a sequence of historical formulations, it does not do so in order to construct a unity out of them, let alone to abstract something common to them all" (46, translation altered).

The most visible and distinguished attacks today on the coherence of period styles come from Sir Ernst Gombrich, who sees the specter of Hegelianism wherever a unified stylistic field-theory rears its head. Gombrich's critical intelligence is powerful, his imagination limited: armed with the blinkered positivism of his friend Sir Karl Popper, he has made out a formidable case against Hegelian historical theory without ever being able to account for its seductions. The trouble with getting rid of these ideas of period and style, as many besides Gombrich have proposed, is that they slink back disguised even from the author and out of his control: a reviewer of Gombrich's recent biography of Aby Warburg commented acidly that for someone so opposed to Hegelian theories of style, Gombrich used the expression "period-flavor" surprisingly often. In any case, Benjamin does not attempt to construct a unity out of his picture of the seventeenth century in *The Origin of German Trauerspiel,* and Gombrich's arguments against theories of period style are harmless if applied to Benjamin's work.

An alternative to coherence is the loosely organized "family" of meanings, the treatment of a period that allows the different tendencies to jostle each other uncomprehendingly in an attempt to give the illusion of vitality that comes from disorder. The emphasis on variety often arrives at a radical distortion of reality in the interests of the critic's convenience. If, to follow a recent suggestion, we treat late eighteenth-century style in music as a loosely organized set of procedures, and abandon the idea of coherence, one crucially important phenomenon remains unexplained and generally unexamined: when one of the stylistic procedures (like treatment of melody) is radically altered, it creates a complementary alteration in at least some of the others (harmonic structure, phrase, rhythm).[25] Nor could a composer like Mozart or Clementi borrow Haydn's technique of thematic fragmentation without being influenced by his large structures and his harmonic rhythm.

In short, these procedures are not independent and not a genuine collection, not a "family" with the loose acceptance of incoherence that that implies. A period style, like baroque, or even a personal style, like Clementi's, is not a collection of procedures and tendencies, but *the interrelationships of these procedures.* Each time we try to discover these interrelationships, we are postulating a configuration which is the object of our research. It is evident that Benjamin's methodology, or some variant of it, is essential in historical criticism.

It is also evident that the interrelationships among stylistic procedures are best discovered when one of the procedures is used in particularly outrageous fashion, provoking a reaction in others. That is why the extreme case gives more information than the average. At any rate, the average cannot give one the range of a style—only the extremes can do that, and they alone can endow the average with its true sense. We may say that the extremes give the outline of the style, and the average gives its center of gravity. A middle-point has no significance until we know what it stands between.

In his picture of seventeenth-century German drama, Benjamin explores the opposing aspects of the figures of the tyrant and the martyr in the plays, the contrast between legal, bureaucratic terminology and pastoral style, the transformation of the *Trauerspiel* both into opera and the later marionette parodies of the plays. This is Benjamin's synthesis of extremes, a dialectical method, but not a Hegelian one. It does not resolve the contradictions in a false unity but represents their relationship as part of a much larger, total pattern.

The technique of representation is derived from Symbolism: Benjamin arranges his extraordinary quotations in an order that seems both to isolate them—to allow for a moment, with a shock, their alien nature to appear unmediated—and to resonate with their context, by forcing the reader to reassess their meaning.

Even his own sentences in their discontinuous arrangement and their aphoristic density seem like quotations. This procedure was defined for poetry by Mallarmé—or, better, evoked by him. From it Benjamin created a poetry of philology.

Here, in Mallarmé's dense prose (next to which Benjamin's style has the limpidity of John Dryden's), is his formulation of Symbolist technique and its relation to a philosophy of language:

Speaking only refers commercially to the reality of things: in literature, it is sufficient to make an allusion to them or to abstract their quality which will be embodied by some idea.

On this condition, the song bounds forth, a joy unburdened.

This aim I call Transposition—another I call Structure.

The pure work implies the elocutory disappearance of the poet: he yields the initiative to the words, mobilized by the shock of their disparity; they light up with reciprocal reflections like a virtual trail of fire on precious stones: replacing the perceptible respiration of the old lyric afflatus or the enthusiastic personal direction of the sentence.[26]

The direct reference of ordinary everyday language attempts to seize reality "commercially," that is, to possess it. Literature transposes it, turns it into structure, by indirection. The pure work of literature is based not on the poet's voice but on the nature of language, considered objectively. The idea must appear to arise solely from the juxtaposition of words as they reflect each other—this implies that more than one facet of the meaning of each word is used to create these reflections. The minute attentiveness to words replaces the coercive rhythm of older poetic styles or the coercive direction of a personal style. The independent initiative of the words is ensured by systematically weakening the linear movement, the flow of the sentence, traditionally cultivated in literary style. The Symbolist poet renounces communication for presentation.

If the words are to exhibit their multifaceted meaning, they must seem to be isolated within the text. By this isolation, they become names. In Mallarmé's words:

Je dis: une fleur! et, hors de l'oubli où ma voix relègue aucun contour, en tant que quelque chose d'autre que les calices sus, musicalement se lève, idée même et suave, l'absente de tous bouquets. . . .
    Le vers qui de plusieurs vocables refait un mot total, neuf, étranger à la langue et comme incantatoire, achève cet isolement de la parole: niant, d'un trait souverain, le hasard demeuré aux termes malgré l'artifice de leur retrempe alternée en le sens et la sonorité, et vous cause cette surprise de n'avoir ouï jamais tel fragment ordinaire d'élocution, en même temps que la réminiscence de l'objet nommé baigne dans une neuve atmosphère.

(I say: A flower! and out of the oblivion where my voice consigns a certain contour, as something other than the known calyxes, rises musically—itself an idea and sweet—the flower absent from all bouquets. . . .
    The verse which, from several terms, remakes a word—total, new, strange to the language and like an incantation—accomplishes this isolation of the word: denying with a sovereign gesture the inessential that remains in the terms in spite of the artifice of retempering them by dipping them alternately into sense and sonority, it causes you that surprise which comes from never having heard this particular ordinary fragment of elocution, at the same time that the reminiscence of the object named bathes in a novel atmosphere.)[27]

Benjamin's distinction between symbolic and profane meaning comes directly from Mallarmé's contrast of poetic and everyday language, and the technique of Symbolist poetry gave him his method of representing the Ideas—justly, as Symbolist theory asserts the independence of language and its emancipation from communication, and it is in language so emancipated that Benjamin placed the Ideas.

He was the last great Symbolist critic—and the first, too, in a way—certainly the first to apply the poetic theory to historical criticism. As Mallarmé treats words, Benjamin treats ideas: he names them, juxtaposes them, and lets them reflect one off the other. Renouncing directed argument, he relies upon the ideas through language to produce their own cross-meanings: his arrangements are material for contemplation, they force the reader himself to draw the meaning from the resonances of the ideas, from the perspectives created by the order of sentences.

Like Mallarmé's poetry, Benjamin's criticism is allusive, not coercive: it does not impose its interpretation on literature, but takes the form of a meditation on the texts that are quoted. Where it goes beyond Symbolism is in the more modern surrealist use of shock. This is particularly evident in his later essays on Baudelaire, inspired by Baudelaire's own fascination with the technique of shock, the yoking-together of incongruities. In Benjamin's "synthesis of extremes," however, the effect of shock is already a latent power, and the Symbolist procedure of allowing language to speak for itself, of "giving the initiative to the words," does the rest. The extremes are juxtaposed with little or no mediating comment, and the Idea arises in the silence between them.

8

L'armature intellectuelle du poème se dissimule et a lieu—tient—dans l'espace qui isole les strophes et parmi le blanc du papier; significatif silence qu'il n'est pas moins beau de composer que les vers.

(The intellectual armature of the poem conceals itself, and takes place—stands—in the space that isolates the stanzas and amidst the white of the paper; significant silence that is no less beautiful to compose than verse.)

—Mallarmé, *Le "Livre"*

A final assessment of Benjamin's Marxist period from his "conversion" in the late 1920s until his death must await publication of a large part of the material—in particular the Goethe essay written for the Moscow Encyclopedia but refused, like the *Trauerspiel* book, and the mass of notes for his last book, *Paris, Capital of the Nineteenth Century.* His new allegiance to a more openly activist philosophy made for an improvement, even a purification, of his style. With the partial disappearance of the idealist terminology went some of the mannerism: the writing is less visibly worked over. The long essay on Leskov, "The Storyteller," which contains a historical theory of narration, is perhaps the most accessible and the most beautiful of his works.

When the evidence is in, however, I doubt if we shall find that Benjamin had considerably altered his old opinions. In the 1930s he turned openly to the sociology of literature and language, above all in his essays on Brecht and in "The Work of Art in the Age of Mechanical Reproduction," but this interest had been implicit in his early work. He never, as Lukács did, retracted or betrayed his earlier insights, and he never ceased to get himself into trouble with those who could have helped and protected him.

The talk he gave at a communist congress in 1934, "The Author as Producer,"[28] was such an open provocation. It was tactless and imprudent to tell a group of communist writers that they ought not to judge a work by its *Tendenz*, by its ideological content, that there was no sense in writing bourgeois novels with communist ideals. His obvious interest in avant-garde art would have found a welcome response in the breasts of the many surrealist artists then in the party, but most of them had learned to temper their surrealist enthusiasm by 1934. Benjamin's efforts to champion Brecht also had a certain bravado, as Brecht was not in the best odor in Moscow. What must have been especially outrageous to the French communists was Benjamin's praise of the interesting experimental movement in Russia which tried to abolish the distinction between reader and writer, and allowed the workers to write their own newspaper: this would have taken some of the press out of state control, and the movement was under heavy attack in Stalinist Russia.

Shortly afterward the movement was suppressed, and then Benjamin repeated his praise of it in "The Work of Art in the Age of Mechanical Reproduction." This was evidently going too far, and Adorno and his friends who published it cut out the offending phrases.

"The Work of Art in the Age of Mechanical Reproduction" is the most influential of Benjamin's writings: it proposes the theory of the *aura*, the traces of history that guarantee the authenticity and uniqueness, the autonomy, in fact, of the traditional work of art. In this essay Benjamin envisages the possibility that art and culture as we know them will disappear, that they will be destroyed by the technology of the new mass arts; he thought that the shock of information relayed by the newspapers was killing the sense of the wisdom conveyed by the oral tradition of the storyteller.

Benjamin was a lover of rare books, with a splendid collection of children's books. He was tied emotionally in many ways to the old forms of culture. He knew, however, how much the conception of the single, isolated work of art, authentic and unrepeatable, owed to religion, which gave it its sacred radiance, and then later, in a secularized form, how much it owed to a system of private property which gave it its value. He knew the dependence of culture upon a world and a society that he felt—with the intensity of an alien Jew in Paris in the 1930s—to be unjust and even indecent.

It may be that Benjamin exaggerated, and certainly he misstated, the complicity of art and culture in the injustice of history. In any case, he could not bring himself to condemn the possible—and even, he hoped, eventual—disappearance of the society he knew, although he understood that much of what he considered art would disappear with it—not only by the destruction of objects, but by the death of the *aura*, the sense of art which was already losing its power.

He was perhaps the only critic who would neither rejoice at

the prospect of the death of art nor—in spite of the deep nostalgia his essay expresses—allow himself to mourn its passing. His dispassionate tone is aristocratic. Perhaps to understand the tragic irony of this famous essay we should need to have the text of the unpublished discussion in which Benjamin, according to Scholem,[29] defended *in Marxist terms* the thesis that art is meant for connoisseurs of art.

In the end, it was probably this aristocratic manner that made the difficulty between Benjamin and the editors of the *Zeitschrift für Sozialforschung*, the one review where, by 1938, Benjamin could still place a substantial essay. The refusal to publish some of his finest work, the three essays on Baudelaire now grouped together as *The Paris of the Second Empire in Baudelaire*, delayed their appearance until the years 1967–71.

The ostensible reason for the rejection, as expounded in Adorno's letters, was Benjamin's faulty Marxism, his pragmatic placing of details from the "superstructure" directly against traits drawn from the "substructure" without the mediation of theory. For example, Benjamin set the stanzas of Baudelaire's *The Ragpicker's Wine* directly alongside a description of the wine tax, without comment. Adorno objected to his "open-eyed wonder in the presentation of the facts" as un-Marxist. There is no doubt, as Habermas has said, that Adorno was the better Marxist of the two—although he, too, was peculiar enough in his own way; what upset him was what he called Benjamin's "ascetic" withholding of theory.

This "asceticism" was central to Benjamin's philosophy. He seized on Adorno's phrase about his "open-eyed wonder":

When you speak of "open-eyed wonder in the presentation of facts," you characterize the true philological attitude. . . . Philology is the close inspection of a text, moving forward by details, that fixes the reader's attention magically onto it. . . .

In your Kierkegaard criticism you say that this wonder gives "the deepest insight into the relation of dialectic, myth and image". . . . This ought to read: "the wonder should be a prominent *object* of such an insight". . . .

If you think back on other works of mine, you will find that a criticism of the philological attitude has been close to me for a long time—and is at its core identical with my criticism of myth. At times this criticism provokes the philological activity itself. It presses, to use the language of the *Elective Affinities,* towards a display of the material content in which the truth content is historically enfolded.[30]

Benjamin was unregenerate. Necessarily so, as what he called philology was at the heart of his style. Philology is the "display of the material content" of a work of literature, the elucidation, element by element, of its historical significance. Theory, however, could only be presented indirectly, unless it was doctrine—that is, unless it was sanctified by tradition, given the authority of "historical codification," as Benjamin put it.[31]

The form of indirect presentation—that, in fact, of Symbolist poetry—Benjamin called the "tractatus." In it the appearance of a mathematical demonstration, of a rigorously ordered chain of reasoning, had to be abandoned.

Presentation as detour—that is the methodical character of the tractatus. Renunciation of the uninterrupted course of intention is its principal mark of distinction. Perseveringly thought begins always afresh, ceremoniously it goes back to the thing itself. This unremitting respiration is the most characteristic existential form of contemplation. (28, my translation)

This is the rhythm of Benjamin's style. Basically, this respiration was his innocent idea of dialectic. Between every sentence there is a moment of silence; as he said, he deliberately renounced the use of all those stylistic equivalents of the manual gestures and the directed glance by which we normally carry over from one sentence to the next when we speak, and which the writer can mimic by rhythm and syntax. This renunciation accounts for Adorno's confusion: he thought that Benjamin was implying a causal connection between the facts of social and economic history and the lines of Baudelaire juxtaposed to them. No such connection exists in Benjamin's text. Adorno had not heard the silences.

9

Die wahre Aesthetik ist die *Kabbala.*
(The true aesthetic is the Kabbalah.)

—Friedrich Schlegel, *Literary Notebooks 1797–1801,* Fragment 1989

The Romanticism of the end of the eighteenth century—of Novalis, Schlegel, Blake, Wordsworth, Coleridge, Senancour, Chateaubriand—is often presented as a religious revival. That is to stand things on their heads. It was a profoundly secularizing movement, an attempt to appropriate what was left of a moribund religious culture and to reinstate it in secular form, most often to replace religion with art. The fact that by 1810 many of these figures had lost their revolutionary fervor and fled into the arms of the Church meant only a temporary setback: the task was larger than one had initially imagined. It has continued. Most of the institutional aspects of religion had already become secularized by the American and French revolutions: the pretense at transcendence within the Church after that time has largely been fraudulent. What had remained almost untouched were the mystical strains in religious thought. It was to the preservation of these mystical elements, giving them a secular form, that Blake, Novalis, and the others addressed themselves, sometimes inventing new mythologies to liberate mysticism from its religious mold, sometimes merely giving it an aesthetic expression that made it once again available.

In this return to early Romantic philosophy and criticism, Walter Benjamin continued that tradition—he was its greatest representative in our century along with Yeats and André Breton. The preservation of mystical forms of thought meant for him not their resurrection but their transformation—just as, in the seventeenth century, allegorical technique preserved the pagan deities by transforming them into emblematic fragments, presenting them as ruins. Philology, the painstaking study of the fragmentary documents of the past, was an act of transforming memory, of translation.

Benjamin held on to the doctrine of the autonomy of the work of art, because it was only by this autonomy that the work could assume an authority that was once the prerogative of the sacred image or text. The doctrine has been misunderstood: it does not imply that a text does not refer outside itself, or, even more absurdly, that it is intelligible without a knowledge of the universe that surrounds it. It merely guarantees that no elucidation of the text—not even the author's own exegesis—can ever attach itself permanently to it, or pretend to be an integral or necessary condition of experiencing it (except perhaps for the elucidation of the explicit, public sense of the words in it). No critical theory whatever has a valid and lasting claim upon the work. This autonomy requires that one return to the work itself, and that the interpretation is never in any way a substitute for it, or even, more modestly, its necessary accompaniment.

This doctrine appears hard to some critics. They have labored diligently and long on some work, and they believe that in some sense it is now theirs, that they have earned it honestly like the squatter who has worked a piece of land for many years. That was why Benjamin claimed that knowledge was possession, something one had, but truth was not, and the work belonged to the realm of truth: this means above all that no critical reading can get a permanent hold upon it. The interpretation remains forever and necessarily outside the work. To take a recent example, an interpretation none the less absurd for having been sanctioned by an offhand remark of the author himself: no amount of critical work will ever succeed in turning *The Waste Land* into a work that *says* it is about a private grouse of the author. As long as it survives, a philosophical or sociological interpretation of it will remain as cogent as a biographical one—more so, in my opinion.

The autonomy of a work has recently been attacked by many critics, but with the greatest distinction and the most considerable panache by Harold Bloom. In a recent book, he has proclaimed:

> Few notions are more difficult to dispel than the "commonsensical" one that a poetic text is self-contained, that it has an ascertainable meaning or meanings without reference to other poetic texts. Something in nearly every reader wants to say: "*Here* is a poem and *there* is a meaning, and I am reasonably certain that the two can be brought together." Unfortunately, poems are not things but only words that refer to other words, and *those* words refer to still other words, and so on, into the densely overpopulated world of literary language.[32]

Bloom is incontrovertible as far as he is willing to go, but he makes a disastrous slip which reveals the cloven hoof of the professional. It may be found in the words "literary language":

it is into the *whole* of language that each work is absorbed. Bloom refuses to isolate the poem, but insists on isolating the literary tradition; he would evidently like to claim that before a poem reaches the larger context of culture as a whole, it must first be integrated into the literary tradition. But although the initial movement of a poem is within a purely literary tradition, long before it can find a secure place in even a part of that tradition it has spilled over into ordinary language. This does not make the teaching of literature any easier.

Bloom himself bears witness to what he refuses to recognize: the self-contained meaning of the poem. As he says, few notions are indeed more difficult to dispel. It is by such a meaning that a poem is supposed to work, it is essential to its function, it is what it has been made for—which is why ordinary and extraordinary readers everywhere find it so hard to give up the idea. In absolute terms, of course, the idea is absurd, but no one holds it on those terms.

For Bloom, "words . . . refer to other words, and *those* words refer to still other words," as indeed they do, but that seems a limited view. In Bloom's systematic criticism a poem by Wordsworth refers above all to a poem by Milton, transforms and overcomes it. But a poem refers beyond words to the totality of the culture that produced it, and as it moves through time it reveals the capacity to refer to the future as well.

In denying autonomy to the work, Bloom has to find another independent object for study. He relocates autonomy in the "literary language" and he thereby blocks the access of the work of literature to the rest of life. The "literary language" or "literature" itself is a fiction if there ever was one, unless it is an Idea in Benjamin's sense. Bloom treats the literature as if it exists in the real world, the world of phenomena, and so it does—in the university. Bloom is today in this country the most powerful force in literary graduate studies: rightly so, as his systematic criticism is both eminently fascinating and easily teachable.

Benjamin cannot be taught. His criticism imposes nothing. His metaphors for the most part glance at and then fall back from the work of literature: when they appear to be absorbed into it, it is only because they are derived directly from it. His interpretations do not give meaning to, but strip meaning from, the work, allowing the inessential to drop off and the work to appear in its own light. He does not place the work historically but reveals its integrity: history in his account finds its way to the work. As he himself said, he appeared to be writing cultural history, but it was not meant as such: the beauty and the distinction of his achievement came about because it was conceived as philosophical criticism.

Notes

*See Hannah Arendt's introduction to *Illuminations.*

1. *TLS,* October 25, 1974, 1198. Review of *Gesammelte Schriften,* Volume I. At the opening of his thesis on Schlegel and Novalis, Benjamin claims that a Messianic vision of history lies at the heart of their criticism, but he does not mention this further. The same thing may be said of his own criticism.

2. I use *Trauerspiel* throughout for the title instead of *Tragedy.* Since Benjamin carefully distinguished between the classical Tragedy and the baroque *Trauerspiel,* it avoids confusion if one keeps the German (as does the translator John Osborne throughout, except in the title).

3. "The Image of Proust," *Illuminations,* 215–16.

4. In an excellent new book, *Walter Benjamin—Der Intellektuelle als Kritiker,* Bernd Witte has pointed out that Benjamin's criticism of Goethe's *Elective Affinities* is a transformation of the metaphors of the original. By working with the elements of the work itself, Benjamin appears to impose his reinterpretation from within. (I did not come upon Witte's book until this review was almost finished, and I regret not being able to give it detailed consideration.)

5. Letter to Florens Christian Rang, December 9, 1923, *Briefe,* 321–22.

6. *Trauerspiel,* 44 (slightly altered—I have preferred to translate *Inbegriff* as "embodiment" instead of "sum total." I have altered the translation of most of the quotations from Benjamin in this review).

7. The present translation by John Osborne is, paradoxically, good—it was made with a real sensitivity to Benjamin's thought and style, and it contains major errors, many of them disastrous, on almost every page.

8. "The Tragedies of Webster, Tourneur and Middleton: Symbols, Imagery and Convention" in *English Drama to 1710,* ed. Christopher Ricks (London: Sphere Books Limited, 1971).

9. The silence of Iago after the crime is a convention, too, going back to Prince Hieronimo's words in *The Spanish Tragedy* after the final murders: "But never shalt thou force me to reveale / The thing which I have vowd inviolate," after which he bites out his tongue. It signifies the irrelevance of motivation against the power of fate.

10. Ricks, 349.

11. Ricks, 309.

12. See also, among many other examples from other dramatists, the final scene of Middleton's *The Changeling*.

Almero: I'll be your pander now; rehearse again
Your scene of lust, that you may be perfect
When you shall come to act it to the black audience,
Where howls and gnashings shall be music to you.
Clip your adulteress freely, tis the pilot
Will guide you to the *mare mortuum*
Where you shall sink to fathoms bottomless.

13. *TLS*, October 25, 1974, 1198.

14. This does not mean that communication is ever completely absent: even when its force is at its lowest point in literature, we find substituted for it a mimicry of its procedures.

15. Benjamin's intransigence was reserved for critics. On the other hand, he wrote about such contemporaries as Hofmannsthal, Gide, Valéry, Brecht, Kraus, and Rilke with open respect and admiration, although he differed radically from all of these both philosophically and politically. His taste in contemporary literature was very sure.

16. Novalis, *Schriften*, edited by P. Kluckhorn and R. Samuel (Stuttgart: Kohlhammer, 1960) 2: 570. Benjamin's doctoral thesis on the concept of the criticism of art of the early German Romantics was written from 1917 to 1919 and based on the fragments of Schlegel and Novalis. This fragment of Novalis was first published in 1901, and Benjamin must therefore have known it.

17. It is this emphasis on representation that distinguishes Benjamin's philosophy of language from Heidegger's; it was elaborated before Heidegger had published any of his major works. Benjamin unfortunately never wrote his projected demolition of Heidegger, whose work he once characterized as a model of how not to do it.

18. Humboldt's anticipation of many aspects of modern linguistics has been celebrated by Chomsky. In one of his *curricula vitae* Benjamin avowed that his interest in the philosophy of language started with a reading of Humboldt, and continued with Mallarmé.

19. All the quotations of Humboldt are from the end of his essay "Latium und Hellas." I have used here (with some changes) the translation by Marianne Cowan in *Humanist Without Portfolio* (Detroit: Wayne State University Press, 1963), 248.

20. "The Task of the Translator," *Illuminations*, 74.

21. Peter Szondi in *"L'Herméneutique de Schleiermacher" (Poésie et poetique de l'idéalisme allemand)* (Paris: Editions de Minuit, 1975) defines Idea "in Benjamin's sense" as "the figure of the unity of the diverse semantic nuances of a word." That gets rid of the mysticism, but also of the required objectivity.

22. See particularly Morris Weitz, "Genre and Style," *Perspectives in Education, Religion and the Arts*, vol. 3 of *Contemporary Philosophic Thought* (Albany: State University of New York Press, 1970), in which concepts of period, style, and some genre concepts are considered as "open," i.e., perpetually debatable.

The Ruins of Walter Benjamin

23. The mechanism of these relationships was to be demonstrated many years later by William Empson in *The Structure of Complex Words* (New York: New Directions, 1951).

24. He accepted with strong reservations the positivistic arguments of Konrad Burdach against treating terms like "Renaissance" or "Humanism" as if they were living individuals with a life of their own: they were, according to Burdach, only convenient fictions, abstract concepts invented "as a consequence of our innate need for systematization" which help us "to come to grips with an infinite series of varied spirtual manifestations and widely differing personalities." While Benjamin, however, agreed on the danger of personifying general concepts, he commented that Burdach's "arguments constitute a private mental reservation, not a methodological defence" (*Trauerspiel*, 40–41).

25. An inordinately short recapitulation section in a sonata movement by Haydn after 1770, for example, implies a development section in which part of the second half of the exposition reappears very exceptionally in the tonic.

26. Parler n'a trait à la réalité des choses que commercialement: en littérature, cela se contente d'y faire une allusion ou de distraire leur qualité qu'incorporera quelque idée.
    A cette condition s'élance le chant, qu'une joie allégée.
    Cette visée, je la dis Transposition—Structure, une autre.
    L'oeuvre pure implique la disparition élocutoire de poète, qui cède l'initiative aux mots, par le heurt de leur inégalité mobilisés; ils s'allument de reflets réciproques comme une virtuelle traînée de feux sur depierreries, remplaçant la respiration perceptible en l'ancien souffle lyrique ou la direction personnelle enthousiaste de la phrase.
    —Mallarmé, *"Crise de vers,"* *Oeuvres Complètes* (Edition de la Pléiade), 366

27. Ibid., 368.

28. *Reflections*, 220–38.

29. *On Jews and Judaism in Crisis* (New York: Schocken Books, 1976), 221.

30. Letter to Adorno, December 9, 1938.

31. *Trauerspiel*, 27.

32. *Poetry and Repression* (New Haven: Yale University Press, 1976), 2–3.

Reflections on the Chapter "Modernity" in Benjamin's Baudelaire Fragments

Hans Robert Jauss

Our difficulty in spotting customary elements of Jauss's aesthetics of reception in the following text can in part be attributed to the fact that it is actually an excerpt from a lengthy essay entitled "Literary Tradition and Contemporary Consciousness of Modernity," which appeared in a collection of essays on aspects of modernity. This essay is an elaborate attempt to fathom the relation between tradition and modernity through an investigation of terminological and conceptual history. Jauss traces the changing meaning of the "modern," delineated against contrasting notions such as "ancient" and "antiquity," in order to understand "how the new consciousness of an epoch takes leave of its preceding tradition." The section published here is the essay's conclusion, which in its revised form (1972) refers to the first version of Benjamin's Baudelaire essay, published in 1969.

While Jauss does attempt to locate a contradiction in Benjamin's Baudelaire interpretation, the inconsistency he would want us to see is in fact no more than an early terminological uncertainty, which does not recur in the second version of Benjamin's essay. But Jauss does detect a genuine ambiguity in Benjamin's treatment of the contrasting pair antiquité/modernité. *On the one hand, Benjamin, in his remarks on Meryon (I:590), follows Baudelaire in specifying antiquity as the point of departure for modernity. On the other hand, Benjamin—contrary to Baudelaire's intention—"turns the* functional *relationship of* modernité *and* antiquité *back into an opposition of content."*

It is paradoxical that Baudelaire's theory of modernity should have been misunderstood by the very critic whose work has done the most to propel us toward a new understanding of that poet. It is thanks to Walter Benjamin that we no longer see the *Fleurs du mal* in the thrall of *l'art pour l'art,* as a withdrawal of poetry into itself; through him we now recognize in it the product of a historical experience, which rendered the social process of the nineteenth century intelligible to art. In view of this indebtedness, it hardly serves the suitable appreciation of Benjamin to overlook (in the Baudelaire fragments of the *Pariser Passagen*) the effect of a prepossession that encumbers his new understanding of Baudelaire and embroils it in contradictions. With this prepossession I do not refer to the program of "The Paris of the Second Empire in Baudelaire" to demonstrate "Baudelaire's unique significance" as the one who "first and most unflinchingly fixed, that is, recognized and concretized, the productive energy of alienated man."[1] This legitimate intention becomes a problematic prejudgment only to the extent that Benjamin's interpretation is one-sided: he interprets the *Fleur du mal* as testimony exclusively to the denatured existence of the urban masses. In the process, he overlooks the dialectical "other face" of alienation, the new productive energy liberated by the repudiation of nature, to which Baudelaire's *Großstadt* (metropolitan) lyric poetry and theory of modernity offer no less significant testimony.

Benjamin's *parti pris* is evident in his near omission from the chapter "Modernity" of the very cornerstone of Baudelaire's theory of modern art: the 1859 essay on Constantin Guys, the *peintre de la vie moderne*. Benjamin's posthumously published chapter is informative on this score. "In Baudelaire's view of modernity"—he concludes an extremely cursory synopsis of the essay on Guys—"the theory of modern art is the weakest point." He continues:

His general view brings out the modern themes; his theory of art should probably have concerned itself with classical art, but Baudelaire never attempted anything of the kind. His theory did not cope with the resignation which in this work appears as a loss of nature and naïveté. Its dependence on Poe down to its formulation is one expression of its constraint. Its polemical orientation is another; it stands out against the grey background of historicism, against the academic Alexandrinism which was in vogue with Villemain and Cousin. None of the aesthetic reflections in Baudelaire's theory of art presented modernity in its interpenetration with classical antiquity, something that was done in certain poems of the *Fleurs du mal*. (82)

Why should a theory of modern art at this time be trying to come to terms with classical art? The question is left open, and one wishes to know how Benjamin would have answered it. His postulate is difficult to accept when one considers that by the nineteenth century the theory of modern art was no longer wont to legitimate itself through a coming to terms with classical art, though this was still routine and obligatory from the eighteenth century up through the German *Klassik*. But what nineteenth- or twentieth-century theory of art of comparable stature might have conformed to Benjamin's specifications? The reason why a confrontation with classical art was superfluous for Baudelaire and the nineteenth-century theory of art is stated clearly enough in the essay on Guys. There Baudelaire develops his *théorie rationnelle et historique du beau* and carries the emancipation of modern art that had begun with historicism a radical step further. Baudelaire's insight into the "dual nature of the beautiful"—for which Benjamin only spares the authoritarian, unsupported judgment that "one cannot say that this is a profound analysis" (82)—not only puts in question *beauté générale* as the essence of classical art and as the prevailing academic norm (as an *élément . . . non approprié à la nature humaine*),[2] but it also restores to its rightful place that "historical," that is temporal, beauty which the classical tradition had suppressed. In Baudelaire's theory modern art can dispense with classical art as its authoritative past because the temporal or transitory beauty implicit in the concept of modernity engenders its own antiquity. Might this theory, whose affinity with other tenets of Baudelaire's antiplatonic aesthetics is undeniable,[3] be capable of mastering "the resignation which in his work appears as a loss of nature and naïveté?"

This question follows upon the observation that, in the chapter "Modernity," the conceptual opposition that serves as the vehicle of all interpretations is none other than the functional relationship of modernity and antiquity which—despite weighty reservations—Benjamin draws from Baudelaire's desire " 'that all modernity really be worthy of someday becoming antiquity'—to him that defined the artistic mission generally" (81). In the original essay on Guys, this passage reads: "En un mot, pour que toute *modernité* soit digne de devenir antiquité, il faut que la beauté mystérieuse que la vie humaine y met involontairement en ait été extraite."[4] A violent tendency of Benjamin's interpretation is betrayed by the effacement of the final-clause construction and by the interpolations "really" and "someday" in Benjamin's rendering. According to Baudelaire, it is the task of the artist to extract from modern life the mysterious beauty that arises from temporality, *in order that* modernity may become "an antiquity." Benjamin not only suppresses *beauté fugitive* as the precondition of this transformation, he also—and contrary to Baudelaire's intention—turns the *functional* relationship of modernity and antiquity back into an opposition of *content;* he fails to mention that, in the essay's relevant passages, *antique* and *antiquité* refer not to classical antiquity but to the functional opposition introduced by Baudelaire, that is, to modernity *become "ancient."*[5] The following sentence shows how Benjamin discreetly moves Baudelaire's conception of modernity back into opposition with antiquity as a historical period: "Modernity designates an epoch, and it also denotes the energies which are at work in this epoch to bring it close to antiquity" (81). This assimilation of modernity to *historical* antiquity, while hardly compatible with Baudelaire's theory, *does* quite aptly characterize a significant aspect of Victor Hugo's lyric poetry, a fact that did not escape Benjamin: "For Baudelaire this could be seen in the works of Victor Hugo" (81). It is hardly accidental that the interpenetration (of modernity) with classical antiquity (82), for which certain poems of the *Fleurs du mal* are extolled, should remain confined to poems whose style or themes are Hugoian.[6] And it is one of Hugo's own works, his poetic cycle "À l'arc de triomphe," which can in fact be said to have brought to light a new, "Parisian antiquity" (84). Is it possible that this classical countenance of the metropolis could be—together with its poet, in whom Benjamin saw a dispossessed modern hero and a stand-in for the ancient *heros*—a view of the urban landscape of the *Fleurs du mal,* but filtered through the work of Victor Hugo?

The question becomes unavoidable when one observes how Benjamin must twice correct his claim that in Hugo's poem "À l'arc de triomphe" "the same inspiration is discernable that became decisive for Baudelaire's idea of modernity" (86). This is contradicted shortly thereafter[7] by Benjamin's remarks on Meryon's engraved vistas of Paris: "No one was more impressed with them than Baudelaire. To him the archaeological view of the catastrophe, the basis of Hugo's dreams, was not the really moving one. For him antiquity was to spring suddenly from an intact modernity, like an Athena from the head of an unhurt Zeus" (87). This last metaphor is difficult to concretize. Its meaning should be illuminated by Benjamin's citation from Baudelaire's Meryon text, which he introduces for its "subtle reference to the significance of this Paris antiquity" (88). That quotation, however—which Benjamin unfortunately left wholly unexplicated—in no way either displays a classical face of the city or makes indisputable that "in Meryon, too, there is an interpenetration of classical antiquity and modernity" (87):

Seldom have we seen the natural solemnity of a great city depicted with more poetic power: the majesty of the piles of stone; those spires pointing their fingers to the sky; the obelisks of industry vomiting a legion of smoke against the heavens; the enormous scaffolds of the monuments under repair, pressing the spider-web-bodies; the steamy sky, pregnant with rage and heavy with rancor; and the wide vistas whose poetry resides in the dramas with which one endows them in one's imagination—none of the complex elements that compose the painful and glorious décor of civilization has been forgotten. (88f.)

Here we have before us a piece of modern *Großstadt* poetry, notable for its provocative rejection of any classical, classicizing, or even Romantic conception of Nature and Art: a landscape without the slightest trace of organic nature, in which the sublimity once reserved for nature (*la solennité naturelle*) is conferred upon the man-made world alone, the *douloureux et glorieux décor de la civilisation*,[8] feature by feature and with an ostentatious gesture against the heavens (which are not man-made). This picture of the metropolis, in which the new pathos of industrial labor celebrates its triumph, testifies to Baudelaire's radical and complete revaluation of nature.[9] Benjamin stubbornly and consistently refused to recognize this as the core of Baudelaire's theory of modern art and as an essential aspect of the *Fleurs du mal*. Need this have been the price of an interpretation that sought to relate Baudelaire's epochal position to dialectical materialism?

Reflections on the Chapter "Modernity"

From our contemporary standpoint we may answer this question in the negative. The contradictions in Benjamin's interpretation of Baudelaire appear in another light if one ceases to explain the "loss of nature and naïveté" in Baudelaire's work as a consequence of an alienation that arose with the commodity-producing society of the Second Empire or that derived from "the resistance which modernity offers to man's natural productive élan" (75). To appreciate the dialectical significance of Baudelaire's repudiation of nature, one must not deny the mark of that productive energy—in his aesthetic theory and in his poetic practice—which is specific to the *vie moderne* in the industrial age: man's *new* productive élan—productive both economically and artistically—with which he aims to overcome his natural state in order to work his way up to a world created by himself alone. The menacing, desolate, and disconsolate aspect of the metropolis, which Benjamin describes so hypnotically, thus has its correlate—in the *Fleurs du mal* as in the *Spleen de Paris*—in the discovery of its own proper poetry, about which Benjamin keeps silent. His citation from Baudelaire's Meryon test is by no means the only evidence against his claim that Baudelaire was a stranger to such perspectives of the urban landscape's sublime beauty—that his poems are distinguished from "almost all later *Großstadt* verse" by a "reservation against the metropolis" (83). Not only are these reservations belied by the programmatic opening poem of *Tableaux parisiens*, "Paysage," which announces—from the viewpoint of the garret—what shall henceforth be called "landscape" and "eclogue." There are also the "Rêve parisien" and other verse and prose poems, whose style-setting influence on consequent modern lyric poetry can hardly be contested. The allegorical "landscapes of ennui," which correspond to Benjamin's "idea of the decrepitude of the metropolis" (83), are incapable alone of calling forth the whole reality of the *vie moderne et abstraite*[10]; for this they must be seen in combination with the new "landscape of ecstasy,"[11] which Baudelaire is fond of evoking through the gaze of the *flâneur*.

Benjamin's appeal to the *flâneur* is problematic for him. This modern figure of lyric subjectivity accords ill with the perspective of the alienated man. Only the "hero in his modern manifestation" (74), whom Benjamin pursues in the figures of the fencer, the apache, the rag collector, the dandy, and the *flâneur*, seems to him to conform to this perspective. It cannot, however, be said of the *flañeur* that "to live in modernity requires a heroic constitution" (74). Must it therefore be concluded that the "revealing presentations of the metropolis" (69) do not derive from him? And yet the motifs associated with this unheroic figure are precisely those of the Paris streets and the urban masses: it was Benjamin himself who opened our eyes to the significance of these for the transformations in sense perception that occurred in the nineteenth century. Indeed, the negative judgment of the *flâneur* is soon corrected:

It is the gaze of the *flâneur*, whose way of living still bestowed a conciliatory gleam over the coming destitution of men in the great city. The *flâneur* still stood at the margin, of the great city as of the bourgeois class. Neither of them had yet overwhelmed himself. In neither of them was he at home. He sought his asylum in the crowd. (170)

Here one will no longer find Benjamin considering this as "the gaze of the alienated man"[12]—the gaze that captured the new experience of the masses in the poem as *bain de multitude* and *universelle communion*. It can only cause confusion to equate the gaze of the *flâneur* with that of the allegorist, as Benjamin descried most convincingly in his reading of the *Fleurs du mal*.

The example of the allegorist's gaze will help to clarify how Baudelaire was able, in his work, to master the "loss of nature and naïvité." *Spleen*—an experience in which things have lost their aura, in which the allegorist's gaze "sees the earth revert to a mere state of nature" (145)—has its counterpart in an experience capable of restoring to things a new, though no longer natural, aura. In the *Fleurs du mal* memory labors against the aura's disintegration. This is apparent in the poem "Le Cygne," Benjamin's primary example for that "decrepitude" of Paris which "constitutes the closest connection between modernity and antiquity" (82). In the first part of "Le Cygne," the somber gaze must follow the destruction of the *forme d'une ville* to its culmination in the recriminatory image of the swan dying of thirst. In the second part, the opposing force of memory calls forth the transfigured "emblems of fragility" (82) in a solemn series of evocations, which come together to compose an autonomous "counter-world" of the beautiful.[13] Like this counteractive poetic process, Baudelaire's *correspondances* also presuppose the harmonizing and idealizing strength of memory; no longer signs of a simultaneous unison of inward contemplation and outward nature, they are "data of remembrance," as Benjamin quite correctly emphasized (141). Benjamin believed that the "fundamental paradox of [Baudelaire's] theory of art" resided in the "contradiction between [his] theory of natural correspondences and [his] repudiation of nature."[14] If, however, Baudelaire's correspondences are no longer natural symbols but commemorating signs of once successful experience, then this is a contradiction, not in Baudelaire's theory of "modern beauty," but in Benjamin's interpretation of this theory. And this contradiction is utterly dispensable, because it subsists only as long as one enters Baudelaire's repudiation of nature on the minus side of the dialectical process of history—as "witness in the historical trial [*Prozeß*] to which the proletariat subjects the bourgeoisie"— and not on the plus side as well—as part of that productivity through which man liberates himself from nature's power over him. The paradox that perhaps remains is embedded in that accomplishment of art most provocative for dialectical materialism: that art not only signifies an already existent constellation of society, but also anticipates a future one. "For without exception," Benjamin writes in *One-Way Street,* "the great writers perform their combinations in a world that comes after them, just as the Paris streets of Baudelaire's poems, as well as Dostoyevsky's characters, only existed after 1900" (*One-Way Street,* 48).

Translated by Jim Gussen

Notes

All quotations from Benjamin's *Baudelaire* (trans. Harry Zohn) are indicated in the text by page numbers in parentheses. The word "modernism" has been replaced throughout by "modernity" (Trans.).

Hans Robert Jauss

1. From Benjamin's letter to Max Horkheimer of April 16, 1938 (*Briefe*, 752). My critique concerns the earlier version of the fragment "Modernity," which forms the third chapter of "The Paris of the Second Empire in Baudelaire" in *Baudelaire*, not its 1939 recasting as "Some Motifs in Baudelaire," which followed Theodor W. Adorno's critique (letter of November 10, 1938, in *Aesthetics and Politics*, 126–33). My arguments, however, are not affected by the revision, since in the later version Benjamin continues to see Baudelaire's "reservation against the metropolis" and retains his alienation thesis intact.

2. Cf. Baudelaire, *Oeuvres* (Paris: Gallimard, 1951), 875.

3. Cf. also the treatise cited in n. 13 (esp. 347ff.)

4. Baudelaire, *Oeuvres*, 885.

5. Cf. Baudelaire, *Oeuvres*, 874 (concerning a series of etchings depicting fashions in dress of the revolutionary years): "Ces gravures peuvant être traduites en beau et en laid; en laid, elles deviennent des caricatures, en beau, des statues *antiques*." See also *Oeuvres*, 866 (following a discussion of the false application of models from the epoch of Titian and Raphael): "Malheur à celui qui étudie dans l'antique autre chose que l'art pur, la logique, la méthode générale! Pour s'y trop plonger, il perd la mémoire du présent; il abdique la valeur et les priviléges fournis par la circonstance; car presque toute notre originalité vient de l'estampille que le *temps* imprime à nos sensations." Here again Benjamin has smuggled classical antiquity—which Baudelaire does not intend—into his rendering: "Woe to him who studies other aspects of antiquity [*Altertum*] than pure art, logic, the general method. He who becomes excessively absorbed in antiquity [*die Antike*], etc." (82).

6. In this context, I shall return to "Le Cygne" momentarily.

7. Benjamin was already forced to concede (on p. 83) the fundamental difference in sources of inspiration for Hugo, with his "chthonian bent," and for Baudelaire, in whose poetry "the capacity to become rigid . . . manifests itself a hundredfold . . . as a kind of mimesis of death."

8. Baudelaire, *Oeuvres*, 840.

9. Hans Blumenberg points to the process in the history of the sciences that preceded the antinaturalism of the nineteenth century's theory of art: "When man could no longer doubt that nature was not created for him or in his service—from that moment on he could only endure it in the form of 'matter,' " *Poetik und Hermeneutik* II (Munich: Fink, 1966), 438.

10. Preface to *Le Spleen de Paris*, *Oeuvres*, 273.

11. Concerning the landscape of ennui and of ecstasy, see Gerhard Hess, *Die Landschaften in Baudelaires "Fleurs du mal"* (Heidelberg: Winter, 1953).

12. Cf. *Le Spleen de Paris* 12: "Les Foules."

13. Cf. also the author's "Zur Frage der 'Struktureinheit' älterer und moderner Lyrik," in R. Grimm, *Zur Lyrik-Diskussion* (Darmstadt: Wissenschaftliche Buchgesellschaft, 1966), 347–67.

14. From Benjamin's letter of April 16, 1938, to Max Horkheimer, in which he discusses plans for his Baudelaire book; cf. *Briefe*, 75.

Walter Benjamin and Franz Kafka: Report on a Constellation

Hans Mayer

For Gershom Scholem

The first text of Benjamin's to appear in the postwar period, "Goethes Wahl-verwandtschaften," *was published by Hans Mayer in his 1949 collection* Spiegelungen Goethes in unserer Zeit. *This work redefined "our times" so as to rescue suppressed traditions of Goethe criticism by great critics from Wölfflin to Lukács to Benjamin. While writing his first book,* Georg Büchner in seiner Zeit, *Mayer met Benjamin at Bataille's Collège de Sociologie. Though both held fellowships from the Institut für Sozialforschung, no substantial relationship evolved. It was to be many years before Mayer would write on Benjamin.*

The following text was written during a semester Mayer spent at the Hebrew University in Jerusalem in 1980. The essay provides a notable summary of Benjamin's texts on Kafka, which range from his major essay to scattered observations in notes and letters. The interest in Benjamin's interpretation of Kafka has been so persistent that Suhrkamp published these materials in a paperback edition in 1981. Mayer's essay, published two years before Benjamin über Kafka, *is thorough and comprehensive.*

If we wish to assess the significance of Benjamin's reading of Kafka for his own life and thought, we must first consider three senses of Benjamin's concept of "constellation." First there is the external constellation of the events of the year 1934, which impelled Benjamin, then an emigré in Paris who had written on Kafka and given a radio talk about him, to take up the project of interpreting Kafka as his second major enterprise, alongside the *Passagen-Werk*. The second constellation is closely related to the first: Benjamin came to understand his Kafka analysis as part of a comprehensive, programmatic appraisal of contempo-

Photograph of Franz Kafka owned by Benjamin. Courtesy of Theodor W. Adorno Archive.

rary German civilization. The situation of Walter Benjamin in exile requires a stock-taking as well. Finally, the third constellation was precipitated by Benjamin's major Kafka essay of 1934, which was published, after much to and fro, in Berlin, in the midst of the Third Reich, in Robert Weltsch's *Jüdische Rundschau*. The published essay was abbreviated by half its original length. The first and third parts were published under the titles "Potemkin" and "The Little Hunchback." Omitted were the second section, "A Childhood Photograph," and the concluding section, "Sancho Panza," which Benjamin's letters reveal as especially significant for him.

Nonetheless, we begin to discern the constellation of an impassioned discussion of Benjamin's interpretation of Kafka. His friends, scattered throughout the world by both deliberate and forced emigration, became acquainted with the complete text through copies of the manuscript which Benjamin—needing an occasion—had written for the tenth anniversary of Kafka's death. From this there emerged the third constellation: a Kafka symposium carried out in letters and occasional conversations among Theodor W. Adorno, Walter Benjamin, Bertolt Brecht, Werner Kraft, and Gershom Scholem.

How it came to this, and what was discussed in that context, are the subjects of this presentation. Benjamin's actual Kafka analysis will therefore admittedly receive only secondary emphasis. This does not, however, constitute an injustice to the text, important as it is for understanding Benjamin, for it is demonstrable that the author himself felt the Kafka analysis to be provisional. He expressly retracted it four years later (1938) in a programmatic letter to Scholem. It was thus appropriate that Hannah Arendt, in her selection of Benjamin texts for an American edition of *Illuminations*, included translations of both the essay of 1934 and the 1938 counterdraft.

Indeed, only the tension between *both* attempts to understand the man and the writer Franz Kafka can clarify what the encounter with Kafka meant for Benjamin and for the individuation process of the last decade of his life. The first-rate philological-historical efforts of Rolf Tiedemann and his colleagues, who compiled a marvelous font of information and documentation, make it possible for us to analyze the confrontation between Benjamin and Kafka as an existential problem for Benjamin as well as a representative controversy within the literature of the German exiles. Only now are we able to realize, it seems to me, that alongside the much-touted "expressionism debate" of the thirties (among Lukács, Bloch, Brecht, and many others), there was another, much more concentrated debate, which was limited to a much smaller circle and which represents a second pinnacle of those years: the debate about Kafka and Benjamin.

Benjamin knew very early who Kafka was. In a letter to Scholem on June 21, 1925, he mentions "Before the Law" and says that he regards the story "today just as ten years ago as one of the best there is in German." A year later, when *The Castle* was published by Max Brod, Benjamin drafted a thoroughly "Kafkaesque" miniature, entitled "Idee eines Mysteriums." In "Kavaliersmoral" in the October 25, 1929, issue of *Literarische Welt*, the Rowohlt literary weekly edited by Willy Haas to which Benjamin was a regular contributor, he defended Brod's Kafka edition against the writer Ehm Welk, who had accused Brod of violating the duties of trust and friendship by publishing Kafka's manuscripts instead of burning them. Benjamin interprets Brod's action along a line of thought that already suggests a great affinity with Kafka:

The author's shyness about the publication of his work derived from the conviction that it was incomplete, and not from the intention of keeping it secret. . . . Not only did he know: "I have to suppress what has been born within me for the sake of that which has not yet been born," he also knew: "another will rescue it and free me from the burden of conscience of having either to give the work my imprimatur or to destroy it."

Two years later, on July 3, 1931, Benjamin broadcast a lecture on the Frankfurt radio with the title "Franz Kafka: The Great Wall of China." Essential elements of the 1934 Kafka essay are already developed here: Kafka's animals, the assistants, the little hunchback, and Sancho Panza.

Shortly after the radio talk, Benjamin must have begun to feel the urgency of preparing his confrontation with Kafka, using methods of a major undertaking rather than of merely occasional writings. When Benjamin met with Brecht in Le

Levandou in the summer of 1931, he was cheered by Brecht's "extremely positive attitude toward Kafka's work." He simply noted, however justifiably, Brecht's consciously simplistic exaggeration, that in Kafka we can recognize "the one truly Bolshevist writer."

The year 1931 brought about a new intellectual constellation that became a determining factor for the prodigious late work of this thinker and writer. It would not be accomplished without great suffering. In 1932, according to Scholem, Benjamin, after revising a will, contemplated suicide for the first time. He was about to turn forty years old and considered himself a total failure. Benjamin's image of Kafka developed concomitant with this experience, once again in the form of an identification, so that his interpretation became stamped with the concept of failure.

The year 1931 simultaneously marked for Benjamin an increasingly resolute turn to Marxism and to Brecht. On March 7, 1931, Benjamin sent his friend Max Rychner, the Swiss critic and editor of *Neue Schweizer Rundschau*, a letter he considered programmatic enough to merit sending a copy to Scholem. And three years later, when discord emerged between Benjamin and Scholem regarding Brecht and Kafka (reinforced by the distance between Jerusalem and Paris), Benjamin expressly referred back to that letter. In *Neue Schweizer Rundschau* Rychner had disparaged the recently published programmatic volume by Bernard von Brentano, *Kapitalismus und Schöne Literatur*. As Rychner knew, Brentano at that time belonged to the Brecht circle. Nor had it escaped Rychner that Benjamin also frequently associated with Brecht—and with Brentano. He sent Benjamin a copy of his negative review and asked in a handwritten note, "Dic, cur hic?" which might be freely translated with a quotation from Goethe's Gretchen:

Es tut mir lang schon weh,
Daß ich dich in der Gesellschaft seh!
(It has oft been painful to me,
to see you in such company!)

Benjamin responded at length to the question about why he associated with Brecht and Brentano. "Not because I am a 'believer' in the materialistic 'Weltanschauung,' but rather because

I am laboring to direct my thinking toward such subjects where the truth always appears most densely concentrated." Put in its topical context, this involved more Franz Mehring than Martin Heidegger. Yet this seemingly dialectical materialist position was once again shaken by the kind of amalgamation that must have seemed wholly inappropriate to a Marxist—and most certainly to Brecht. Benjamin wrote Rychner: "And if I should express it in a word: I have never been able to research and think other than—if I may call it this—in a theological spirit, namely, in accord with the Talmudic doctrine of the forty-nine levels of meaning of every passage in the Torah."

This, then, is the new intellectual constellation that leads to the 1934 Kafka essay. It immediately caused an abrupt regrouping within the communities of interest to which the writer had hitherto belonged. To be specific, it meant, on the one hand, Benjamin's parting from Hofmannsthal. On the other hand, it must have inevitably alienated him from Scholem. Scholem sensed, because he knew his close friend so well, the impending threat not merely to a friendship, but to the productivity which he had always loved and admired in the thinker. He accordingly responded quite brusquely from Jericho on March 30, 1931, after reading the letter to Rychner: "Since my first acquaintance with more or less extensive samples from your pen of those reflections on literary matters in the spirit of dialectical materialism, I have realized ever more clearly and distinctly that with this production you are engaging in a singularly intensive kind of self-deception."

Rychner's reply to the letter is not known. Rychner was a friend of Hofmannsthal and was especially close to Carl J. Burckhardt. His early admiration for Benjamin was directed at the author of the study of Goethe's *Elective Affinities* (which Hofmannsthal published), the author of that great baroque book on the origin of the German *Trauerspiel*, and the practically apologetic interpreter of Hofmannsthal's late tragedy *The Tower*. Benjamin therefore made an effort in the letter to claim continuity where both Rychner and Scholem believed they observed retraction and disavowal. To be sure, Rychner, who maintained good relations with Karl Kraus, was ready to accept the essay on Karl Kraus, which Benjamin published in the

Frankfurter Zeitung (March 10, 17, and 18, 1931). The essay came out shortly after Benjamin wrote the letter to Rychner and seemed consistent with his earlier views. Scholem was not taken in, however. He not only perceived the transition from Hofmannsthal to Brecht but also detected, however indirect and discreet, Benjamin's decision against Zionism and for Marxism.

That was it, and yet that wasn't it. Once again Benjamin came very close to Kafka's way of thinking and acting. He knew why he had earlier been in a position to explain so eloquently the instructions Kafka had given Brod to destroy his literary estate though secretly wishing he would not. A rejection of Hofmannsthal was imminent and with that a disavowal of Benjamin's own preceding *oeuvre*. Clearly Kafka was to be allied with Brecht: historical materialism with the Haggadah; Marxism with a subtle, denominationally indeterminate theology. This was a new constellation, which Benjamin first internalized amidst the accustomed regular setbacks and modest hopes for successes, in journals and via commissions that rarely materialized. He now proceeded to design an external, historical-social formation for his internal constellation—unconcerned as to whether this constellation, composed of the living and dead, of friends and enemies, would be in a position to emerge as a group and social force.

Such then was the spirit of that strange venture to which Benjamin devoted himself—in exile in Paris in March 1934, three years after his programmatic letter to Rychner and his conversations with Brecht about Kafka—once again, understandably, without success.

Benjamin announced his plan to secure some income in a letter to Brecht on March 5, 1934: "I am announcing a series of lectures on "L'avantgarde allemande" to circles accessible to me and to a few other French circles. A succession of five lectures—tickets will be sold only to subscribers to the entire series. I plan to choose a single figure who personifies the current situation in each domain of study." The series would of course be presented in French, and Benjamin therefore included in his letter the French titles of his five projected *confé-*

rences. The introduction would be called "Le public allemand." Thereafter Benjamin would carefully introduce and interpret the most notable protagonists of the German novel, essay, theater, and journalism. If we consider this combination "in the light of present-day knowledge," then the precision of Benjamin's literary judgment is once again astonishing. The German avant-garde novel was to be demonstrated through Kafka, avant-garde theater via Brecht. Benjamin designated Ernst Bloch as the most important representative of a new German essay style and as the avant-gardist of journalism, none other than Karl Kraus.

Benjamin seems to have derived great pleasure from his project. He provided further details in another letter from that same period: "A (quite small) salon will be made available for some of the talks." He hoped to "mobilize" all his Parisian connections for this project. Yet of course the little hunchback was also at his post, and once again Benjamin's plans came to naught. Rolf Tiedemann notes in his discussion of Benjamin's Kafka essay, where he also considers the Paris project, that none of the lectures were ever written.

That is true only in a narrow sense because the 1931 essay on Karl Kraus, for example, would presumably have provided the basis for the Kraus interpretation in Paris. The extent to which Benjamin continued to stand by his analysis can be deduced from several remarks he made in the context of the Kafka project. This observer of the German literary avant-garde thought he recognized interrelations and elective affinities everywhere that connected the finished Kraus essay, albeit as a preliminary stage, to the projected momentous study of Franz Kafka. Benjamin even possessed ample material for the lecture on Brecht. As early as 1929 he had written a first version of "What is Epic Theater?" and had sent it to the *Frankfurter Zeitung.* It had in fact already been typeset; but the only editorial protest, from Bernhard Diebold, the paper's theater critic and an advocate of the Expressionists ridiculed by Brecht, resulted in the article's being rejected. The galley proofs, which Benjamin had already corrected, were returned to him in the mail. Undaunted, he continued working on this increasingly fascinating project. He was able to publish a revised version of the study shortly before the war's outbreak in 1939 in the journal *Mass und Wert*, which Thomas Mann edited in Zurich. Today we are also acquainted with Benjamin's commentary on Brecht's poetry (from the summer of 1938) as well as his analysis of Brecht's *Threepenny Novel* (written about 1935), which was published posthumously. Finally, at the same time Benjamin was working on the lectures for the small art *salon*, he was composing his renowned Brechtian study "The Author as Producer." We are therefore able to definitely reconstruct the French lecture on Brecht and his theater.

A reconstruction of the train of Benjamin's thoughts on his planned monographic studies of Kafka, Brecht, and Karl Kraus is thus possible. His study of Ernst Bloch remained unwritten, in contrast, and was not, as far as we know, preceded by any substantial preliminary work. Equally unlikely is that Benjamin began work on his introductory lecture.

We are nevertheless able to discern from this project—the project of an impoverished German emigré writer—Kafka's prominence within the planned constellation. Benjamin understood Kafka above all as part of a new and welcome turning point within the literary development of the German language. By placing him together with Brecht, Bloch, and Kraus, Benjamin achieves a comprehensive negation. These four stand against all others in the domains of the novel, the theater, the essay, and the feuilleton. Kafka, and not Thomas Mann. Brecht is understood as the retraction of the ecstatic Expressionist theater as well as of the *Neue Sachlichkeit* of a Carl Zuckmayer. The reference to Karl Kraus was meant as a negation of nearly all previous German and Austrian journalism: of course, a reader of the magnificent Kraus might sense deep-seated resistances to Benjamin's "hero." The working notes which have survived disclose that Benjamin was more critical of Kraus than the 1931 essay suggests. Kraus himself must have suspected this. His reaction to that heretofore most important and compelling interpretation of *Die Fackel* and its editor was both defensive and embarrassed. Kraus claimed that he did not understand the text, thereby avoiding—probably even for himself—a more detailed response.

Finally, the choice of Ernst Bloch as the representative foun-

der of the modern essay must be understood by anyone familiar with Benjamin's development—even if one knows that
Benjamin and Bloch had both a close and distanced relationship, a mixture of friendly admiration and distrustful aversion—as a posthumous rejection of the essayist Hugo von
Hofmannsthal.

This group of five, then (plausibly adding Benjamin himself),
was by and large cohesive. There was reciprocity, above all in
the relationship between Benjamin and Brecht, and to a lesser
extent between Brecht and Bloch as well. Karl Kraus—who was
influenced not least of all by his own feuds and lawsuits against
Alfred Kerr, the professional disparager of Brechtian theater—had repeatedly stood up for the young writer from Augs-
burg. Brecht had succeeded in getting Kraus invited to Berlin
for lectures, in getting his plays performed by actors close to
him, and in having him broadcast over the Berlin radio, where
friends and students of Brecht were influential. Brecht and
Kraus, Benjamin and Bloch. How did Franz Kafka find his way
into this intellectual context? Even more, how did he enter this
literary community, introspectively constituted by Benjamin,
for himself? Benjamin's conversations with Brecht had undoubtedly inspired him. Benjamin might have expected that
the resolute, often disparaging Brecht, who was proud of his
newly acquired Marxism, would classify the author of *The Penal
Colony* and *Metamorphosis* as the scum of late-bourgeois decadence, just as readily as he had scorned the author of *The Magic
Mountain*. The Brecht of 1931, despite his reservations about
Georg Lukács as the then semi-official literary theorist
of Communism, would conceivably remain obdurate against
Lukács's veneration of Thomas Mann and nonetheless confirm
Lukács's almost incomprehensible rejection of Kafka.

That, as Benjamin ascertained (probably with relief), was not
the case. Brecht's keen artistic sensibility, his perception of
quality in writing, resisted all injudicious pseudo-ideology in
the matter of Franz Kafka. Nonetheless, Benjamin was too in-
tensely engaged with Kafka's writings to approve of Brecht's
cliché of the "truly Bolshevist writer." Since in the earlier studies Benjamin had focused his interpretation on Kafka's failure
as a writer, he would, if he had agreed with Brecht, have had to

interpret Kafka's literary "Bolshevism" as ill-conceived and un-successful, which would have amounted to a negation of Bol-shevism per se. This interpretation must now be brought into harmony with Benjamin's later thoughts on the philosophy of history and on the Angelus Novus, who turns his back to the future and fixes his gaze upon the ruins of previous history.

More important for Benjamin was his increasingly unmistak-able vacillation between the two poles of Gershom Scholem and Bertolt Brecht. This can be understood as a delicate journeying between the realms of the Haggadah and of Marxism. That is how Benjamin meant it from the outset. The letter to Rychner, when properly interpreted, campaigns for the possibility of a theologized Marxism. The origins of the friendship between Bloch and Benjamin presumably went back to this common undertaking, to fuse secularized theology with a proletarian-ized bourgeois enlightenment. During those first years of exile, Kafka became for Benjamin a figure of perhaps total identification. He sought to demonstrate through Kafka's fail-ure the necessity of his own failure—and probably its justification. The little hunchback was always of autobiograph-ical significance for Benjamin. Hannah Arendt did justice to this in her major essay on Benjamin (otherwise contestable on many issues) when she titled a chapter "The Hunchback," just as Benjamin himself had done in the third section of his 1934 Kafka interpretation.

The great works of Karl Kraus, Marcel Proust, Julien Green, or Bertolt Brecht were brought to bear as the interpretation and evaluation of a strange world. Only once before had Benja-min spoken of an Other, a dead person, in order to render a psychogram of his own self: in the *Elective Affinities* essay, whose partial obscurity must be understood as obscuration within autobiography.

The second attempt at a self-explication through interpreta-tion was undertaken with the help of someone only ostensibly a stranger: Kafka. Benjamin waited, as he repeatedly wrote, for two external inducements before actually carrying out an al-ready exigent task. He needed, as he often had in previous cases, productive exasperation with the unsuccessful works of others. Friedrich Gundolf's book on Goethe had helped him in this way with "Goethe's *Wahlverwandtschaften.*" Now, too, Benjamin found abundant incitement to polemic, for instance, in the endeavors of the psychoanalysts and in the work of Max Brod. Under the heading of "The Little Hunchback" we find the gruff decree: "There are two ways to miss the point of Kafka's works. One is to interpret them naturally, the other is the supernatural interpretation. Both the psychoanalytic and theological interpretations equally miss the essential points." Benjamin dismisses Brod's theological interpretation—which culminates in a categorization of Kafka's *oeuvre* as works about the realm of grace and works about the realm of courts and damnation—with the trenchant observation: "This interpretation is a convenient one; but the further it is carried, the clearer it becomes that it is untenable. . . . This theology falls far behind the doctrine of justification of St. Anselm of Canterbury into barbaric speculations which do not even seem consistent with the letter of Kafka's text." Benjamin's reply does not contest the interpreters' method of questioning, yet sharply differs with their attempts at harmonization. Courts and grace? Benjamin replies: "And who can say under what names they appeared to Kafka himself? Only this much is certain: he did not know them and failed to get his bearings among them. In the mirror the prehistoric world held before him in the form of guilt, he merely saw the future emerging in the form of the court of judgment."

This is one aspect. The other is Benjamin's effort to characterize what he interprets as Kafka's effort toward both deferment and postponement, which he would also like to claim for himself as the deferment and postponement of a conceivable decision between Scholem and Brecht. The little hunchback is once again the vehicle of the plea for deferment. The folksong quoted in the Kafka essay ends with a request also to pray for the little hunchback. It continues: "Thus ends the folksong. In his depth Kafka touches the ground with what neither 'mystical divination' nor 'existential theology' could supply him. It is the core of folk tradition, German as well as Jewish."

Benjamin published his essay one year after the outbreak of the Third Reich, in the *Jüdische Rundschau,* a Zionist journal.

Concurrent with his distressing, awkward attempt to organize the Paris lectures ran his ambition to acquire the official contract for a Kafka book, with the help of Scholem and of Kafka's publisher Schocken. That plan foundered mainly on Benjamin's critical attitude toward Max Brod. Yet we need not interpret the 1934 Kafka essay only as a polemic against Kafka's "natural" and "supernatural" interpreters, as Benjamin mockingly called them. The large autobiographical identification process must also be understood as a confrontation with Scholem's image of Kafka.

Consideration of Scholem and his reflections on Kafka is unavoidable. Taken as a whole, the correspondence between the two friends becomes an incomparable intellectual document that lets us confirm what the fragmentary first attempt to publish Benjamin's letters suggested: Scholem, in the course of the discussion with his friend, supplied important ideas that have since, somewhat superficially, been commonly designated as "typical of Benjamin."

Several of Benjamin's formulations illustrate this argument. To return to the programmatic letter to Rychner, Benjamin interprets his work there, even as a Marxist, as "according to the Talmudic doctrine of the forty-nine levels of meaning in every passage of the Torah." That was a central notion that Scholem had gleaned from his efforts to interpret kabbalistic Jewish texts. Scholem's text "Religious Authority and Mysticism" explicitly compares the possibility of exegetically deciphering biblical texts, which are too fertile and thus permit endless possible interpretations, with the corresponding impossibility of breaking the codes of Kafka's texts. Scholem explains: "The situation is not only that in which the writings show the mystical powers—arrived at the *null point,* and yet in the *null point,* where they seem to vanish—to be so infinitely effective. It is already the situation of the Talmudic mystics of Judaism."

Scholem argued for this fundamental relation between Kafka and Jewish mysticism with his friend at precisely the time when Benjamin seemed to have arrived at the crossroads between Jewish mysticism and Marxism. During that intellectual crisis of 1931, Benjamin requested from his friend a summary of his "independent thoughts" on Kafka—just as seven years hence Benjamin himself, at pains to retract his 1934 position, offered anew "independent thoughts" on Kafka.

Shortly after Benjamin's radio presentation on the posthumous *The Great Wall of China*, Scholem answered the request with a letter, which was sent on August 1, 1931. Scholem had already touched on the subject in 1927—the occasion being a note on the modern Hebrew poet and later Nobel Prize laureate Samuel Agnon—and maintained "that in Agnon's writings the appeal of Kafka's trial is being deliberated." The letter to Benjamin explains what is meant: "I advise you to begin any inquiry into Kafka with the Book of Job, or at least with a discussion of the possibility of divine judgment, which I regard as the sole subject of Kafka's production." Scholem continued: "It would be an enigma to me how you as a critic would go about saying something about this man's world without placing the *Lehre* (the teaching), called *Gesetz* (law) in Kafka's works, at the center. . . . Here, for once, is a world articulated, in which redemption cannot be anticipated—go and explain this to the goyim!"

A dual identification is thus achieved. Stéphane Moses asserts in his penetrating study of Scholem and Kafka (whose conclusions I have incorporated): "On the one hand Scholem uses concepts from Jewish mysticism to decipher Kafka's world. On the other hand reading Kafka's writings is precisely what can best open up the symbolic world of the Kabbalah for modern man."

While Benjamin, who was already in exile, was working on his Kafka analysis, Scholem did his utmost to protect his friend from his aspired theological-Marxist symbiosis. He composed a telling didactic poem (*Lehrgedicht*), which he sent from Jerusalem to Denmark, where Benjamin was consulting with Brecht. The title of the poem, which approaches classical form, reads: "With a copy of Kafka's *Trial*." Because Scholem was aware that Benjamin had been deeply moved by Franz Rosenzweig's book *The Star of Redemption*, the poem reads:

Keinem kann Erlösung frommen,
Dieser Stern ist viel zu hoch,
Wärst du auch dort angekommen,
Stündst du selbst im Weg dir noch.

(Redemption—no use trying to gain it,
That star's too high, beyond our grasp;
And even once you did attain it,
Your self would still obstruct your path.)

From our vantage point, we can more precisely understand the affinities and divergences between Scholem's and Benjamin's Kafka interpretations. They shared profound irritation toward Max Brod and, apparently, also toward Martin Buber. They sharply reject a theological harmonization of Kafka via concepts such as "grace" and "judgment," as well as the inclusion of Kierkegaardian motifs. Benjamin points out, correctly, that any attempt to extol the world of *The Castle* as heavenly must collide with the text, which has many negative things to say about the castle and its inhabitants.

On the other hand, Benjamin opposes equating the law with the Jewish *Lehre*, whether in the form of the Halaka as the actual dogma or in that of the Haggada as the mystical-poetic manifestation of the "law." He underscores the contradictions in a letter to Werner Kraft on November 12, 1934, without mentioning Scholem: "I do, in fact, believe that every interpretation that—in contrast to Kafka's own, in this case sincere and incorruptible feeling—derives from the assumption of a body of mystical writings, realized through him, instead of the author's own feelings, his accuracy, and the reasons for his own failure, misses the historical nodal point of his whole work."

The historical nodal point. Benjamin's self-critical distance from his own interpretation of Kafka is evident in that same letter to Kraft: "The form of my work can indeed be perceived as problematic. But his case permitted me no other form; I wanted to keep a free hand; I didn't want to terminate anything." This decision of the interpreter is probably linked with a historical constellation, which Benjamin seemed to assume for himself as well as for Kafka. Kafka's failure necessitated the failure of the Kafka interpreter as well. Nothing more than a "pragmatic," provisional solution would be expected. Thus he writes very sympathetically in his text about Kraft's candid, philological textual analysis and with deep aversion toward Brod's certitudes. This would become even more pronounced in the fresh approach of 1938.

On the other hand, Benjamin's actual rebuff to Scholem, that is, the refusal to subsume any single "teaching" as the basis of the law in Kafka, also implied a renewed, albeit hidden, concurrence of views. It was Scholem who had continually insisted—in his Kafka letter and in his own work on Jewish theology—that according to the classical conception of Judaism, human life must be interpreted as a single, lengthy trial which, because of the innumerable interpretations ascribable to all deeds, has to be extended from day to day, this postponed (*vertagt*) in the literal sense.

In his 1934 text Benjamin follows up these thoughts on the crucial role for Kafka of "postponement." His separation from Scholem is never completed: here too the law of postponement holds sway.

It is conceivable that Benjamin's indecision between Kafka interpretation and autobiography, between a representation of Kafka's historical situation and avoidance of any theologization—an indecision the interpreter held up to himself as pragmatic—explains that feeling of a deep dissatisfaction which a reader senses in Benjamin's painstakingly researched, reflective text. It is not a well-structured composition, comparable to this prodigious essayist's works on Proust, Shestov, Kraus, or Brecht. The four "hooks" of the four sections are inadequate and are consequently forgotten in the middle of the analysis, or at least are replaced by new, and better, symbol-laden stories. In the end there is no discernible path leading from the Potemkin story to Kafka's assistants; the story does not permit the intended conclusions. The Hamsun anecdote is in itself irrelevant; it too is soon forgotten. It turns out that the little hunchback has to help out in person. We are severely taxed to get from Kafka's childhood photograph to Benjamin's theses on Kafka's world theater. The most telling part of the analysis, viz., the fourth and last one, which was omitted from the 1934 publication, begins with a Hasidic legend Benjamin had discovered, as it happens, through Buber, whom he thoroughly disdained. Thus the conception proceeded, even for Benjamin, messianically, in Scholem's sense of that term. There we read: "No one says that the distortions, which it will be the Messiah's mission to set right someday, affect only our space. Surely they are distortions of our time as well. Kafka must have had this in mind."

Must he have? Scholem had this in mind when he denied the possibility, in historical contexts, of the anticipation of redemption—not only of Christian messianism, but also of the heretical outsider position of a "nihilistic messianism," which can likewise be inferred in Kafka's texts.

Benjamin's pragmatism gives way here as well. His essay's conclusion, departing from the Hasidic story in order to arrive at Kafka's Sancho Panza, suddenly gets serious about situating the phenomenon of Kafka historically. He is said to be the counterpart of the Good Soldier Schweik: "The one is astonished at everything, the other at nothing." Brecht's influence is unmistakable: "The invention of film and the phonograph came in an age of maximum alienation of men from one another, of unpredictably intervening relationships, which have become their only ones. Experiments have proved that a man does not recognize his own gait on the screen or his own voice on the Gramophone. . . . The situation of the subject in such experiments is Kafka's situation."

Benjamin's theory of art in the age of reproducibility is already adumbrated here. Kafka's parable of the relationship between Don Quixote and Sancho Panza is supposed to serve as the building of a bridge to Brecht and to ascribe new meaning, with Kafka's help, to modern art. Yet it is precisely here that Benjamin's work on Kafka breaks off.

What Benjamin held up as pragmatism would be better characterized as syncretism. Kafka's failure was supposed to ideologically legitimate the essayist's failure. The author of the Kafka essay did not delude himself. His letter to Scholem on June 12, 1938, contains a harsh sentence about the 1934 Kafka study: "What makes me resist it today most is its inherent apologetic character."

In order to understand this strange formulation, we must more closely consider the ideological constellation that emerged through Benjamin's work—in the form of a rebellion against this type of Kafka interpretation. Benjamin kept an extensive archive in which he preserved all written communications and conversations that could be construed as reactions to the essay. His goal was a projected "revision," in accord with the above-mentioned formulation, which he meant both ironically as well as quite seriously. First of all, it was a proposal to revise the negative judgments; next, a parody of a "trial" in Kafka's sense; finally and most importantly, a revision of Benjamin's own first pinning-down of a Kafka interpretation.

When we examine the positions, which Rolf Tiedemann has again so thoroughly documented in the editorial apparatus to the *Gesammelte Schriften*, we are struck by a long letter Werner Kraft sent Benjamin on September 16, 1934. Kraft, whose authority in matters concerning Kafka Benjamin respected (confirmed by his handwritten notes on Kraft's letter), kept to the elements of a real Kafka interpretation in Benjamin's text, except for a denial of the autobiographical elements. The charge of esotericism is not omitted. Kraft expressed the wish "to reread the essay as a judicious lecture." He felt that the parables, such as Potemkin, were expendable; he shrewdly suggested that Benjamin would not make headway as an interpreter of Kafka with his parable. Yet Kraft's main suggestion addresses Benjamin's interpretational methods: "I have indeed no doubt that for you Kafka's work is identical with an outer, phenomenal layer, as it were, and that you can only maintain your position by adamantly refusing to recognize a deeper level of meaning." Kraft regarded as false and insufficient exactly what Benjamin considered of most consequence: the provisional, unfinished nature of the interpretation—once again its failure. Kraft would have liked, perhaps without knowing it, to correct the identification relation between Kafka's failure and Benjamin's failure with Kafka.

Kraft further conjectured, it should be noted, that neither Scholem nor Brecht could agree with this kind of interpretation.

Benjamin confirmed this in an important letter to Kraft on November 12, 1934. The letter-writer is unusually frank with Kraft, whose role is solely that of the correspondent, and not that of a friend or superego: "The experiences this study has yielded, at a *carrefour* of my thoughts and reflections—and precisely those thoughts I've devoted to this experience—hold the promise of a compass needly in uncharted territory." Both Kraft and Benjamin correctly foresaw that Scholem would have to reject the essay. Benjamin's letter to Kraft contains the already-quoted thesis that it is misguided to postulate as underlying Kafka's works a "mystical body of texts that he actualized." The letter continues: "Scholem, in any case, quite clearly perceived the limits which the present version does not intend to move beyond, when he reproached me for passing over Kafka's concept of the 'laws'."

Kraft further "accurately guessed the opposition . . . to the study that was expected from Brecht, even if you hardly conceive of its temporary vehemence." As is well known, Benjamin kept a detailed diary of his debates with Brecht in Svendborg. For weeks Brecht maintained a silence toward his guest regarding the article. When the author requested the return of his manuscript, the debate broke loose:

Even I could not be completely acquitted of a diaristic style *à la* Nietzsche. My Kafka essay, for instance. It treats Kafka purely from the phenomenal point of view—the work as something that had grown separately, by itself—the man, too—it detached the work from all connections, even with its own author. In the end, every thing I wrote always comes down to the question of the *essence*.

Brecht's objections coincide in principle with those of Kraft. Both disapprove of Benjamin's phenomenological approach. Brecht sees it as a kind of "Husserlian intuition of essences," which has nothing to do with historical materialism. Precisely the historical "situating" of Kafka, to which Benjamin supposedly aspired, remained unachieved.

Brecht seems to have gone still further in the course of the debate. He expressed his displeasure with the method of Benjamin's essay on Karl Kraus. Benjamin appears to have accepted the objection: "It is true that the study of the frontier area defined by Kraus, and in another way by Kafka, preoccupies me a great deal." The study on Kafka was admittedly less successful than the one on Kraus.

Brecht, strangely enough, perhaps without having known more of Benjamin's plan for the Paris lectures, rejected precisely what Benjamin intended by that constellation. Brecht perceived himself as expressly *not* belonging to an avant-garde—together with Kraus and Kafka. In a further conversation in Svendborg on August 29, 1934, the controversy was transformed into a political polemic. Benjamin noted: "A long and heated debate about Kafka. Its foundation: the charge that it promotes Jewish fascism. It increases and spreads the darkness surrounding this figure instead of dispersing it. Yet it is necessary to bring light to Kafka, that is to say, to formulate the practicable suggestions that can be gleaned from his stories."

Scholem rejected a Kafka whose laws and teachings were mere appearance. Brecht dismissed the apology of failure. A prophetic writer like Kafka must be made visible in his teachings, not further obscured by his darkness. The autobiographical element of Benjamin's identification with Kafka appears to have similarly disturbed Scholem, Brecht, and Kraft.

The long, almost tract-like letter of Theodor Wiesengrund Adorno of December 16, 1934, could be characterized in this controversy as Adorno's desire to come to understand both of Benjamin's hesitant, ambivalent positions in the Kafka interpretation—the theological-mystical and the historical-material—as a double negation. He approved of Benjamin's polemic against Brod, his experimentation with Kierkegaard, and even Pascal; he noted parallels to his own work. On the other hand he sees in Benjamin's analysis "close relations . . . to Hegel," which, carefully examined, appear inconclusive and contrived. Adorno is then very conclusive: "If Kafka is not a founder of a religion—and how right you are! How little he is that!—he is certainly not in any sense a poet of Jewish *Heimat.* Here I find most decisive your sentences on the intertwining of the German and the Jewish elements." We might of course object to Adorno that Benjamin's text definitely allows a German-Jewish native-born (*heimatliche*) symbiosis. Benjamin could by no means recant his anthology *Deutsche Menschen,* which he had just published under the pseudonym Detlev Holz.

Adorno formulates his most clear-cut divergence from Benjamin's viewpoint in this way: "The one thing that strikes me as foreign to the substance of the work is the inclusion of categories from the epic theater. For this world theater, since it is performed only for God, does not tolerate any outside viewpoint, with which it would ally itself as stage."

Benjamin avoided—in contrast to the very considered defense he presented to Kraft and to the rebuttal forced upon him in the conversations with Brecht—all controversy in his reply to Adorno from San Remo on January 7, 1935. Here we once again find the principle of postponement and deferment. There is nothing to prevent a reworking of the Kafka essay. Benjamin writes that he missed Adorno's comments on the concluding section, "Sancho Panza"—meaning the treatment of the artist's relation to all reality. He considers the essay to have set many things in motion: "And thus all in all a tonal figure (*Klangfigur*) has developed around it from which I still have much to emulate. For the time being I have begun a collection of reflections without yet considering how they project onto the original text."

The process must then be deferred. The defense sifts through its dossiers and prepares the appeal. Benjamin's work, which he had halfway retracted, had, under the sign of Franz Kafka, led from the first hearings on identity to a most peculiar trial of identification for German (mainly Jewish) emigrants (Brecht being the exception). Scholem and Adorno, Brecht and Kraft and Benjamin: none intends to negate the author of *The Penal Colony* and *A Hunger Artist*. Each seeks and discovers himself in Kafka. Perhaps there will never be a Kafka symposium capable of leading to any other result.

Benjamin's second Kafka essay, composed in the form of a letter to Scholem with the corresponding "separate thought," was precipitated by the publication of Max Brod's biography of Kafka. Benjamin appears to have been very agitated upon reading it. In a letter to Scholem on April 14, 1938, he is enraged "because the said biography, with its interweaving of Kafkaesque incertitude with Brodesque certainties, appears to open a district of the intellectual world where the interplay of humbug and white magic is said to be most edifying." What Benjamin had already implied in his earlier Kafka essay—that Kafka's friendship with Brod must either be regarded as suspect or be understood as part of a life strategy—is explicitly formulated in the epistolary essay of June 12, 1938. There he wrote that it was a friendship that "could not possibly belong to the smallest of riddles in Kafka's life." Benjamin's basic charge against Brod is of course correct, that an interpreter cannot simultaneously present Kafka as a saint and as a simple fellow citizen. Benjamin also humorously glosses the attempt to bring the author of *The Castle* close to Martin Buber: "When Brod says of Kafka that he was more or less in line with Martin Buber, this amounts to looking for a butterfly in the net over which it casts its hovering shadow. Zionists ought to be the first to view this edification with suspicion."

In that late pre-war period in Paris, Benjamin once again stood between the poles of a renewed search for mystical experience and a materialistic-dialectical examination of history. At that time Benjamin regularly attended the meetings of the Collège de Sociologie in Paris, a free and informal association of sociologists whose attention to phenomena of the *"sacré"* included the "wicked" as well as the "sacred." The Collège was headed by Georges Bataille together with Roger Callois and Michel Leiris. Denis de Rougemont was a regular there, as were the philosophers Jean Wahl and Jean Hyppolite. Discussions proceeded somewhat differently from historical-materialist discussion, even though probably all of the circle's members (as was later established) rejected contemptuously the cheap magic of propagandistically fabricated *"sacré"* in the Third Reich.

Benjamin's collaboration with members of the Collège de Sociologie was clearly important for him in connection with his studies of Paris as the capital of the nineteenth century. Contact with Brecht continued. Benjamin's work for Horkheimer and the emigré Institute for Social Research at the same time tested the historical-materialist approach, which occasionally led to conflicts with the Institute's leadership in New York.

Once again, the thinker and writer worked elliptically in his longstanding, artfully organized state of permanent tension. This affected his renewed attempt to interpret Kafka. His procedure was once again clandestinely autobiographical, in the form of an empathetic attitude, wholly without alienation. Benjamin seeks and of course finds in Kafka what he constantly practiced himself: "Kafka's work is an ellipse with foci that are far apart and are determined, on the one hand, by mystical experience (in particular, the experience of tradition) and, on the other, by the experience of modern urban man." Brecht, presumably, would have used the formulation "city-dwellers." At any rate, the new study is much more precise than the earlier one; above all it is consistent. At both foci, however, the analyst believes to have discovered mere negations (which must have pleased Adorno). This time Benjamin unrestrainedly declared that in Kafka's case "a negative characterization is probably altogether more fruitful than a positive one." That is, Kafka's experience with tradition presents itself as the transmission of something that, as truth, and consequently as Teaching or doctrine (*Lehre*), is no longer transmissible. Benjamin again equates doctrine with Jewish religious tradition. And he attempts, as he did with Scholem, to explain Kafka's relation to Jewish tradition by way of the dualism of the Halakah and the Haggadah, though admittedly with a crucial difference from the 1934 text. There Benjamin still claimed that Kafka's writings "are to Teaching, as the Haggadah is to Halakah." This image is taken up again four years later, though decisively modified, when it is said of Kafka's parables: "They do not modestly lie at the feet of the doctrine, as the Haggadah lies at the feet of the Halakah. Though apparently reduced to submission, they unexpectedly raise a mighty paw against it."

Beasts, then. They are in opposition to the doctrine and to traditional law because both, according to Benjamin's formula, signify nothing other than a "sickening of tradition." This is now proclaimed as a thesis: "Kafka's work represents a sickening of tradition."

The same negativity is found at the other focus of the ellipse: Kafka as the modern city-dweller and urban man. One could venture to approach Benjamin's coeval work and speak of Kafka within the world of arcades. The motif of Kafka as *flâneur* had already come up earlier.

In this negative dialectic, an emptied doctrine is associated with a vacuous and meaningless existential experience of man in modern society. Here Benjamin was probably answering Brecht's thesis of Kafka as a "prophetic" writer. But he continued:

What I mean to say is that this reality can virtually no longer be experienced by an *individual*, and that Kafka's world, frequently of such playfulness and interlaced with angels, is the exact complement of his era, which is preparing to do away with the inhabitants of this planet on a considerable scale. The experience which corresponds to that of Kafka, the private individual, will probably not become accessible to the masses until such time as they are being done away with.

This time everything has become equivocal, in Benjamin's answer to Scholem as well as to Brecht. Kafka's writing, his Haggadah as it were, reaches up indignantly like a beast of prey against a fetishistic and sickened tradition. But Kafka's experience of the modern world and the processes of alienation are to be understood as a prophecy, though as a prophecy without hope. Benjamin captured this in a beautiful image: "No farsightedness of any sort, not any 'prophetic vision.' Kafka listened to tradition, and he who listens hard does not see." With this comparison, Kafka is directly assimilated into the *Angelus Novus* of Paul Klee. This happens quite consciously, for only a few lines earlier Benjamin expressly drew a parallel between Kafka and Klee. Both, the new angel of history and the listening non-seer Kafka, are shaken by the storms of something in the future. Yet the angel's gaze in Benjamin's theses "On the Concept of History" is meant for the ruins of a past; Kafka listens to this past, though he does not see.

And *hope*? Benjamin was shaken from the start by Brod's report of a conversation with Kafka in which he is said to have answered that there is "an infinite amount of hope—but not for us." This was already echoed in the essay of 1934. Now it is thus interpreted: "So there is, then, as Kafka puts it, an infinite amount of hope, but not for us. This statement really contains Kafka's hope; it is the source of his radiant serenity." With this it becomes understandable why Benjamin rejected the earlier interpretation as "apologetic," for it had still nurtured the dream of a hope "for us." The profound gravity of the thesis of Kafka's failure had not been truly felt and followed. This time Benjamin makes up for that. Negation at both foci: in the mystical experience and in the contemporary experience of society.

I was strangely disturbed—why deny it?—by the absence of Kafka's name in the more than 1600 pages of Ernst Bloch's *Principle of Hope*. Bloch, of course, knew this writer's work intimately. In *Erbschaft dieser Zeit*, he discovers in Kafka's novels and stories the uncanny return of a sunken world. In the analyses of moral philosophy and philosophy of right in his book *Natural Law and Human Dignity*, he places Kafka as one of the "great self-haters" alongside Luther, Kierkegaard, and Dostoyevsky. Kafka's world should be interpreted as a "mythology of the incurring of guilt." Kafka, as Bloch formulates it, "gave to all of that its ultimate and basic form: that of naked violence, which is the most disguised, and open violence, which is the most insidious." Bloch thus knew his way around in the realms of the *Penal Colony* and *The Trial,* with Kafka's animals and with his gates. Nevertheless, Kafka was of no use to Bloch within the system-world of the Principle of Hope: an infinite amount of hope, but not for us? Bloch would have asked, "for whom then?"

Translated by Gary Smith and Thomas S. Hansen

Walter Benjamin:
From Rupture to Shipwreck

Pierre Missac

The rescue of the principal manuscript of Benjamin's Passagen-Werk *is due to the efforts of Georges Bataille and Pierre Missac. Both were acquainted with Benjamin during his last years in Paris, and since the end of the war, Missac has been the most visible interpreter of Benjamin's works in France. He published a translation of Benjamin's theses "On the Concept of History" in Sartre's* Les Temps modernes *as early as 1946, four years after its first printing in the Institut für Sozialforschung's commemorative* Gedächtnis-schrift. *For many years he wrote on Benjamin when scarcely anyone else was doing so in France, publishing essays in such journals as* Critique, La Quinzaine littéraire, La Revue de littérature comparée, *and* Nouveaux cahiers. *At the same time he was working on a book on Benjamin,* Passage de Walter Benjamin, *an original and penetrating study that was finally published only months after his death in October 1986. His is the unique voice of an* homme de lettres *(as Hannah Arendt described Benjamin himself), moving intelligently between Benjamin's life and works. He fixes on certain of Benjamin's prominent motifs, such as glass architecture, but also takes a truly Benjaminian approach to other phenomena, such as the atrium, that appeared after Benjamin's death. His analyses are typically judicious and aphoristic.*

1

The chronology of the translations into French of Walter Benjamin's works reveals a pattern analogous to the one that marked his reception in Germany. In both cases emphasis was placed first on his "later" work (if such an adjective may be applied to an author who died at the age of forty-eight), that is, on his political orientation. In the late 1960s this emphasis gave rise in Germany to an unfortunate polemic in which those who most actively served Benjamin's memory were accused of concealment and misrepresentation.[1] In France Benjamin began to arrive on the scene with the rise and subsequent fading of the Spirit of May 1968 and before translations of works by other Frankfurt School figures began to appear.[2] The situation has since changed. "A l'écart des courants,"[3] that is, "Apart from the Currents" and without any futile references to Violence or to Revolution, French readers now have access to such texts as *Deutsche Menschen,* the chiseled prose of *Berliner Kindheit,* the short pieces of *Einbahnstraße,* and finally the two volumes of *Briefe,* in a careful translation. In Germany, even if Werner Fuld finds it necessary to reiterate—in a most inauspicious and incongruous way—the accusations from discussions long out of date, and that despite the exemplary character of the edition of Benjamin's *Gesammelte Schriften,* there are also studies by Liselotte Wiesenthal, Bernd Witte, and Jean-Pierre Schobinger, which devote themselves above all to the writings of Benjamin's first "period."[4] After being first read as a philosopher of history and politics, Benjamin is now being studied as the writer, the man of letters, he had become and whose social role drew his concern. I shall therefore take up Benjamin translations recently made available to the French public as well as several recent studies in German, mainly from the perspective of literature. At the risk of falling prey to the dangers of thematic criticism and statistical analysis, I shall adopt as landmarks several notions that seem fundamental or constant in Benjamin's writings. These notions, while little used in France, to my knowledge, recur insistently in the studies published in Germany and Switzerland. Emphasis, therefore, will be placed on the tension (*Spannung*) between two poles; on the dialectic that claims to resolve this tension; on the destruction and the rupture (*Bruch*) that seek to make do with or take advantage of it; and finally on the two most prominent notions: *Rettung,* which is distinct from redemption (*Erlösung*), and *Bruchstück.* The translation problem posed by these two notions will not be resolved here.[5]

2

Faced with the complexity of Benjamin's personality and the difficulty of classifying his *oeuvre,* exegetes readily fall back on the theme of opposites. They portray their author as either seated "between two chairs" (*zwischen den Stühlen*) or as oscillating between atheism and theology. One such interpreter underscores the contradictions in the Baudelaire studies, while another, in an analysis and explanation based on oxymoron, characterizes Benjamin as a mystic, or Marxist rabbi—as a sort of hermetic socialist. His gaze is said to be Manichean. Even the two people who knew and understood Benjamin best follow this practice: Scholem, convinced that his friend's adherence to dialectical materialism undermined his most profound genius, sees his work as moving along two separate tracks (*Zweigleisigkeit*), one political and the other theological: parallel, yet impossible to harmonize in counterpoint. Rather than opposition, Adorno prefers the notion of periods: distinguishing the theological from the materialist periods.[6]

Of course, this situation is primarily due to Benjamin himself, and first of all, let me repeat, to the complexity of his work and the ambiguity of his positions. Did not Benjamin himself speak of his "Janus face" in a letter to Scholem dated February 14, 1929 (*Briefe*, 489)? This difficulty is also attributable to the specific importance that Benjamin—as philosopher, critic, and writer—attaches to the notions of division, polarity, and tension. This is the case regarding his studies of Baudelaire and Kafka. Referring to the *Passagen-Werk*, Benjamin wondered whether he would have the strength to "string the bow," to forge a connection between two opposed views (*Briefe*, 687). But he also gives way to rhetorical flourishes and hazards the "profane illumination" induced by hashish or systematized by surrealism. Even more often he ventures into the domain of rhetoric. I have elsewhere emphasized the function of genitive reversals in his writing, which is undoubtedly related to the fact that chiasmus is seen to represent the progressiveness of dialectical operations as compared to the methods of classical logic.[7]

"Dialectic is the philosopher's stone of modern thought." This observation by Fougeyrollas only restates a call to order handed down from Nietzsche to Merleau-Ponty, passing by way of Popper.[8] Benjamin is not exempt from such criticisms, perhaps because he perceives in the dialectic a way to resolve his internal septum. The triadic structure of the dialectic explicitly provides the schema for a provisional outline of his *Elective Affinities* study (I:1075) and, in a less obvious way, for its final outline. He would later hope to realize a similar structure in the *Passagen-Werk*, subsequently confessing that "such fortuitous dialectical constructions" (as those he encountered in a text by Jochmann, for instance) could be used only by authors who knew nothing of Hegel (II:583).

Yet another reason to take recourse to dialectic should be added—on a more conscious level this time, indeed too conscious for the taste of some, in the sense that when brought down to earth the dialectic overcomes contradictions at the practical level and allows for the concretion (*Konkretion*) so dear to Adorno. The most acrimonious exchanges with Adorno at the time of the work on Baudelaire concerned the use Benjamin made of dialectical method and the absence in it of adequate mediation; but the legitimacy or relevance of the dialectic is never contested or called into question, either by Adorno, who calls for more ("ein *Mehr* an Dialektik," I:1004) or by Benjamin. The question is, then, did Benjamin do so shortly before his death? At first, Benjamin expected—not without a certain naiveté, according to Scholem[9]—that he could eliminate the contradictions discovered by his friend in the essay on the technical reproducibility of art. The sublation of these contradictions would be accomplished by a third, genuinely materialist term—the proletarian revolution. Later on Benjamin went even further by resorting to the miraculous. The third term was now placed in the realm of theology, or perhaps that of mysticism: the Messiah is assigned the task of vanquishing the Antichrist, of interrupting the historical chain of catastrophes at every moment—*hic et nunc*—for there is not a moment to lose. As I will repeat below, this reversal at the eleventh hour, this return to criteria that continue to be cherished despite the objective judgment of them as outmoded, appears to be mainly, if not entirely, a testimony of despair, or perhaps despair mingled with that quality of irony so lacking in Blanqui (I:1071), or despair mixed with a humor blacker than that of the surrealists. At the moment of greatest danger, the absurd appears merely as illusory. If hope lies only in the intervention of a messianic figure, it would be better to withdraw from the game by taking one's own life.

One might contend that Benjamin overestimated dialectics as an ontology or as a method, that he adhered blindly to its Marxist form without ever managing to rid himself of the traces of nondialectical positivism, indeed of magic,[10] and that prevented him from making sufficiently convincing use of it. Or, conversely, one could argue that he was more or less conscious of the inadequacies of his position vis-à-vis dialectics, or of the shortcomings of dialectics itself in relation to truth. In any case, however, Benjamin's equivocal relationship to dialectics seems to lead to certain slippages or displacements of emphasis in the interpretation of several of his works.

Irving Wohlfarth wonders[11] whether it would be appropriate to consider the description of "the destructive character" as applicable to Benjamin himself (his friend Gustav Glück would, from this point of view, be seen to serve as a kind of straw man, a "whipping boy"). To this, one can certainly respond in the negative, at least if one takes the notion of "destruction" in a sufficiently radical sense. Benjamin demanded an immense inner effort of himself—or was driven by an extreme situation, such as the one accompanying the writing of the final "Theses"—before he would declare himself a "partisan," much less the instigator, of radical change, of a clean slate. As he says of Baudelaire (I:666), his tendency toward destruction never implies the elimination of what it claims to ruin. This observation has been taken up by recent critics who freely characterize him as a *conservateur*. The issue is no longer to "erase traces," to use Brecht's phrase (which was admired and also probably dreaded by Benjamin), but instead to maintain them, indeed to reconstitute them. To destroy or to shatter is not to annihilate[12]— to return to dust soon dispersed by "the winds of history" —but rather to unsettle, "to break into pieces." This notion of "rupture" (*Bruch*) is plainly crucial to Benjamin's life and thought. In a recent interview,[13] Scholem admitted that while he had always been able to detach himself with relative ease from what had been close to him, this was not at all the case for Benjamin. For Benjamin, separation implies a kind of flight: it requires that brutality take the place of strength. His last letter to Wyneken (*Briefe,* 120–22) has as its objective "to burn all bridges behind him," to irrevocably excavate and widen the gap separating them. He was able to act similarly toward Herbert Belmore, if not toward Werner Kraft.[14] With the women he loved or believed he loved, separation was enough; he did not feel the need to make more radical breaks. One wonders, from this point of view, whether his attitude toward prostitutes is at least in part explained by the interplay between the "commodity" and the "ever new but ever the same" in his thought. Within the realm of "ideas" as well, "rupture" takes precedence over "destruction." Essential is the notion of shock, which, by no accident, becomes a characteristic of the modern. Under the impact of shock, what existed before collapses, but without being lost to the future. The "aura" gives way to shock and to a new concept of the work of art, now perceived more heterogeneously as dependent and as requiring reconciliation.[15] The ruins, celebrated by the baroque (I:353), also mark the preservation of the past. In a similar way the notions of rupture and of *Rettung* are inextricably connected.

Even if these terms are closely related (indeed for critics this relation is an obsession[16]), it does not necessarily follow that they are not subject to differing interpretations. This is especially the case regarding *Rettung.* Even Benjamin questioned the placement of *Rettung* between the "too early" and the "too late" ("Central Park," I:683) and thought that the notion "could become a problem" (letter to Adorno, I:1077). In anticipation of misunderstanding, he mentioned on various occasions his intention to clarify his ideas on this subject, particularly by opposing *Rettung* to *Würdigung,* that is, to apology in the sense of justification. The latter strives to conceal in history precisely those revolutionary elements that *Rettung* wants to rescue from the forgotten and to keep alive (I:658, 1074, 1150, 1162). *Rettung* can be seen to assert its originality in its difference from— if not opposition to—the notion of redemption. It neither issues from the Beyond, the Paradise from which, on the contrary, the tempest blows that carries the Angel of History away, nor does it possess any transcendental character. *Rettung* is, Wohlfarth's claim notwithstanding,[17] more atheological than

theological: it is the work of man. Rather than the "tiger's leap
. . . beneath the open air of history" (*Illuminations*, 263), *Rettung*
prefers a more modest springing (*kleiner Sprung*) to interrupt
the flow of catastrophes (I:683).[18] Its intervention only has the
look of brutality: it can in fact still manifest itself in the phenomenon of fashion.[19] *Rettung* is a confiscation and secularization of that "weak Messianic power" (*Illuminations*, 254) granted
every generation. *Rettung* sees its opportunity in a moment that
differs radically from the one in which the hosts of angels,
having extolled God, destroy themselves. Instead of the specu-
larity of the symbol, *Rettung* addresses itself, in the final analysis, to the possibilities as well as to the limits of allegory.

Woven tightly together, the preceding notions converge in
the *Bruchstück*. A product of the rupture, the *Bruchstück* differs
from the fragment—a difference that leads to the problem of
translation alluded to above—in its less suggestive implications
or in its less ambitious origins, at least from the perspective of
Romanticism.[20] But however little the allegorist may put its
powers of limitation into play (*Trauerspiel*, 183f., I:359), the
Bruchstück can rival the fragment, can blossom into aphorism,
can unfold in itself, perhaps dialectically, the ensemble of concealed tensions that ask nothing more than to experience Cin-
derella's awakening. An epigrammatic text from "Central
Park" (I:676) opens up such perspectives: "The brooder whose
startled gaze falls upon the fragment in his hand becomes an
allegorist."[21] Amidst all the associations thus suggested, and
almost in spite of them, the *Bruchstück* evokes a *Rettung* that
could also be the *Rettung* of a dialectics reduced to more appropriate proportions.

3

The primary feature of the *Bruchstück* is obviously its brevity—
that conciseness which Benjamin regarded as evidence of mystery (*Trauerspiel*, 180f.). But in a letter written to Scholem in
July 1932, on the day before he planned to commit suicide,
Benjamin characterized his writings as "small-scale victories
[which] . . . correspond to large-scale defeats" (*Briefe*, 556). Six
years earlier he had tried to correct, or at least to avenge, the

forced withdrawal of his study on baroque drama with an apologue of a few lines, which he regarded as one of his "most accomplished texts" (I:901f.). At a time when circumstances necessitated a fragmented production, it must have been reassuring for him to know that his genius would accommodate itself to such a constraint. In the end, his predilection for the small-scale, for miniaturization, as evidenced by his handwriting as well as the anecdote about the two grains of wheat reported by Scholem,[22] served him as a justification for the difficulty of development, which can only recall a similar difficulty that faced Georges Bataille. Benjamin is not the only one who wavers between the too short and the too long. Adorno even alternates between reproaching him for bringing motifs together without ever fully developing them (I:1094) and declaring that the best thoughts are those that cannot be thought through to completion (I:1132).

And so they are, at least in the marvelous and intimidating act of writing. For in the presence of his circle of friends, Benjamin, brilliantly loquacious, could extemporize theories "ex abrupto" so that a listener would approach him afterward to ask him to take up the subject in writing—"the gambler,"[23] for example, or "progress" (letter from Gretel Adorno, February 10, 1940; I:1226). Benjamin knew the value of spontaneity: "Strength lies in improvisation. All the decisive blows are struck with the left hand" (*Reflections,* 65).[24] Fascinated by Lichtenberg, he knew the value of *Einfall,* of *Eingebung* (insight, inspiration) that has to be caught without being crushed, to be preserved—in a word, to be saved.

This task becomes particularly delicate when the insight consists of or expresses itself in an image, a metaphor. It has often been noted that these rhetorical devices play an essential role in Benjamin's mode of thought. Liselotte Wiesenthal made this the point of departure for a somewhat exaggerated comparison between Benjamin's "scientific" thought and the thought of the early Wittgenstein.[25] Others have more or less held this style against him. Whether good or bad, this approach may have found an adequate mode of expression in what has been called the *Denkbild.* But a misunderstanding is possible here. In fact, despite the interpretations given by Adorno and the editors of the *Gesammelte Schriften,* it appears that the designation *Denkbild* is most often applied to the "pieces" that are by nature more closely related to those of the *Berliner Kindheit* than to those of *One-Way Street,* not to mention "Central Park." While these latter two are certainly consummated texts, works of an unparalleled conciseness or "concentration,"[26] they no less belong to a form of *discourse* based on the two-fold duration of event and writer than they are manifestations of the budding of metaphor in a brute state. They describe or recount (*beschreiben, erzählen*) more than they show (*zeigen*) or present (*darstellen*), this last designation being by far the one that best corresponds to Benjamin's intentions and accomplishments. In any case, at the end of his life and in the final stage of his reflections, Benjamin resorts to the notion of the "dialectical image" to synthesize the "rescue" he proposes, that of an *Einfall,* which, in this new form, allows for the rescue of the idea as well.[27]

Beyond the innate virtues that short prose reveals to the person who knows how to mold it, the short prose piece bears in its "ruptured" nature qualities to which Benjamin was very sensitive. Significantly, he copied, among the notes taken during the last months of his life, a remark by Focillon about the work of art: "At the instant when it is born, it is a phenomenon of rupture . . . to mark a momentous event is to disturb, startlingly, the moment" (I:1229f.). Elsewhere he stresses that "the finest prose sentence imaginable" undoubtedly results from the disruption of a single poetic period (*Reflections,* 79). Thus the shock that destroys the "aura" in order to take its place and that provides a foundation for a "modern" aesthetic becomes the necessary means of saving what time inexorably distances from us and of making us responsible for it.

The origin of such *Bruchstücke* is often uncertain. Many seem to be the mere vestiges of an edifice that was never constructed and that hovers like a mirage before the dreamer's mind. It would be the ambition of each element, thus saved from limbo, to replace that from which it was said to have issued, to render it useless, even to render it forgotten for the benefit of some new totality. Benjamin, who attached the greatest importance to questions of form, of genre definition, and of a work's composition, was not in the least inferior to the Nietzsche of a hypothetical *Will to Power* in his concern for *disposition* (not necessarily dialectic), that is, for those "combinations" repeatedly returned to the workshop. The exercise reached its greatest complexity within the framework of the *Passagen-Werk*, when Benjamin was revising the outline and approach required by the studies on Baudelaire. No commentator, to my knowledge, has tried to analyze the secret architecture intended by the author for *One-Way Street*. In this respect, it is perhaps at a substructure—that of the sentence—that his success is evident. In certain passages of the *Trauerspiel* book or in the final "Theses," the text appears to be constructed in a sequence, as a kind of linear mosaic of formulas so strikingly formed that they have on occasion been criticized as apodictic.

It is well known that Benjamin often dreamed of constructing a work that would be nothing but a mosaic of quotations.[28] One unavoidably thinks here of the practice attributed to the ancient Egyptians who, following the precise rules for constructing new temples, drew their materials from edifices that had just been demolished. In this way, the debris left by certain literary works would become a quarry (*Steinbruch*) for new works. With Benjamin the ingenuity of the method is accentuated by the arbitrary choice of the authors he cites—arbitrary in that his readings appear to have been far from systematic. The works that inspired him or caught his attention were not necessarily the works he read to the end (of which he scrupulously kept a list). Whether it happened to be Jochmann or Blanqui, Benjamin frequently found the subjects for his studies and fresh paths of thought as a consequence of his *flâneries* in libraries with his collector's eye or of the sort of "objective chance" so dear to the surrealists. For him, reading and writing were accompanied by quotation that was now a *citation á l'ordre du jour* (*Illuminations*, 256),[29] the conclusion of a chain for fortuitous accidents, and of no less fortuitous *Rettungen*.

If we transpose the discussion onto the map of Benjamin's own destiny and that of history, then the *Bruchstück* takes on a new range and amplitude—as a sign of quality, indeed of greatness, as hope for renewal after the destructive shock, preserving something of the dialectic in the midst of literature. Here again *Rettung* acquires its full meaning in recognizing its own limits, that is, in becoming, above all, a rescuing. An extended metaphor will make this apparent—that of the shipwreck. Rather traditionally applied to literature, especially since Mallarmé,[30] and to literature only within the frame of the sheltered existence of the petit-bourgeois-turned-great-writer, its participation in the dramas of the era caused the "shipwreck," along with Benjamin himself, to "rise to new tasks," to don a dramatic or tragic significance, in view of misfortune's effacement of all nuance. From 1931 on, under the twin pressures of personal difficulties and the evolving political situation, *Rettung* referred to the struggle for survival. In a letter to Scholem (*Briefe*, 532), Benjamin portrays himself as "someone shipwrecked, who climbs the crumbling mast of his boat's wreckage . . . to signal for rescue." His signals not being received, understood, or recorded, the shipwrecked figure clings hopelessly to the most fragile debris, to the last straw (I:1243). In vain, of course, as he knew: his existence cannot be saved. As such, returning to literature, he had already tossed a bottle to the sea. It did not contain a call for help or the coordinates of Robinson's Island. The necessarily brief message, in the form of a *Bruchstück,* renounced once more any immediate communication (*Trauerspiel,* 208). Only later would its meaning be penetrated and reconstituted, the ensemble recovered of which it was the sign or allegory.

Adorno insists, as the afterword to the French translation of *Negative Dialectics* indicates, on preserving the finest testimonies of our culture in a secure place.[31] This idea, and many others, was common to Adorno and Benjamin, who referred to it with pleasure at the end of his life.[32] From this perspective, his *Bruchstücke* would be condensed versions of what he wanted to say, of what he finally, in many cases, was able to say, thanks to them. We can apply to Benjamin what he had hoped for Rang—the rescue through posthumous works, through the *Nachlaß* (*Briefe*, 371). We can apply this to him and to all the components of the universe of ideas and images that was his own, despite the catastrophe which he judged imminent and which indeed had already begun.

4

The catastrophe occurred. It was of course partial, leaving room for future catastrophes, or, for Utopians, the hope of redemption. "En attendant," as Benjamin and his friends at the Institute used to say occasionally in French. If Benjamin fulfilled his own fateful role as victim, predestined for misfortune, then his work remains incomplete as a whole— fragmentary, in most precious individual components—by vocation as well as by necessity, seeming thereby to offer itself up to the fury of commentators. Yet it only seems so. For a new reversal happens here, once again, at the level of literature. Critics are free to take their scalpel to the completed works: death comes but once. As for the other works, the *Bruchstücke*, they are answerable instead to silent contemplation and meditation, and they evoke the beautifully turned phrase at the close of Karl Kraus's collection *Nachts*: "Patience, seekers, the secret will come clear of itself." The present mission of the *Bruchstück*—one might almost say its duty to the one who contributed to making a genre of it and who, in doing so, made it illustrious—would be to rescue Benjamin's work from the tide of exegesis.

Translated by Victoria Bridges, Larry Cohen, Kevin McLaughlin, and Gary Smith

Notes

This essay was originally written as a response to the French translations of three of Benjamin's works—*Correspondance* (Paris: Aubier-Montaigne, 1979), *Sens unique précédé d'Enfance berlinoise* (Paris: Les Lettres Nouvelles, 1978), and *Allemands* (Paris: Hachette, 1979)—and two books on Benjamin—Werner Fuld, *Walter Benjamin. Zwischen den Stühlen. Eine Biographie* (Munich: Carl Hanser, 1979), and Jean-Pierre Schobinger, *Variationen zu Walter Benjamins Sprachmeditationen* (Basel: Schwabe, 1979). (Ed.)

1. Regarding this controversy, see my essay "Du nouveau sur Walter Benjamin," *Critique* 267–268 (August–September 1969). Fuld's book was severely criticized by Walter Boehlich in *Der Spiegel* 21 (1979).

2. This was especially due to the collection *Critique de la politique*, edited by Miguel Abensour.

3. This is a play on the title of Adorno's last publication on Benjamin, "A l'écart de tous les courants," which was first published in Missac's translation in *Le Monde* (May 31, 1969). See Theodor W. Adorno, *Über Walter Benjamin*, 96–99. (Ed.)

4. See Liselotte Wiesenthal, *Zur Wissenschaftstheorie Walter Benjamins* (Frankfurt a.M.: Athenäum, 1973); Bernd Witte, *Walter Benjamin. Der Intellektuelle als Kritiker* (Stuttgart: Metzler, 1972); and Schobinger, *Variationen*.

5. Rather than translating *Rettung* as *salut*, written in lower case and halfway between a kind of rescue and salvation nearer to redemption, the German word was chosen. By the same token, the word *Fragment*, which bears too many overtones of Romanticism, has a brittle relation to *Bruchstück*. This last is raised, if perhaps too briefly, in the exemplary book by Ph. Lacoue-Labarthe and J.-L. Nancy, *L'Absolu littéraire* (Paris: Editions du Seuil, 1978).

6. See especially Gershom Scholem, "Walter Benjamin and His Angel," this volume, and Theodor W. Adorno, "A Portrait of Walter Benjamin," in *Prisms* (Cambridge, MA: MIT Press, 1982). Included among those who make use of the eclectic designations mentioned here are Oskar Sahlberg, J.-P. Stern, and Jürgen Habermas.

7. See my study of rhetoric in *Critique* 378, as well as "Eloge de la citation," *Change* 22. It should be noted that Irving Wohlfarth, in a study noted below (note 11), refers expressly to the notions of oxymoron and chiasmus in I:57, 64.

8. See Pierre Fougeyrollas, *Contradiction et totalité* (Paris: Edition de Minuit, 1964), 9. Nietzsche, in fact, treats the formal or rhetorical aspect of the dialectic with more precision. By Popper, see "What is Dialectic?" *Mind* 49 (1940): 402–26.

9. See the collection, Adorno et al., *Über Walter Benjamin* (Frankfurt a.M.: Suhrkamp, 1968), 152.

10. Letter to Benjamin of November 10, 1938. (See *Aesthetics and Politics*, 128, 130). In the same letter Adorno also speaks of Benjamin's mythicizing or archaicizing tendencies.

11. Reference is made to the following essays by Irving Wohlfarth: "No Man's Land: On Walter Benjamin's 'Destructive Character,' " *Diacritics* (June 1978): 47–65; "On the Messianic Structure of Walter Benjamin's Last Reflections," *Glyph* 3 (Baltimore: Johns Hopkins, 1978): 148–212.

12. "Great innovators" often know, however, how to "make a clean sweep of things" (II:215). It is this duality of aspects that inspires those, such as Wohlfarth, who suggest comparison between the "destruction" of Benjamin and the "deconstruction" of Derrida.

13. See Gershom G. Scholem, *Fidélité et Utopie* (Paris: Calmann-Lévy, 1978), 55.

14. Regarding the controversy with Werner Kraft concerning the discovery of Jochmann, see II:1397ff.

15. This tendency recalls the will, underscored by Adorno, to reconcile the disappearance of individuality with the salvation of man. See Adorno, "A Portrait of Walter Benjamin," *Prisms*, 231.

16. See especially Witte, *Walter Benjamin. Der Intellektuelle als Kritiker*, 127–29.

17. For whom it is neither one nor the other (see I:172). See Witte, 110–11.

18. *Sauter/springen/saut/sprung* contains a double signification of jumping or leaping like a tiger *and* that of a cracking or splitting such as "springing a leak." Missac's use of the word "interrompre" (interruption) just after the second occurrence of "saut" in the sentence emphasizes this distinction and connects the latter usage to his definition of "rupture" in Benjamin's work. Missac selects a good example in his reference to a sentence from "zentralpark" (I:683): "Die Rettung hält sich an den kleinen Sprung in

der kontinuierlichen Katastrophe," which can be rendered "Redemption seeks the small fissure in the ongoing catastrophe." (Ed.)

19. "Fashion is the eternal recurrence of the new. Are there nevertheless motifs of redemption (*Rettung*) precisely in fashion?" (I:683; "Central Park," 47).

20. See note 5 above.

21. A new problem of translation arises here. As early as 1928 the critic Werner Milch (*Berliner Tageblatt*, November 11, 1928) referred to Benjamin as *Fragmentist*, a term that can be translated only imperfectly as "author of fragments." And what would one make of "*Allegoriker*"? In refusing a cigarette, while an Englishman or Frenchman will say: "Je ne fume pas" (I don't smoke), a German or Swiss-German will more likely say: "Ich bin kein Raucher" (I am a nonsmoker).

22. G. Scholem, "Walter Benjamin" in *On Jews and Judaism in Crisis* (New York: Schocken, 1976), 176f.

23. See Adorno, "Portrait," 238.

24. "In der Improvisation liegt die Stärke. Alle entscheidenden Schläge werden mit der linken Hand geführt werden" (IV:89). J. Lacoste translates this as "seront portés comme en se jouant" (will be brought into play), which is not inexact but leaves nothing of the image. We preferred to retain the image in "C'est du gauche que seront portés tous les coups décisifs," even at the cost of invoking the context of sports, which was obviously foreign to Benjamin. In both cases, the political connotations suggested by "la gauche" ("the left") is lacking.

25. Wiesenthal, *Zur Wissenschafttheorie Walter Benjamins*, 88–97.

26. It is in this manner that they are notably described by H. Schweppenhäuser; see "Physiognomie eines Physiognomikers," in S. Unseld, ed. *Zur Aktualität Walter Benjamins* (Frankfurt a.M.: Suhrkamp, 1972), 146.

27. The dialectical image readily invites commentary. See on this subject, Adorno's famous letter of August 2, 1935 (*Aesthetics and Politics*, 110–20) and Rolf Tiedemann, *Studien zur Philosophie Walter Benjamins* (Frankfurt a.M.: Suhrkamp, 1965), 126ff. See above all a passage from "Central Park," *New German Critique* 34 (Winter 1985): 49.

28. Even if it remains unaccomplished, the design takes strength and becomes more radical from the moment of the *Trauerspiel* book to the *Passagen-Werk*. Benjamin's treatment of quotation seems so important and so original that one deplores its not being cited in the otherwise so attractive work of Antoine Compagnon, *La Seconde main ou le travail de la citation* (Paris: Seuil, 1979).

29. "Only for a redeemed mankind has its past become citable in all its moments. Each moment it has lived becomes a *citation á l'ordre du jour*—and that day is Judgment Day." (Ed.)

30. See the poems "Au seul souci . . ." and "A la nue accablante . . . ."

31. See H.-G. Holl's afterword, "Emigration dans l'immanence le mouvement intellectuel de le dialectique négative," in *Dialectique négative* (Paris: Payot, 1978), 325–40.

32. In conversations and sometimes in letters (*Briefe*, 727f.).

Resentment Begins at Home: Nietzsche, Benjamin, and the University

Irving Wohlfarth

Wohlfarth has long ranked among the most schooled and original readers of Benjamin's writings. Since the 1960s, when he first heard Adorno lecture in Frankfurt, Wohlfarth has published extensively on Benjamin and Adorno in French, English, and German. He introduced the French translation of the Trauerspiel *book and helped organize the large Paris colloquium on the* Passagen-Werk *in 1983. In his forthcoming collection of essays,* No-Man's Land *(which includes the following essay and which reviews several of the essays in this collection), Wohlfarth shows how Benjamin always took up a tactical position* between *existing camps, official fronts, constellations of friends, and the like.*

Wohlfarth's most public contribution to the West German discussion came during the 1982 colloquium in Frankfurt celebrating the publication of the Passagen-Werk. *There he showed, through a close reading of the "Theologico-Political Fragment," that the tensions between the "early, theological" and "late, materialist" Benjamin—two entrenched camps in Benjamin criticism—were in crucial respects already productively resolved within an early "theological" text.*

In the essay published here, Wohlfarth takes up Benjamin's metaphor of the "rendezvous" between past and present. Through an exegetical reading of texts that evince Benjamin's exasperation with the academy, he shows that there was never a "meeting of the minds" between Benjamin and Nietzsche and questions where our rendezvous with Benjamin may be.

Meanwhile my Frankfurt plans have been practically scotched, and it is being put to me that I should voluntarily withdraw my application for the *Habilitation.* Looking back over this tortuous course of events, I have every reason to take comfort in the inner and outer conviction which increasingly forbade me to respect the present-day university as a place of fruitful, and above all uncorrupted, activity. For how much fruitless indignation, how much gall would the treatment to

which I have been subjected have awoken in me under any other circumstances. . . . To be able to step before the young and win them over through living speech no doubt has its value and appeal. *Where* this happens and *whom* it reaches are not, however, a matter of indifference. And certain though it is that there does not yet exist outside the university another place where fruitful activity is assured, it seems no less certain to me that the university is itself today increasingly muddying its own wellsprings.
Benjamin, *Briefe*

FÜR MÄNNER
Überzeugen ist unfruchtbar.
Benjamin, *Einbahnstraße*

The problem [of resentment] is not exactly easy: one has to have experienced it both from a position of strength and from a position of weakness.

The scholar—a *décadent*.
Nietzsche, *Ecce Homo*

All active interpretations, all strong acts of reading, take the form, according to Walter Benjamin, of a "secret rendezvous" between an ineluctable present and a no less determinate past.

This present may, admittedly, be a meager one. Be that as it may, one has to have it firmly by the horns to be able to ask questions of the past. The present is a bull whose blood must fill the pit if the spirits of the departed are to appear at its edge. (III:259)

What we usually mean when we speak of "sacrificing" the present to the past, or vice versa, is that the one has to be disregarded, at least provisionally, in favor of the other. We tend to assume that their conflicting claims cannot be met at one and the same time. Such an assumption is, the above quotation suggests, in neither's interest. The sacrifice involved is an unnecessary one; a different, more compelling sacrifice is called for. Only by offering up its own blood and guts can the present hope to summon up the spirits of the dead. There is, in short, sacrifice and sacrifice—in Benjamin's terminology, mythical and nonmythical sacrifice. If you want to relive the past, you should not, according to Fustel de Coulanges, let yourself be distracted by anything that happened in the meantime (*Illuminations*, 256). You must, in other words, stop living the present. *That* would be "mythical" self-sacrifice. Instead of summoning up the shades of the departed, the historian joins them, and thereby sacrifices his best energies on the altar of (what he takes to be) historical objectivity. By contrast, the "materialist historian" after Benjamin's heart "leaves it to others to be drained by the whore 'Once upon a time' in the brothel of historicism" (*Illuminations*, 262). *His* task is to seize the day, that is, to grasp the "constellation" it forms with a particular past. Dialectics, as Hegel conceived it, is a matter of "entering the enemy's strength," the better to harness it. Likewise, the materialist historian's task is, according to Benjamin, both to dream the dream of history and, neither succumbing to nor forgetting the unconscious past, to awaken from—but also with—it. This double task prompts the composite metaphor of taking the proverbial bull by the horns and then ritually slaughtering it, as in ancient times, in order to resuscitate the bloodless shades of the dead. The present may be a rather anemic bull, a "bad new" day as opposed to the "good old" ones (*Reflections*, 219), but its horns are the horns of *our* dilemma. That dilemma entails no alternative between past and present. Its solution depends rather on the right interaction between the two.

Or, as Nietzsche had it, the "use" to which history should be put depends on the "strength"[1] we bring to it. Like a drug, it is subject to abuse. "We need history, but we need it differently than the spoiled idler in the garden of knowledge."[2] It is no accident that this sentence from the preface to the second of the *Untimely Meditations*, "On the Use and Abuse of History for Life," should have found its way into Benjamin's theses "On the Concept of History." For the relation between these texts is so far-reaching that the parallels could be shown to extend all the way from deep structural affinities to strikingly analogous metaphorical formulations. But the idea of such a "parallel" is itself anything but far-reaching. It smacks of that "history of ideas" which both Nietzsche and Benjamin saw as a symptom of historicist impotence and vaguely conjures up harmonious visions of great thinkers finally meeting at infinity. The notion of a parallel is too straightforward a metaphor to account for more

complex types of interrelation which might, for instance, fluc-
tuate imperceptibly between intimacy and distance. Such is the
relation of Benjamin's and Nietzsche's writings to one another.
One cannot read them side by side without being struck by the
intricate patterns of simultaneous divergence and convergence
that regularly result from such juxtapositions. It is beyond the
scope of this essay to attempt to formulate the law that governs
so elusive and shifting a relationship, or even merely to describe those moments when Benjamin comes closest to a rap-
prochement or engagement with Nietzsche.[3] Suffice it to say,
for our present purposes, that if there exists a "rendezvous"
between Benjamin and Nietzsche it is *so* "secret" that one can
never be entirely sure whether a meeting of the minds actually
does take place. It may be of relevance in this context that
Benjamin's phrase "secret rendezvous" went through various
revisions and was to have been "clandestine" (*heimlich*) or "temporal" (*zeitlich*) before becoming a "secret" (*geheim*) assignation.
From here it is not far to the "uncanny" (*unheimlich*)—a word
dear to Nietzsche, though not to Benjamin, and one which
might be applied to their particular rendezvous, especially in
light of the complex relationship Freud traces between *heimlich*
and *unheimlich* in his recently much-discussed essay "The Uncanny." According to Gershom Scholem, there were two thinkers with whose work Benjamin conspicuously failed to come to
terms—namely, Nietzsche and Freud; Freud's own failure to
acknowledge his debt to Nietzsche has in turn been much remarked upon.

Not that the secret to all this uncanniness is necessarily to be
found in some unvaryingly Oedipal "anxiety of influence." If
Benjamin's rendezvous with Nietzsche never quite comes
about, this is perhaps because more pressing appointments take
precedence. "I have not yet had the time," he writes to Scholem
in 1932, "to consider what meaning Nietzsche's writings might
yield if put to the critical test [*im Ernstfall*]" (*Briefe*, 554). There
is no need to act on Nietzsche now. He looms on the horizon,
but for the time being he can wait. Benjamin decides he can, in
this case, afford to keep his options open until such time as he
will be forced to make more critical decisions. But when that
Ernstfall does arrive—one which, in their respective ways,

both Nietzsche and Benjamin saw coming—Benjamin will, of course, have still less time to devote to Nietzsche.

He will thus continue to refer to him only in passing. These glancing allusions serve, however, to exemplify his theory and practice of quoting others out of context. This very method could, moreover, itself be considered as citing Nietzsche out of context. Its point is, after all, to liberate both the text and the act of quotation from their authoritarian contexts. And had not Zarathustra already sought to turn his own authority against itself? "One repays a teacher badly," he warns his would-be disciples, "if one always remains a mere pupil. And why will you not pluck at my wreath?"[4] He is, in effect, instructing them to bury him so that, instead of being mummified for all time, he can one day be at least partially resurrected: "Now I bid you lose me and find yourselves; and only when you have all denied me will I return to you."[5] Benjamin was, of course, never Zarathustra's disciple, or for that matter anyone else's, but across the great divide that separates them Zarathustra might conceivably have recognized in Benjamin one of his own. Benjamin did, moreover, deny what was perhaps the most Nietzschean phase of his development—namely, his association with the *Jugendbewegung*—in order to find his own way. Along that way a certain Nietzsche periodically returned to him. This Nietzschean moment didn't always come directly from Nietzsche's own writings; and even when it did, it was so thoroughly assimilated to Benjamin's own way of thinking as to be virtually unrecognizable. But never less so, perhaps, than where his texts prescribe the emancipation of the reader from their own authority.

So much, in all too general terms, for Benjamin's relation, or nonrelation, to Nietzsche. But what about resentment and the university? What has been said thus far may give us an initial grip on the horns of this dilemma. In instructing us, their would-be pupils, to terminate our dependency, to place "history" in the service of "life," our masters are plainly telling us to take the present by the horns. The present is, as usual, a meager one, and it is, as always, the only one we've got. How, then, might we go about obeying (that is, disobeying) our masters' instructions—the present being, in this instance, an academic conference entitled "Nietzsche and the Psychology of Resentment"? We might begin by recognizing the massive irony, the inherent falsity, of our situation. Brecht once sketched the following satire on the Frankfurt Institut für Sozialforschung. A sick and aging capitalist sets aside a small portion of his profits to fund research into the causes of poverty in contemporary society—only to be led to the inevitable conclusion that capitalism is itself the root of the problem. Closer to home, an analogous scenario might go more or less as follows. A hand-picked group of far-flung academics is paid to attend a conference on the "psychology of resentment," which cannot but confirm what they all knew already, from bitter experience, without needing to read Nietzsche on the subject—namely, that resentment breeds more efficiently wherever two or three academics are gathered together.

Benjamin and Nietzsche, both of whom turned their backs on the university, might momentarily have savored our little dilemma, and it seems likely that this conference will be punctuated by ghostly gusts of hysterical laughter or biblical wrath as they turn in their unquiet graves.

Let me, at the risk of placing myself in its line of fire, reenact one such posthumous salvo by recalling Benjamin's response to the fate that his now-famous *magnum opus, The Origin of German Trauerspiel,* suffered at the hands of the University of Frankfurt when he submitted it as a postdoctoral thesis, a *Habilitationsschrift* which, without guaranteeing him a salaried position, would, if accepted, have at least gained him the credentials he needed to obtain an academic appointment. The following account will be necessarily anecdotal—but Nietzsche and Benjamin were among the first to teach us the cognitive value of anecdotes.

Here, to begin with, is Benjamin's description of the professor on whose good offices official acceptance of his work depended:

This Professor Schultz, while intellectually insignificant, is an experienced man of the world who probably has a better flair in many literary matters than young coffeehouse regulars. That is, however, all that can be said for his phony cultural pretensions. He is a mediocrity in every other respect. What skills he has for diplomacy are paralyzed by a pusillanimity that clothes itself in the correct forms. As yet I know nothing, or rather nothing good, about the reception of my manuscript. When I handed him the second part a week after delivering the first, I found him cool and touchy, in addition to being obviously ill-informed. . . . Thereupon I traveled here, and meanwhile he too has left town or else is lying low. . . . A year and a half ago, he gave me very definite hopes—without making any firm promises—that he would support my candidacy in literary history. . . , but even before receiving the manuscript he had withdrawn his support and was arguing in favor of aesthetics. In that case, of course, his voice would not carry quite as much authority. However that may be, my *Habilitation* is doomed to failure unless he gives me his complete backing. Despite his astonishment at the extraordinary precision of my scholarly apparatus, I certainly cannot count on such support. After all, so many factors are involved, including resentment. As he said to Salomon, not without decent self-irony, the only thing he has against me would be that I am not a student of his. (*Briefe*, 375f.)

Academic politics with a vengeance! Professor Schultz—or *homo academicus! Homo academicus*—or *der Mensch des Ressentiments!* Benjamin's portrait of an academic dean could, in effect, be matched point for point by Nietzsche's psychology of resentment. Consider, for example, the following passage from *Beyond Good and Evil*:

The worst and most dangerous things a scholar is capable of stem from an instinct for mediocrity which works to destroy the exceptional human being, and seeks to break—or, still better, to slacken—every tautened bow. To sap all intensity, and to do so with tender loving care (*Abspannen nämlich, mit Rücksicht, mit schonender Hand natürlich,—mit zutraulichem Mitleiden abspannen*)—this truly jesuitical art has always managed to pass itself off as a religion of compassion.[6]

Both Nietzsche and Benjamin have a healthy respect for the sick politics of resentment—for politics *as* resentment. *Personal* resentment is only one factor in the situation that Benjamin describes ("Denn schließlich spielt tausenderlei hinein, und auch Ressentiment"); its precondition is a larger, institutionalized resentment. The psychology of resentment is, as in Nietzsche, no *mere* psychology. Schultz is, above all, a political animal who knows how to change his tack, blow hot and cold, keep a low profile, stay out of trouble, pass the buck, play the rules, etc. Not merely do his "jesuitical" ploys exemplify Nietzsche's various accounts of resentment in (re)action, but his whole behavior can hardly be explained *except* in terms of a Nietzschean psychology of resentment. Schultz's calculated duplicity toward an exceptional candidate who might, if admitted to the profession, refuse to play the game is a tactical response to two contradictory pressures—the old-boy network which administers the status quo and the candidate's appeal to the standards by which the academic institution legitimizes itself.[7] Careful not to expose himself to reproach from either quarter ("Schultz," writes Benjamin in his next letter, "der sich zwar mir gegenüber keine Blösse geben will"), he maneuvers between both. Whether or not he merely wants to keep his bases covered, or whether he also has a bad conscience toward Benjamin, we will never know. But if "hypocrisy is the homage vice pays to virtue" (La Rochefoucauld), resentment represents a similarly devious, and still more dangerous, tribute. It cannot openly acknowledge what it secretly admires. Resentment not merely says no to the world; it also denies its own existence. It negates its own nihilism, and thereby compounds it. It thus consists of layer upon layer of (k)nots. Chief among them is what Freud termed "denial." One spectacular instance of this would be Nietzsche's celebrated account, in *The Genealogy of Morals,* of the Jewish hatred that lurks beneath Christian love. Another would be the final touch in Benjamin's portrait of Schultz. His "only" objection to Benjamin, Schultz allows, is that he isn't one of his pupils. A disingenuous remark if ever there was one. Schultz cannot outwardly admit to his multiple resentments. Not merely is that objection clearly *not* the only one he has against Benjamin, but he also knows better than to leave himself without the possibility of dissociating himself from it. (In the wake of the Watergate trial, such tactics came to be known as "deniability.") Hence the "decent self-irony," which, by partly denying resentment, partly admitting to it, and partly admitting its inadmissibility, gets away with it. Such alleged decency is, of course, highly ambivalent. Schultz may be decent enough to have qualms about saying what he does, but his bad conscience is calculated to demonstrate his good faith, and thus to enable him, by way of self-irony, to vent resentments he is evidently afraid, or ashamed, to express more directly.

Irving Wohlfarth

It is tempting to see the opposition between Benjamin and Schultz in terms of the interplay between "active" and "reactive" forces, which, in Nietzsche's account, constitutes the whole history of European nihilism. In each case, the opposition of contrary forces forms a chiasmus, inasmuch as power turns out to be weakness, and vice versa. The threat that Benjamin's work poses to the academic establishment is at once real and symbolic, as powerful as it is powerless. Unlike the powers that be ("Schultz, der sich . . . keine Blösse geben will"), genuine power is essentially defenseless. Its defeats at the hands of the powers that be are, however, never final. The virtues of the defeated, Benjamin writes in the "Theses," "have retroactive force and will constantly call in question every victory, past and present, of the rulers." His own life and work will prove to be a case in point. But such retroactive force threatens both sides in turn. Each is vulnerable to the other's power. *"Even the dead,"* Benjamin also writes, "will not be safe from the enemy if he wins. And this enemy has not ceased to be victorious." Here too Benjamin's own posthumous reputation may well illustrate his thesis. What if his eventual triumph over a *benighted* establishment coincided with the rise of an *enlightened* one, which proceeded to enlist him, as a token spokesman for the defeated, in "the triumphal procession where the present rulers step over those who are lying prostrate" (*Illuminations*, 255f.)? But let us not anticipate.

It isn't by breaking their bows but by slackening them that, according to Nietzsche, the weak disarm the strong. The politics of resentment are those of attrition. They count on the difficulty of maintaining tension indefinitely and reckon that the laws of time, inertia and gravity are on their side. They avoid open confrontation, play a waiting game, and let things take their course. This is precisely how Benjamin's bow (a metaphor he often applies to his writings) was slackened. The manuscript was, as we say, referred from one department to another, like a dossier in a Kafkaesque trial; various referees claimed not to—or, as Benjamin put it, "not to want to"—understand it (a familiar detail, this, in the annals of resentment: those who "don't understand" modern music, Adorno was to observe, understand it all too well); and Benjamin was finally advised—

mit Rücksicht, mit schonender Hand natürlich—to withdraw his candidacy in order to be spared the embarrassment of official rejection.

In his capacity as Dean, Schultz had assured me that, whatever happened, he wanted to spare me such rejection. But no word was forthcoming. I have sound reasons for assuming that he let me down. I have not, however, withdrawn my candidacy, for I would like to see the faculty assume the whole risk of reaching a negative decision. (*Briefe*, 392).

Much though the idea of forcing resentment into the open appealed to Benjamin, he regretfully decided against it, not so much to avoid embarrassing the faculty as to spare himself resentment. "How much fruitless indignation, how much gall" the treatment he had received would have provoked in him, he writes, had he not meanwhile been forced to abandon hope in the intellectual possibilities offered by the contemporary university (*Briefe*, 399). Benjamin's verdict on the university, like Nietzsche's before him, is motivated in part by considerations of personal hygiene. His own regimen will, however, never include the *superhuman* exercises that Nietzsche had prescribed as an antidote to modern cultural decadence.

One of the inalienable rights left out of democratic constitutions was, according to Baudelaire, "le droit de s'en aller." Benjamin left the university in style. If we examine his style in closer detail, we will, in the process, find ourselves squarely confronted with our present dilemma. Benjamin's parting shot was a time bomb. Even as we pore over it, it may explode in our face.

That time bomb was, of course, a text. Benjamin conceived it as a retrospective preface to *The Origin of German Trauerspiel*— an apocryphal, unpublished preface, not to be confused with the notorious "Epistemo-Critical Prologue," whose difficulty had contributed to the failure of Benjamin's attempted *Habilitation*. Hence it is in English translation, which tends, alas, to muffle its resounding onomatopoeic echoes:

I would like to tell the story of Sleeping Beauty a second time.
She sleeps in her hedge of thorns. And then, after so and so many years, she awakens.
But not from the kiss of some Prince Charming.

The cook it was who awoke her, when he gave the scullery boy a resounding slap that echoed throughout the castle with the pent-up force of so many years.

A beautiful child lies sleeping behind the thorny hedge of the following pages.

Let no Prince Charming clad in the shining armor of modern scholarship venture too close. For as he embraces his bride, she will bite him.

To awaken her, the author has, instead, reserved for himself the role of the cook. Too long has the slap been overdue that is intended to send reverberations through the corridors of academic scholarship.

Then this poor truth will also awaken, having pricked herself at an old-fashioned spinning wheel when she trespassed into the lumber room in order to weave herself a professorial gown.

Frankfurt a/M, July 1925[8]

This retelling of "Sleeping Beauty" is based on Grimms's version of that time-honored fairy tale. Let us quickly recall the salient details of the traditional story in order to verify where Benjamin's version departs from the original.

After waiting many a long year, the Queen finally gives birth to a Princess. The whole Court is invited to the celebrations, including the twelve fairy godmothers (or, as the brothers Grimm call them, "the wise women"). By some oversight, the unlucky thirteenth fails to get invited, and vows in revenge that the Princess shall die. The other twelve are, however, able to mitigate the sentence: the Princess will merely fall into a perpetual sleep when she pricks herself at a spinning wheel. The King thereupon orders the destruction of all the spinning wheels in the realm. One day, however, the Princess ventures into a remote attic of the castle, where an old woman is seated at a spinning wheel. . . . No sooner has the inevitable occurred than the whole kingdom enters a state of suspended animation. The palace cook, for example, had just been about to box the scullery boy's ears; his arm is now arrested in midair. As time passes, a hedge of thorns, which no Prince succeeds in penetrating, grows around the kingdom. After a hundred years, however, it yields magically to the approaching footsteps of a fairy Prince who, on discovering the Princess, awakens her with a kiss. Thereupon the whole kingdom returns to life. The cook promptly finishes boxing the scullery boy's ears. And the story duly ends with the marriage of the Prince and Princess, who live happily ever after.

All's well that ends well. But Benjamin's *Habilitation* had ended badly, under circumstances hardly reminiscent of a fairy tale. Hence his transformation of a goodnight story intended to lull children to sleep into a cautionary tale calculated to awaken the university from its dogmatic slumber. It is, according to Benjamin, historicism that reduces history to the fairy-tale dimensions of the "once upon a time." Abruptly skipping over that ritual invocation of simpler, more innocent days, Benjamin introduces the jarring present into the never-never land of Sleeping Beauty. The resulting version of Grimms's fairy tale, while not exactly its "transvaluation," has an energy that Nietzsche would surely have saluted. *Abspannen*—this is, we recall, the technique whereby lesser minds defuse the intellectual intensity they fear and envy. Conversely, Benjamin's version of Sleeping Beauty enacts a symbolic explosion that is to send shock waves through the corridors of power. This condemnation of the academic establishment has the same "transcendent thrust" (*transzendente Wucht*) as the salvation of the baroque allegorist at the end of the manuscript that Benjamin had feigned to submit to temporal powers.

It could in fact be shown that the magisterial tone with which Benjamin here takes on the university has theological overtones, indeed that it contains a whole theology of language. The resounding slap that is to echo through the groves of academe is, in effect, an apocalyptic performative, a self-fulfilling prophecy, a quasi-divine speech act intended to dismiss the university, once and for all, from the presence of the Word. It is as if the Logos in person were announcing its presence, and were doing so by the heaviness of its breathing. "To interrupt the course of the world," writes Benjamin, "such was Baudelaire's deepest wish (*Wille*). The wish of Joshua" (I:667). Such too was Benjamin's wish—a wish for (re)percussion(s). Like the trumpets that brought down the walls of Jericho, that extramural slap is intended, by sheer acoustic force of will, to bring the academic world, at least momentarily, to a "Messianic standstill" (*Illuminations*, 263). And, like the Last Trump, it sounds the Resurrection, the triumphant reawakening, the return of a "poor truth" which the university had, at its own risk, presumed to turn away. This definitive verdict on the university both anticipates the Last Judgment and recalls God's original act of judgment, the expulsion of Adam and Eve from Paradise. For the Fall was, according to Benjamin, the Fall of language into "chatter," a fall from "names" into "signs," and, synonymously, from "truth" into "knowledge" (*Erkenntnis, Wissen*).[9]

Are, then, academics at all competent to pronounce on matters of truth? Isn't bourgeois scholarship (*Wissenschaft*) merely another form of fallen knowledge, idle chatter masquerading as the Word?[10] It is, at all events, no accident that the "lumber room" into which the "poor truth" ventures in order to weave herself academic garb recalls nothing so much as the "bleak confusion of Golgotha" (*trostlose Verworrenheit der Schädelstätte*), which, according to that selfsame "truth" (e.g., *Ursprung des deutschen Trauerspiels*), represents the recurrent baroque emblem for the "desolation" (*Trauerspiel*, 232) of an unredeemed world; or that the same word (*Öde*) should sum up Benjamin's view of the academic scene (*Briefe*, 523). Far from radiating *lux et veritas*, the university is here presented as a dark and dusty lumber room, an allegory of the Fall. And it is no accident that it is in such lumber rooms that Kafka's *Trial* takes place.

Benjamin's revised version of Sleeping Beauty is not merely implicitly underwritten by a Jewish metaphysics of language; such a metaphysics is already explicitly contained in the original manuscript—the "beautiful child"—which he had submitted to the university for its stamp of approval. It is, moreover, chiefly contained in the prologue, which, as its title, "Erkenntniskritische Vorrede," already indicates, formulates a critique of mere knowledge in the name of truth. That notoriously thorny preface is, in fact, the "hedge of thorns" its author had erected in order to protect his "poor truth" against unwelcome encroachment; and its original motto read: "Über Stock und über Steine/ Aber brich Dir nicht die Beine." Its author may have trespassed upon private (or privatized public) property when he entered the lumber room to weave himself the semblance of an academic gown, an idiosyncratic patchwork composed of the most recondite scholarly materials. But his academic readers were in turn placed in the position of potential trespassers. They were kept out by a strategically placed hedge of thorns—a rhetorical precaution more readily associated with hermetic poetry than with the methodological introduction to a scholarly treatise. Thus, the second, apocryphal preface repeats the gesture of the first. Both turn the tables on their academic judges by stripping them of all authority. They do so on their *own* authority, but also by appealing to the millennial authority of Judaic tradition. In its own way, each preface speaks on behalf of the monotheistic, monological, paternal Logos and reserves the right to monopolize the Word. Thus, the author of the second preface has, in effect, reserved for himself *all* the roles, that of watchful father, sleeping daughter, and executive cook, leaving out only the members of the other side, Prince Charming and the kitchen boy, who are left to stew in their own chatter. Where Hannah Arendt was to speak of the "banality" of evil, Benjamin's theology of the Fall reduces it to sheer vanity, arbitrary despotism, and nameless nonentity.

The story that is here being retold is thus a new variant not merely of Sleeping Beauty but also of Western metaphysics. Certain resources of that ancient legacy are being mobilized against the upstart university. What Heidegger and Derrida have termed the "ontotheo-eschato-teleology of presence" is being trained on its own places of higher learning. More paradoxical yet, Benjamin—a wandering Jew if ever there was one—can, in a letter to Hofmannsthal, describe modern scholarship as having a "nomadic" relation to the "oldest logoi" of our culture (*Briefe,* 329).[11] His wayward version of Western logocentrism is not, needless to say, mainstream metaphysics, but rather an attempt to go against the current. "Genuinely theological thinkers," "heretically inclined men" such as Florens Christian Rang and Franz Rosenzweig, Benjamin writes in 1932, "transport the tradition on their own back, instead of administering it from a sedentary position" (III:320). His own untenured theology takes the form of an anarchic messianism which, from the outset, contains the elements of his subsequent materialism.

This could be shown by a close reading of his "Theologico-Political Fragment," which might also furnish the basis for a far-reaching confrontation between Benjamin and Nietzsche.

Here, in lieu of such a commentary, is the conclusion of that elliptical fragment.

> To the spiritual *restutio in integrum,* which introduces immortality, corresponds a worldly restitution that leads to the eternity of downfall (*eines Untergangs*), and the rhythm of this eternally transient, worldly existence, transient in its totality, in its spatial but also in its temporal totality, the rhythm of Messianic nature, is happiness. For nature is Messianic by reason of its eternal and total passing away (*Vergängnis*). To strive after such passing, also for those stages of man that are nature, is the task of world politics, whose method has to be called nihilistic. (*Reflections,* 313)[12]

Such is the method at work in Benjamin's nihilistic response to *academic* politics. It is, we said, animated by an active Nietzschean energy. Still more Nietzschean is the yes-saying, indeed dithyrambic nihilism of the "Theologico-Political Fragment," which, with its repetitive, orgasmic celebration of transience, its "approbation de la vie jusqu'à la mort" (Bataille), invites comparison with Nietzsche's doctrine of the eternal return. But how can this be so? How can any valid comparison be possible between Benjamin's thought, steeped as it is in Jewish theology, and Nietzsche's atheist project to *free* European philosophy from its Judeo-Christian legacy? How compatible are Dionysus and the Messiah? And what can conceivably be meant by a yes-saying nihilism? Does not nihilism primarily refer, in Nietzsche's terminology, to the hateful burden of Jewish theology, the concomitant sickness of European civilization, the life-denying forces of reaction? It is, in this perspective, synonymous with the *ressentiment* of those Jewish pharisees who invented truth, theology, and the other world in order to avenge themselves on this one. If, then, Jewish theology is a *symptom* of resentment, how can it also provide the wherewithal to diagnose and cure it?

The answer to these questions does not, surely, lie in some philosemitic variant of Max Scheler's egregious argument that Nietzsche spoiled his noteworthy discovery of the connection between moral judgment and *ressentiment* when he extended it to include *Christian* ethics.[13] A more convincing response could, perhaps, be elicited from our earlier claim that the relation between Benjamin's and Nietzsche's thought is best character-

ized neither by some overall affinity nor by standard oppositions, but rather by fluctuating patterns of convergence and
divergence. Such a demonstration would have to be elaborate,
and this is not the place to attempt it. Let us, instead, return to
Benjamin's version of Sleeping Beauty in order to find out what
Jewish messianism has to say about the psychology of resentment. Here too Benjamin and Nietzsche would, on the face of
it, seem to be worlds apart. Where Nietzsche reduces the whole
history of Judeo-Christian metaphysics, as a metaphysics of
subjectivity, to a "psychology of resentment," Benjamin invokes
Jewish messianism not merely against the metaphysics of subjectivity but, more or less synonymously, against all psychology
as well. Nietzsche accounts for theology in terms of psychology;
Benjamin explains psychology in terms of theology. Their
respective versions of academic *ressentiment* will nevertheless
prove to be uncannily similar.

Resentment makes a twofold appearance in Benjamin's
story—both as the evil godmother and as Prince Charming.
While the former is, it is true, conspicuous by her absence, the
fact that the Princess pricked herself at an "old-fashioned spinning wheel" tells us all we need to know. Dean Schultz, Benjamin's disloyal patron and godfather of the local academic
mafia, has been cast as the absent godmother, whose existence
is to be inferred from the trap she left behind.[14]

What, then, is an evil godmother, and why does she pronounce a curse on the newborn child? Her animosity derives,
according to the brothers Grimm, from the fact that no one
invited her to the party. To this Benjamin adds a further explanation. What the old witch resents is that Sleeping Beauty
merely wanted to use her spinning wheel for her own purposes.
Benjamin failed, in other words, to defer to Schultz as "his"
pupil; he didn't behave as a would-be *protégé* in need of a godfather's protection; he merely wanted to camouflage his brain-
child in the requisite academic paraphernalia. The university
would, in this case, have no real part to play in the conception,
gestation, or delivery of the child. It would have no gift to
bestow except a degree. Hence its resentment. And resentment
is, according to Nietzsche, endowed with an instinctive intelligence that it would be reckless to underestimate. One cannot

therefore reasonably expect to outmaneuver it on its own turf. The godmother's impotent resentment can thus be understood, in entirely Nietzschean terms, as a reactive response to active generative powers with which she cannot hope to compete. What she resents is the child's very existence, which serves as a reminder of her own infertility. This the evil old crone can neither forgive nor forget; and it is this inability that makes her so evil and so old. She accordingly withdraws her blessing, and, by the same token, her *imprimatur,* thereby in effect putting Benjamin's "beautiful child" to sleep by delaying its publication.

In Benjamin's version, the godmother's habitat has been significantly changed from an attic to a lumber room. For Benjamin, as for Nietzsche, the proliferating disorder of a lumber room is a metaphor for a disorder of the mind, an intestinal blockage, an inability to forget, that both thinkers identify with modern historical *Wissenschaft;* and it is this inability to forget that makes historicism synonymous with resentment. Baudelaire's second "Spleen" poem ("J'ai plus de souvenirs que si j'avais mille ans") similarly describes such hypertrophic memory as a cluttered drawer, a pyramid, a cave, a cemetery, and an overstuffed boudoir. Likewise, both Nietzsche (in "The Use and Abuse of History") and Benjamin (in the theses "On the Concept of History") explore the profound connection between historicism and spleen. Historicism is, in Nietzsche's perspective, one of the terminal symptoms of "European nihilism," a "sad science," unquickened by the exigencies of the present, a terrible will to "knowledge" that wants to know nothing of "life" itself. And while Benjamin's "angel of history" stares in horror at a single uninterrupted catastrophe "which keeps piling wreckage upon wreckage" (*Illuminations,* 257), historicism vainly tries to pass off the "bleak confusion of Golgotha" as an orderly progression of events. The image of the lumber room is, however, one of *dis*order. Historicism unwittingly reflects the chaos of history, but it does not reflect intelligently *upon* it.[15]

If historicism is a form of spleen, spleen is in turn closely related to resentment and nihilism. Does not Baudelaire, in a celebrated line, describe *Ennui* as wanting to swallow the world in a yawn? All these afflictions are essentially disorders of the memory. The connections between them are constantly made throughout Nietzsche's writings by a series of interrelated metaphors of insomnia, dyspepsia, and various other inner disorders. A useful exposition of these interrelations is to be found in Gilles Deleuze's book *Nietzsche and Philosophy*.[16] In the chapter "From *Ressentiment* to the Bad Conscience," he shows how Nietzsche's model of the psychic apparatus, like Freud's, divides the mind into two clearly distinct but interdependent systems. On the one hand, consciousness acts as a self-clearing receptor that is always available to register new impressions. On the other hand, memory stores the traces of past impressions in the unconscious. Consciousness is the active, memory the reactive faculty, and psychic equilibrium depends on the quality of their interaction. Where Freud, however, tends to dwell on the pathology of repression, Nietzsche asserts the necessity of healthy inhibition. A certain "active forgetting" is needed to ensure that unconscious memory-traces do not clog the system:

The man whose apparatus of inhibition is damaged and breaks down is comparable to a dyspeptic . . .—he can never "have done" with anything (*er wird mit nichts "fertig"*).[17]

Such too is the chronic indigestion of *der Mensch des Ressentiment*, who refuses ever to "get over" anything.

This topological model of the psychic apparatus can, as in Freud, be restated in terms of the energies at work in it. Deleuze describes them as follows:

Resentment designates a type in whom the reactive forces prevail over the active ones. But they can only prevail in one way: by ceasing to be acted (*agies*). We should on no account define resentment by the force of a reaction. If we want to know what the man of *ressentiment* is, we should not forget the following principle: he does not re-act. And the word *ressentiment* itself suggests as much: *reaction ceases to be acted and becomes something felt (senti)*. The reactive forces prevail over the active ones by escaping their action.[18]

This disequilibrium of active and reactive forces is the very definition of sickness. And *ressentiment* is not merely a sickness; all sickness is, Nietzsche boldly proposes, inherently *ressentiment*:

If any fundamental objection is to be made against sick or weak states, it is that man's healthiest instincts, his instinct to defend and arm himself (*der Wehr- und Waffen-Instinkt*), are thereby enfeebled. One never gets rid of anything, can never have done with it, never repels it—everything hurts. . . . Memory is a festering wound. Illness is itself a kind of resentment.[19]

Or, as Deleuze puts its, resentment would not merely be an illness of the memory. Powerless to escape the stimuli to which it is passively exposed, memory would be inseparable from resentment.[20]

Benjamin's vindictive godmother is a case in point, and we can now better understand the connection between the godmother and the attic, between refuse and refusal. For the lumber room, which we earlier identified as an allegory of historicism,[21] can also be read as the topological representation of a dysfunctional memory-system, a hopeless clutter of inert memory-traces that merely congest the mind. It is, in short, the ideal breeding ground for *ressentiment.*

If, then, resentment is here personified as an evil godmother stubbornly ensconced, like a spider in its web, amidst the accumulated bric-à-brac of her own cavernous memory, how might one visualize someone who is—as Nietzsche himself claimed to be in *Ecce Homo*—*devoid* of all resentment? Consider the following two paragraphs from Benjamin's portrait "The Destructive Character":

> The destructive character knows only one watchword: make room; only one activity: clearing away. His need for fresh air and open space is stronger than any hatred.
>
> The destructive character is young and cheerful. For destroying rejuvenates by clearing away the traces of our own age; it cheers because everything cleared away means to the destroyer a complete reduction, indeed eradication (*Radizierung*) of his own condition. But what contributes most of all to this Apollonian image of the destroyer is the realization how immensely the world is simplified when tested with a view to its destruction. This is the all-embracing bond uniting all that exists. It affords the destructive character a spectacle of the deepest harmony. (*Reflections*, 301)[22]

Here too it could be shown that such peculiarly affirmative nihilism is, for all its pragmatism, deeply informed by messianic theology. We are once again in the presence of the Word as deed, of a summary justice which brooks no delay, a pneuma that has the force of a pneumatic drill, and is, as in Benjamin's essay "The Critique of Violence," ultimately directed against the bourgeois state and its legal apparatus. The destructive character may thus be said, like the author-cook of Sleeping Beauty, to implement the "world politics, whose method," according to the "Theologico-Political Fragment," "has to be called nihilism." The cheerfulness with which he assents to the provisional nature of his work is, likewise, not unrelated to the messianic celebration of transience in which that fragment culminates. Such an "Apollonian image of the destroyer," who decimates the world without the least trace of guilt or animosity, is the diametrical opposite of the Nietzschean *Mensch des Ressentiments,* whose contrary, Judeo-Christian nihilism has reduced Europe to its present mess. There is, clearly, nihilism and nihilism. Unlike the *decadent* nihilist, the "destructive character" is the very picture of health. The secret of his perpetual youthfulness is contained in his Brechtian motto: "Efface the traces" (*Verwisch die Spuren*). Conversely, resentment is, according to Nietzsche's diagnosis, a crippling inability to efface the traces, and this is in turn the telltale symptom of a moribund culture. If the "destructive character" is miraculously devoid of resentment, this is because he has seemingly limitless powers of evacuation. "He is the eater with the iron jaw who empties the house of the world" (II:554). There is nothing that he cannot ingest, because there is nothing that he cannot expel from his system. *Ressentiment,* by contrast, is an anal fixation: it rehashes everything, stews in its own juice, cannot rid itself of its own shit. Thus, if the resentful godmother lurking in her lumber room represents a cancerous memory-system no longer kept in check by the "inhibiting apparatus" of consciousness, the "destructive character" would seem to be the very embodiment of such an apparatus. Having achieved a "complete reduction" of his condition, he enacts the Freudian or Nietzschean model of consciousness: pure practical preparedness which adapts to the world the better to change—and not merely, like philosophical consciousness, to interpret—it. Not that he has divested himself of *all* memory-traces. He is, on the contrary, described as standing "in the vanguard of the traditionalists." But he occupies that strategic position in order to subordinate memory to consciousness. (Or, in Nietzschean terms, "history" to "life," except that life has meanwhile—between *Lebensphilosophie* and existentialism—become a matter of sheer physical survival.) If the godmother's lumber room is a bourgeois interior only dimly illumined by the light of the day, the destructive character is, by contrast, associated with glass architecture. A man unencumbered by interiority,[23] whose element is the light and air of the outside world, he is the precise opposite of the bourgeois individual *qua* "windowless monad."

A final parenthetical word at this point about the Benjamin-Nietzsche connection. Whenever Benjamin celebrates the effacement of traces, there is something at once messianic, Brechtian, *and* Nietzschean in the air. "On this sofa the aunt cannot but be murdered."[24] It is in the name of a "new, positive barbarism," and with a barbaric Nietzschean laugh, that Benjamin welcomes the various efforts of a certain avant-garde to clear away the clutter of bourgeois culture.[25] His impulse to be rid of the "phantasmagorias" of the bourgeois interior, with all its things and souvenirs and traces and claustrophobia, corresponds to Nietzsche's will to free the superman of all traces of human interiority. But wherever such resemblances suggest themselves, the differences are all the more instructive. Both Zarathustra and the destructive character quell resentment so effectively because they harbor none within themselves. But whereas Zarathustra destroys inherited values in order to "transvalue" them, the destructive character would also make *tabula rasa* of any newly created tablets. "The destructive character does his work; the only work he avoids is being creative." While no less opposed than Zarathustra to the impotent negativism of a merely critical stance, he says amen only to destruction. His all-embracing yes is inseparable from an all-encompassing no. "The destructive character has the consciousness of historical man, whose deepest emotion is an insuperable mistrust of the course of things." Just as theology, according to the "Theses," has today "to keep out of sight," the affirmation of life can only take the form of a double negative: "The destructive character lives from the feeling, not that life is worth living, but that suicide is not worth the trouble" (*Reflections*, 303).[26] If he is explicitly described as "Apollonian," he is by the same token no disciple of Zarathustra.

So much, then, for the *first* figure of resentment in Benjamin's fairy tale—the proprietress of an "old-fashioned spinning wheel." The *second* figure is much more up-to-date, and will, as promised, serve to confront us with our present dilemma.

Let no Prince Charming clad in the shining armor of modern scholarship venture too close. For as he embraces his bride, she will bite him.

It might seem paradoxical to describe Prince Charming, of all people, as a living embodiment of resentment. But the paradox is an all-too-real one. Behind the discreet charm of *la nouvelle bourgeoisie* lies what Marx once alluded to as *die alte Scheisse*. The originality of Benjamin's version of Sleeping Beauty is to have opened up the possibility that, appearances to the contrary, Prince Charming is a not-so-distant *relative* of the evil godmother. His shining armor comes from the same lumber room as her spinning wheel; it has merely been dusted off. His stance might, accordingly, be described as neo-historicism, and his charm as neo-resentment. Nothing, in fact, is more authentically historicist than his tentacular embrace. What Nietzsche and Benjamin have against historicism is, precisely, its impotent promiscuity, its indiscriminate "empathy with the victor" (*Illuminations*, 256),[27] its willingness to embrace *anything* as long as it happened "once upon a time." The Prince is, in Nietzsche's phrase, a "Don Juan of knowledge." "Qui trop embrasse," Baudelaire observed of an emerging eclecticism, "mal étreint." And he added that any criticism worth its salt is "partial, passionate, and political."[28] "Tout comprendre, c'est tout pardonner": such contrary wisdom masks unforgiving *ressentiment* behind a condescending doctrine of universal love and/or objectivity. The Prince's wide-open arms recall nothing so much as that gaping, abysmal, nihilistic *Ennui* which "would swallow up the world in a yawn." Such is the liberal embrace of the "open society." No wonder that Nietzsche and Benjamin identified an all-embracing historicism, an all-comprehending resentment (*mit zutraulichem Mitleiden abspannen*) as their most insidious, their most dangerously empathetic enemy. Prince Charming was, they knew, waiting in the wings, an omnivorous culture-vulture biding his time. The title of Karl Popper's book

The Open Society and Its Enemies sums up conventional liberal wisdom. What, though, if the open society turned out to be a *variant* of the authoritarian enemy?

It is true that the Prince is as gallant and progressive as the godmother is forbidding and reactionary. But this merely heightens the disguise. For the history of resentment, as Nietzsche tells it, is one of unfolding self-concealment. Already Judaic morality was, according to a celebrated passage in the *Genealogy of Morals,* the sublimated revenge of the slaves against the masters; as such, it constituted the original "transvaluation of all values."[29] But such self-denying vengeance cannot, Nietzsche argues, compare for duplicity with the New Testament gospel of Christian love, which, by posing as the opposite of a pharisaical spirit of vengeance, was able to perpetuate it all the more effectively. Christ the Redeemer is thus cast as the Trojan horse in a Jewish world conspiracy, as the ruse of Jewish reason; and Christianity emerges as "the secret black art of a truly grandiose politics of revenge," "seduction in its most uncanny and irresistible form."[30]

What if we were to superimpose Nietzsche's story on Benjamin's? Isn't the moral in this instance much the same? The godmother would then be, as it were, the *Jewish,* the Prince the *Christian* phase of *ressentiment.* Now the former, in Nietzsche's argument, masterminds the latter. The good Christian Prince would thus be the puppet of the absent Jewish witch. Alternatively, he would be that selfsame godmother in appropriately modern disguise—"seduction in its most uncanny and irresistible form."

Let us pause to consider just *how* uncanny this situation is. In so doing, we may also be reminded of a more recent description of it—namely, Pierre Bourdieu's account of the pseudo-liberalization of our educational institutions.[31]

The *godmother* represents the old, illiberal university that deviously rejected Benjamin's candidacy for the *Habilitation.* The *Prince* is the representative of some later, more liberal policy, who will come, still more deviously, to right the wrongs of the past. Illiberal professors such as Schultz were, after all, already capable of charming liberal self-irony; conversely, their enlightened, liberal successors are still basically illiberal at heart. The new is, for all its shining reforms, the perpetuation of the old. What Hegel said of the Spirit—that it "heals its own wounds"— cannot, therefore, be claimed on behalf of the university. To manage to persuade us that history *is,* as Hegel alleged, "progress in the consciousness of freedom" would indeed be the cunning of academic reason. It would be the Prince's version of the story. Benjamin's own account rests on a far more somber speculation. At the very moment that his *Habilitation* is being aborted by the university, he anticipates a much worse fate— namely, the day when it will be *re*habilitated. Not merely will such belated restoration to academic favor come at a moment when the original scandal has receded far enough into the past to have become, in its turn, a historicist fairy tale that happened once upon a time. Worse yet, later rehabilitation, as Benjamin visualizes it, hardly marks any improvement on the original verdict. It seems merely to be a new, improved version of the old treatment—a friendly historicism in lieu of a hostile one, resentment that is still more self-effacing. Even as he regrets past aberrations, the Prince will merely vary Schultz's routine. In rescuing the Princess from the godmother, he will still be recuperating her for the university. All his charm, his openness and his newfangled *Wissenschaft* will merely represent a better-equipped attempt by the forces of reaction to bring a genuinely active force to heel. The Prince might thus be ironically described as a "good European." As all good liberals know, a certain relaxation of control (*Abspannen nämlich*) will, in the long run, prove to be the more efficient way of maintaining it. Inclusion does the job better than exclusion. How much difference is there, moreover, between the original rejection and posthumous honors? Isn't such inclusion merely a softer form of exclusion—exclusion, as it were, *en rose*? Don't the two, whatever their private differences, actually work together, always either rejecting or swallowing outsiders *en bloc*? And isn't commemoration (*Würdigung*) another way of putting them to sleep? In rescuing Benjamin's work from academic neglect, the Prince would, moreover, seem to be parodying Benjamin's own messianic theory and practice of "redemptive criticism" (*rettende Kritik*). The fact that such perverse reappropriation is even possible is perhaps the uncanniest aspect of the whole business, since it raises the question of what it is about active forces that allows reactive ones to pervert their best impulses.[32]

His dormant child, Benjamin assures us, will not remain oblivious to such all-embracing perversion. She will not lie idly by while Mr. Progress makes his advances. To misquote the "Theses": not even future victors will be safe from the defeated past. Sleeping Beauty will bite any Bluebeard who comes too close. Is it to avoid the point—namely, her teeth—to wonder whether that bite might not nevertheless pose a delicate hermeneutic problem? The *threat* it poses requires no gloss: it is clearly intended to keep would-be rescuers at arm's length. But as a *Gewissensbiss*, a *morsus conscientiae* calculated to instill remorse, isn't it, at least in a Nietzschean perspective, an all-too-*Jewish* bite? Doesn't re-morse have the same telltale genealogy as re-sentment? But does not Nietzsche also champion the avenging God of the Old Testament against the compassionate God of the New?[33] And does not the resounding vengeance that Benjamin vows to visit on his false friends have a similar ring of biblical prophecy about it?[34]

But the point is, after all, to let that bite sink in, perhaps even to resent it. For Benjamin's little fable surely contains a moral; and as long as there are morals, there will doubtless be resentment. "Rehabilitate me if you dare," it warns, and the warning is plainly addressed to *us*. "Our coming was expected on earth" (*Illuminations*, 254). If there *is* a predestined rendezvous, messianic or otherwise, between past generations and our own, Benjamin is not merely *waiting*, he is *lying in wait* for us. Reserving for himself the role of cook, and demoting his academic superiors to the scullery, he has cast us as Prince Charming, the savior from whose all-too-eager clutches the Princess will henceforth need to be saved. Anyone who, like the present writer, makes an academic living off Walter Benjamin will be the first to cringe. No sooner will one have done so, however, than one may be tempted to convert guilt (*Schuld*) into profit by capitalizing on it:

Et nous alimentons nos aimables remords,
Comme les mendiants nourrissent leur vermine.

Nos péchés sont têtus, nos repentirs sont lâches;
Nous nous faisons payer grassement nos aveux . . .[35]

In letting ourselves be bitten by the bride we barter, we ought not, clearly, to wallow in remorse (which, Nietzsche teaches, is inimical to life) or in "left melancholy" (which, Benjamin argues, is inimical to socialism).[36] For, despite all protestations to the contrary, such emotions have a vested interest in the status quo. As both etymology and Baudelaire's anatomy lesson clearly indicate, re-morse is business as usual, the ritual of confession, the routinization of the bite. Like re-sentment, it is a repetition compulsion calculated to maintain things as they are.

How, then, *are* we to take the bull by the horns? I have, of course, studiously avoided that crucial issue. Let me, in conclusion, sidestep it one last time and propose instead the following interim observation. To listen well to Benjamin and Nietzsche, to do justice, as they demand of us, to the demands of the present, is to recognize, for a start, that we cannot speak, cannot *command* their language. For if both of them teach emancipation from authority, each does so with an authority of his own, for which each paid in blood. They thus both repel and invite discipleship, especially among disaffected academics who resent the university—Blake's "horses of instruction" dreaming of the great outside. We cannot, surely, help envying them their extraterritorial power, or wanting to tap into it, but we also cannot ignore the historical distance that separates us from it. Such distance, while in itself a merely contingent fact, perhaps offers a renewed opportunity for reading them against themselves.

Both Benjamin and Nietzsche posit clear-cut distinctions between truth and scholarship, active and reactive forces, masters and slaves, the original and its travesty, biblical vengeance and petty resentment, fresh and musty air, the inside and the outside of the university. They can, on this basis, walk out on it. They can be great outsiders. If our presence at this conference is anything to judge by, our own predicament would seem at once more comfortable and more ambiguous. While the old oppositions remain as indispensable as ever, they also carry somewhat less conviction than they once did. If Nietzsche and Benjamin cannot be emulated today, this is perhaps because the faith that used to sustain such oppositions has meanwhile dwindled. Such a process of erosion is, indeed, diagnosed in certain of their own writings.[37] To say that times have changed is, however, merely to perpetuate historicism: Prince Charming is perfectly capable of sporting the postmodern look. We need to understand better why those oppositions—which feel so urgent at one moment, and so dated the next—can no longer quite sustain us. But do we need to make a business out of blurring them?[38] That might suit the purposes of the present-day university all too well. As he preys, from inside, on the outside, Prince Charming has a stake in obfuscating the difference between them. And which of us can nowadays be sure that (s)he *isn't* a Prince Charming—even, and perhaps above all, those of us who claim to bite the hand that feeds us?

Postscript

The preceding paper was written for a symposium on "Nietzsche and the Psychology of Resentment." In the ensuing discussion, the inevitable objection was raised that Benjamin's denunciation of the university can itself hardly be considered devoid of resentment. This was argued by neo-historicists on psychological and by deconstructionists on textual grounds. The pros and cons of the psychological case, which seem, if anything, to reflect their proponents' own psychology, can perhaps be set aside as being basically unarguable. Wouldn't Nietzsche, however, suspect the psychologist who exempts *no one* from resentment of *exemplifying* the psychology of resentment? And isn't the "realism" of the historicist's unhistorical assumptions about "human nature" in fact a "phantasmagoria"[39] which, as Marx remarked of the bourgeoisie, "makes the world in its own image"? The deconstructive case, relying as it does on a closely argued reading, is less easily ignored. The type of questions it raises might include the following. Doesn't Benjamin's text, *qua* text, inevitably belie its own implicit metaphysics of the Word? Doesn't it, despite its brevity, repeat its punishment rather too often (slap, bite, slap) to be able to pretend to the status of divine judgment exercised once and for all?[40] Is its convoluted temporal structure reducible to such an instantaneous present? Are we not rather in the presence of a theological *desire* for presence, for a "consummation devoutly to be wished?" How, after all, "reserve" the role of cook and still maintain the fiction of *un*reserved immediacy? Doesn't the "accumulated force" (*aufgesparte Kraft*) of his pent-up anger point to what Nietzsche would call a *Hintergedanke,* to malice aforethought and delayed gratification, in short to *ressentiment*?[41] To salvation on a savings plan? Doesn't Benjamin already anticipate the epiphany, the festive metaphysical release, that will redeem the past—namely, the resentment he will have saved up in the meantime—in much the same way that one redeems a savings bond? By proposing to lie in wait for us, isn't he laying the same trap the evil godmother laid for him? And doesn't all this amount, precisely, to the metaphysics, the psychology, the economy, and the temporality of resentment? In mobilizing Nietzsche against Benjamin, a deconstructive reading would seem to provide the psychological case against him with the arguments it lacks—at the risk, however, of collapsing into it.

At the conference, neo-historicists and deconstructionists were, at all events, unwilling to grant Nietzsche and Benjamin the immunity they both occasionally claimed for themselves. Such unwillingness to make exceptions seems fair enough, and one could stumble into any number of pitfalls by rejecting it out of hand. But fairness is itself a pitfall; it is, after all, the Prince's forte. Will it do to spread resentment around, like so much manure? Is *ressentiment* now to replace Cartesian *bon sens* as *la chose la mieux partagée*? If democracy merely amounted to such equitable distribution, Nietzsche's tirades against it wouldn't sound nearly so shrill as they do. Who, Nietzsche would want to know of his evenhanded critics, is diagnosing whom, and to what end?[42] Is it in order once again to reduce exceptions to the all-too-human rule? And thereby to insure oneself against the disaster they continue to represent?

What, then, if the claim to be "free of resentment" and "healthier than one would like to allow us"[43] were not as idle as a certain wary, weary nihilism seems to need to believe? Or if the "sublime malice and extreme exuberance of revenge" to which Nietzsche himself freely admits were in no way a refutation of his philosophy?[44] "For *that man be delivered from revenge,*" says

Zarathustra, "that is the bridge to the highest hope for me, and a rainbow after long storms."[45] Here too it is a question of *biting* the knowledge (*Wissen*) that threatens to stick in one's gullet:

But the shepherd bit, as my cry bade him; he bit with a good bite! Far away did he spit the head of the snake—and sprang up.

No longer a shepherd, no longer a man, but someone transfigured, who *laughed*. Never on earth did any man every laugh as *he* laughed!

Oh my brothers, I heard a laugh that was no man's laugh—and now a thirst eats away at me, an unquenchable longing.[46]

It is his disgust at the eternal return of human pettiness that Zarathustra's *alter ego* is here almost choking on.[47] Not to spit it out is to gag on it. But there is nothing to prevent such choking resentment from mouthing Zarathustra's own teachings. "Where one can no longer love," Zarathustra tells one such "foaming clown," "one should—*pass on*."[48] Rewriting "Sleeping Beauty" was Walter Benjamin's way of spitting the system out of *his* system and passing on. The last line reads: "Frankfurt a/M, July 1925." "Because," as Baudelaire had put it, "I want to date my anger."[49] To remember, but also to forget.

June 1983

Second Postscript

The academic mill grinds slowly. The above text, written in the heat of the moment, is coldly going to press three years later. Its author, on rereading it, is somewhat uneasy with its apocalyptic tone, its anti-institutional mimicry. To brandish good, epic fathers in order to belittle the bad ones down the hall— does such an Oedipal scenario really point a way out of the psychology of resentment? How free oneself from those ghostly fathers without simply reincarnating those one set out to depose? Shades of 1968 . . .

"Geist kann man nicht habilitieren." Thus, decades later, a German professor, on Benjamin's failure to gain admittance to his club: the man was clearly too clever by half, too extraordinary to be an *Ordinarius* like himself. Scholem rightly denounced Erich Rothacker's remark as unconscionable.[50] But what if, as a matter of fact, Rothacker were right? For what is unconscionable about his remark is not so much its content *per se* or the recourse to a category that is fraught with an anti-Semitic potential (as in *Der Geist als Widersacher der Seele*) as the cynical tone which inflects it, stands behind it, and thus reaffirms the original exclusion. "The tone and correctness of these words," observed Benjamin in a related context, "counterbalance one another" (II:81). Stated with a somewhat different emphasis, however (on, say, *kann* instead of *Geist*), it becomes an entirely different proposition. Such a shift of emphasis has been audible in recent years. I have heard genuinely thoughtful colleagues (such as Albrecht Wellmer and Gerhard Kaiser) doubt out loud, in all honesty, without embarrassment or resentment, whether Benjamin's work was ever really *intended* for academic acceptance;[51] whether it *was* indeed acceptable to the university as it then was; and whether, God forbid, they in Schultz's shoes would or could have accepted it. To raise such questions is not necessarily to rehabilitate Schultz[52] instead of Benjamin. Here too it is all matter of tone. Perhaps, indeed, it is time to cool it for a while as we search for other alternatives. For the alternative between academic epigones of Nietzsche/Benjamin and the university seems fraught at present with resentment on either side. To try to see the university for what it is—whatever that may be—without waxing either apocalyptic or defensive on the subject: this may be the best chance we academics have at present of inching our way out of our mutual resentments. At the end of a tortuous letter to his father, Kafka, for his part, did not dare to hope for more.

September 1986

Notes

1. *"You can explain the past only by what is most powerful in the present. . . .* The language of the past is always oracular: you will only understand it as builders of the future who know the present," Friedrich Nietzsche, *Werke* (hereafter *W*), ed. Karl Schlechta, vol. 1 (Munich: Hanser, 1966), 250f.

2. *W*, 1:209.

3. For example, Benjamin's early affiliation with the *Jugendbewegung*, when he echoes Nietzsche's question "But where are those in need?" (*Briefe*, 86); the critique of Nietzsche's theory of tragedy in the *Trauerspiel* book (101–10); and the affinity he

claims between Auguste Blanqui's cosmological treatise *L'Eternité par les Astres* and Nietzsche's doctrine of the eternal return, as read by Karl Löwith (V:169–77). Cf. also Benjamin's comment on the paradoxical affinity between Nietzsche and Kierkegaard in *Briefe*, 47; and notes 12, 15, and 26 below.

4. "Von der schenkenden Tugend," *W*, 2:339. This instruction does not preclude its opposite: in *Ecce Homo*, Nietzsche visualizes, seemingly without irony, the day when institutions and professorships will be set up to explicate Zarathustra's teachings (*W*, 2:1099), after having cited the above-quoted passage from *Zarathustra* in the Foreword (1068).

5. *W*, 2:340.

6. *W*, 2:667.

7. Benjamin was later to write that his treatise had been a "test" designed to measure the distance that separated a "strict compliance with genuine academic methods of research" from the malpractice of existing scholarship (*Briefe*, 523). *How* strict that compliance was is debatable. Benjamin himself refers both to the "eccentric meticulousness" (*Briefe*, 339) of his preparatory labors and to his "remarkably—indeed uncannily—narrow" base: "acquaintance with a few dramas, by no means all the relevant ones. An encyclopaedic reading of the works in the tiny space of time available to me would have inevitably produced in me an invincible dégoût" (*Briefe*, 326). Like Nietzsche, Benjamin claims to be a philologist ("I want to present myself by way of a Romantic notion of philology," *Briefe*, 342), yet knows that the occupational hazard of such scholarly retentiveness is intestinal disorder. Given the aforementioned lack of time, the whole enterprise was in any case bound to be a "reckless escapade" (*Briefe*, 339f.); and its "academic intentions" were in the nature of an "ironical" challenge calculated to ascertain to what extent university requirements were compatible with his own (*Briefe*, 387). The whole venture might best be summed up as a "sociological experiment" (V:426)—Benjamin's own description of Baudelaire's candidacy for the French Academy. One may in this context recall Brecht's *Dreigroschenprozess*, which was calculated to turn a lost legal case into a test case, an occasion for public instruction. More relevant still is the whole debate, set off by Sartre, around Baudelaire's alleged "failure," which, Blanchot and Bataille claimed, was inseparable from his success. Benjamin had come to a similar conclusion about Kafka. "Once he was certain of eventual failure," he wrote in 1938, "everything worked out for him *en route* as in a dream" (*Illuminations*, 145).

8. First published in *Briefe*, 418:

Ich möchte das Märchen vom Dornröschen zum zweiten Male erzählen.

Es schläft in seiner Dornenhecke. Und dann, nach so und so viel Jahren wird es wach.

Aber nicht vom Kuß eines glücklichen Prinzen.

Der Koch hat es aufgeweckt, als er dem Küchenjungen die Ohrfeige gab, die, schallend von der aufgesparten Kraft so vieler Jahre, durch das Schloß hallte.

Ein schönes Kind schläft hinter der dornigen Hecke der folgenden Seiten.

Daß nur kein Glücksprinz im blendenden Rüstzeug der Wissenschaft ihm nahe kommt. Denn im bräutlichen Kuß wird es zubeißen.

Vielmehr hat sich der Autor, es zu wecken, als Küchenmeister selber vorbehalten. Zu lange ist schon die Ohrfeige fällig, die schallend durch die Hallen der Wissenschaft gellen soll.

Dann wird auch diese arme Wahrheit erwachen, die am altmodischen Spinnrocken sich gestochen hat, als sie, verbotnerweise, in der Rumpelkammer einen Professorentalar sich zu weben gedachte.

Frankfurt a/M, Juli 1925

Schallend . . . hallte . . . schallend . . . gellen soll: the German text enacts the reverberations it invokes.

9. This is originally expounded in the essay "On Language as Such and on the Language of Man" (*Reflections*, 314–32) and taken up again in the prologue and concluding pages of *The Origin of German Trauerspiel*. Cf., on this theology of language, my essay "Sur quelques motifs juifs chez Benjamin," *Revue d'Esthétique* 1 (Paris 1981): 141–61; and, on its connection to Sleeping Beauty, my "Hors-d'Oeuvre," in Walter Benjamin, *Origine du Drame Baroque Allemand* (Paris: Flammarion, 1985), 7–21, especially 11f.

10. Benjamin's radical indictment should not, however, be confused with the kind of ultra-radicalism that stands "to the left of all possibility" (III:281). At once "immanent" and "transcendent," his extraterritorial critique of the academy does not dismiss all *Wissenschaft* as such, *ex cathedra*, from some lofty theological vantage point. (Only a few years later Benjamin will indeed anatomize such "better knowlege" in a review entitled "Privileged Thinking," III:315–22). Benjamin does not oppose theology to philology. He *does* oppose an authentic theologico-philological "science of origin" (*Wissenschaft vom Ursprung*, I:227) to a degraded "academic commerce" (*Wissenschaftsbetrieb, Briefe*, 532), which is as oblivious to theological origins as it is to the best traditions of philological research (e.g., the brothers Grimm). Theology and philology, like past and present, do not pose an alternative; rather, by performing their respective tasks, they inform one another. Such too is the relation between theology and politics, the messianic and the profane orders, as described in the "Theologico-Political Fragment" (*Reflections*, 312f.). Benjamin can thus write in 1931 that all his research has so far been carried out within a theological perspective (*Briefe*, 523). "For the scholarly (*wissenschaftlich*) approach in the present-day sense," he will later write, "is not the salient feature of my essay" (*Briefe*, 400) on the German baroque.

11. This passage is also quoted by Hannah Arendt in *Illuminations*, 47.

12. Such unreserved affirmation of transience is Nietzsche's answer to *ressentiment*: "This, yet this alone is revenge itself: the will's aversion (*Widerwille*) to time and its 'It was' " (*W*, 2:394). *Ressentiment* is *Wider-wille*: a negation of the will to power. The—joyful—task is thus to un-negate it, to undo the (k)nots. And nothing is more knotted—and hence more metaphysical—than its relation to time. In *harboring* resentment and *never forgetting* its cause, we are at odds with time itself. Nietzsche's affirmation of time extends even, and above all, to the past ("its 'it was' "): the will to power embraces, without *Widerwille*, the idea of its eternal return. It is here that Nietzsche and Benjamin once again part ways. Benjamin sets his sights on the messianic redemption of the past. Nietzsche assents, no less retroactively, to the past such as it was. This is the only "redemption"—an anti-redemptive one—he will allow: the rest is the metaphysics of resentment.

13. Cf. Max Scheler, *Ressentiment*, ed. Lewis A. Coser (New York: Free Press of Glencoe, 1961).

14. As Benjamin's letters make clear, Schultz had originally encouraged him to write a thesis on the German baroque, only to withdraw his patronage once it was completed.

15. "Where [historicists] perceive a chain of events, [the angel of history] sees one single catastrophe which keeps piling wreckage upon wreckage" (*Illuminations*, 257). However neatly he may arrange his "mass of data" (*Illuminations*, 262), the positivist piles up facts the way "progress" piles up debris; the busy work of what Benjamin calls the *Wissenschaftsbetrieb* is part of the catastrophe we call "business as usual." The sadness of this spectacle is quite different from the spleen of those who perpetuate it. Another major difference between Benjamin and Nietzsche looms up at this point. Where Nietzsche opposes his own "joyful wisdom" to the "sad science" of historicism, Benjamin distinguishes between the alienated "sadness" or *"accidie"* of the latter (*Illuminations*, 256) and the authentic melancholy of the angel's gaze. *Melencolia 'illa heroica'*; heroism resides here in sustaining melancholy, not in overcoming it. There is no place

in Nietzsche for an *angelus novus* who "would like to stay, awaken the dead, and make whole what has been smashed" (*Illuminations*, 257). Where the angel's staring eyes remain glued to the past, Zarathustra has his sights set on the future—the new age of the superman. What Zarathustra wants to make whole is the dismembered body of "Man" strewn over the "battlefield" of history—not that battlefield itself. Cf. *W*, 2:393f. and, on the difference between Benjamin's and Nietzsche's critique of historicism, my "Hors-d'Oeuvre," 13f.

16. Paris: Presses Universitaires de France, 1962 and, in English translation, Columbia University Press, 1983.

17. *W*, 2:799.

18. Deleuze, 127f. (111f.) He proceeds to formulate the following rules: "A reaction becomes something acted (*devient quelque chose d'agi*), by taking conscious excitation as its object, at the same time that a reaction to traces remains in the unconscious as something insensible" (*insensible*) (129). And conversely: "A reaction to traces is felt (*devient quelque chose de sensible*) at the same time that a reaction to stimuli ceases to be acted" (130; 114).

19. *W*, 2:1077. On the basis of his own experience, Nietzsche recommends two ways of dealing with resentment. For the sick, he prescribes "fatalism," inasmuch as any dissatisfaction or "revolt" drains energies and is itself tantamount to resentment. The healthy, on the other hand, need good, strong opponents and should not stoop to fight something that is beneath contempt (1077–79). The only effective way of dealing with resentment is, in short, to have no dealings with it. One voids it by avoiding it.

20. "And, more profoundly, the memory of traces is hate-laden (*haineuse*) in and by itself" (Deleuze, 133; 116). Benjamin, for his part, is too committed to a Jewish concept of remembrance to assent to so unqualified a statement.

21. Cf., on historicism as a "lumber room," I:1237f. and *W*, 2:676.

22. Cf., for further analysis, my "No-man's-land: On Walter Benjamin's 'Destructive Character'," *Diacritics* (June 1978): 47–65.

23. Cf., on the inseparability of resentment, interiority, and bad conscience in Nietzsche, Deleuze, 146–52 (124–29): "It is by interiorizing itself, by turning against itself, that the active force becomes truly reactive."

24. Cited in "Manorially furnished ten-room apartment," *Reflections*, 64f.

25. Cf. "Experience and Poverty" (II:213–19).

26. Cf. also the following paragraph: "No vision inspires the destructive character. He has few needs, and the least of them is to know what will replace what has been destroyed. First of all, for a moment at least, empty space, the place where the thing stood or the victim lived. Someone is sure to be found who needs this space without taking it up (*ohne ihn einzunehmen*)" (301f.). The destructive character is better described as an *Unmensch* than an *Übermensch*. Cf., in this connection, the end of Benjamin's essay on Karl Kraus (II:367).

27. Benjamin describes historicism as a "bordello" inhabited by "the whore called 'Once upon a time' " (*Illuminations*, 262); Nietzsche calls its practitioners "eunuchs"; and Baudelaire equates spleen with impotence: "Je suis comme le roi d'un pays pluvieux,/ Riche, mais impuissant, et pourtant très-vieux" ("Spleen III").

28. *Oeuvres Complètes,* ed. Y.-G. le Dantec (Paris: Gallimard, 1968), 930.

29. *W,* 2:780f.

30. *Ibid.* While Nietzsche usually derives the "birth of Christianity" from "the spirit of resentment" (*W,* 2:1143), he occasionally exempts its founder from resentment. In this argument, Christ's death was, like his life, a positive act of love. It was his disciples who turned it into something negative, a martyrs' revolt against the existing order, which they sought to avenge, thereby reproducing the mentality they opposed (*W,* 2:1202). It would be in this reactive sense that Christianity was born of *ressentiment.*

31. Cf. P. Bourdieu and J.-C. Passeron, *Reproduction: In Education, Society and Culture* (Beverly Hills: Sage, 1977). "Inasmuch as it more fully masks the ultimate foundations of its pedagogic authority . . . , the 'liberal university' conceals the fact that there is no liberal university more effective than a theocratic or totalitarian educational system, in which the delegation of authority is objectively manifested in the fact that the same principles directly establish political authority, religious authority and pedagogic authority" (66). In vindicating pedagogic authority against "academic freedom," Nietzsche's early lectures "On the Future of Our Educational Institutions" already denounce the state controls hidden behind liberal appearances. Cf. *W,* 1:225, *passim.* So does Benjamin's early essay "The Life of the Students."

32. Jacques Derrida has posed this question in connection with the Nazi appropriation of Nietzsche. What needs to be explained is that such "reactive perversion can exploit the same words, statements and slogans as the active forces they oppose" ("Nietzsche's Otobiography," in *Fugen,* ed. M. Frank, F. Kittler, and S. Weber [Olten: Walter, 1980, 89]). Some powerful, anonymous, and as yet little-understood machine must, Derrida argues, be programming such uncanny family likenesses between opposite forces and opposed versions of the same force (89–91). Hence the need to "deconstruct" such oppositions. Deleuze, by contrast, organizes his whole account of Nietzsche's philosophy around an "anti-dialectical" opposition between active and reactive forces. This subsequently leads Deleuze to champion Nietzsche, undialectically enough, in the name of the counterculture: in his statement "Pensée nomade" (in *Nietzsche aujourd'hui?* [Paris, 1973] 1:159–74), Nietzsche stands for "nomadic" exteriority versus bureaucratic institutionalization, "intensity" versus the law, in short, for an apocalyptic anarchism not unlike that of Benjamin's Sleeping Beauty.

33. Cf. *W,* 2:614–15.

34. Similarly, Benjamin rallies to Marx's conception of the "struggling, oppressed class" as "the avenger that completes the task of liberation in the name of generations of the downtrodden," as opposed to the Social Democratic alternative, which would have the working class "forget both its hatred and its spirit of sacrifice" (*Illuminations,* 260). One might speak here of an opposition between vengeance (" 'Vengeance shall be mine,' saith the Lord") and *ressentiment,* between Judaic and Judaeo-Christian, Old and New Testament versions of socialism. It is because Nietzsche essentially equates socialism with the latter that he denounces it as a perpetuation of the "slave revolt in morality."

35. Baudelaire, "Au Lecteur."

36. Cf. III:279–83. That socialism is itself, according to Nietzsche, a seething mass of resentment points once again to the gaping—but bridgeable—differences that separate his thought from Benjamin's.

37. E.g. Benjamin's letter on Kafka (*Illuminations,* 141–45) and statements such as the following: "The basic belief of the metaphysicians is *the belief in the opposition between*

Irving Wohlfarth

values" (*W*, 2:568). If both Benjamin and Nietzsche oppose conventional *oppositions,* neither appears to lose faith in *extremes* ("the *magic of the extreme,* the seduction exerted by the ultimate," *W*, 3:601: Nietzsche's faith in the absolute is clearly less absolute than Benjamin's). In the above-mentioned letter, which describes an ailing theological tradition, Benjamin sums up Kafka's work as an "ellipse" between the two extremes of modern urban experience and the mystical tradition: the crisis of theology is still seen in terms of an essentially theological model. A metaphysics of tension and intensity pervades both Nietzsche's and Benjamin's writings; the metaphor of the tautened bow is one indication among many.

38. Only a vulgar deconstructionism *effaces* the differences. In *Positions* (Chicago: University of Chicago Press, 1981, 41), Derrida himself stresses the need both to refuse the given alternatives and to intervene within them, to suspend *and* invert existing oppositions without sacrificing one element of this "double strategy" to the other.

39. Cf., on the notion of "phantasmagoria," "Paris, Capital of the Nineteenth Century," *Reflections,* 146–62.

40. Cf., on the "pure immediate violence" of a summary revolutionary justice modeled on "pure divine violence," "Critique of Violence," *Reflections,* 300.

41. Before deciding that such "accumulated force" belongs, in Bataille's terms, to a "restricted" rather than a "general" economy, one should, however, remember that every potlatch rests on prior accumulation and thus amounts, in Bataille's phrase, to a "shady" compromise with the calculations it seems to flout. Cf. Derrida's essay "De l'Economie Restreinte à l'Economie Générale," in *L'Ecriture et la Différence* (Paris: Seuil, 1967), 369–407.

42. Cf., on Nietzsche's substitution of the Sophists' *Who?* for the Socratic *What?,* Deleuze, 86–88.

43. Cf. *W*, 2:1077.

44. Cf. Heidegger's essay "Who Is Nietzsche's Zarathustra?" in Allison, ed., *The New Nietzsche* (Cambridge, MA: MIT Press, 1985), 76.

45. *W*, 2:357.

46. *W*, 2:410.

47. *W*, 2:464–65.

48. *W*, 2:428.

49. Or, according to a variant, "my sadness" (1265).

50. Cf. *Über Walter Benjamin* (Frankfurt, 1968), 146–47 and Gershom Scholem, *Walter Benjamin. The Story of a Friendship* (Philadelphia: JPS, 1982), 119.

51. Benjamin confided to Scholem that he had "a thousand reasons" for not embarking on an academic career, and would in any case have begun by asking for a leave of absence (*Briefe,* 379, 393). But this does not mean that he never intended to try academia out—only that he could not do so except on his own terms. Likewise, his subsequent encounter with communism prompted him to ask four years later whether the "new function" that now fell to the bourgeois artist did not require the "interruption" of his " 'artistic career' " (*Reflections,* 191).

52. It has been alleged that Schultz subsequently wore his academic robes to a Nazi book-burning ceremony. Cf. Werner Fuld, *Walter Benjamin. Zwischen den Stühlen. Eine Biographie* (Munich: Hanser, 1979), 161. This can be documented at least in a metaphorical sense: Schultz's literary scholarship effortlessly incorporates a euphemistic proto-Nazi vocabulary not unlike the kind unmasked by Benjamin in his essay "Literaturgeschichte und Literaturwissenschaft" (III: 286–87). Cf. in this context Burkhardt Lindner, "Habilitationsakte Benjamin," in *Walter Benjamin im Kontext,* ed. B. Lindner (Königstein: Athenäum, 1986), 324–41. This circumstantial account of Benjamin's abortive *Habilitation* adds further details, culled from hitherto inaccessible university archives, to the editorial account in III:868–84 and 895–914. It only now turns out that Max Horkheimer, later to be Benjamin's financial patron as head of the Institut für Sozialforschung and at the time a young *Assistent* at the University of Frankfurt, was asked by his professor, Hans Cornelius, who was, as a result of Schultz's evasions, the first referee of Benjamin's manuscript, to submit a short written opinion of his own. This he did, dutifully confirming Cornelius's verdict that it was unintelligible, on the basis of a three-page summary that Cornelius had requested of Benjamin (Lindner, 335). Such, then, are the surprises and convolutions, the secrecy and banality of resentment, its obscene, shifting interplay of private and public, psychological and institutional factors, most of them excusable peccadillos protected by extenuating circumstances, but cumulatively adding up to what Lindner rightly calls a "scandal" (324). Cf., on relations between Benjamin and Horkheimer, Scholem, 206, 210, 215–16.

Dialectics at a Standstill: Approaches to the *Passagen-Werk*

Rolf Tiedemann

When Rolf Tiedemann came to study with Adorno at the Institut für Sozialforschung in 1958, his interest in Benjamin's work was already established. Six years later, he became the first person to dedicate a book-length scholarly study to Benjamin's writings, Studien zur Philosophie Walter Benjamins, *for which he received his doctorate. Adorno at that time stressed the importance of Tiedemann's study for our critical perspective: "After this work it will no longer be possible to entrench oneself behind the argument that the essence of what Benjamin inaugurated is aperçus-like or rhapsodic."*

Tiedemann collaborated closely on various editions of Benjamin's works with Gershom Scholem, Gretel Adorno, and Theodor Adorno; after Theodor Adorno's death in 1969 he became the editor in charge of Benjamin's collected papers. The edition aims to present Benjamin's writings comprehensively, organized by genre, and in accord with the highest philological standards. Its critical apparatus was designed to enable much other material, especially letters, to be made public, since even at the beginning of the 1970s it was hard to imagine that one day Benjamin's letters might find publishing support for a collected edition, such as the one now being prepared.

His intimate knowledge of Benjamin's entire corpus put Tiedemann in a position to shape the fragmentary complex of material from Benjamin's Arcades project into a book. He has reassembled the pieces of a puzzle that will never yield a whole picture. But his authoritative introduction convinces us that he has taken us as close to constructing the picture as is possible at this time.

It was Benjamin himself who set the myth of the Passagen-Werk *in motion through repeated, grand statements about the project; the publishing of two volumes of his letters in 1966 revitalized the expectations Benjamin had created more than three decades earlier. It became Tiedemann's task to present Benjamin's long-anticipated* chef d'oeuvre, *although he knew that it would meet with much disappointment and confusion. Thousands of excerpts overwhelm most signs of Benjamin's conception. In his introduction, Tiedemann resists any temptation to make this material something other than it is and convinces us instead of the significance of the project's fragmentary status. The* Passagen-Werk *becomes the ruins of a construction Benjamin never built, although he collected vast amounts of building materials and he twice drew up blueprints. Its most fitting epitaph may well be the Delphic line at the close of the* Trauerspiel *book: "In the ruins of great buildings the idea of the plan speaks more impressively than in lesser buildings, however well preserved they are."*

There are books whose fate has been settled long before they even exist as books. Benjamin's unfinished *Passagen-Werk* is just such a case. Many legends have been woven around it since Adorno first mentioned it in an essay published in 1950.[1] Those legends became even more complexly embroidered after a two-volume selection of Benjamin's *Letters* appeared, which abounded in statements about his intentions for the project. But these statements were neither complete nor coherent.[2] As a result, the most contradictory rumors spread about a book that competing Benjamin interpreters persistently referred to in the hope that it would solve the puzzles raised by his intellectual physiognomy. That hope has remained unrealized. The answer that the fragments of the *Passagen-Werk* give to its readers instead follows Mephisto's retort, "Many a riddle is made here," with Faust's "Many a riddle must be solved here."

In fact, for some years the texts that provide the most reliable information about the project Benjamin worked on for thirteen years, from 1927 until his death in 1940, and that he regarded as his masterpiece have been available. Most of the more important texts he wrote during the last decade of his life are offshoots of the *Passagen-Werk.* If it had been completed, it would have become nothing less than a materialist philosophy of the history of the nineteenth century. The exposé entitled "Paris, Capital of the Nineteenth Century" (1935) provides us with a summary of the themes and motifs Benjamin was concerned with in the larger work. The text introduces the concept of "historical schematism" (V:1150), which was to serve as the basic plan for Benjamin's construction of the nineteenth century. On the other hand, "The Work of Art in the Age of Mechanical Reproduction" (1935–36) has no thematic connection with the *Passagen-Werk* (dealing with phenomena belonging to the twentieth rather than to the nineteenth century), but is nevertheless relevant from the point of view of methodology. In this essay Benjamin tries to "pinpoint the precise spot in the present [his] historical construction would take as its vanishing point" (V:1149). The great, fragmentary work on Baudelaire, which came into being between 1937 and 1939, offers a "miniature model" of the Arcades project. The methodological problems raised by the "Work of Art" essay were, in their turn, addressed once more in the theses "On the Concept of History." In Adorno's opinion these theses "more or less summarize the epistemological considerations that developed concurrently with the *Arcades Project.*"[3] What survives of this project—the countless notes and excerpts that constitute the fifth volume of Benjamin's *Gesammelte Schriften*—rarely go theoretically beyond positions that have been formulated more radically in the texts mentioned above. Any study of the *Passagen-Werk* (Benjamin's intentions hardly lay themselves open to a simple perusal) must therefore deal with the "Work of Art" essay, the texts devoted to Baudelaire, and the theses "On the Concept of History." These must always be present to the student's mind, even though they are manifestly autonomous, writings either introductory to the *Passagen-Werk* or distinct from it.

The published volumes of the *Passagen-Werk* begin with two texts in which Benjamin presents the project in summary, first in 1935 and again in 1939. Together with the early essay "The Saturn Ring, or Some Observations on Iron Mining," these texts are the only ones belonging to the Arcades complex that may be said to be complete. They were not, however, intended for publication. The earlier German one was written for the Institut für Sozialforschung which, as a result, accepted the *Passagen-Werk* as one of its sponsored research projects. The other text, written in French, came into being at Horkheimer's instigation: Horkheimer hoped to make use of it to interest an American patron in Benjamin. The most important part, as well as the lengthiest section of volume five of the *Gesammelte Schriften,* consists of the manuscript of the "Notes and Materials," which is subdivided thematically. This is the manuscript that had been hidden in the Bibliothèque Nationale during the war.

Benjamin probably worked on this manuscript from the fall or winter of 1928 until the end of 1929, and then again from the beginning of 1934. The last entries were made in the spring of 1940, immediately before Benjamin fled Paris. The present order of the notes does not correspond to the order in which they were originally entered. It seems that Benjamin would begin a new *Konvolut,* or sheaf of notes, whenever a new theme suggested itself and demanded to be treated. Within the different sheaves that were composed simultaneously, the notes may evince the chronological order in which they were written down. Yet even this chronology is not always identical with that of the notes' actual conception. At the beginnings of those rubrics that had guided his research in its earliest stage, we find notes Benjamin incorporated from older manuscripts. Here the notes have been rearranged, and therefore the first pages of the respective collections of material follow certain clear principles. By contrast, rubrics either added to or newly begun from 1934 onward generally owe their order to the coincidences of Benjamin's studies or, even more so, to his reading.[4] —The section "First Notes" (V:991–1038) consists of consecutive notes that were begun about the middle of 1927 and terminated in December 1929 or, at the latest, by the beginning of 1930. They are published in their entirety, even though their contents have for the most part been incorporated into the larger "Notes and Materials." It is only with their help that we can trace the "transformation process" that determined the transition from the first stage of the work to the second. The first of the "Early Drafts," entitled "Arcades," dates back to the very first phase of the work, mid-1927, when Benjamin intended to collaborate with Franz Hessel on a journal article. The sketch may well have been written by Benjamin and Hessel together. "Paris Arcades II" shows Benjamin's attempts in 1928 and 1929 to write the essay he thought the *Passagen-Werk* would become. Benjamin wrote these texts in a format totally unusual for him and on very expensive handmade paper, which he never used before or after. One can easily imagine that he approached their composition as he would a festive occasion. But he did not get very far. The discrete texts, whose sequence he did not establish, are soon interspersed with and finally overgrown by quotations and bibliographical notes, and in places with commentary. Both the "Notes and Materials" and the "First Notes" are published in extenso as they are found in the manuscript, but "Paris Arcades II" is treated in a different manner. The notes and quotations in this manuscript were never really worked out: they must have either been transferred to the "Notes and Materials" or been discarded. They have therefore not been included in this edition. Only fully formulated texts have been published; their order has been established by the editor. These texts, among the most important and, if I may say so, the most beautiful of Benjamin's texts, surface again at various places in the "Notes and Materials." Published as a whole, however, they convey an impression of the essay Benjamin mulled over but never actually wrote. The last text, "The Saturn Ring, or Some Observations on Iron Mining," also belongs to the first phase of his project. It may, in fact, be a journal or newspaper article, an offshoot of the *Passagen-Werk* which never made it into print.

The fragments of the *Passagen-Werk* can be compared to the materials used in building a house, the outline of which has just been marked in the ground or whose foundations are just being dug. In the two exposés that open the fifth volume of the *Gesammelte Schriften,* Benjamin sketches broad outlines of the plan as he had envisaged it in 1935 and in 1939. The five or six sections of each exposé should have corresponded to the same number of chapters in the book or, to continue the analogy, to the five or six floors of the projected house. Next to the foundations we find the neatly piled excerpts, which would have been used to construct the walls; Benjamin's own thoughts would have provided the mortar to hold the building together. The reader now possesses many of these theoretical and interpretative reflections, yet in the end they almost seem to vanish beneath the very weight of the excerpts. It is tempting to question the sense of publishing these oppressive chunks of quotations; if it would not be best to publish only those texts written by Benjamin himself. These texts could have been easily arranged in a readable format, and they would have yielded a poignant collection of sparkling aphorisms and disturbing fragments. But this would have made it impossible to guess at the project attempted in the *Passagen-Werk*, such as the reader can discern it behind these quotations. Benjamin's intention was to bring together theory and materials, quotations and interpretation, in a new constellation compared to contemporary methods of representation. The quotations and the materials would bear the full weight of the project; theory and interpretation would have to withdraw in an ascetic manner. Benjamin isolated a "central problem of historical materialism," which he thought he could solve in the *Passagen-Werk* namely:

By what route is it possible to attain a heightened graphicness (*Anschaulichkeit*) combined with a realization of the Marxist method. The first stage in this voyage will be to carry the montage principle over into history. That is, to build up the large structures out of the smallest, precisely fashioned structural elements. Indeed, to detect the crystal of the total event in the analysis of the simple, individual moment (N 2,6).[5]

The structural elements are the countless quotations, and for this reason they cannot be omitted. Once familiar with the architecture of the whole, the reader will be able to read the excerpts without great difficulty and pinpoint in almost every one that element which must have fascinated Benjamin. The reader will also be able to specify which function an excerpt would have served in the global construction, how it might have been able to become a "crystal" whose sparkling light itself reflects the total event. The reader will, of course, have to draw on the ability to "interpolate into the infinitesimally small," as Benjamin defines the imagination in *One-Way Street* (75). For the reader endowed with such an imagination, the dead letters Benjamin collected from the holdings of the Bibliothèque Nationale will come to life. Perhaps even the building Benjamin did not manage to build will delineate itself before the imaginatively speculative eye in shadowy outlines. —These shadows, which prevent us from making a surveyable, consistent drawing of the architecture, are often traceable to problems of a philological nature. The fragments, which are mostly short and often seem to abbreviate a thought, only rarely allow us to glimpse how Benjamin planned to link them. He would often first write down ideas, pointed scribbles. It is impossible to determine whether he planned to retain them in the course of his work. Some theoretical notes contradict each other; others are hardly compatible. Moreover, many of Benjamin's texts are linked with quotations, and the mere interpretation of those citations cannot always be separated from Benjamin's own position. Therefore, to assist the reader in finding his bearings in the labyrinth this volume presents, I shall briefly sketch the essentials of Benjamin's intentions in his *Passagen-Werk*, point out the theoretical nodes of his project, and try to approach explication of some of its central categories.

The *Passagen-Werk* is a building with two completely different floor plans, each belonging to a particular phase of the work. During the first phase, from about mid-1927 to the fall of 1929, Benjamin planned to write an essay entitled "Paris Arcades. A dialectical fairyland (*féerie*)."[6] His earliest references to it in letters characterize the project as a continuation of *One-Way Street* (V:1083), though Benjamin meant less in terms of its aphoristic form than in the specific kind of concretization he attempted there: "this extreme concreteness which made itself felt there in some instances—in a children's game, a building, and a situation in life" should now be captured "for an epoch" (V:1091). Benjamin's original intention was a philosophical one and would remain so for all those years: "putting to the test (*die Probe auf das Exempel*)" as "to what extent you can be 'concrete' in historical-philosophical contexts" (V:1086). He tried to represent the nineteenth century as "commentary on a reality" (V:1028) rather than construing it in the abstract. We can put together a kind of "catalogue of themes" from the "First Notes" about the *Passagen-Werk*. The catalogue shows us what the work was supposed to treat at this level: streets and warehouses, panoramas, world fairs, types of lighting, fashion, advertising and prostitution, collectors, the *flâneur* and the gambler, boredom. Here the arcades themselves are only one theme among many. They belong to those urban phenomena that appeared in the early nineteenth century, with the emphatic claim of the new, but they have meanwhile lost their functionality. Benjamin discovered the signature of the early modern in the ever more rapid obsolescence of the inventions and innovations generated by a developing capitalism's productive forces. He wanted to recover that feature from the appearances of the unsightly, *intentione recta,* the physiognomic way: by showing rags, as a montage of trash (V:1030). In *One-Way Street* his thinking had similarly lost itself in the concrete and particular and had tried to wrest his secret directly, without any theoretical mediation. Such a surrender to singular Being is the distinctive feature of this thinking as such. It is not affected by the rattling mechanisms of undergraduate philosophy, with its transcendental tablets of commandments and prohibitions. Rather it limits itself to the somewhat limitless pursuit of a kind of "gentle empirical experience (*Empirie*)." Like Goethe's *Empirie* it does not conjecture the essence behind or above the thing—it knows it in the things themselves. —The surrealists were the first to discover the material world characteristic of the nineteenth century and in it a specific *mythologie moderne.* It is to that modern mythology that Aragon devotes the preface to his *Paysan de Paris,* while Breton's *Nadja* reaches up into its artificial sky. In his essay "Surrealism," which he called an "opaque folding screen placed before the *Passagen-Werk*" (V:1090), Benjamin praised surrealism as "the first to perceive the revolutionary energies that appear in the 'outmoded,' in the first iron constructions, the first factory buildings, the earliest photos, the objects that begin to be extinct, grand pianos in the salon, the dresses of five years ago, fashionable restaurants when the vogue has begun to ebb from them" (*One-Way Street,* 229). This stratum of material, the alluvium of the immediate past, also pertains to the *Passagen-Werk.* Just as Aragon, sauntering through the Passage de l'Opéra, was pulled by a *vague de rêves* into strange, unglimpsed realms of the Real, so Benjamin wanted to submerge himself in hitherto ignored and scorned reaches of history and to salvage what no one had seen before him.

The nearly depopulated *aquarium humain,* as Aragon described the Passage de l'Opéra in 1927, two years after it had been sacrificed to the completion of the inner circle of boulevards—the ruins of yesterday, where today's riddles are solved—was unmatched in its influence on the *Passagen-Werk* (cf.

V:1117). Benjamin kept quoting the *lueur glauque* of Aragon's arcades: the light that objects are immersed in by dreams, a light that makes them appear strange and vivid at the same time. If the concept of the concrete formed one pole of Benjamin's theoretical armature, then the surrealist theory of dreams made up the other. The divagations of the first Arcades sketch take place in the field of tension between concretization and the dream.[7] Through the dream the early surrealists deprived empirical reality of all its power; they maltreated empirical reality and its purposive rational organization as the mere content of dreams whose language can be only indirectly decoded. By turning the optics of the dream toward the waking world, one could bring to birth the concealed, latent thoughts slumbering in that world's womb. Benjamin wanted to proceed similarly with the representation of history, by treating the nineteenth-century world of objects as if it were a world of dreamed objects. Under capitalist relationships of production, history could be likened to the unconscious actions of the dreaming individual, at least in so far as history is man-made, yet without consciousness or design as if in a dream. "If we want to understand the most fundamental sense of the arcades, we must immerse them in the deepest layer of dreams" (V:1009). If the dream model is applied to the nineteenth century, then it will strip the era of its completeness, of that aspect that is gone forever, of what has literally become history. The means of production and way of life dominant in that period were not only what they had been in their time and place: Benjamin also saw the image-making imagination of a collective unconscious at work in them. That imagination went beyond its historical limits in the dream and actually touched the present, by transferring "the obviously fluctuating condition of a consciousness divided at all times and in many ways between waking and sleeping," which he had discovered in psychoanalysis, "from the individual to the collective" (V:1012). Benjamin wanted to draw attention to the fact that architectonic constructions such as the arcades owed their existence to and served the industrial order of production, while at the same time containing in themselves something unfulfilled, never to be fulfilled within the confines of capitalism: in this case the glass architecture of the future Benjamin often alludes to. "Each period" has a "side it turns toward the dream, its infant side" (V:1006). The scrutiny this side of history was subjected to in Benjamin's observation was designed to "liberate the enormous powers of history . . . which have been put to sleep in the 'once upon a time' of the classical historical narrative" (V:1033).

Almost concurrently with his first notes for the *Passagen-Werk,* Benjamin included in his writings many protocols of his own dreams; this was also when he began to experiment with drugs. Both represented attempts to break the fixations and the encrustations in which thinking and its object, subject and object, have been frozen under the pressure of industrial production.[8] In dreams as in narcotic intoxication, Benjamin watched "a world of particularly secret affinities" reveal itself, a world in which things enter into "the most contradictory ties" and in which they could display "indefinite affinities" (V:993). Intoxication and the dream seemed to unlock a realm of experiences in which the Id still communicated mimetically and corporeally with things. Ever since his earlier philosophical explorations, Benjamin sought a concept of experience that would explode the limitations set by Kant and regain "the fullness of the concept of experience held by earlier philosophers," which should restore the experiences of theology.[9] But the experiences of the surrealists taught him that it was not a matter of restoring theological experience but of transporting it into the profane:

These experiences are by no means limited to dreams, hours of hashish eating or opium smoking. It is a cardinal error to believe that, of "surrealist experiences," we know only the religious ecstasies or the ecstasies of drugs. . . . But the true, creative overcoming of religious illumination certainly does not lie in narcotics. It resides in a *profane illumination,* a materialistic, anthropological inspiration to which hashish, opium, or whatever else can give a preliminary lesson. (*One-Way Street,* 227)

Benjamin wanted to carry such profane illuminations into history by acting as an interpreter of the dreams of the nineteenth-century world of things. The epistemic intention manifest here seems to fit in with the context of Benjamin's soon to be formulated theory of mimetic ability, which is, at its core, a theory of experience.[10] The theory holds that experience rests on the ability to produce and perceive similarities, an ability that underwent significant change in the course of species history. In the beginning a sensuous, qualitative type of behavior of men toward things, it later transformed itself phylogenetically into a faculty for apperceiving nonsensuous similarities, which Benjamin identified as the achievements of language and writing. Vis-à-vis abstracting cognition, his concept of experience wanted to maintain immediate contact with mimetic behavior. He was concerned about "palpable knowledge" (*gefühltes Wissen*), which is "not only nurtured by what appears sensorily before the eyes, but which is also able to assimilate mere knowledge, even dead facts as if they had been lived and experienced" (V:1053). Images take the place of concepts: the enigmatic and vexing dream images which hide all that falls through the coarse mesh of semiotics, and yet those images alone balance the exertions of cognition. The nineteenth-century language of images represents that century's "most thoroughly dormant stratum" (V:1012)—a level that should be awakened by the *Passagen-Werk*.

Benjamin knew that this motif of awakening separated him from the surrealists. They had tried to abolish the line of demarcation between life and art, to shut off poetry in order to live writing or write life. For the early surrealists both dream and reality would unravel to a dreamed, unreal Reality, from which no way led back to contemporary praxis and its demands. Benjamin criticized Aragon for "remaining in the realm of dreams" and for allowing mythology to "stay" with him (V:1014). Aragon's mythology remains *mere* mythology, yet it is unpenetrated by reason. Surrealist imagery evens out the differences separating Now from Then; instead of bringing the past into the present, it puts "things into the distance again" and remains close to "the Romantic perspective in the historical realm" (V:998). Benjamin, on the other hand, wanted "to [bring] things closer" to allow "them to step into our lives" (V:1014). What linked his methods to surrealist ones, the immersion of what was before into layers of dreams, did not represent an end in itself for the *Passagen-Werk*, but rather its methodological arrangement, a kind of experimental set-up. The nineteenth century is the dream we must wake up from; it is a nightmare that will weigh on the present as long as its spell remains unbroken. According to Benjamin, the images of dreaming and awakening from the dream are related as expression is related to interpretation. He hoped that the images, once interpreted, would dissolve the spell. Benjamin's concept of awakening means the "genuine redemption from an epoch" (V:1058), in the double sense of Hegel's *Aufhebung*: the nineteenth century would be transcended *in* that it would be preserved, "rescued" for the present. Benjamin defines "the new, the dialectical method of history writing" as "to live through the past (*das Gewesene*) with the intensity of a dream, in order to experience the present as the waking world that dream relates to" (V:1006). This concept is based on a mystical conception of history that Benjamin was never to abandon, not even in his late theses "On the Concept of History." Every present ought to be synchronic with certain moments of history, just as every past only becomes "legible" in a certain epoch, "namely the one in which mankind, rubbing its eyes, suddenly recognizes the dream image as such. It is at that point that the historian takes up the task of dream interpretation" (N 4,1). Toward this end we do not need a dragging of the past into the mythological, but, on the contrary, a "dissolution of 'mythology' in the historical" (V:1014). Benjamin demanded a "concrete, materialist meditation on what is closest to us" (*das Nächste*); he was interested "only in the representation of what is kin to us, what determines us" (V:998). In this way the historian should no longer try to enter the past; rather, he should allow the past to enter his life. A "pathos of what is close" should replace the vanishing "empathy" (V:1015). For the historian past objects and events would not then be fixed data, an unchangeable given, because "dialectical thinking throws them about, revolutionizes them, turns them upside down" (V:1001); this is what must be accomplished by awakening from the dream of the nineteenth century. That is why for Benjamin the "attempt to awaken from a dream" represents "the best example of dialectic reversal" (V:1002).

The key to what may have been Benjamin's intention while working on the first phase of the *Passagen-Werk* may be found in the sentence "Capitalism was a natural phenomenon which brought a new dream sleep over Europe, and with it a reactivation of mythical powers" (V:494). Benjamin shares his project, the desire to investigate capitalism, with historical materialism, from which he may well have appropriated the project in the first place. But the concepts he uses to define capitalism—nature, dream, and myth—originate from the terminology of his own metaphysically and theologically inspired thought. The key concepts of the young Benjamin's philosophy of history center around a critique of myth as the ordained heteronomous, which kept man banished in dumb dependence throughout prehistory and which has since survived in the most dissimilar forms, both as unmediated violence and in bourgeois jurisprudence.[11] The critique of capitalism in the first Arcades sketch remains a critique of myth, since in it the nineteenth century appears as a domain where "only madness has reigned until now." "But," Benjamin adds, "the soil must be mixed with reason and cleansed of its undergrowth of myth and madness. That is what I propose to accomplish here for the nineteenth century" (V:1010). His interpretation recognizes forms still unhistorical, still imprisoned by myth, forms that are only preparing themselves, in such an interpretation, to awaken from myth and to take its power away. Benjamin identifies them as the dominant forms of consciousness and the imagery of incipient high capitalism: the "sensation of the newest, the most modern" as well as the image of the "eternal recurrence of the same"—both are "dream forms of what has happened," dreamed by a collective that "knows no history" (V:1023). He speaks in direct theological terms in his interpretation of the modern as "the time of hell":

The point is that the face of the world, that enormous head, never changes, certainly not in what is the newest, that this "newest" remains the same in all its parts. This constitutes both the eternity of hell and the sadist's desire for innovation. To define the totality of the features by which the modern expresses itself means to represent hell. (V:1010ff.)

Since it is a "commentary on a reality," which sinks into the historical and interprets it as it would a text, theology was called upon to provide the "main scientific foundation" of the *Passagen-Werk*, though at the same time politics was to retain its

"primacy over history" (V:1057). At the time of the first Arcades sketch, Benjamin was less concerned with a mediation of
theological and political categories than with their identity. In
this he was very much like Bloch in the *Spirit of Utopia,* which he
explicitly took as his model. He repeatedly took recourse to
Blochian concepts to characterize his own intentions, as in
"fashion stands in the darkness of the lived moment, but in the
collective darkness" (V:1028). Just as for Bloch the experiencing individual has not yet achieved mastery over himself at the
moment of experiencing, for Benjamin the historical phenomena remain opaque, unilluminated for the dreaming collective.
In Bloch's opinion individual experience is always experience
of the immediate past; in the same way Benjamin's interpretation of the present refers to the most recent past: action in the
present means awakening from the dream of history, an "explosion" of what has been, a revolutionary turn. He was convinced that "all the facts the project had to deal with" would "be
illuminated in the process of the proletariat becoming conscious of itself" (V:1033). He did not hesitate to interpret these
facts as part of the preparation for the proletarian revolution.
"The dialectical interpenetration and actualization of past contexts is a test of the truth of the present action" (V:1026f.)—not
of the action itself—but it serves as a contribution to its theory.
This defines the task of the historian as "rescuing" the past or,
as Benjamin formulated it with another concept taken from
Bloch, "awakening a knowledge, not yet conscious, of what has
been" (V:1014) by applying the "doctrine of knowledge which
is not yet conscious . . . to the collective in various epochs"
(V:1031). At this stage Benjamin conceived of the *Passagen-
Werk* as a mystical reconstitution: dialectical thinking had the
task of separating the future-laden, "positive" element from the
backward, "negative" element, after which it had "to subject
the tentatively isolated, negative part to another division, such
that with a shifting of perspective . . . it reveals a new, positive
element, different from the one previously indicated. And so
on, in infinitum, until all of the past has been brought into the
present in an historical apocastasis" (N 1a,3). In this way the
nineteenth century should be brought into the present inside
the *Passagen-Werk.* Benjamin did not think revolutionary praxis

should be allowed at any lesser price. For him revolution was, in its highest form, a liberation of the past, which had to demonstrate "the indestructibility of the highest life in all things" (V:1025). At the end of the 1920s theology and communism converged in Benjamin's thought. The metaphysical, historical-philosophical, and theological sources that had nurtured both his esoteric early writings and his great aesthetic works until *The Origin of German Trauerspiel* were still flowing and would also nurture the *Passagen-Werk*.

The *Passagen-Werk* was supposed to become all of that, and it became none of that—to echo a famous phrase of Benjamin's. He interrupted work in the fall of 1929 for various reasons. Retrospectively, he placed responsibility on problems of representation: the "rhapsodical nature" of the work, which he had already announced in the first sketch's subtitle, "a dialectical fairyland" (V:1117). The "illicit 'poetic' " formulation he then thought he was obliged to use was irreconcilable with a book that was to have "our generation's decisive historical interests as its object" (V:1137). Benjamin believed that only historical materialism could safeguard those interests; the *aporias* he encountered while composing the *Passagen-Werk*, then, undoubtedly culminated in the project's position in relation to Marxist theory. Though Benjamin professed his commitment to Communist party politics to begin with, he still had to convince himself of the necessity to proceed from a political creed to the theoretical study of Marxism, which he thought could be appropriated for his purposes even prior to his actual study. His intention was to secure the *Passagen-Werk* "against all objections . . . provoked by metaphysics"; "the whole mass of thought, originally set into motion by metaphysics," had to be subjected to a "recasting process" which would allow the author to "face with equanimity the objections orthodox Marxism might mobilize against the method of the work" (V:1118). Benjamin traced the end of his "unconcernedly archaic philosophizing, imprisoned by nature," which had been the basis of the "romantic form" and the "rhapsodical naiveté" of the first draft, to conversations with Adorno and Horkheimer that he characterized as "historical" (V:1117). These took place in September or October 1929 in Frankfurt and Königstein. In all probability both Hork-

heimer and Adorno insisted in discussions of the submitted texts
—mainly the "Early Drafts" published with the *Passagen-Werk*—
that it was impossible to speak sensibly about the nineteenth
century without considering Marx's analysis of capital; it is entirely possible that Benjamin, who at that time had read hardly
anything by Marx, was influenced by such a suggestion.[12] Be
that as it may, Benjamin's letter to Scholem of January 20,
1930, contains the statement that he would have to study certain features of both Hegelian philosophy and *Capital* in order
to complete his project (V:1094). Benjamin had by no means
concluded such studies when he returned to the *Passagen-Werk*
four years later. The "new face" (V:1103) the work unveiled,
not in the least due to Benjamin's political experiences in exile,
revealed itself in an emphatic recourse to social history, which
had not been wholly relinquished in the first sketch but which
had been concealed by that sketch's surrealist intentions. None
of the old motifs were abandoned, but the building was given
stronger foundations. Among the themes added were Hauss-
mann's influence, the struggles on the barricades, railways, con-
spiracies, comradeship, social movements, the stock exchange,
economic history, the Commune, the history of sects, the Ecole
Polytechnique; moreover, Benjamin began assembling excerpts
on Marx, Fourier, and Saint-Simon. This thematic expansion
hardly meant that Benjamin was about to reserve a chapter for
each theme (he now planned to write a book instead of an
essay). The book's subject was now defined as "art's fate in the
nineteenth century" (V:1151) and thus seemed more narrowly
conceived than it had been. That should not be taken too literally, however: the 1935 exposé, after all, in which Benjamin
most clearly delineates his intentions in his work's second stage,
still lists every theme the *Passagen-Werk* was to treat from the
outset: arcades, panoramas, world fairs, interiors, and the
streets of Paris. This exposé's title, "Paris, Capital of the Nineteenth Century," remained the definitive title and was appropriated for another exposé—a French prospectus—in 1939.
This prospectus contains a decisive reference to "the new
and far-reaching sociological perspectives" of the second
sketch. Benjamin wrote that these new perspectives would
yield a "secure framework of interpretive interconnections"

(V:1118). But his interpretation was now supposed to trace the book's subject matter—the cultural superstructure of nineteenth-century France—back to what Marx had called the fetish character of commodities. In 1935 the "unfolding of this concept" would "constitute the center" of the projected work (V:1112), and by 1938 the "basic categories" of the *Passagen-Werk* would "converge in the determination of the fetish character of commodities" (V:1116). This notion surfaces only once in the first sketch (V:1030); it was then by no means clear that commodity fetishism was destined to form the central schema for the whole project. When Benjamin wrote the first exposé in 1935, he was probably still unfamiliar with the relevant discussion in Marx's writings. He apparently only began to "look around . . . in the first volume of *Capital*" after completing the exposé (V:1122). He was familiar with the theory of commodity fetishism mainly in Lukács's version; like many other left-wing intellectuals of his generation, Benjamin largely owed his Marxist competency to the chapter on reification in *History and Class Consciousness*.

Benjamin wished to treat culture in the era of high capitalism like Lukács's translation back into philosophy of the economic fact of commodity fetishism as well as his application of the category of reification to the antinomies of bourgeois thought. Marx showed that capitalist production's abstraction of value begets an ideological consciousness, in which labor's social character is reflected as objective, thing-like characteristics of the products of that labor. Benjamin recognized the same ideological consciousness at work in the then dominant "reified conception of culture," which obfuscated the fact that "the creations of the human mind . . . owe not just their origin, but also the ways in which they have been handed down, to a continuing social labor" (V:1255). The fate of nineteenth-century culture lay precisely in its commodity character, which Benjamin thereupon represented in "cultural values" as *phantasmagoria*. Phantasmagoria: a *Blendwerk*, a deceptive image designed to dazzle, is already the commodity itself, in which the exchange value or value-form hides the use value. Phantasmagoria is the whole capitalist production process, which constitutes itself as a natural force against the people who carry it out. For Benjamin cultural phantasmagorias express "the ambiguity inherent in the social relationships and the products of this epoch" (V:55). In Marx the same ambiguity defines "the economic world of capitalism": an ambiguity "that becomes very obvious where machines e.g. are concerned, since they intensify exploitation rather than alleviate man's fate" (V:499). The concept of phantasmagoria that Benjamin repeatedly employs seems to be merely another term for what Marx called commodity fetishism. Benjamin's term can even be found in Marx's writings: in *Capital*'s first chapter (on fetishism), in the famous passage about the "definite social relation" which molds labor under capitalist conditions of production, that very relation is said to "assume . . . the phantasmagoric form of a relation between things" for the people concerned.[13] Marx had in mind the circumstances of the bourgeois economy's "necessarily false" consciousness, which is no less false for being necessary. Benjamin's interest in culture was less for its ideological content, however, whose depth is unearthed in ideology critique, than for its surface or exterior, which is both promising and deceptive. "The creations and life-styles that were mainly conditioned by commodity production and which we owe to the previous century" are "sensuously transfigured in their immediate presence" (V:1256). Benjamin was interested in that immediate presence; the secret he was tracking in the *Passagen-Werk* is a secret that becomes visible. The "luster with which the commodity-producing society surrounds itself" (V:1256) is phantasmagorical—a luster that hardly has less to do with the "beautiful appearance" of idealist aesthetics than with commodity fetishism. Phantasmagorias are the "century's magic images" (I:1153); they are the *Wunschbilder*, the wish symbols or ideals, by which that collective tried "both to transfigure and to sublate the unfinished nature of the social product and the defects in the social order of production" (V:46f.). To begin with, the phantasmagoria seems to have a transfiguring function: world exhibitions, for example, transform the exchange value of commodities by fading, as in a film, from the abstractness of their valuation. Similarly the collector transfigures things by divesting them of their commodity character. And in this same way iron construction and glass architecture are transfigured in the arcades because "the century could not match the new technical possibilities with a new social order" (V:1257). As Benjamin in late 1937 came across Blanqui's *L'Eternité par les Astres*—a cosmological phantasmagoria written by the revolutionary while in prison—he reencountered his own speculation about the nineteenth century as Hades. The "seemingness" (*Scheinhafte*) of all that is new and that the century liked to show off as modern *par excellence* became consummated in its highest concept, that of progress, which Blanqui denounced as a "phantasmagoria of history," as "something so old it predates thinking, which struts about in the clothes of the New," as the eternal recurrence of the same, in which mankind figures "as one of the damned" (V:1256). Benjamin learned from Blanqui that the phantasmagoria embraced "the most bitter criticism," the harshest indictment of society" (V:1256f.). The transfiguring aspects of phantasmagoria change to enlightenment, into the insight "that mankind will remain under the power of mythical fear as long as phantasmagoria has a place in that fear" (V:1256). The century always transcends the "old social order" in its cultural phantasmagoria. As "wish symbols," the arcades and interiors, the exhibition halls and panoramas are "residue of a dreamworld." They are part of Blochian dreaming ahead, anticipating the future: "Every epoch doesn't merely dream the next epoch, but in dreaming it propels itself toward awakening. It carries its end in itself." Insofar as dialectical thinking tries to define as well as to expedite this end of decaying bourgeois culture, it became for Benjamin the "organ of historical awakening" (V:59).

"The feature that is attributed to the commodity as its fetish character is inherent in the commodity-producing society itself, not as that society is in itself, but rather as it always portrays itself and believes to understand itself when it makes abstraction of the fact that it produces commodities" (V:822). That was hardly Marx's opinion. He identifies the fetish character of the commodity through the fact that the features of man's labor *appear* to him as what they *are:* "as material relations between persons and social relations between things."[14] The analysis of capital establishes the *quid pro quo* of commodity fetishism as objective, not as a phantasmagoric. Marx should have rejected the notion that the commodity-producing society might be able to abstract the fact that it produces commodities in any other way than by really ceasing to produce commodities in the transition to a higher social formation. It is not difficult—though also not very productive—to point out Benjamin's miscomprehensions of Marxist theory. —Benjamin showed little interest in a Marxist theory of art, which he considered "now swaggering, now scholastic" (N 4a,2). He valued three short sentences by Proust more highly than most of what existed in the field of materialist analysis (V:498f.). The majority of Marxist art theorists explain culture as the mere reflection of economic development; Benjamin refused to join them. He viewed the doctrine of aesthetic reflection as already undercut by Marx's remark that "the ideologies of the superstructure reflect relations in a false and distorted manner." Benjamin followed this remark with a question:

If the substructure defines the superstructure to a certain extent in its materials of thought and experience, but if that definition is not a simple reflection, then how should it be characterized? As its expression. The superstructure is the expression of the base. The economic conditions in which society exists are expressed in the superstructure, just as the dream-contents of someone sleeping on a full stomach—although causally "contingent" on that full stomach—are not its mirroring but its expression. (V:495)

Benjamin did not set out according to ideology critique;[15] rather he gave way to the notion of materialist physiognomics, which he probably understood as a complement, or an extension, of Marxist theory. Physiognomics infers the interior from the exterior, it decodes the whole from the detail, it represents the general in the particular. Noministically speaking, it proceeds from the tangible object; inductively it commences in the realm of the intuitive. The *Passagen-Werk* "deals basically with the expressive character of the earliest industrial products, the earliest industrial structures, the earliest machines as well as the earliest department stores, advertisements, etc." (N 1a,7). In that expressive character Benjamin hoped to locate what eluded the immediate grasp: the *Signatur*, the mark, of the nineteenth century. He was interested in the "expressive relationship": "the expression of the economy in its culture will be described, not the economic origins of culture" (N 1a,6). Benjamin's trajectory from the first to the second draft of the *Passagen-Werk* documents his efforts to safeguard his work against the demands of historical materialism; in this way motifs belonging to metaphysics and theology survived undamaged in the physiognomic concept of the epoch's closing stage. To describe the expression of economics in culture was an attempt "to grasp an economic process as a concrete source phenomenon, from which all the manifestations of the arcades (and consequently the nineteenth century) proceed" (N 1a,6). Benjamin had already enlisted Goethe's primal phenomenon (*Urphänomen*) to explicate his concept of truth in *The Origin of German Trauerspiel*[16]: the concept of "origin" in the *Trauerspiel* book would have to be "a strict and compelling transfer of this Goethean first principle from the realm of nature to that of history." In the *Passagen-Werk,* then:

I am also involved in fathoming origin. That is to say, I am pursuing the origin of the construction and transformation of the Paris arcades from their rise to their fall, and am laying hold of this origin through economic facts. These facts, seen from the viewpoint of causality, that is, construed as causes (*Ursachen*), would not, however, constitute originary phenomena (*Urphänomene*); they become this only insofar as in their own development (*Entwicklung*)—unfolding (*Auswicklung*) might be a better word—they allow the whole series of the arcade's concrete historical forms to emerge; like a leaf unfolding forth from itself the entire wealth of the empirical plant kingdom." (N 2a,4)

Metaphysical subtleties and theological moods reappear here in the theory of epistemology, even though they seemed vanquished after they learned of their ironic unmasking by economics. How could *Ur*-phenomena, which represent themselves as the expression of economic facts, distinguish themselves from those ideas in Benjamin's *Trauerspiel* book which represent themselves by empirical means? Benjamin resolves this problem with his early notion of a monadological truth, which presides at every phase of the *Passagen-Werk* and remains valid even in the theses "On the Concept of History." Whereas in the *Trauerspiel* book the idea as monad "contains the image of the world" in itself (48), in *Passagen-Werk* the expression as *Ur*-phenomenon contains the image of history in itself. The essence of capitalist production should be comprehended vis-à-vis the concrete historical forms in which the economy finds its cultural expression. The abstractions of mere conceptual thinking were insufficient to demystify this abhorrent state of affairs, such that a mimetic-intuitive corrective was imposed to decipher the code of the universal in the image. Physiognomic thought was assigned the task of "recognizing the monuments of the bourgeoisie as ruins even before they have crumbled" (V:59). —The prolegomena to a materialist physiognomics that can be gleaned from the *Passagen-Werk* counts among Benjamin's most prodigious conceptions. It is the programmatic harbinger of that aesthetic theory which Marxism has not been able to develop to this day. Whether Benjamin's realization of his program could fulfill its promise, whether his physiognomics would have been equal to its materialist task, could only have been proven by the actual composition of the *Passagen-Werk* itself.

Modified concepts of history and of the writing of history are the link between both Arcades drafts. Their polemical barbs are aimed at the nineteenth-century notion of progress. With the exception of Schopenhauer—by no coincidence his objective world bears the name "phantasmagoria"—idealist philosophers had turned progress into the "signature for the course of history *in its totality*" (N 13,1) and by doing so deprived it of its critical and enlightenment functions. Even Marx's trust in the unfolding of the productive forces hypostasized the concept of progress, and it must have appeared untenable to Benjamin in light of the experience of the twentieth century. Similarly, the political praxis of the worker's movement had forgotten that progress in terms of proficiency and information does not necessarily mean progress for humanity itself—and that progress in the domination of nature corresponds to societal regress (*Illuminations,* 260f.). In the first Arcades draft Benjamin already demanded "a philosophy of history that surmounts the ideology of progress at every point" (V:1026), such as he later worked out in the historical-philosophical theses. There the image of history reminds the reader more of Klages's lethal juggling with archetypal images (*Urbilder*) and phantoms than of the dialectic of the forces and the relations of production. It is that Angel of History who appears in one of the theses as an allegory of the historical materialist (in Benjamin's sense)[17] and who sees all history as a catastrophe "which keeps piling wreckage upon wreckage and hurls it in front of his feet" (*Illuminations*, 259). The Angel abolishes all categories which until then have been used for representing history: this materialist sees the " 'gradualness' of becoming" as refuted, and "evolution" is shown to be only "seeming" (V:491, 1006). But more than anything else he denounces the "establishment of continuity" (N 9a,5) in history, because the only evidence of that continuity is that of horror, and the Angel has to do with salvation and redemption. The *Passagen-Werk* was supposed to bring nothing less than a "Copernican Revolution" of historical intuition (V:490f., 1006). Past history would be grounded in the present, analogous to Kant's epistemological grounding of objectivity in the depths of the subject. The first revolution occurred in the relationship in which subject and object, present and past meet in historical perception:

The "Then" has always been interpreted as "fixed" and the present's efforts were to gropingly lead knowledge up to this fortress. The time has come to invert that relationship, and the Then should become a dialectical turning-over (*Umschlag*); it should become the sudden thought in an awakened consciousness. Politics achieves primacy over history. Facts turn into something that just happened to us, to establish them is the task of memory." (V:490f.)

The historical line of vision no longer falls from the present back onto history; instead it travels from history forward. Benjamin tried to "read today's life, today's forms out of the life and the apparently secondary, forgotten forms" of the nineteenth century (N 1,11). Our contemporary interest in a historical object seems "itself preformed in that object, and most of all" it feels "that object concretized in itself, promoted from its being from that time into the higher concretization of being now (*Jetztseins*) (of being awake!)" (V:494f.). The object of history goes on changing, it becomes historical (in that word's emphatic sense) only when it becomes topical in a later period. The continuous relationships in time, with which history deals, are superseded in Benjamin's thought by constellations in which the past coincides with the present to such an extent that the past achieves a "Now" of its "recognizability." Benjamin developed this "Now of Recognizability," which he sometimes referred to as his theory of knowledge (V:1148), from a double frontal position against both idealism and positivistic historicism. While the latter tried to move the historical narrator back into the past, so that he could comprehend "emphatically" (solely from within) the whole of the Then, which filled "homogenous, empty time" as a mere "mass of data" (*Illuminations*, 264), idealist constructions of history, on the other hand, usurped the prospect of the future and posited in history the existence of the natural plan of a process, which runs on autonomously and can in principle never be completed. Both relegate "everything about history that, from the very beginning, has been untimely, sorrowful, unsuccessful" (*Trauerspiel*, 166) to forgetting. The object of that materialist historical narrative Benjamin wanted to try out in the *Passagen-Werk* would be precisely what history started but did not carry out. That the lineaments of the past are first detectable after a certain period is not due to the historian's whim; it depicts an objective historical constellation:

History is the object of a construct whose site is not homogenous, empty time, but time filled by Now-Time (*Jetztzeit*). Thus, to Robespierre ancient Rome was a past charged with Now-Time, which he blasted out of the continuum of history. The French Revolution viewed itself as Rome incarnate. It quoted ancient Rome. (*Illuminations*, 263)

Benjamin wished to continue along this line in the *Passagen-Werk*: the present would provide the text of the book, history the quotations in that text; "to write history . . . means to *quote* history" (N 11,3).

Benjamin's Copernican Revolution of historical intuition also (and above all) meant that the traditional concept of truth was to be turned upright:

An emphatic refusal of the concept of "timeless truth" is in order. Yet truth is not—as Marxism maintains—just a temporal function of knowledge; it is bound to a time kernel (*Zeitkern*) that is planted in both the knower and the known. This is *so* true, that the "eternal" is in any case far more a frill on a dress than an idea. (N 3,2)

The temporal core of history cannot be grasped as really happening, stretching forth in the real dimension of time, but rather where evolution halts for a moment, where the *dynamis* of what is happening coagulates into *stasis,* and where time itself is condensed into a differential, wherever a Now identifies itself as the "Now of a specific recognizability." In such a Now "truth is loaded to the bursting point with time" (N 3,1). The Now would have thus shown itself to be the "innermost image" (V:1035) of the arcades themselves, of fashion, of the bourgeois interior—appearing as the image of all that had been, and whose cognition is the pith of the *Passagen-Werk.* Benjamin invented the name "dialectical images" for such configurations of the Now and the Then; he defined their content as a "dialectic at a standstill." Dialectical image and dialectic at the standstill are, without a doubt, the central categories of the *Passagen-Werk;* their meaning, however, remained iridescent, it never achieved any terminological consistency.[18] We can distinguish at least two meanings in Benjamin's texts; they remain somewhat undivulged, but even so cannnot be brought totally in congruence. Once—in the 1935 exposé, which in this regard summarizes the motifs of the first draft—Benjamin localized dialectical images as dream and wish images in the collective subconscious, whose "image-making fantasy, which was stimulated by the new" should refer back to the "*Ur*-past": "In the dream, in which every epoch displays itself in images to the subsequent epoch, the previous epoch appears wedded to elements of *Ur*-history, i.e., of a classless society. Their experiences, deposited in the collective's unconscious, generate utopia when they are penetrated by the new" (V:47). The modern quoted *Ur*-history "by means of the ambiguity characteristic of the social relations and products of this epoch." In turn, "Ambiguity is the appearance of dialectic in images, the law of the dialectic at a standstill. This stasis is utopia, and the dialectical image is therefore a dream image. Such an image unmasks commodities at once by revealing them as fetish" (V:55). These statements drew the resolute criticism of Adorno, who could not concede that the dialectical image could be "the way in which fetishism is conceived in the collective consciousness," since commodity fetishism is not a "fact of consciousness"

(V:1128). Under the influence of Adorno's objections, Benjamin abandoned such lines of thought; the corresponding passages in his 1939 exposé were dropped as no longer satisfactory to their author (cf. V:1157). By 1940, in the theses "On the Concept of History," "dialectic at a standstill" seems to function almost like a heuristic principle, a procedure that enables the historical materialist to maneuver his objects:

A historical materialist cannot do without the notion of a present which is not a transition, but in which time stands still and has come to a stop. For this notion defines the present in which he himself is writing history. . . . Materialist historiography . . . is based on a constructive principle. Thinking involves not only the flow of thoughts, but their arrest as well. Where thinking suddenly stops in a configuration pregnant with tensions, it gives that configuration a shock, by which it crystallizes into a monad. A historical materialist approaches a historical subject only where he encounters it as a monad. In this structure he recognizes the sign of a Messianic cessation of happening, or, put differently, a revolutionary chance in the fight for the oppressed past. (*Illuminations*, 264f.)

In fact, Benjamin's thinking was invariably in dialectical images. As opposed to the Marxist dialectic, which "regards every . . . developed social form as in fluid movement,"[19] Benjamin's dialectic tried to halt the flow of the movement, to grasp each becoming as being. In Adorno's words, Benjamin's philosophy "appropriates the fetishism of commodities for itself: everything must metamorphize into a thing in order to break the catastrophic spell of things."[20] His philosophy progressed imagistically, in that it sought to "read" historical social phenomena as if they were natural historical ones. Images became dialectical for this philosophy because of the historical index of every single image. "In the dialectical image" of this philosophy "the Then of any given epoch is always also the past from time immemorial" (N 4,1). By so being, it remained rooted in the mythical. Yet at the same time the historical materialist who seized the image should possess the skill to "fan the spark of hope in the past," to wrest historical tradition "anew . . . from a conformism that is about to overpower it" (*Illuminations*, 255). By immobilizing dialectic, the historical "victors" have their accounts with history cancelled, and all pathos is shifted toward salvation of the oppressed.

For Benjamin, freezing the dialectical image was obviously not a method the historian could employ at any time. For him, as for Marx, historiography was inseparable from political practice: the rescuing of the past through the writer of history remained bound to the practical liberation of humanity. Contrasted with the Marxist conception, however, according to which "capitalist production begets, with the inexorability of a law of nature, its own negation,"[21] Benjamin's philosophy preserves anarchist and Blanquian elements:

> In reality there is not one moment that does not carry *its own* revolutionary opportunity in itself. . . . The particular revolutionary opportunity of each historical moment is confirmed for the revolutionary thinker by the political situation. But it is no less confirmed for him by the power this moment has to open a very particular, heretofore closed chamber of the past. Entry into this chamber coincides exactly with political action. (I:1231)

Political action "no matter how destructive," should always "reveal itself as messianic" (I:1231). Benjamin's historical materialism can hardly be severed from political messianism. In a late note, perhaps written under the shock of the Hitler-Stalin pact, Benjamin formulated as "the experience of our generation: that capitalism will not die a natural death" (V:819). In that case, the onset of revolution could no longer be awaited with the patience of Marx; rather it had to be envisaged as the eschatological *end* of history: "the classless society is not the ultimate goal of progress in history but its rupture, so often attempted and finally brought about (I:1231). Myth is liquidated in the dialectical image to make room for the "dream of a thing" (I:1174); this dream is the dialectic at a standstill, the piecing together of what history has broken to bits (cf. *Illuminations*, 257), the *tikkun* of the Lurian Kabbalah.[22] Benjamin did quote the young Marx, who wanted to show "that the world has long possessed the dream of a thing that, made conscious, it would possess in reality" (N 5a,1). But for the interpreter of dialectical images, true reality cannot be inferred from existing reality. He undertook to represent the imperative and the final goal of reality as "a preformation of the final purpose of history" (N 5,3). The awakening from myth would follow the messianic model of a history immobilized in redemption as the historican of the *Passagen-Werk* had imagined it. In his dialect-ical images the bursting of time coincides with "the birth of authentic historical time, the time of truth" (N 3,1). Since the dialectical images belong in such a way to messianic time, or since they should at least let that time reveal itself as a flash of lightning, messianism is introduced as a kind of doctrine of historical methodology—an adventuresome undertaking if ever there was one. "The subject of historical knowledge is the struggling, oppressed class itself" (*Illuminations*, 260); one may imagine the historism of the dialectic at a standstill as the herald of that class. Benjamin himself did not hesitate to call him "a prophet turned backward," borrowing a phrase from Friedrich Schlegel (I:1237); he did not dismiss the Old Testament idea that prophecy precedes the Messiah, that the Messiah is depen-dent on prophecy. But Benjamin's historiographer is "endowed with a *weak* messianic power, a power to which the past has a claim." The historian honors that claim when he captures that "image of the past that is not recognized by the present as one of its own concerns" and thus "threatens to disappear irretriev-ably" (*Illuminations*, 256f.) Benjamin was able to recognize only the mythical Ever-Same (*Immergleiche*) in historical evolutions and was unable to recognize progress, except as a *Sprung*—a "tiger's leap into the past" (*Illuminations*, 263), which was in reality a leap out of history and the entry of the messianic kingdom. He tried to match this mystical conception of history with a version of dialectics in which mediation would be totally eclipsed by change, in which atonement would have to yield to criticism and destruction. His "blasting" the dialectical image "out of the continuum of the historical process" (N 10a,3) was akin to that anarchistic impulse which tries to stop history dur-ing revolutions by instituting a new calendar, or by shooting at church clocks, as during the Paris revolution. The gaze, which exorcized images from objects blasted loose from time, is the Gorgon gaze at the "*facies hippocratica* of history," the "petrified primordial landscape" of myth (*Trauerspiel*, 166). But in that mystical moment when Past and Present enter "lightning-like" into a constellation—when the true image of the past "flashes" in the "Now of recognizability" (N 9,7)—that image becomes a dialectically changing image, as it presents itself from the messianic perspective, or (in materialistic terms) the perspective of the revolution.

From this perspective of "messianic time" Benjamin defined the present as catastrophe (I:1243), as the prolongation of that "one single catastrophe" which meets the Angelus Novus when he looks back on past history. It might appear as if Benjamin wished to reintroduce the "large hyphen between past and future,"[23] which was thought to be eradicated after Marx. Yet even Benjamin's late work does not fully forgo historical indication. Henri Focillon defined the classical in art as "*bonheur rapide*," as the *chairou achme* of the Greeks, and Benjamin wanted to use that definition for his own concept of messianic standstill (cf. I:1229). The dialectic at a standstill, the final coming to rest, the ending of the historical dynamic which Hegel, following Aristotle, wished to ascribe to the state, was, for Benjamin, prefigured only in art. A "real definition" of progress, therefore, could only emerge from the vantage point of art, as in the *Passagen-Werk*:

In every true work of art, there is a place where anybody who positions himself within it encounters the cool breeze of a coming dawn. Which therefore demonstrates that art, which has often been considered as resisting any connection to progress, can serve to give the latter its true definition. Progress does not reside in the continuity of temporal succession, but rather in its moments of interference. (N 9a,7)

In that sense it may even be possible to save that problematic definition from the first exposé, according to which in the dialectical image the mythical, *Ur*-historical experiences of the collective unconscious generate "utopia when they are penetrated by the new"—and that utopia "has left its traces in a thousand configurations of life, from lasting buildings to fleeting fashions" (V:47). Benjamin devised his dialectic at a stillstand in order to make such traces visible, to collect the "trash of history," and to "redeem" them for its end. He undertook the equally paradoxical and astonishing task of representing history in the spirit of an anti-evolutionary understanding of history. As a "messianic cessation of the event," it would have devolved upon the dialectic at a standstill to bring home in the *Passagen-Werk* the very insight Benjamin had long assimilated when he began that project: "the profane . . . although not itself a category of this (Messianic) Kingdom, is at least a category, and one of the most applicable, of its quietest approach" (*Reflections*, 312). Benjamin's concept of profane illumination would remain "illuminated" in this way to the end; his materialist inspiration would be "inspired" in the same way, and his materialism became theological in the same way, despite all "recasting processes." Benjamin's historical materialism was only historically true as the puppet, "which enlists the services of theology." Nevertheless, it was supposed to "win" (*Illuminations*, 253). One can be excused for doubting whether this intricate claim could ever be honored. In that case, the reader, who has patiently followed the topography of the *Passagen-Werk*, including all the detours and cul de sacs this edition does not veil, may think he is, in the end, faced with ruins rather than with virginal building materials. What Benjamin wrote about German *Trauerspiel* however, holds true for the *Passagen-Werk*: namely, that "in the ruins of great buildings the idea of the plan speaks more impressively than in lesser buildings, however well preserved they are" (*Trauerspiel*, 235).

Translated by Gary Smith and André Lefevere

Notes

For the convenience of the reader who wishes to refer to the English translation of Konvolut "N" of the *Passagen-Werk*, references to this sheaf are made to the particular excerpt number (for example [N 4,1]), rather than to the page number in the German text.

1. Translated as "A Portrait of Walter Benjamin" in T. W. Adorno, *Prisms*, trans. Samuel and Shierry Weber (Cambridge, MA: MIT Press, 1981), 229–41.

2. Cf. Walter Benjamin, *Briefe*, passim. The author provides, in V:1081–1183, a complete compilation of Benjamin's statements in letters about the *Passagen-Werk* (within the limits of available correspondence).

3. Adorno, *Prisms*, 239.

4. Cf. Rolf Tiedemann, *Dialektik im Stillstand* (Frankfurt a.M.: Suhrkamp, 1983), 190f., n. 18a, on the current legend of a "rearrangement" of the notes and materials of the *Passagen-Werk*.

5. According to Adorno, Benjamin's intention was "to eliminate all overt commentary and to have the meanings emerge solely through a shock-like montage of the material. . . . His magnum opus, the crowning of his antisubjectivism, was to consist solely of

citations" (Adorno, *Prisms*, 239). Though this thought may seem typical of Benjamin, I am convinced that Benjamin did not intend to work in that fashion. There is no remark in the letters attesting to this. Adorno supports his position with two notes from the *Passagen-Werk* itself (see N 1,10 and N 1a,8), which can hardly be interpreted in that way. One of the notes already turned up in the "First Notes" of 1928 or 1929 (cf. V:1030), when Benjamin stated that he was still considering an essay, which he had begun in the "Early Sketches"—by no means, however, in the form of a montage of quotations.

6. This had been preceded by the plan—which probably did not last long—to collaborate with Franz Hessel on an article about arcades. Cf. V:1341.

7. Here and in what follows, references to the first and second sketch are in the same manner that Benjamin referred to them in his letter to Gretel Adorno of August 16, 1935: merely in quotation marks, so to speak. No single text is meant by "sketch"; the second sketch especially does not denote the 1935 exposé. Benjamin had in mind the concept of the work, such as it can be inferred from an interpretation of the totality of the notes from both stages of his work.

8. Cf. Hermann Schweppenhäuser, "Propaedeutics of Profane Illumination," this volume.

9. Cf. mainly "Program of the Coming Philosophy," *The Philosophical Forum* 15, 1–2 (Fall–Winter 1983–84): 41–51; this citation originates from an early fragment, "Über die Wahrnehmung" (VI:33–38).

10. Cf. "Doctrine of the Similar," *New German Critique* 17 (Spring 1979): 65–69, and "On the Mimetic Faculty," *Reflections*, 333–36. One of the latest texts in the "First Notes" to the *Passagen-Werk* seems to be a germinating cell of Benjamin's theory of mimesis (cf. V:1038).

11. Cf. the author's *Studien zur Philosophie Walter Benjamins*, 2nd ed. (Frankfurt a.M.: Suhrkamp, 1973), 76f., 98f.

12. In the "First Notes," in which economic categories are used either metaphysically or in a desultory fashion, we find uncommented references to two passages in the first and third volumes of *Capital*, and these references are to the "original edition" (cf. V:1036). This could be especially instructive in the case of the first volume, whose first edition of 1867—the original edition referred to—is very rare and is almost never cited. We may surmise that Horkheimer or Adorno referred Benjamin to the pages in question during the "historical conversations" in the fall of 1929. The library of the Institut für Sozialforschung owned, at that time, a copy of the original edition, and at least Horkheimer was wont to quote from scarce editions. This conjecture is corroborated when one checks the relevant passage in the first edition of *Capital*: it deals with the definitive formulations of commodity fetishism, that is, the very concept whose "unfolding" would be "the central core" of the second *Passagen-Werk* draft (cf. above, p. 276). Since the manuscript of the "First Notes" was abandoned shortly after this entry, it is very possible that Benjamin's abandoning the manuscript may have been caused by the obstacles created by the suggestion that it was necessary for him to read *Capital*. Finally, a letter from Adorno to Horkheimer from June 8, 1935, which is absent from the fifth volume because it was made available only after the edition's publication, may well turn speculation into certainty. Adorno characterizes the first prospectus as "an attempt to unlock the nineteenth century as 'style' by means of the category of 'commodity as dialectical image'." He adds:

This concept owes as much to you as it is close to me (and as I have been beholden to it for many years). In that memorable conversation in the Hotel Carlton [in Frankfurt] which you, Benjamin, and I had about dialectical images, together with Asja Lacis and Gretel, it was you who claimed that feature of a historical image as central for the commodity; since that conversation both Benjamin's and my thoughts on this matter have been reorganized in a decisive way. The Kierkegaard book [by Adorno] contains their rudiments, the "Arcades" draft embraces them quite explicitly.

13. Karl Marx, *Capital,* vol. I, trans. Samuel Moore and Edward Aveling (New York: International Publishers, 1975), 72.

14. Marx, 73.

15. Cf. Jürgen Habermas, "Walter Benjamin: Consciousness-Raising or Rescuing Critique," this volume.

16. Cf. Tiedemann, *Studien,* 79–89.

17. Cf. Tiedemann, "Historical Materialism or Political Messianism?" in *The Philosophical Forum* 15, 1–2 (Fall–Winter 1983–84): 71–104.

18. Benjamin never brought himself to define these categories at length, and yet they are the basis of all his thoughts on the *Passagen-Werk,* which he identified with the "world of dialectical images" and for which the dialectic at a standstill was to be "the quintessence of method" (V:1035). He apparently developed the theory of dialectical images mainly in conversations with Adorno. Although both concepts are absent from Benjamin's publications during his lifetime, the "dialectical image" appears—with reference to its Benjaminian origins—in Adorno's *Habilitationsschrift* on Kierkegaard, which was published in 1933 (cf. Adorno, *Kierkegaard: Construction of the Aesthetic,* trans. Bob Hullot-Kentor [Minneapolis: University of Minnesota Press, 1988]). I shall here only allude to the fact that Adorno's interpretation of the concept differs from Benjamin's in more than mere nuances. In his Kierkegaard book, Adorno equated the dialectical image with allegory, and later he also seems to liken it to phantasmagoria (cf. N 5,2, and V:1136). Benjamin characterized Adorno's definition of the "antinomy of appearance and meaning" as "fundamental" for both allegory and phantasmagoria, but he found it "confusing" in its application to the "dialectical image" (I:1174). The difference might be found in the connection Benjamin made between the dialectical image and elements of messianism—a connection to which Adorno, the more scrupulous Marxist, could not accede. One may try to put it this way: the phantasmagorias of the arcade or the collector as such are not dialectical images in Benjamin's sense; both the arcades and the collector become dialectical images only when the historical materialist *deciphers* them *as* phantasmagorias. But in Benjamin's opinion the key that allows the historical materialist to unlock the code remains connected to the discovery of a messianic force in history (cf. I:1232).

19. Marx, 20.

20. Adorno, *Prisms,* 233.

21. Marx, 763.

22. Cf. Gershom Scholem, *Major Trends in Jewish Mysticism,* 3rd. ed. (London: Thames and Hudson, 1955), 283–87; and, *On the Kabbalah and Its Symbolism,* trans. Ralph Manheim (New York: Schocken, 1965), 126ff; cf. also Tiedemann, *Dialektik im Stillstand,* 102ff.

23. Marx, *Briefe aus den 'Deutsch-Französischen Jahrbüchern',* in Karl Marx/Friedrich Engels, *Werke,* Vol. I, 2nd ed. (Berlin: Dietz, 1957), 346.

Walter Benjamin's
Theory of Myth

Winfried Menninghaus

Winfried Menninghaus is the scholar who has furnished us with the most scrupulous account of Benjamin's views on language and their origins. In 1980 Menninghaus made his debut with a dissertation published as two books—the first on Benjamin's theory of Sprachmagie *(language's magic) and the second an interpretation of Paul Celan's poetry erected largely on this theory of language.* The book on Benjamin gave close readings of his three major theoretical essays on language and demonstrated their importance for a reading of Benjamin's two major literary-historical complexes—the* Trauerspiel *book and the studies on Baudelaire. When Menninghaus later received his* Habilitation *at the Institut für Allgemeine und Vergleichende Literaturwissenschaft (which Szondi had founded) of the Freie Universität Berlin with a monograph on the early Romantic grounding of art theory in the concept of absolute self-reflection, a central chapter of his* Habilitationsschrift *was on Benjamin's Romantic work.†*

The occasion for the paper published here was a conference in Paris, "Walter Benjamin et Paris," which followed the German publication of Benjamin's Passagen-Werk.‡ *Treating the arcades as acts as well as places, Menninghaus explores both temporal and spatial forms in Benjamin's experiences of "thresholds." Both forms are elements of Benjamin's concept of myth and produce a wealth of metaphors even where the term threshold does not explicitly occur. Menninghaus traces the semantic configurations between Benjamin's concept of myth and the concepts of beauty, language, freedom, and the tragic throughout Benjamin's works and also compares them with several other influential traditions of the interpretation of myth.*

"In the course of its history," according to Walter Benjamin, "philosophy is—and rightly so—a struggle for the representation of a limited number of words which always remain the same" (*Trauerspiel*, 37). Benjamin shared with the major philosophers he most often cited (Leibniz, Kant, and Hegel) a refusal to introduce new terminology as well as a preference for creating new contexts for older sets of concepts. The way in which Benjamin accomplished his terminological objectives separates him, however, from the "traditional" philosophers, since his terminological struggle engaged not only canonical philosophical words (such as truth, freedom, nature, appearance, being, beauty), but also terms of popular culture (such as fashion, commodities, *flâneur*), as well as conceptual reflections about more occult regions of experience (magic, intoxication, aura). The interpenetration of these sets of concepts determines the physiognomy of Benjamin's thought. One of its central motifs is given in a single term, *myth,* which belongs to all three realms: philosophy narrowly defined, the reflection of quotidian reality, and the reflection of "archaic" forms of thought and behavior now considered marginal. To reconstruct Benjamin's use of the term "myth" is to present a comprehensive portrait of his thought.

Seven Oppositions

Each new use of a concept entails an opposition with previous uses. An "external" comparison is often able to stipulate a strategic grid, which is essential for the immanent construction of a concept's meaning. Such polemical orientation points also become perceptible when we compare Benjamin's concept of myth with characteristic features of seven of the most noteworthy modern traditions of reflections about myth: the eighteenth-century *Enlightenment* concept of myth; the *Romantic* concept, which asserted itself against the Enlightenment concept from about 1795 onward and largely determined the nineteenth-century view of myth; mythical reflection in the *philosophy of religion,* such as Benjamin encountered it in Hermann Cohen; Sigmund Freud's *psychoanalytic* concept of myth; C. G. Jung's *deep-psychological* notion of myth as archetype; Aragon's *surrealistic* mythology; and the radically unhistorical, formal *semiological* concept of myth of twentieth-century structural anthropology.

The idea of a new mythology without its old content allowed the Romantics to formulate the beginnings of a theory of the general form of mythical signifying. The structuralist concept of myth severed such attempts (which it naturally drew less from Romantic semiology than from that of Saussure) from their historical-philosophical and poetological background and achieved an equivocation of myth and language: both essentially function according to a structuralist logic of oppositions, and both have at their disposal—less from their respective concrete contents than from their formal quality—an analogous life-structuring and/or life-interpreting ordering ability. This theory does not imply any particular phase of mythical development; on the contrary, its efficacy can be ascertained in analogous forms everywhere and at all times.

Even though Benjamin could not know of the mature structuralist concept of myth, the boundary between both concepts makes this implicit designation most appropriate. Benjamin dissociated himself from all definitions of myth that he viewed as indifferent to philosophy of history. In this regard his remarks on Nietzsche's and Cassirer's theories of myth simultaneously anticipate a critique of the formal universalism of the definition of myth in Lévi-Strauss. Viv-à-vis Nietzsche's theory of the tragic myth, Benjamin speaks of a dubious "aestheticism": Nietzsche's "purely aesthetic conception of myth," which leads to his "renunciation of its understanding . . . in historical-philosophical terms," is "a high price to pay" for its innovative, productive achievements in the context of Nietzsche's theory of tragedy, that is, tragedy's "emancipation" from ethos, from "the stereotype of a morality" (*Trauerspiel*, 102).

A conception of myth that exclusively stresses the difference between abstract, conceptual thought and myth's capacity to provide more concrete and figurative forms of sense and meaning is ultimately for Benjamin also a "purely aesthetic" and ahistorical view: "Some time ago I read Cassirer's *Begriffsform im mythischen Denken* with much interest. I still question, though, the practicability of an attempt to illuminate mythical thought . . . solely by contrast with the conceptual" (*Briefe*, 407). We may leave the question open, as we have in Nietzsche's case, whether or not this criticism does justice to Cassirer's theory of myth, particularly its elaborated form in the *Philosophy of Symbolic Forms*.[1] In any case, it provides clear indications of Benjamin's viewpoint: as many parallels as his definitions find in Cassirer's work, and as much as he himself, especially in the *Passagen-Werk*, links the theory of myth and its blasting apart to a theory of the image, these features (*Formcharaktere*) alone still did not suffice for a "profane illumination" of the mythical. This could only be accomplished in the realm of philosophy of history. We may ascertain Benjamin's view of the task of a philosophy of history of myth by examining his criticisms of Nietzsche and Cassirer: it must countermand the de-historicization of the concept of myth without simultaneously reverting to the one-sided evolutionary schema myth–religion–theoretical knowledge, a schema rooted in Cassirer, despite his structuralistic tendencies. Benjamin, in contrast to this evolutionary scheme, universalizes the concept of myth, insofar as he relates it to phenomena of the modern *Merkwelt*, the perceptual world. Reduced to a formula: Benjamin wants to appropriate the universalizing capacity of a purely formal conception of myth, to the extent it is compatible with a specific historical-philosophical orientation, which sharply separates him from structuralists, especially Lévi-Strauss.

The Romantic concept of myth differs from the hitherto mentioned forms of the concept's universalization by possessing the element Benjamin found lacking in the others: the embeddedness of its formal theoretical considerations in a historical-philosophical horizon. This makes it all the more surprising, then, especially in view of his extensive, largely positive reception of Romantic theories of art and language, that Benjamin's concept of myth probably most clearly dissociates itself from the Romantic concept. The Romantic concept of myth first of all occurs in reflections on the history of poetry: modern art's confounding chaos and detachment, freed from all confining genres, was attributed to the lack of a collective foundation (which the Romantics considered necessary for poetical freedom) such as that given to Greek art in ancient mythology. This demand for a collective image-character and meaningfulness of the (poetic) cosmos derives not least from an analogous experience and critique of social relations: traditional mythical and religious world views were dissolved equally through the Enlightenment as the feudal class barriers increasingly receded behind the "freedom" and "equality" of the bourgeois economy; the enlightened world of free merchants, wage-laborers, and capitalists was no longer able, however, to shape a new cosmos of meaningful images and ideas that were as generally respected as those of myth and religion. To be able to read in this the currently notorious "crisis of meaning" hardly requires a divinatory critique. Manfred Frank represented the Romantic idea of a "new mythology" and the forms of the contemporary "search for meaning" as esoteric and exoteric forms of the same problem: as answers to the increasing brittleness or even absence of stable, binding horizons of justification or legitimation.[2] Against this background (in contrast to the modern "crisis of meaning"), the myth as form is attributed a genuine synthetic potential, the ability to endow with meaning (*Sinnstiftung*).[3]

Countering an Enlightenment that understood myth—whether as a pre-scientific explanation of nature, as a (hindering rather than revealing) disguise of timeless truth, or as a mere delusion—in all cases as a wholly superfluous form of thought with respect to the "light of reason," the Romantics restored to myth an autonomous, irreducible *Objektivationsleistung*, its ability to objectify. Benjamin's relationship to the Romantic conception of myth takes itself the form of a "dialectic of Enlightenment." If the leitmotif of Enlightenment reflection about myth is that of dissolution and displacement, and if the Romantics by contrast call for a restitution of myth (directed toward the future rather than toward the past), then in the utopian horizon of Benjamin's reflections on myth stands the motif of its *Sprengung*, its blasting apart. Far be it from Benjamin to wager on the "stabilizing and consoling function of myth"[4] in times of crisis of social legitimization; violence and delusion remain integral parts of this concept of myth throughout his early and late works. But does this imply a regression to an Enlightenment position?

The following considerations may place Benjamin's almost polemical anti-reception of the Romantic concept of myth in the context of the history of ideas. Whereas the Romantic apologia of myth opposed itself to the Enlightenment's rationalistic negation of myth, there was no comparable polemical context for Benjamin. He had to deal, rather, with the "depraved" forms of the Romantic conception he encountered in politics and theory. The Romantics' originally critical, progressive intentions had changed into their opposite. The restitution of mythology had become the province of political reaction and of irrationalism. Whether or not the false heirs of the Romantic concept of myth hindered understanding of its "original" essence, Benjamin had every reason to resort to the traditional "arms" of the Enlightenment in his struggle with these concepts and to demarcate his concept of myth against its pseudo- or post-Romantic resurrections rather than against its decayed Enlightenment form. Our search in Benjamin's works for its more primitive forms is to no avail. This is consistent with his thesis of the "uncriticizability of the inferior" (I:78), which dissuades even a disapproving critical mention of what is beneath a dignified notice. Nevertheless, he wants to define his theory of collective dream images, which is central to his concept of myth in the *Passagen-Werk,* against the reactionary, mythologizing features of the comparable theories in Klages and Jung (I:1157). Yet Benjamin even criticizes the model for his *Passagen-Werk,* Aragon's mythology of the "Passage de l'Opéra," in Enlightenment terms, so to speak: surrealist mythology, according to Benjamin, puts things at a distance, transports them to the realm of dream, and leaves them there; by contrast, materialistic mythology illuminates the realm of dreams—the collective *Bildphantasie* or image-making capacity—in order to bring us to the verge (*Schwelle*) of awakening. Its aim is to sharpen our eye for "the Next," for the time and space of each present history (N 1,9; V:998).

Is Benjamin, then, even though the most caustic critic imaginable of Enlightenment beliefs in reason and progress, its advocate with respect to the theory of myth? The following note from the *Passagen-Werk* sounds like an Enlightenment call-to-arms:

To clear fields, where until now only delusion (*Wahnsinn*) ran rampant. Forge ahead with the whetted ax of reason, looking neither left nor right, in order not to fall victim to the horror beckoning from the depths of the primeval (*Ur-*)forest. At a certain point, reason must clear the entire ground and rid it of the underbrush of delusion and myth. Such is the goal here for the nineteenth century. (N 1,4)

The ax of reason in battle against the "primeval forest" of entangled and underdifferentiated "underbrush of delusion and myth": this is so similar, even in its metaphors, to a passage from Benjamin's *Elective Affinities* essay, that the formulation in the *Passagen-Werk* is a kind of self-quotation. Benjamin's vehement critique of Gundolf's attempt "to present Goethe's life as a mythical one" (I:158) culminates in this locution:

No attitude of mind is more disastrous than that mentality which bewilderingly turns back to myth even having begun to outgrow it and which indeed, through the accompanying forced immersion into the monstrous, would have warned every intelligence unwilling to stay in the tropical wilderness, in a primeval forest where words swing like chattering apes from bombast to bombast, avoiding at all costs the ground which would disclose their inability to stand—for this is the Logos, where they should stand and give an account of themselves. (I:163)

The juxtaposition of reason and truth with myth seems to wholly comply with the canon of Enlightenment reflection. Yet it is precisely here that we can measure the extent to which Benjamin—in the guise of Enlightenment terms and tropes—departs from their theoretical foundation. Benjamin's rejection of "the identification of truth and myth," which he regards as a key assumption of Gundolf's book on Goethe (I:162), holds true for all Romantic resurrections of "myth" that attribute to it a truth beyond reason, or even just an ultimate grounding of meaning. By contrast, however, the Enlightenment saw in myth in part direct falsehoods, in part corrupted truths—or those still obscured by ignorance. Benjamin's definition of "the relation of truth and myth" as "that of mutual exclusion" (I:162) is contrary to both of these. Its point is hardly the Enlightenment critique that the truth of myth is absent or only partial, but instead the claim of myth's wholly "indifferent attitude toward truth"—that they have nothing to do with each other, neither in a negative nor an affirmative respect. As a consequence, the concept of truth has to be set aside rather than used as a standard if we wish to arrive at a satisfactory concept of myth.

While the Enlightenment, by confronting myth with an abstract concept of theoretical truth, failed to realize any genuine form and function of myth, Benjamin refuses to reduce myth to either a form of truth or of falsehood, and thus rescues the autonomous dimension of myth. This productive separation of terms often related to one another is obstructed somewhat by Benjamin's retention of the Enlightenment, as well as religious-philosophical, hierarchization of the realms of myth and truth (religion); the cognition of myth's "indifference" to truth remained fixed to a vertical schema of evaluative classification. Although later Benjamin would disclaim comparable hierarchical classifications of the "mutually exclusive" domains of myth and truth, he nevertheless retains an analogous interpretative structure by virtue of his systematic reference of the mythology of technical and cultural objects (the *Dingwelt* or "thing-world") to the category of fetishism. He accomplishes this, however, only at the cost of unambiguousness: just as fetishism and ideology in Marx are an amalgam of the false and the true, Benjamin also recognizes a duality of "utopian" and "cynical" elements in the mythological image and dream worlds (V:51). The clear hierarchy of myth and truth is at least upset; and therein persists another of myth's essential characteristics, from the *Elective Affinities* essay through the *Passagen-Werk*: "ambiguity" (V:55). What Benjamin defers is less the phenomenal description of myth than the evaluative accent, which is attributed to it. Benjamin's formulation in the *Elective Affinities* essay is negative ("no unequivocal clarity in myth," *keine Eindeutigkeit*, I:162), whereas in the *Passagen-Werk* he speaks of the more positive term, "ambiguity" (*Zweideutigkeit*, V:55).

Benjamin's critique of the "identification of truth and myth" thus attempts to transcend analogous Enlightenment arguments while employing the same terms. This presents us with a general formula of the relation between Benjamin's and the Enlightenment's concepts of myth: though Benjamin adopts *topoi* of Enlightenment argumentation, especially in his dissociation from pseudo-Romantic affirmations of myth, he does not resort to their content.

I will now consider Benjamin's understanding of the concept of myth in the philosophy of religion, such as he encountered it in the writings of Hermann Cohen. This variant of reflection about myth—in the motif of the blasting apart of myth—converges more than just formally with the rationalistic, Enlightenment critique of myth; indeed it was already one of its theological variants. In Benjamin's essay on the *Elective Affinities,* the Enlightenment opposition (even in its rhetorical tropes) of logos and truth on the one hand, myth on the other, sometimes becomes a theological opposition because Benjamin attributes a theological character to logos and truth. That is precisely Cohen's thinking: to liberate thought "from the entanglement with myth" from the perspective of monotheistic revelatory religion—or, better yet, to make way for it.[5] Above all, Benjamin's early contraposition of divine power and mythical violence is nourished by such a critique of "myth" *sub specie* religion. In his later writings, God and religion gradually lose their prominence as critical antipodes of myth. They are already relativized by the affinity to Enlightenment argumentation in "Goethe's *Elective Affinities,*" and by the time Benjamin is composing his *Passagen-Werk,* they have been fully worn out as a medium of contrast. Nevertheless, theological concepts, at least, remain on the horizon of the blasting apart of myth: redemption and the messianic realm. Whether we interpret that "merely" metaphorically or not, there is in any case a strict line of demarcation between Benjamin's and Cohen's concepts of myth. Cohen's notion, just as the religious-philosophical concept, emphasizes exclusively the negative. Benjamin's "dialectic" of blasting apart *and* redeeming is radically unfamiliar to Cohen's as well as to the Enlightenment notion.

We can also consider Sigmund Freud's *psychoanalytic* interpretation of myth as a variant of Enlightenment reflection about myth. Both strive to present a theory of myth's origin: the latter from structures of phantasmagorical (mis)understanding of human intellectual faculties, the former from a logic of displacement and condensation in the human soul. Both reductively interpret myth *as* myth: myth is derived from something that is not in itself mythical; it is transcended to another reality of which it is supposed to be the mere representation. The affinity as well as the distance between the Freudian and Benjaminian concepts of myth may be determined by considering two paradigms. The first is the correlation of myth, guilt, and fate, which equally stamp Benjamin's early concept of myth and Freud's interpretation of Oedipal "parricide."[6] The line separating their theories is clear: whereas Benjamin interprets the mythical entanglement in a supra-individual context of fate, guilt, and expiation primarily in terms of the philosophy of history—as a socially coercive relation, a sort of "second nature," which is to be broken apart by the intervention of moral action as the form of freedom's realization—Freud sees "the sense of guilt" and the "compulsion by a destiny that is alien to him" as psychological projections of unconscious motives.[7] Above all, however, what Freud merely extrapolates from the interpretation of the *specific content* of the Oedipus myth, Benjamin regards as a *universal* element of myth's form.

A second paradigm of affinity and distance is Freud's analogy between myth and dream, which Benjamin adopts in the *Passagen-Werk*. For Freud as well as Benjamin, the analogy rests on two points: both myth and dream proceed according to similar principles of form, and both evince an especially "deep" expressive character. Just as the psychoanalyst seeks a privileged entrance to the unconscious, by reading the dream rebus, Benjamin searches for the determining forces of an epoch in the physiognomy of "its side facing the dreams" (V:490):

The economic conditions of society's existence achieves expression in the superstructure; just like the sleeping person's overstuffed stomach finds in the contents of his dreams, although they may causally "determine" it, not its reflection, rather than its expression. (V:495)

Just as Freud does for the dream rebus, Benjamin imputes "expressive character [to] the earliest industrial products, the earliest industrial structures, the earliest machines, as well as the earliest department stores, advertisements, etc." (V:574). The task of "interpret[ing] the nineteenth century in fashion and advertising, buildings and politics, as the consequence of its dreamlike visions" (V:492) emerged from this amalgam of theory of myth and Marxist adoption of the psychoanalytic concept of dream. That is why Benjamin asserts—referring to the arcades as well as "winter gardens, panoramas, factories, wax figure cabinets, casinos, and railway stations" (V:511)—that "in order to understand their essence, we submerge them into the deepest layer of dream" (V:1009). Benjamin differs from Freud, however, on the issue of what is to be sought and found in this dream layer: the latter searches for explanations of the patient's inner life or for universal laws of individual dream work, whereas the former seeks the physiognomy of the material culture of an epoch—the collective's concrete dream images. Benjamin explicitly drew this line: he wished to "translate" psychoanalytic findings "from the individual to the collective" (V:1012), so that he is "more on the track of things than of the soul" (V:281). (The representation of the *Dingwelt*, however, is *ipso facto* a representation of social relations, without being reducible to the Marxist doctrine of reification.)

Benjamin's criterion of opposition to the psychoanalytic concept of dream—"dreaming collective" (V:1012) versus dreaming individuum—seems to neglect Freud's own remarks about myth and dream. For Freud as well, only those dreams that form a collective tradition could be called myths; in this sense, he characterized myths as "distorted residues of the wishful fantasies of entire nations."[8] The plot of the Oedipus tragedy, moreover, even represents "sweeping and universally valid efficaciousness." What legitimizes Benjamin's contrast, nevertheless, is that Freud does not see any genuine collective content in myth. Freud predicates validity for all single individuals by means of and based on a schema extrapolated from the individual psychological level. This has as little to do with a concrete historical concept of specific collectives as does C. G. Jung's "deep-psychological" metaphysics of collective unconscious archetypes. Benjamin intended to distance himself from Jung as well as from Freud, but his "dispute with Jungian doctrine, especially that of the archaic images and the collective unconscious" (V:1161) remained unwritten. His implicit opposition to Jung's concept of myth, however, is unmistakable: whereas Jung perceives myths as collective dream images, suprahistorical archetypes of human existence absolute, Benjamin is concerned with the specific *historical* signature of collective image and thing worlds. (The theoretical groundwork of Benjamin's discussion of a dreaming collective, unfortunately, is deficient.)

Benjamin directs his theorem of the "dissolution of 'mythology' in the space of history" (N 1,9) not only at Jung, but also to a polemical addressee, whose approach to myth is antithetical to Jung's approach: surrealism. Aragon is not in the least interested in a metaphysical and collective validity of myth; he tends to separate myth from any claim of collective validity. In Aragon's works, "the mythical functions to found and legitimate a collective world of binding values survive, if not wholly cut off, then only as a vacant space which cannot be occupied at the present. The mythical is individualized to the experience of images by single persons."[9] Benjamin's mythology of the arcades is nevertheless first and foremost beholden *in concreto* to the surrealistic approach to the thing world. He appropriates less the surrealist's theory than their praxis of *mythologie moderne*—though only as a single element that is integrated into a thoroughly divergent theoretical concept. The border between this concept of mythology and Benjamin's concept is drawn not only by Benjamin's retention of a collective subject of mythology, but equally in the instrumentalization of dream images: for Benjamin the realm of dreams is not an end in itself but is charged with a "teleological moment. This moment is that of waiting. The dream clandestinely waits for the awakening" (V:492). The surrealist's mythology, by comparison, lacks this (historical-philosophical) function as an organon: it "persistently remains in the realm of dreams" (N 1,9).

Space in Myth: Science of Thresholds

All theories of myth concur that mythical objects and phenomena can acquire a significance that transcends the scientific view of these objects and phenomena. This has less to do with a subsequent "animation" or "enlivening" of things than with the construction of a space of living and perceiving *before,* that is, *beyond* the sharp differentiation between inside and outside, self and world, life and death. Benjamin himself speaks (somewhat unfortunately) of a mythical "life of seemingly dead things" (I:139). The "real" world, in myth, is at the same time an interpreted world, a world of symbols, and in fact throughout the realms of nature and culture. In his interpretation of Goethe's

Elective Affinities, Benjamin above all sheds light on the mythical signifying power of natural phenomena: in the function of the landscape, the magnetism, the lakes, and even the wind for the novel's events (I:132f.). Besides this exception, which occurs in interpreting a poetic work, Benjamin's interest in the mythical fundamentally turns away from *nature.* He discusses myth in the highly developed civilization in terms of *language,* on the one hand (more on this later), and in terms of a physiognomic significance of respective *technische Dingwelten,* on the other. It is the ever more rapid change of technical perceptual worlds (*Merkwelten*) that reveals the mythical image character of each single one that much more clearly (N 2a,2). The ontogenetic recurrence of myth in the child's conquest and interpretation of new experiential domains serves for Benjamin as only *one* paradigm of the permanent transformation of social thing worlds, which had seemed restricted to their purposive facticity, into meaningful images (V:576). "That correspondences are at work between the modern technical world and the archaic symbol world" (V:576) is a reflection fundamental to the entire *Passagen-Werk.* Its more precise formulation resulted from the obviously predominant role architecture plays for the "sensual-supersensual" image of social life: "Architecture is the most important witness of latent mythology. And the most significant architecture of the nineteenth century is the arcade" (V:1002).

Through his orientation toward buildings and architecture as the prime *contents* of modern mythology, Benjamin particularly reactivates one element of myth as *form:* the construction of a significant arrangement of space. According to Cassirer, the mythical space is "as closely related to the perceptual space as, on the other side, it is rigorously separated from the conceptual space of geometry."[10] Objects inform their location in space with a meaningful "accent," and, conversely, the spatial arrangement influences the apprehension of the things it contains. In his *Elective Affinities* essay, Benjamin had already reconstructed such a mythical topography, not only of nature, but also of buildings and of the cultural "landscape." This becomes programmatical is his *Passagen-Werk:* "Kinship of myth and topography. Aragon and Pausanias. (Also include Balzac.)" (V:1031). Aragon explicitly conceived his "mythology" of the "Passage de l'Opéra" as a "metaphysics of places,"[11] and Benjamin spoke of Balzac and Pausanias in a note for the *Passagen-Werk* (V:134):

> Balzac secured the mythical condition of his world through its particular topographical contours. Paris is the soil of his mythology—Paris with its two, three great bankers (Nucingen, du Tillet), Paris with its great doctor Horace Bianchon, with its entrepreneur César Birotteau, with its four or five great coquettes, with its usurer Gobseck, with its several advocates and military. Above all, however, it is always the same streets and recesses, chambers and corners, from which the figures of this circle step into the light. What does that signify other than that the topography is the outline of this, as every, mythical space of tradition, even becoming the key, as Pausanias became for Greece, as the history and location of the Paris arcades would become for the century of an underworld into which Paris sank.

In the framework of a mythical topography of borders and transitional areas, Benjamin attributes a prominent significance to the gestalt of the Between, the threshold. Cassirer introduced the mythical concept of the threshold in this manner:

> A primordial mythical-religious feeling is linked with the fact of the spatial "threshold." Men's veneration of the threshold and awe of its sanctity are expressed almost everywhere in similar usages. Even among the Romans Terminus was a special god, and at the festival of the Terminalia the boundary stone itself was crowned with a garland and sprinkled with the blood of a sacrificial beast. From the veneration of the temple threshold, which spatially separates the house of the god from the profane world, the fundamental juridical-religious concept of property seems to have developed along similar lines in totally different cultural spheres. Just as it originally protected the house of the god, the sanctity of the threshold (in the form of land markings) safeguarded house and fields against hostile trespass and attack. (Cassirer, 103)

We can already read Benjamin's *Elective Affinities* essay as a kind of *Schwellenkunde,* a science or connoisseurship of thresholds (V:147). The essay treats the mythical forces which emerge from the violated threshold of matrimonial law and which in turn manifest themselves in a cosmos of ambiguous thresholds: spatial thresholds such as the lake's surface thought of as the border between the upper and nether worlds (I:133); or the cemetery, whose grounds are violated, and then restituted, by the death of the violator (V:132); and temporal thresholds such as the rites of passage from one year to the next, or from one qualitative situation to another (the birthday, the laying of a cornerstone, the roofing ceremony). We can read not only Benjamin's *Elective Affinities* essay, but most of his literary-critical works as a "science of thresholds." Benjamin himself left undisguised traces of this more than once. In his "Surrealism" essay he writes of the "threshold between waking and sleeping," which "was worn away" in Breton and Aragon (*One-Way Street*, 226), and in his portrait of Proust "we are guests who cross a threshold beneath a swaying sign, a threshold behind which eternity and rapture (*Rausch*) await us" (*Illuminations*, 212). In his portrayal of Karl Kraus, oddly enough, Benjamin locates his "object" in "the landscape of Austria, which fills unbroken (*schwellenlos*) the captivating expanse of Stifter's prose" (*One-Way Street*, 264). In this thresholdless landscape, Kraus constructs or reveals several kinds of thresholds: the "threshold" of one's own "private existence" (*One-Way Street*, 266); "the threshold between dying and rebirth . . . joy and soul, but also language and Eros, also rhyme and name" (*One-Way Street*, 285); and, finally, "the threshold of the Last Judgment" (*One-Way Street*, 271). Benjamin explicitly anticipated his *Schwellenkunde* of the Parisian metropolitan landscape in the *Berliner Kindheit* (cf. Menninghaus, *Schwellenkunde*, 33–43) and the 1929 review of Franz Hessel's *Spazieren in Berlin*. From the review's title alone—"The Return of the *Flâneur*"—we can identify its affinity to the thematic coterie in the *Passagen-Werk*. The following passages on the "*rites de passage*" and "thresholds" might have been taken from the *Passagen-Werk* itself:

Paris created the *typus* of the *flâneur*. That it wasn't Rome is the wonderful thing about this. Yet in Rome, does not even dreaming move through streets that are far too prefigured? And isn't the city too full of temples, enclosed *piazzas*, national shrines, in order to enter the dreams of the passerby, undivided in itself with every cobblestone, every shop sign, every step, and every gateway? The grand reminiscences, the historical shudder, are even rubbish to the *flâneur*, who gladly relinquishes them to the traveler. And he gives away all of his knowledge about artist's lodgings, birthplaces, or royal domiciles, for the scent of a single threshold or for the tactile sensation of a single tile, as any house dog carries it away. Further reasons may be found in the character of the Romans. For it is the Parisians—and not the strangers—who have made Paris the promised land of the *flâneur*, the "landscapes formed of sheer life," as Hofmannsthal once characterized it. Landscape—Paris becomes that in the act of sauntering (*flânerie*). Or more precisely: the city comes apart in its dialectical poles for the *flâneur*. It opens itself up to him as landscape, it encloses him as a parlor. (III:195)

Beneath the *plebs deorum* of the caryatids and atlantes, the Pomonas and putti, with whose discovery he receives the reader, are his favorite figures, those at one time ruling, now having become penates, unseeming Gods of private thresholds, who are the guardians of the *rites de passage*, dusty on stairway landings, namelessly quartered in corridors; who once accompanied every step across a wooden or metaphorical threshold. He cannot break free from them and he still feels the breath of their presence, where their likenesses have long since disappeared or become unrecognizable. Berlin has few gateways, but this great threshold connoisseur knows the minor crossings which contrast city against lowland, and one quarter of the city against the other: construction sites, bridges, city railroad loops, and city squares. They are all honored and respected here, not to speak of the thresholds within certain hours, the sacred twelve minutes or seconds of the meager life, which corresponds to the macrocosmic "twelve nights" and at first glance can seem so portentous. "Friedrichstadt's *thés dansants*," as the author knows, "have their most edifying hour when nearing twilight, the *danseuse*, next to the still-packed instruments, has a bite to eat while conversing with the cloakroom girl or the waiter (III:197).

Two years prior to these sentences, Benjamin had already authored a brief sketch entitled "Passagen." Even during this initial stage of his project, when Benjamin still planned to collaborate with Franz Hessel on a journal article (V:1341), we encounter spatial forms of the threshold: "thresholds of sandstone," "the inscriptions and signs on the entrance gates (one can just as well say exit gates)," "mosaic thresholds in the style of the Palais Royal's old restaurants," for example (cf. V:1041).

Analogous to the constellation of *passage*, threshold, and gate, Benjamin displays the concept of threshold in various folios of the subsequent *Passagen-Werk*, especially with reference to the city gates and triumphal arcs. He cites a work by Ferdinand Noack, according to which for the Romans, in the context of doors and arches, "a sacrally understood concept such as border or threshold was effective everywhere" (V:157). Furthermore:

> Marching through the triumphal arch as a rite of passage: "the marching through of the military, pressing through narrow gateways *en masse,* is compared to the 'pushing through a narrow opening', to which one has attributed the meaning of a rebirth." Ferdinand Noack: *Triumph und Triumphbogen* (Vorträge der Bibliothek Warburg V Lpz 1928 p 153). (V:151f.; cf. also V:521f., 139)

Benjamin's "science of thresholds" (V:147) attains a genuinely modern significance by its application to the nineteenth century:

> These gates, the entrances to the *Passagen,* are thresholds. No stone step marks them. Only the tarrying of a few people does so. Sparingly measured steps reflect, unconsciously, that a decision is about to be made. (V:142)

> A mailbox in front of the arcade's entrance: a last chance to signal the world one is leaving. (V:141)

> The doorbell's despotic terror, which holds sway over the household, draws its power from the magic of the threshold as well. With its piercing announcement, something is ready to cross over the threshold. (V:141)

The arcana of Benjamin's "science of thresholds" are the arcades themselves, the "*Passagen* myth" (V:516f., 995). The French terminus for the rites of crossing over thresholds, "rites de passage" (V:617), marks the relation between *passage* as arcade, and threshold. The arcade is a threshold, which—as a transitional zone between the street and the individual shops—displays a "phantasmagoria" of goods, not via theoretical ideology but in their "immediate presence" (V:1256). And on this arcade as threshold Benjamin himself undertakes a dual rite of passage: he wants to lead sensuously present "dream images" to the "threshold of awakening" by constructing a rite of passage with quotations extracted from the cultural history of the nineteenth century. His work is *Passage* in three senses: in its historical-philosophical intention, in its scientific form (resembling a *rite de passage*), and as the principal subject of his latest major work. Resorting to the terminology of Benjamin's philosophy of language, the word *Passage* thereby becomes a "symbolic" word in the context of his "science of thresholds": a *name*—exactly as it was demanded and realized for the term *"Trauerspiel"* in his baroque book (*Trauerspiel*, 36f.). In the following excerpt, Benjamin most clearly articulates the configuration of mythology, rites of passage, and *Schwellenkunde*, in the name and image of the *Passage*:

> In ancient Greece one could show places where one descended into the nether world. Our waking existence is likewise a terrain in which places are concealed leading to the underworld, inconspicuous places where dreams flow to the surface. During the day we pass them by, unsuspectingly, but sleep hardly arrives and we swiftly feel our way back to them, losing our way in their dark passages. In daylight, the city's labyrinth of houses resembles consciousness; the *Passagen* (being the galleries, which lead into its past existence) flow unnoticed into the streets during the day. At night beneath the dark masses of houses, however, its more condensed darkness alarmingly leaps out; and the late passerby hastens by it, unless it happens that we have encouraged him to the trip through the narrow passageway. (V:1046)

Can Benjamin's work be plausibly construed as a multifarious "study of thresholds"? What predetermines the threshold's spatial and temporal forms to become a prototypical subject of Benjamin's thought? I wish to propose two conjectural answers to this question. The first concerns philosophy of history. Benjamin differs from the customary triadic orientation of philosophical concepts of history, which—between lost and rediscovered paradise, between happy primordial state and utopia—recognizes a long period of negativity, in which at some point a gradual progress toward a better period commences, by strictly rejecting mere "periods of decline" (N 1,6) and by asserting the virtually permanent possibility of a revolutionary "tiger's leap" (*Illuminations*, 263) into the past or into the future. The messianic is always one mere step away, so to speak: "Every second of time," wrote Benjamin about a conception of time anchored in Jewish theology, is "the strait gate through which the Messiah might enter" (*Illuminations*, 266). This formulation, of the step through a narrow gate, unequivocally satisfies the *Passagen-Werk*'s paradigm of the transfiguring crossing of a threshold, the mythical rite of passage. Hence we might argue: Benjamin regards every time and every space as a *potential* threshold, one step away (indeed a decisive step) from the messianic kingdom—just as at the verge of awakening sleep and wakefulness are contiguous, or at the threshold of the temple the domains of the profane and of the holy closely touch one another. The threshold's form as a temporally or spatially nonextended gestalt of betweenness corresponds, then, with Benjamin's particular conception of the triad of philosophy of history.

This corresponds equally to Benjamin's conception of a medium, a mediating betweenness, which he ultimately grounds in his philosophy of language. Benjamin's point, namely, is that a medium is not merely a space of instrumental mediation between existent extremes—for example, the mediation of a nonverbally conceived "content" between two speakers. He would argue that, what is more, the medium first *produces* what it seemingly "mediates." Benjamin formulated these thoughts most articulately in his theory of the medium of reflection in the thought of Schlegel and Novalis. The movement between a reflecting pole and a reflected pole first creates, constitutes, according to this theory, that which seems only retrospectively reflecting or moving back and forth (I:37, 63, 65). In the Romantics' own words, the movement between apparently preexisting extremes "produces the extremes, between which the movement of suspension takes place."[12] By way of analogy we might ask whether it is the temple's threshold that first "creates" the regions of the profane and the holy, whether the verge of awakening (or falling asleep) makes sleeping and waking what they are, and whether or not the rites of passage constitute that between which they are the passage. It is at least consistent with Benjamin's "mediumistic" philosophy that forms of betweenness undergo a certain upward valuation and advance from mere mediation components to producers of the mediated. Herein also presumably abides one incentive for Benjamin's remarkable interest in *Schwellenkunde*.

Mythical and Anti-mythical Language

The mythological topography of Paris has another object besides its arcades and the arrangement of its *quartiers*, streets, and catacombs: their *names*. One motive for Benjamin's interest in the names of streets, etc., can be found in his (anti-)-hermeneutical thesis that the truth-content of an artwork emerges to the same degree that its material content disappears (I:125f.) In the later terminology of the *Passagen-Werk*: the mythological image-character of a configuration of cultural objects first merges through their displacement by the next configuration (or "thing world"). Where the sole relics of the objects are often their names, they become the springboard of physiognomic interpolation. On Benjamin's view, all that remains given of the increasingly swift dissipation of perceptual worlds is "nothing other than their names: *Passagen*, and: *Passage du Panorama*. The forces of subversion work deep within these names, which is why we maintain a world in the names of the old streets" (V:1001). In addition to the more hermeneutical motive, a second, cognitive motive for the orientation toward names appears and even provides grounds for the first: whether or not the "named" perishes, the names constitute a domain of mythical significance on par with that of images. Under the sign of topography, Benjamin's interest in this world's mythical image-character coincides with his preoccupation with language's mythical character:

What before was restricted to very few words, to a privileged class of words, the city has rendered possible for all, or for at least a great number of them: to be elevated to the nobility of names. This revolution of language was effected by what is most common: the street—the city has become a cosmos of language through the names of its streets. (V:650)

Benjamin dedicates nearly ten pages of the *Passagen-Werk* to the mythical "expressive character of street names" (V:647) as "intoxicating substances that enrich our perceptions by spheres and categories" (V:645). The street names are followed by company names:

Surrealist poetry treats words like company names and their texts are basically brochures of enterprises not yet in business. Today's fantasies nest deep within the names of companies, whereas in former times these fantasies were believed to be hoarded in the vocabulary of "poetic" words.

As was the case with Benjamin's mythical concept of space, his "charging" of the concept of language shares features of Cassirer's theory of myth. Cassirer speaks of a mythical "concrescence of name and thing (*Sache*)," of a nonseparatedness of "material aspect" (*Dingmoment*) and the "signifying aspect" (*Bedeutungsmoment*).[13] Cassirer has been criticized, however, precisely with reference to such definitions, for blurring the boundary between magic and myth. According to this criticism, only in magic is there an immediate and substantial participation of (especially ritual) language with the essence of "mana"; myth, by comparison, tends to distance itself from magical forms of immediate (direct) participation by developing more complex, mediated, and structural orders of world and language.[14] Of the moment of an "immediate" expression of meaning in a language, Benjamin spoke invariably of its "magic" (I:142f., 208) and never of its mythical character. Despite this, his theory of myth and his theory of language's magic (*Sprachmagie*) correspond in many of their features. The distinction between two basic forms of language's magic—the "concrete" magic of name and symbol, and the "abstract" magic of word and allegory (I:153f.)—closely relates to the polarity of myth and its *Sprengung*, which Benjamin relates to different forms of artistic language as well. This can be ascertained from a careful analysis of Benjamin's use of terms in both his early and late works on language and literature.

By way of contrast to Benjamin's conceptual "grammar" of magic, myth, symbol, and allegory, Friedrich Creuzer's canonical *Symbolik und Mythologie der alten Völker* serves as an appropriate foil.[15] Benjamin already grappled with this work's "important theoretical expositions" explicitly in his baroque book (*Trauerspiel*, 163–68) and implicitly in other reflections. He criticized "the banal older doctrine that survives" in Creuzer's works, due to a distinction between symbol as being-in-itself (presence) and allegory as a standing for something else (representation).[16] Creuzer provided two theoretical innovations, however, one of which Benjamin appropriated for his own purposes and the other of which he turned into its direct contrary: (1) his determination of the different temporal structures in symbol and in allegory, as well as (2) the correlation of these concepts to the spheres of mysticism (magic) and the plastic arts on the one hand, and of myth and epos on the other. For both Creuzer[17] and Benjamin the symbol's temporal form is "momentary totality"; the temporal form of allegory is "progression in a series of moments" (*Trauerspiel*, 165) or, to use another term, "history." Creuzer attributes momentary (instantaneous) totality to the symbol in the plastic arts, and particularly to the "mystical," the *pre*-mythological symbol.[18] In this symbolic form of time, the sacred is immediately, and yet unfathomably, present. For Creuzer myth, by comparison, differentiates and mediates the opaque density of mystical symbols into manifold and well-distinguished elements, such as gods, demigods, heroes, and their stories. Myth, emerging from the exegesis of "mystical symbols," divides their momentary totality into "series of moments" and thereby takes on the allegorical form.

Although Benjamin agreed with Creuzer about the temporal structures in symbol and allegory, he rejected the theory that the form of myth is allegory and that both derive from the unfolding of pre-mythical symbols. He undertook to establish the opposite association: symbol relates to both magic and myth, whereas allegory figures in the blasting apart of myth. The correlation between myth and symbol reveals Benjamin's use of metaphors, as well: just as in his *Elective Affinities* essay he criticizes the world of myth, confronting it with the distinct orders of rational comprehension (*Verstand*), as an underdifferentiated "primeval forest" (I:563; N 1,4); and as he later analogously cited Baudelaire's "forêts de symboles" (I:638), Benjamin speaks in his *Trauerspiel* book, in reference to Görres, of an unfathomable "and if one might say so, forest-like interior" of the symbol (165). In "Goethes *Wahlverwandtschaften*," he saw his thesis of a mythical world of the novel proven by the "*symbolism* of death" (I:135, 137; my italics). And in the *Passagen-Werk*, he tersely refers to the world as a "symbol world" (N 2a,1; cf. V:218, 493). Benjamin, like Cassirer, saw no reason for a clear-cut, semiotic distinction between magical and mythical symbolism; both were taken as similar in their contrast to conceptual (and allegorical) thinking, in their merging of being and signifying, and in their capacity to produce or incorporate sensuous totality. With respect to this, allegory becomes myth's direct antagonist (utterly antithetical to Creuzer's view) in its correlation to a sharp distance between image and meaning and through the dispersion of every appearance of totality (*Trauerspiel,* 177ff.):

The antithesis between allegory and myth should be clearly developed. Baudelaire owes it to the genius of allegory that he did not fall victim to the abyss of myth, which accompanied him along the way. (V:344)

The antidote to myth is to be demonstrated in allegory. Myth was the easy path, which Baudelaire forbade himself. A poem such as *La vie antérieuré,* whose title suggests every compromission, shows just how remote Baudelaire was from myth. (I:677)

In this way, the field of tension between myth and anti-myth— for Adorno *the* field of tension in Benjamin's thought[19]— reverberates to the decisive poles of Benjamin's philosophy of language. What Benjamin's early essay on language abstractly introduced (concrete and abstract linguistic elements, name and word, symbol and allegory), and what the subsequent essays on literature divided into the analysis of differing poles (myth and symbolism in the *Elective Affinities* essay versus anti-mythical allegory in the *Trauerspiel* book),[20] are finally reunited on an advanced level in the *Passagen-Werk*: this work deals with both the mythical symbolism of technical thing worlds and street names *and* with the anti-mythical allegory in Baudelaire's poetry. And precisely this dialectic of the afterlife of mythical and anti-mythical motifs in the field of linguistic theory confirms Adorno's suggestion that Benjamin's intentions were not realized in the mere destruction of myth, but in its reconciling redemption.[21]

The characters of linguistic thought and mythical thought converge in their concrete forms of meaning as well as in their general intentions: Benjamin's theory of language deals with the "magical side of language" (II:208) yet also aims toward a "liquidation" of magic insofar as it is incompatible with a rational conception of the world (*One-Way Street,* 163). Benjamin's theory of myth seeks a blasting apart of myth but at the same time does not want to relinquish the whole potential of its forms of experience. These forms include, even more than language, the *image,* and that is why the theory of dialectical images, too, bears witness to the field of tension in Benjamin's reflections on myth. The dialectical image, on the one hand, tends to break up the mythical power of images (*Bildkraft*) by means of the dialectic of knowledge, and, on the other hand, it implies that the genuine form of knowledge itself is, at least in part, based on images and thereby on myth.

Myth and Beauty

Benjamin's theory of *beauty* is also a theory of the saving and the blasting apart of myth: "the period of beauty is fixed from the earliest decay of myth until its blasting apart."[22] To the extent myth deceives in terms of being the all-governing form of life, its formal characteristics, on Benjamin's view, devolve upon beauty. In this process the mythical forms—the merging of sensuousness and meaning, of "veil" and "what is veiled," ambiguity, secret—cease to be frightening and become the reconciling forms of beautiful appearance. Benjamin saw "the problem of Homeric poetry" already in the decaying myth's inheritance to the beautiful: "How do mythological motifs become 'beautiful'?" (VI:128). Ultimately all beauty, understood in this way, "has myth's latent efficacy as its presupposition" (VI:128). The attribution of myth and beauty also withstands a cross-check: allegory as the antithesis of myth was for Benjamin at the same time the antithesis of beautiful appearance; its "field" lies "beyond beauty" (*Trauerspiel,* 176,178). The perspective of an anti-mythical art, beyond beauty, already stamped Benjamin's theory of beauty with dialectical features: as long as no additional moment supervenes upon "mere" beauty, it remains, as does myth, which it succeeds, beyond truth and the morality of the word. Benjamin does not view either myth or beauty as transforming pre-mythical "chaos" into "veracity" in the "world" (that is, putting an end to the chaos), but rather as giving it the appearance of "life" by differentiating "elements" (I:180f.). This explains Benjamin's differences with the idealistic theory of the appearance, (*Er-*)*Scheinens,* of truth in beauty. It is not beauty itself, but the objection to it, which lets art partake of "truth": "What puts a stop to this beautiful appearance, blocks its movement, and disrupts its harmony, is the

Ausdruckslose, the expressionless [that which is without expression, the inexpressible]. The secret of the work is based on that life (of beautiful appearance), its substance is based on this ossification" (I:181). Comparable to Kant's differentiation between the beautiful and the sublime, Benjamin attributes "the sublime power of truth" to the *Ausdruckslose* (I:181)—whereas myth and beauty for him are excluded from the sphere of truth. In his *Trauerspiel* book, Benjamin not only did without the erratic term of the expressionless, but he also reclaimed the thesis of "truth" as the "essential content of beauty." The appearance of self-contradiction vanishes, however, after a more careful reading: "beautiful" for Benjamin is "the truth . . . not so much in itself, as for whomsoever seeks it." Conversely, beauty enters the sphere of truth only in a process of critical "incineration" (*Verbrennung*) or "mortification of the works" (*Trauerspiel,* 31, 182). Thus we are able to combine two seemingly contradictory theses on beauty and truth: for Benjamin, at the moment of myth's decay, beauty inherits the mythical forms of meaning, but does not "explode" myth, and therefore requires objection or critique in order to take part in the sphere of truth. And in the process of such criticism, beauty, as myth's successor, is able to mediate the realms of "myth and truth," which are otherwise said to be "mutually exclusive" (I:162). Hence it is also true of beauty that its poles arbitrate the tension in Benjamin's reflections about myth. In his late work we can find an only slightly transposed analogue to the dialectical grammar of his early concept of beauty: the concept of *aura.* Aura is essentially of mythical character; its "decimation"—for example, via technical reproduction or via allegory—blasts apart myth not only in the negative sense of destruction, but also in the positive sense of "enlightening," of the honing of critical consciousness.

Mythical "Nature" versus Freedom

In the domain of *philosophy of history,* the ultimate source of the trend or undertones of Benjamin's definition of "myth," myth's poles are nature and freedom. Their juxtaposition refers both to the Enlightenment critique of myth and to Kant's doctrine.

The powerlessness in the face of (first and second) nature and the (necessarily) false consciousness of it characterize the mythical forms of life and thought, from the perspective of reason and freedom, as rooted in nature in a pejorative sense: in the context of the mythical derivation and interpretation of all occurrence, "freedom" of the "person" (*One-Way Street,* 130) exists as little as a conscious mastering of nature and society by human power and self-determination. With respect to his *post-* or *trans*-mythical utopia, Benjamin does not take into account that, in relation to *pre*-mythical cultures, myth already accomplishes an alleviation of human powerlessness, as Horkheimer and Adorno[23] and Hans Blumenberg[24] have pointed out. And he stands particularly in opposition to any modern mythical world view—whatever its content may be—that promises a solution to the modern crises of meaning and legitimation. Benjamin considered the categories "fear" (I:151) and "sacrifice" inseparable from "myth" (I:164f., 140; *Trauerspiel,* 107ff.). His perhaps best-known utterance about myth is unthinkable without a rather diffuse amalgamation of the above-mentioned facets of meaning: "Myth will continue to exist as long as there is a single beggar" (V:505).

In his later works Benjamin related the concept of myth's rootedness in nature to bourgeois society's unmastered natural laws, which produce false consciousness: "Capitalism was a natural phenomenon with which a new dream-laden sleep came over Europe, and with it a reactivation of mythical powers" (V:494). Whereas this late application of the concept of myth corresponds closely to the theory of Marx, Benjamin's earlier explications drew upon the doctrine of Kant.[25] Kant contrasted the domain of morality and freedom as intelligible and transcendent over nature, on the one hand, with inflexible laws of nature, on the other. Quite similarly, Benjamin distinguished "natural" and "supranatural (*übernatürlichen*) life" (I:138f.; *Trauerspiel,* 129 f.): "Natural" or "mere life" stays fully under the spell of the fateful laws, which abstractly lie ahead of it in nature and society. The mythical spell of the superior "natural laws" can first be broken by the intervention of a "supranatural" life in such a "natural life"—modeling a world according to the notion of moral self-determination. The heroes of Greek tragedy, who make the alien fatality of mythical fate their own, and thereby allow, in the moral actualization of utopia, an "end" of myth to come into view, undertake precisely this (*Trauerspiel*, 107–17, 135f.). The materialist historian and the revolutionary attempt this as well by seeking to break up the fateful, deluding character of bourgeois society's "natural laws."

Time in Myth: Eternal Recurrence

In addition to *space, language,* and *beauty,* Benjamin's aesthetic of myth harbors another topic, which is at home in his philosophy of history: his theory of *time* in myth. As the "basic form" of mythical temporal experience, it determines the "eternal recurrence" (V:178) and thereby bears a central motif of the *Passagen-Werk*:

The essence of all mythical occurrence is recurrence. Futility is the concealed figure inscribed on it, such as it is written on the foreheads of some heroes of the netherworld (Tantalus, Sisyphus, or the Danaides). (V:178)

Benjamin's theory of time in myth applies only to the sense of myth as a whole rather than to the temporal form in the narrative genesis of individual mythological structures. Its principal categories are cyclical recurrence and the Moira, the mythical fate. Benjamin interprets their relation to one another as follows: "The 'eternal recurrence of all the same' . . . is the sign of fate" (I:137). With the concept of fate in mind, Benjamin views the literary reshaping of myth in tragedy as an "extreme phenomenon" (*Trauerspiel,* 35) in the sense that it does not lead away from original myth, but (dis)arranges it in a way that reveals its essential elements all the more clearly. In tragedy, the morality of the hero as a free individual and the power of mythical fate diverge. The hero is led into a predetermined guilt, without offending morality from the viewpoint of individual responsibility. An attribution of guilt to ancestry demands expiation in the interest of the damaged order. This cyclical structure of guilt (offending of a valid order) and expiation (retribution, punishment) reveals for Benjamin the fundamental relationship of mythical fate and law (I:174f., 187f.).[26] The mythical retribution, however, produces, as in the case of the revenge of the spouse's murder by matricide, a new guilt; and in this way the fateful cycle of guilt and expiation virtually eternalizes itself, unless the tragic hero can somehow, by means of his "supranatural life," break through fate's natural cycle, in a final fulfillment of it. Yet in this breaking apart of mythical fate—the "undermining of a dated body of laws" by a last "restoration" (*Trauerspiel,* 115), mythical law's revision in its "depiction" (*Trauerspiel,* 116)—the tragic hero enters upon the threshold of a new time, in which the power of repetition over existence comes to an "end" (*Trauerspiel,* 116). In the time frame of mythical fate, however (whose statutes, like that of law, find purpose in sustaining the status quo, the existing order which gives them meaning and validity), there is, for Adorno and Blumenberg, as well as for Benjamin, "latent identity, the closed-circle pattern, the recurrence of the same."[27] The following passage from the *Dialectic of Enlightenment* serves both as reception of and commentary on the conceptual correlation of myth, law, fate, and guilt in Benjamin's works; Horkheimer and Adorno's universalization of elements of *Strafmythen,* myths about punishment, to characteristics of myth in general could be read as a direct reference to the passage from the *Passagen-Werk* quoted above:

The formula for the cunning of Odysseus is that the redeemed and instrumental spirit, by resigning itself to yield to nature, renders to nature what is nature's, and yet betrays it in the very process. The mythic monsters whose sphere of power he enters always represent ossified covenants, claims from prehistory. Thus in the stage of development represented by the patriarchal age, the older folk religion appears in the form of its scattered relics: beneath the Olympian heavens they have become images of abstract fate, of immaterial necessity. The fact that it was impossible to choose any route other than that between Scylla and Charybdis may be understood rationalistically as a mythic representation of the superior power of the currents over the small, antique ships. But in the mythic, objectifying transition, the natural relation of strength and impotence has already assumed the character of a legal connection. Scylla and Charybdis have a right to what comes between them, just as Circe does to bewitch those unprepared with the gods' antidote, or Polyphemus to eat the bodies of his guests. Each of the mythic figures is programmed always to do the same thing. Each is a figure of repetition: and would come to an end should the repetition fail to occur. All bear traces of something which in the punishment myths of the underworld—those of Tantalus, Sisyphus and the Danaans—is founded upon Olympian justice. They are figures of compulsion: the horrors they suffer are the curse upon them. Mythic inevitability is defined by the equivalence between the curse, the crime which expiates it, and the guilt arising from that, which in its turn reproduces the curse.

All justice in history to date bears the mark of this pattern. In myth each moment of the cycle discharges the previous one, and thereby helps to install the context of guilt as law.[28]

Neither Horkheimer and Adorno's nor Benjamin's theory of eternal recurrence originates from studies of classical mythology. They were formed, as is well known, in a theory of capitalistic modernism. The *Passagen-Werk,* which we may construe as an (anti-)mythology of the nineteenth century, treats not only figures of mythical space, but also modern equivalents of mythical time. Hence its second principal motif (next to that of "topography"): the return of (the theory of) the return of the same, especially in the canonical variations this notion underwent in Baudelaire, Blanqui, and Nietzsche:

It is to be demonstrated with every possible emphasis how the idea of eternal recurrence intrudes into the world of Baudelaire, Blanqui, and Nietzsche at approximately the same moment. In Baudelaire the accent is on the new which is won with heroic effort from the "ever-always-the-same"; in Nietzsche it is the "ever-always-the-same" which the person faces with heroic composure. Blanqui is much closer to Nietzsche than to Baudelaire, but with him resignation prevails. In Nietzsche this experience projects itself cosmologically in the thesis: there will be nothing new anymore. (I:673)

It is hardly possible to find a common denominator in Benjamin's plethora of notes that attempt to secure a precise historical meaning for the doctrine of the eternal recurrence of the same. Some notes correlate the "splendor" of this theory to the actual disappearance of recurrence in "everyday constellations," to the accelerated displacement of life worlds through capitalism (V:430). In other notes Benjamin claims the effectiveness of recurrence not only in the "fundamental structure" of capitalist society, but also in its "most minute details." At yet another point he places the "idea of eternal recurrence" on a level with the "belief in progress," not as a correction to the latter but as its equally shallow complement. In this context, and before the judgment seat of a "dialectical concept of historical time," both are rejected as "belonging to . . . the mythical mode of thought," in a precritical sense (V:178). But what on the one hand, "despite everything (despite its acute, internal viewpoint), in the sphere of theory," is said to promise only a "tired and faded truth" (V:677) is on the other hand highly esteemed as a *Wahrtraum*, a prophetic dream—"the doctrine of eternal recurrence as a dream of uncanny discoveries still to come in the field of technology of reproduction" (I:680)—or as its consequence: "the idea of eternal recurrence transforms historical events themselves into mass-produced articles" (I:663).

As unequivocal and even self-contradictory as these modern transpositions of the theory of mythical time may be, they all partake equally of the fundamental dialectic of Benjamin's thought on myth: the eternal recurrence of the same characterizes the historical compulsory relation *to be broken apart,* but equally the temporal form of the "happiness" of the *exploded* mythical fate:

Eternal recurrence is an attempt to link two antinomic principles of happiness with each other: namely that of eternity and that of the yet once again.—The idea of eternal recurrence conjures up out of the misery of time the speculative idea (or phantasmagoria) of happiness. (I:682f.)

Only with this duality does the theory of mythical *time*—in addition to the theories of mythical *space, language,* and *beauty*—become a genuine element of Benjamin's "science of thresholds." Benjamin writes of thresholds, that is, of places and moments of passage, of *rites de passage,* as a passerby in a double sense: he passes through the phantasmagoric zone between "dreamful sleep" and "awakening" in the nineteenth century by resolving to make passage through fundamental categories of myth. And insofar as the revision of these categories of myth already determined his early philosophical reflections on language and history, as well as their application in the *Elective Affinities* essay and *Trauerspiel* book, Benjamin's *entire* corpus is a passage of passages. His emphatic concept of experience (*Er-*

fahrung), which next to "myth" is the second concept determining Benjamin's entire corpus, means nothing other than this figure of a self-reflective *passage* through myth. *Erfahrung* in Benjamin's sense means, on the one hand, an ultimately messianic category of unrestricted synthesis, from his opposition to the determination of consciousness and action by the mythical constraints, which reproduces always the same and does not permit anything new. On the other hand, experience distinguished itself from abstract knowledge through its link to mythical forms of meaning. Experience, then, breaks apart myth by its own means—a dialectical *passage de mythe*.

Variance and Invariance in Benjamin's Concept of Myth

The integration of Benjamin's various uses of the term "myth" in a *single* coordinate system involves, to a certain extent, the supposition that there is only *one constant* (stable) use of the term. This contradicts, however, a hardly deniable development in Benjamin's thought; in this essay I already mentioned several divergent inflections of his concept of myth. I conclude this essay by projecting the systematically extrapolated elements of this concept, if only sketchily, upon the diachronic axis of the development of Benjamin's thought.

My results are the following, admittedly rough, findings: whereas the synoptically extrapolated moments form a largely constant reservoir of Benjamin's conceptions of myth, these moments are neither activated at the same time, with identical consequences, nor equally explicit. Benjamin's formulation of the relation between myth and beauty, as well as myth and language, are hardly affected by any alteration. His various reflections on myth and beauty, which extend from his earliest writings to the essay on Goethe's *Elective Affinities,* are consistent with one another. Afterward, however, this theme receives no further mention, yet Benjamin does not signal any change in his position. He never directly associates myth with language. Since Benjamin similarly correlates both myth and magic to the concept of symbol, however, the concept of *Sprachmagie,* which Benjamin employs throughout his early and late works, may be considered as a witness to a vicarious continuity in Benjamin's conception of the relation between language and myth as well. What determines the developmental dynamic of Benjamin's use of the concept are above all the temporal and spatial moments of myth. Benjamin's earliest remarks (in "Fate and Character" and "Critique of Violence") frame "myth" almost exclusively in terms of the fateful time structure, of the constraint of the always-the-same. In Benjamin's *Elective Affinities* essay, a mythical temporal structure explicitly coincides, for the first time, with a captivating (*bannhaft*) arrangement of space. This concept of a unitary, captivating, and all-affecting myth in time and space becomes transformed into a multiplicity of various and limited mythologies in *Berliner Kindheit, One-Way Street,* and the *Passagen-Werk.* To a certain degree, however, the concept of a captivating and unitary mythical time in the *Passagen-Werk* remains valid as a moment of Benjamin's reception of Marx's theory of capitalism as a kind of "second nature." But the sphere of symbolizing, social thing worlds is no longer the strictly closed symbolizing space of the *Elective Affinities,* but is a looser framework of multifarious myths. Benjamin also localizes utopian attributes in the mythological spatial forms as collective dream images. In accord with this relativization of the closed, captivating character of myth, it is first in Benjamin's late work that the positive and negative accents of his concept of myth can be said to be approaching equilibrium and that the motif of blasting apart myth becomes transfigured into the dialectic of breaking apart *and* rescuing myth.

Translated by Gary Smith

Notes

* *Walter Benjamins Theorie der Sprachmagie* and *Paul Celan. Magie der Form* were both published by Suhrkamp Verlag, Frankfurt a.M.

† *Unendliche Verdoppelung: Die frühromantische Grundlegung der Kunsttheorie im Begriff absoluter Selbstreflexion* (Frankfurt a.M.: Suhrkamp, 1987).

‡ This essay is a preliminary study to Menninghaus, *Schwellenkunde: Walter Benjamins Passage des Mythos* (Frankfurt a.M.: Suhrkamp, 1986).

1. Ernst Cassirer, *Philosophy of Symbolic Forms,* vol. 2, *Mythical Thought,* trans. Ralph Manheim (New Haven: Yale University Press, 1955).

2. Manfred Frank, *Der kommende Gott. Vorlesung über die Neue Mythologie* (Frankfurt a.M.: Suhrkamp, 1982).

3. Cf. Frank, 156, 185.

4. Frank, 208.

5. Hermann Cohen, *Religion und Sittlichkeit,* cited from Cohen, *Jüdische Schriften,* vol. 3, *Zur jüdischen Religionsphilosophie* (Berlin: 1924), 158.

6. Cf. Gertrud Höhler, "Die Schlüsselrolle des Ödipusmythos. Zu Sigmund Freuds Mythos-Begriff," in Helmut Koopman, ed., *Mythos und Mythologie in der Literatur des 19. Jahrhunderts* (Frankfurt a.M.: Klostermann, 1979), 333f.

7. Sigmund Freud, "Dostoevski and Parricide," trans. James Strachey, in Freud, *Collected Writings,* vol. 21 (London: Hogarth Press, 1961), 177–96, esp. 188ff.

8. Freud, "The Relation of the Poet to Day-dreaming," in Freud, *On Creativity and the Unconscious,* ed. Benjamin Nelson (New York: Harper & Row, 1958), 53.

9. Hans Freier, "Odyssee eines Pariser Bauern: Aragons 'mythologie moderne' und der Deutsche Idealismus," in Karl Heinz Bohrer, ed., *Mythos und Moderne* (Frankfurt a.M.: Suhrkamp, 1983), 164.

10. Cassirer, *Mythical Thought,* 83.

11. Louis Aragon, *Paris Peasant,* trans. Simon Watson Taylor (London: Cape, 1971), 27.

12. Novalis, *Schriften,* vol. 2 (*Das philosophische Werk* 1), Richard Samuel et al., eds. (Stuttgart: Kohlhammer, 1981), 266.

13. Cassirer, *Mythical Thought,* 24f.

14. Ulrich Gaier, "Hölderlin und der Mythos," in Manfred Fuhrmann, ed., *Terror und Spiel. Probleme der Mythenrezeption* (Munich: Fink Verlag, 1971), 306f. Ulrich Gaier does not mention Cassirer by name, but speaks summarily of "many researchers" who fail to draw a sharp enough distinction between "magical-substantial and mythical-polar structures."

15. Friedrich Creuzer, *Symbolik und Mythologie der alten Völker, besonders der Griechen* (Hildesheim: Olms, 1973); reprint of the third, revised edition of 1837–43. Both Benjamin's and my references are from volume four, 496–569.

16. Creuzer, 540.

17. Creuzer, 541.

18. Creuzer, 535f.

19. Theodor W. Adorno, "A Portrait of Walter Benjamin," in Adorno, *Prisms,* trans. Samuel and Shierry Weber (Cambridge, MA: MIT Press, 1981), 234,

20. This disjunction has only limited validity. In the *Elective Affinities* essay Benjamin develops both the idea of mythical symbolism and its counterpart: the "arcanum of hope" (I:201), the "expressionless" (I:181), and above all the romance of the "peculiar

Walter Benjamin's Theory of Myth

neighbor's kids" as the antithesis of myth (I:171). The reverse holds as well: anti-mythical allegory in the *Trauerspiel* book is to some extent immanently mediated with its counterpart, mythical symbolism. For what was left out of discourse as *object* is smuggled back in as *form*. Benjamin intends his "portrayal" to disclose the "symbolic character of the term" *Trauerspiel*, its quality as the "name" of an "idea." Cf. Menning-haus, *Walter Benjamins Theorie der Sprachmagie* (Frankfurt a.M.: Suhrkamp, 1980), 90f.

21. Adorno, *Prisms*, 233. Jürgen Habermas first treated this relation extensively; see Habermas, "Consciousness-Raising or Rescuing Critique," this volume.

22. Benjamin, "Zu einer Arbeit über die Idee der Schönheit," VI:128.

23. Max Horkheimer and Theodor W. Adorno, *Dialectic of Enlightenment* (New York: Herder and Herder, 1972).

24. Hans Blumenberg, *Work on Myth*, trans. Robert M. Wallace (Cambridge, MA: MIT Press, 1985), especially 14, 31–32.

25. Cf. Adorno, this volume,

26. I have attempted elsewhere a more extensive representation of Benjamin's correla-tion of the concepts of fate, right, guilt, expiation, and sacrifice: "Romeo und Julia auf dem Dorfe. Eine Interpretation im Anschluß an Walter Benjamin," in Menninghaus, *Artistische Schrift. Studien zur Kompositionskunst Gottfried Kellers* (Frankfurt a.M.: Suhr-kamp, 1982), 97–104, 112–15.

27. Blumenberg, 70.

28. Horkheimer and Adorno, 57.

Recollections

Benjamin with Maria Speyer or Gert Wissing, Saint-Paul, 1932. Collection of Gary Smith.

Benjamin the Letter Writer

Theodor W. Adorno

When Scholem proposed to Adorno that they edit a collection of Benjamin's letters, they anticipated no great difficulties in tracing a sufficient number of documents. They were nonetheless astonished at the abundance of letters saved by Benjamin's friends and acquaintances, many throughout exile. Scholem attributed this phenomenon to the fact that "to almost all who knew him more intimately, Benjamin was a much too impressive and significant figure for them not to have saved some or all of what he wrote." Furthermore, "the natural gracefulness and lustre of a power of formulation evident even in his spontaneous communication . . . must have made these letters precious to the addressees."

These letters provide our richest documentation of Benjamin's personal and intellectual biography, from his leading role in Gustav Wyneken's faction of the youth movement to his desperate last years as an emigré. Benjamin's highly stylized epistles evince the "tact and tactics"* of a letter writer who accommodates himself in each case to the recipient and whose attentiveness to the role of the correspondent characterizes the selection of classic German letters he made in his Deutsche Menschen. *It was the publication of Benjamin's* Briefe *that carried the interest in Benjamin's biography to the threshold of a personality cult. It also generated a series of subsequent publications of letters, most notably Scholem's correspondence with Benjamin from 1933 to 1940, as well as a collection of all of his available letters, which is currently being prepared.*

Walter Benjamin the person was from the very beginning so completely the medium of his work—his felicity was so much one of the mind—that anything one might call "immediacy of life" was refracted. Not that he was ascetic, or even gave such an impression by his appearance; but there was something almost incorporeal about him. Master of his ego as few others have been, he seemed alienated from his own *physis*. That is perhaps one root of his philosophical intentions: to render accessible by rational means the range of experience that announces itself in schizophrenia. Just as Benjamin's thinking constitutes the antithesis of the existential concept of the person, he seems empirically, despite extreme individuation, hardly to have been a person at all, but rather an arena of movement in which a certain content forced its way, through him, into language. It would be idle to reflect on the psychological origin of this trait; to do so would be to postulate precisely the standard image of a living being that Benjamin's speculation exploded, and to which general consensus clings all the more obdurately the less of a life life becomes. A remark about his own handwriting (Benjamin was a good graphologist), namely that its object was above all to pretend that nothing had happened, attests at any rate his attitude toward this dimension of himself; but otherwise he never bothered much about his psychology.

It is doubtful whether anyone else ever succeeded in making his own neurosis—if indeed it was a neurosis—so productive. The psychoanalytic concept of neurosis implies the fettering of productive forces, the misdirection of energies. Nothing of the sort in Benjamin's case. His productivity in spite of self-alienation can be explained only by the fact that the *difficile* subjective mode of his reactions was the precipitate of an objective historical reality, which enabled him to transform himself into an organ of objectivity. What he may have lacked in immediacy, or what must soon have become second nature to him to conceal, is forfeit in a world subject to the abstract law of relations between people. Only at the price of the severest pain, or else untruthfully, as tolerated nature, may it show itself. Benjamin had acknowledged the consequences long before he was consciously aware of such matters. In himself and his relations with others he insisted unreservedly upon the primacy of the mind; which, in lieu of immediacy, became for him immediate. His private demeanor at times approached the ritualistic. The influence of Stefan George and his school, with whom Benjamin had nothing in common philosophically even as a youth, amounts to this: from George he learned the patterns of ritual. In the letters this ritual element extends to the graphic image, indeed even to the selection of writing paper, about which he was uncommonly particular; during the period of emigration his friend Alfred Cohn continued a longstanding practice of presenting him with a specific grade of paper. Benjamin's ritual behavior was most pronounced in his youth, and only toward the end of his life did it begin to relax; as if the apprehension of catastrophe, of what was worse than death, had awakened the long-buried spontaneity of expression that he had banished through mimesis to the hour of death.

Benjamin was a great letter writer, and obviously he wrote letters with a passion. Despite two wars, the Hitler Reich, and emigration, very many of them have been preserved; it was difficult to make a selection. The letter became one of his literary forms; as such, it does transmit the primary impulses, but interposes something between them and the addressee: the process of shaping the written material as if in conformance with the law of objectification—in spite of the particular occasion and also by virtue of it—as though the impulse were otherwise not legitimate. Thinkers of major significance and power will often produce insights that address their objects with utmost fidelity and yet at the same time are insights into the thinkers themselves. This was the case with Benjamin; a model would be the well-known remark about the old Goethe as chancery clerk of his own interior. Such second nature has nothing affected or posed about it, though Benjamin would have taken the reproach with equanimity. The letter form suited him because it predisposes to mediated, objectified immediacy. Letter writing simulates life in the medium of the frozen word. In a letter one can disavow isolation and nonetheless remain distant, apart, isolated.

One anecdote that does not directly involve correspondence at all may shed some light on Benjamin's distinctive features as a letter writer. The conversation once came round to differences between the written and the spoken word; for instance, the fact that in lively conversation, for the sake of humaneness, one speaks somewhat less formally and uses the comfortable perfect tense where German grammar would strictly require the simple past. Benjamin, who had a very delicate ear for linguistic nuances, was unreceptive to this idea and challenged it with some intensity, as if a sore spot had been touched. His letters are figures of a speaking voice that writes when it speaks.

For the renunciation that bears them, however, these letters have been richly rewarded; and the reward justifies their being made accessible to a wide readership. It is true that Benjamin experienced the present moment in the "prismatic splendor" of reflection;[1] but he was granted power over the past. The letter form is an anachronism and was already becoming one in Benjamin's lifetime; his own letters are not thereby impugned. Characteristically, he wrote them by hand whenever possible, long after the typewriter had prevailed. The pleasure he took in the physical act of writing—he loved to prepare excerpts and fair copies—was as great as his aversion to mechanical expedients; in this respect the essay "The Work of Art in the Age of Mechanical Reproduction," like many another stage of his intellectual biography, was an act of identification with the aggressor. Letter writing registers a claim of the individual, but is nowadays quite as ineffectual in advancing that claim as the world is set against honoring it. When Benjamin remarked that it was no longer possible to caricature anyone, he was dealing with a closely related issue; likewise in the essay "The Storyteller." In a total constitution of society that demotes every individual to a function, no one is now entitled to give an account of himself in a letter as though he were still the uncomprehended individual, which is what the letter claims; the "I" in a letter has something about it of the merely apparent.

Subjectively, though, in the age of disintegrating experience people are no longer disposed to write letters.[2] For the time being it seems that technology is undercutting their premise. Since letters are no longer necessary, in view of the speedier means of communication and the dwindling of space-time distances, their very substance is dissolving. Benjamin brought to them an uninhibited talent for antiquities; he celebrated the wedding of a vanishing institution to its utopian restoration. What enticed him to write letters was thus connected with his habitual mode of experience; for he regarded historical forms—and the letter is one such form—as nature that required deciphering, that issued a binding commandment. His posture as a letter writer inclines to that of the allegorist: letters were for Benjamin natural-history illustrations of what survives the ruin of time. His own letters, by virtue of not at all resembling the ephemeral utterances of life, develop their objective force: that of formulation and nuance indeed worthy of a human being. Here the eye, grieving for the losses about to overtake it, still lingers over things with a patient intensity that itself needs to be restored as a possibility. "I am not interested in people; I am interested only in things"—this private remark of Benjamin's broaches the secret of his letters. The energy of negation that emanates from it is identical with his productive energy.

The early letters are all to friends from the Free German Youth Movement, a radical group headed by Gustav Wyneken that came closest to realizing its program in the Free School Community at Wickersdorf. Benjamin was also an influential contributor to that circle's periodical publication *Der Anfang*, which attracted much attention in 1913–14. It is difficult to imagine him, with his thoroughly idiosyncratic reactions, involved in such a movement, or in fact in any movement. That he plunged in so unreservedly, that he took so very seriously the controversies of the "discussion halls" and all who participated in them—by now the issues are incomprehensible to an outsider—was surely the result of psychic compensation. Benjamin was by nature inclined to express the general through an extreme of the particular, through what was proper to himself; and he suffered so acutely on that account that he searched for collectivities—to be sure, fitfully and in vain—even in his maturity. Furthermore (and on the other hand!) he shared the general tendency of young intellectuals to overestimate the people they first associate with. As a matter of course he credited his friends with the same intentness upon achieving the utmost that animated his own intellectual existence from its first to its final day; such confidence befits the pure will. It cannot have been the most trifling of his painful experiences to discover that most people do not have the power of elevation that his own example led him to assume in others; and what is more, they do not even aspire to that utmost of which he considered them capable, because it is the potential of humanity.

To be sure, Benjamin's experience of young people, with whom he fervently identified, and also his experience of himself as a youth were already in the mode of reflection. Being young became for him an attitude of consciousness. He was supremely indifferent to the contradiction here: one negates naiveté by adopting it as a standpoint, let alone contemplating a "Metaphysics of Youth."[3] Later, Benjamin's melancholy observation that he "revered youth" aptly named the trait that left its distinguishing mark on the early letters. Between his own proclivities and the circle he joined there was a gulf that he seems to have attempted to bridge by indulging his need to dominate; even afterward, while working on the baroque book, he once remarked that images such as that of the king had attracted him very strongly from the beginning. Flashes of imperiousness dart through the often nebulous early letters like lightning bolts in search of tinder; the gesture anticipates what intellectual energy will later accomplish. Benjamin must have typified the behavior that young people, say university students, are so quick to censure in the most gifted among them as arrogant. And such arrogance is not to be denied. It marks the difference between what persons of the highest intellectual rank know to be their potential and what they already are; a difference for which they adjust by means of behavior that necessarily gives the surface appearance of presumption. Later, the mature Benjamin exhibited as little arrogance as desire to dominate. His politeness was consummate and extremely gracious; it is documented also in the letters. In this quality he resembled Brecht, and without it the friendship between them could hardly have lasted very long.

With a sense of abashment at his beginnings, such as commonly overtakes those of high aspiration—an abashment quite the equal of the earlier self-assessment—Benjamin closed accounts on the period of his participation in the Youth Movement when he came to full self-awareness. He stayed in touch with only a handful of friends, like Alfred Cohn. And of course with Ernst Schoen; that was a lifelong friendship. Schoen's indescribably distinguished bearing and sensitivity must have touched him to the quick, and certainly Schoen was among the first acquaintances to match him in caliber. If Benjamin enjoyed a few years of more or less secure income between the collapse of his academic plans and the outbreak of fascism, he owed them in no small measure to the solidarity of Ernst Schoen, who as program director of Radio Frankfurt commissioned his regular and frequent contributions. Schoen was one of those profoundly self-assured individuals who loved to yield the limelight—without a trace of resentment and to the point of self-effacement; all the more reason to remember him when speaking of Benjamin's personal history.

Aside from the marriage to Dora Kellner, the friendship with Scholem was of decisive importance during the period of Benjamin's emancipation; Scholem was his intellectual peer, and the friendship probably the closest he ever contracted. Benjamin's talent for friendship resembled his talent for letter writing in many features, even in such eccentric ones as the mystery-mongering with which he kept his friends apart whenever possible; although, within a necessarily limited circle, they did as a rule eventually make each other's acquaintance. Out of aversion to clichés of the human sciences, Benjamin rejected the idea that there had been any development in his work; but the difference between his first letters to Scholem and all the previous ones, as well as the trajectory of the *oeuvre* itself, demonstrates how much he did in fact develop. Here, suddenly, he is free of all contrived superiority; which is replaced by the infinitely delicate irony that made him so extraordinarily charming also in private life, despite his strangely objectified and untouchable personality. That irony resides in part in the incongruousness of a touchy and fastidious Benjamin toying with folksiness, say with the Berlin idiom or with typically Jewish expressions.

The letters from the early twenties on have not dated as much as those written before World War I. Benjamin unfolds himself in loving reportage and narrative, in precise epigrammatic formulations, and occasionally also—*not* altogether too often!—in theoretical argument. To the last of these he felt compelled whenever his extensive travels prevented personal discussion with the correspondent. His literary relations are widely ramified. Benjamin was anything but a misunderstood writer who would not be rediscovered until today. His quality remained hidden only from the envious; through journalistic media like the *Frankfurter Zeitung* and the *Literarische Welt* it became generally visible. Not until the eve of fascism was he rebuffed; and even in the first years of Hitler's dictatorship he was still able to publish pseudonymously here and there in Germany. The letters convey a progressive picture not only of him, but also of the spiritual climate of the age. The breadth of his professional and personal contacts was not restricted by politics of any sort. These contacts ranged from Florens Christian Rang and Hofmannsthal to Brecht; the intricate texture of theological and social motifs becomes perspicuous in the correspondence. Time and again he adapted himself to the recipient without thereby diminishing his individuality; reserve and a sense of etiquette, the constituents of any Benjamin letter, then enter the service of a certain diplomacy. There is something touching about that diplomacy when one remembers how little the sometimes artfully considered sentences actually facilitated his life; how incommensurate he remained with existing conditions and how unassimilable, in spite of temporary successes.

I should like to mention the dignity and, until it became a question of sheer survival, the patient self-possession with which Benjamin endured the period of emigration, although the first years imposed upon him the most pitiful material circumstances, and although he never for a moment deceived himself about the danger of sojourning in France. For the sake of his magnum opus, the Paris Arcades project, he accepted the danger. In maintaining such an attitude at that time, he benefited greatly from his impersonality and disregard of private concerns: since he understood himself as the instrument of his thought, and refused to set up his life as an end in itself—in spite, or rather because, of the unfathomable wealth of substance and experience that he incorporated—he never bemoaned his fate as a private misfortune. Insight into the objective conditions of that fate gave him the strength to raise himself above it; the very strength that allowed him in 1940, doubtless with thoughts of death, to formulate the theses "On the Concept of History."

Only by sacrificing life did Benjamin become the spirit that lived by this idea: there must be a human estate that demands no sacrifices.

Translated by Howard Stern

Notes

* The phrase is Irving Wohlfarth's, from his review essay of the Benjamin/Scholem *Briefwechsel 1933–1940* in *Merkur* 35, issue 2 (February 1981): 170.

1. The reference is to Goethe's *Faust*, Act 2, scene 1, line 4727 (Trans.).

2. The word for "experience" is *Erfahrung;* Benjamin's formulation of the distinction between *Erfahrung* and *Erlebnis* is developed, for example, in the essay "On Some Motifs in Baudelaire," *Illuminations*, 163 (Trans.).

3. II:91 (Trans.).

Recollections of Walter Benjamin

Ernst Bloch

Bloch's recollections of Benjamin are both intimate and reserved, qualities of their relationship almost from its beginning. The tensions and fluctuations produced by their contact surface repeatedly in letters to third parties and in other documents. In 1919 Bloch, who was writing several articles a month for Berne's emigré paper, the Freie Zeitung, *pressed Benjamin hard to be more politically active as a writer. He responded to Benjamin's intransigence by labeling him, in a conversation with Scholem, an "analyst of form."*

The political texts Benjamin produced two years later—the "Critique of Violence," "Theologico-Political Fragment," and the lost "Wahren Politiker" (True Politician)—shows signs of his exchange of ideas with Bloch. But their friendship was beset by resentments and suspicions, the most damaging being that of plagiarizing ideas. One of many examples has Benjamin writing a friend in 1935 on his reticence to speak about his Arcades project: "You will appreciate that Bloch's nineteenth-century Hieroglyphs [*referring to Bloch's* Erbschaft dieser Zeit] *has made me somewhat wary." Bloch's correspondence is no less strewn with critical observations; he wrote to Joachim Schumacher in July 1935: "Quite interesting and fruitful conversations with the rediscovered Benjamin, whose fussiness* [Verschrulltheit] *has reached a degree where it has become productive."*

It requires little effort to map a number of intersections in their work: One-Way Street *and* Spuren, *for example, are similarly constructed fragments of cultural criticism. Their joint experimentation with hashish left traces in the writings of both. And the messianic remained a central element of the philosophical thought of both men.*

Yet their relationship remains puzzling, in part because we possess very few direct documents of their contact. Benjamin's long review of the Geist der Utopie *was never printed and has since disappeared. His letters to Bloch are lost, except for the unpublished draft of a single letter from 1934; the few surviving letters of Bloch's are late ones, written in exile. Benjamin does receive frequent mention in Bloch's letters to Kracauer and Krenek, both of whom Benjamin met through Bloch. But aside from a single, scant review of* One-Way Street, *which was first published in 1928 and underwent Bloch's customary cosmetic recension in 1935 and 1962, the following recollection is the sole first-hand testimony of their relation. It is an account in which tensions and disaffection have been tempered, not merely by the friend's death and the intervening decades, but by the acclaim the thought of both men had received.*

I first met Benjamin in Bern in 1918. He was living a secluded life, keeping himself—as his wife Dora said—up to his ears in books. I met him again a few years later in Berlin, where he was living unhappily and unsuitably in the family villa. Our meetings were therefore all the more lively and frequent. Benjamin was occupied at that time (as he would be for a long while) with his book *The Origin of German Trauerspiel.* We met again in Capri and Positano. Asja Lacis, the Latvian theater director, was there as well; she influenced Benjamin insofar as she acquainted him with Marxist trains of thought. Later, following this stay in a southern Italian landscape well suited to both of us, we experienced a true symbiosis in Paris in 1926 that lasted half a year. We were quite close, saw each other daily, or rather especially nightly. So close, in fact, that as is usual with excessive proximity and enforced dependence upon one another in a great city (even being Paris, her intellectuals and celebrities had turned a cold shoulder to Benjamin at that time), our relationship gave rise to a sort of trench fever, or at least this had its place in our relationship. I mean: we had a bit too much of one another due to this enforced proximity. This came to a halt and faded in consequence, as it should have, when we met again in Berlin in the twilight of friendship, which was then interrupted by Hitler in 1933.

I did not see Benjamin in the time just before his death. Our last meeting was again in Paris, in 1935. That made the news of his death seem that much more terrible and unexpected. His sort of death, though, was not so unsuited to him if one views it in the context of a sentence of Benjamin's which I remember: "It is only over the dead that no one has power!"

I am asked about our most frequent topics of discussion. Because of our shared sense for the particular (*Einzelheit*) and for the so often overlooked meaning of the peripheral (*Neben-bei*) in our observations of the small and the unnoticed—or to say all this without pathos, of the cornerstone that the masons have thrown away and that is found everywhere—well, because of this shared sense for the detail from which the most important conclusions can be drawn, our conversations covered—I will express myself in the style of the eighteenth century—*de omnibus rebus et de quibusdam aliis*. A sense for the peripheral: Benjamin had what Lukács so drastically lacked: a unique gaze for the significant detail, for what lies alongside, for those fresh elements which, in thinking and in the world, arise from here, for the individual things (*Einzelsein*) which intrude in an unaccustomed and nonschematic way, things which do not fit in with the usual lot and therefore deserve particular, incisive attention. Benjamin had an incomparable micrological-philological sense for this sort of detail, for this sort of significant periphera, for this sort of meaningful incidental sign. (Lichtenberg had this characteristic as well, though admittedly without the same metaphysical stature.) I say philological because Benjamin read as well as observed; he read for meaning, even in a corrupt text. And not in *books,* but rather through books. He was not only up to his ears in books, but up to his ears in the experience of a *world* that had to be read with the greatest care. His was a special philological sense—at the same time his most graphic faculty—that made external appearances and precisely the strikingly unnoticed (or rather that which is striking and yet goes unnoticed) in this perception and the structures of appearance appear to him as written signs. This happened in a slightly uncanny manner, as if the world were a text, as if the course of things, when tracing (*beschreiben*) a circle or something else, were writing an unknown book out of mere emblems, and as if this describing, in the double sense that the word "describing" has (that one describes something and that a pen describes a circle), made ciphers that had to be read, read in a micrological-philological way. Just these sorts of meanings lie on the surface, but not only on the surface. Rather, and this is wholly characteristic of Benjamin, they must be read and at the same time opened up. Opened up through vivid concepts, through a boring which goes beneath the thing, but in a wholly new way, so that one may well have to replace the word "boring" here: it is more of a cut that Benjamin undertakes here, a diagonal cut such that even the type of cutting reveals something peripheral, something unusual. A diagonal cross-cut, to use Benjamin's term, such as one makes in agate. The structures, the figures, and the figurines, which then appear on the agate, first emerge adequately on the cutting surface due to this cross-cut. Precisely the "text" structure emerges here, and only, as Benjamin thought, because the objective hieroglyphics of the thing become visible to us in this way.

Benjamin could be quite self-deprecating about his own keen sensibility for the eccentric (*Ausgefallene*). The first question he addressed to my fiancée is telling. We saw him strolling pensively, so to speak, with his head bowed, on the Kurfürsten-damm—and my fiancée Karola, who was seeing him for the first time after having heard so much about him from me, asked him what he had been thinking about. He answered: "Dear lady, have you ever noticed the sickly appearance of the marzipan figures?" A truly Benjaminian question, self-ironic, but nothing was too odd or ludicrous (*skurril*) (in the eyes of others) as to prevent his gazing at and looking through. Micrology of the most left-handed sort was at work—"left-handed sort," I say, according to a sentence Benjamin himself wrote in *One-Way Street*: "Today no one should have pretensions as to what he can do. The decisive blows are being delivered with the left hand." Here then, attention to the peripheral is extended from observation and theory to include *praxis*. But observation must of course precede praxis, and in this way Benjamin started off from the *skurril*—or better yet, went into it—with an uncannily philosophical detective's art. This detective work produced, moreover, a *Realmontage,* that is, a bringing together—but a *real* bringing together—of things that were far removed from each other superficially. What was close together became separated, while things that, in the normal sphere of experience, stood at an extreme distance from one another were suddenly jolted, through this montage, into the closest proximity. We have epic examples of this—pictorial examples within the epic works of Joyce and especially Proust (whom Benjamin revered, a substantial portion of whose work he translated, and upon whose handling of images he was dependent). This montage of things, then, grew out of apparently quite disparate, peripheral things, as did the opposite of montage: the separation or divorce of characteristics from the objects that bear these characteristics, which in the normal sphere of experience seem to coexist quite closely. This extended even into psychology, so that Benjamin could say things to many people which had the approximate form or were from the same family as a sentence found in *One-Way Street*: "Gifts ought to have such an effect on the recipient that he takes fright." And another, more methodical example, with a comparable mixture of bizarre and not so bizarre images: "A good historian does not exhaust his energy in the boudoir of the odalisque 'Once upon a time'; he knows, instead, how to explode the continuum of history and so gain power over the 'Now-Time' and its correspondences."

"Now-Time" (*Jetztzeit*), a concept Benjamin liked to use in a completely new way, was a concept that Schopenhauer—to say nothing of Karl Kraus—had mocked savagely from a purely linguistic perspective because of its ugliness. Benjamin never denied its ugliness, but found even here something unusual: Now-Time signifies a time when what is long past suddenly becomes a Now. Not, however, as a Romantic reprise: the *polis*, say, in the French Revolution, was a Now. What is long past touches itself in an odd, enveloping, circular motion, in which even the narrow and indifferent Now of 1925 or 1932 suddenly acquired correspondences or concordances that no longer remained in history. In short: the continuum was exploded, so that the suddenly raw citation rises before our eyes. This method was related, as Benjamin loved to point out, to a sort of varied gardening, in which the same bouquet or the same dish is never offered twice. The giving self never remains the same, the self of the philosopher especially, and things likewise never remain true to themselves. A good cook never makes a dish the same way twice. The philosopher must proceed in the same way, with an eye constantly attentive to the changing and wholly incomparable periphery of a thing, that is to say, with a procedure suited to its object; nonetheless even then with a pluralism over which a distant, questionable, ponderable star— indeed a star only worthy of questions—only then begins to form. Apart from the way in which details seized us, about which I learned a great deal from Benjamin, our deepest affinity lies in the realization that this star presupposes dark- ness. It needs, then, as a precondition or as its preferred envi- ronment what I called in the "Philosophy of Music" section of *The Spirit of Utopia* "the deep joyousness of the darkness that is closing in." This occurred in the middle of an interpretation of Bach, a section of which Benjamin, significantly, later para- phrased.

Yes, the other question, what I thought of Benjamin, or bet- ter, what I admired in him. Precisely and at least most visibly this: that, under the light shed on them by Benjamin, the cen- trality of things that are peripheral, out of the way, and even eccentric could emerge with some precision, and that they then, illuminated as a real written image, become "emblematic." Goethe once said of Lichtenberg that one could use him as one used the best divining rod. Wherever he tells a joke, a problem lies buried. Something almost parallel can be said of Benjamin: where he creates a paradox by his emphasis on details, through his unusual gaze that paints the world in a new way, in this highly metaphysical quality of the peripheral, there arises a Now and a Here with features that penetrate allegorically, sug- gestive of one of the many "most central" meanings, to use Benjamin's favorite phrase. Precisely in the astonished and most peculiar, when it was least expected, one suddenly has been led to the heart of the matter, which the usual big words or all-too-broad and ready-made contexts did not reveal.

The other question, what we—his circle of friends and I— expected of his later works. As we know, the documentation lies unfinished for a book that was to have been called *Paris, Capital of the Nineteenth Century*. Brimming with miscellany, a tortuous piece of work, in which he even wanted to obliterate all traces of himself as author and let the mere documents speak for themselves, if I have been informed correctly. Documents that are nonetheless still miscellany, but that are seen in passing by a philosophical, metaphysical *flâneur*. Here I can say, especially with regard to this work and our expectations, that we would have been in for major surprises with this book, in which so much stone and so many stone houses appear, ornaments of a past age. One can comment on this question with a sentence of Benjamin's from *One-Way Street*: "The climber of facades must make the best use of every ornament." Benjamin had the best reputation in our small circle of friends: Adorno, Kracauer, Weill, Brecht, I, and a few others. Otherwise, however, the larger public of the so-called "Golden Twenties" accorded Benjamin a scandalous neglect that followed him to his grave. And this despite the fact that—besides the appearance of his own books and brilliant essays—Benjamin's reviews appeared almost weekly during the twenties, at least twice monthly, most visibly in the *Frankfurter Zeitung* and in the *Literarische Welt*. All for nothing. And the universities, what was their response? It is enough to say this: a fellow named Schultz, a Germanist in Frankfurt at the time, let the thirty-five-year-old Benjamin—with great book on the baroque drama in hand— fail in his attempt to receive the *habilitation*.

Now to the last point of your questions—I've already told you a good bit that may be characteristic of Benjamin—let me tell a short, revealing, and appropriate story about him.

After I had written down my reflections on his book *One-Way Street* and given it to him to read—in one of the large Berlin cafés on the Kurfürstendamm, where we met one another in the evenings—he expressed his pleasure that I had noted an odd relationship in this *One-Way Street*. Here was—as I wrote them—a store opening of philosophy, something wholly unprecedented, with the latest spring models of metaphysics in the window display. A slice of the surrealism of lost glances, of the most intimate things; and just for this reason the best thing lay behind or among the others, disturbing and unhappy, inviting, challenging, enticing, avoided, sought again, the best found again in the unlikely, but also this: "Don't forget the best"—a small, distant, hushed-up glimmer of the heavenly Jerusalem. I mention this because of Benjamin, because of the sight of his joy at that time, a tiny joy, as was proper, at such an unexpected comparison, a comparison with the "final condition" which lay embedded everywhere, as Benjamin wrote pointedly elsewhere, because this tiny joy at such an extraordinary and lofty comparison at the same time reveals the elegance of Benjamin's understatement.

Translated by Michael W. Jennings

Walter Benjamin in the Internment Camp

Hans Sahl

Benjamin is reported to have said in 1938, on the last evening he was with Adorno, that "there are still positions left to defend in Europe." His reluctance to leave the locus of his Passagen-Werk, *the metropolis whose language and culture he had been close to for most of his life, kept him there until September 3, 1939, when placards went up announcing that all "ressortissants d'Allemagne et d'Austriche" had to report, with a blanket, to the Stade le Colombe. Benjamin and about five thousand others were held there, in dreadful conditions, for ten to fourteen days, after which he and several hundred others were transported to an internment camp in Nevers.*

Among those who recognized Benjamin in this camp was a young Berlin critic, Hans Sahl, who is perhaps best known today for his memorable poem "We Are the Last." His report is a literary account that uncannily harmonizes with other descriptions of Benjamin's personality and demeanor. Sahl could not suspect—even when writing his account almost three decades later—just how quintessentially Benjaminian the strategy of starting a literary journal was. We now know that Benjamin played a leading role on a number of other journal projects, two of which, despite elaborate preparations, never published an issue. His camp journal was to be the third. The first failed journal project, Angelus Novus, *of which he was sole editor, fell victim to inflation and an unreliable publisher. That journal was to be wilfully "ephemeral" and thereby assured of the "kind of actuality which alone is the true kind." The second,* Krisis und Kritik, *a collective venture with Bertolt Brecht and others in 1930, was to be "of political character. That is, its critical activity is anchored in the lucid awareness of the critical underlying situation of the present society."*

Both of these programmatic statements are appropriate to Benjamin's final journal project, as described by Sahl. An interesting footnote to this story is that one of the penciled suggestions Benjamin had made to the list of collaborators for Krisis und Kritik *includes "Sahl?".*

The portrait of Walter Benjamin drawn here by some of his friends would be incomplete without a description of his behavior in the internment camp. In extreme situations people may continue to behave exactly as one might expect—or they may react in completely uncharacteristic ways. In Benjamin's case, the confrontation with the reality of the camp revealed personality traits that had probably always been present but that under the pressure of this situation came to predominate in a peculiar though typical way. There was something about the nature of the system of his thought that caused it to metamorphose into pedantry in the face of a reality that mocked this system. As he tried to orient himself to reality using his intelligence and his historical-political understanding, he distanced himself ever further from it. He took reality "at its word" in order to unmask it, but instead unmasked the impotence of the word worn by reality as a facade. Never have I been made so conscious of the tragic conflict between thought and action in a person, who, especially as a Marxist, attempted to unify the two. And never have I been so conscious of the painful failure of a method, which in sympathetic unworldly innocence thought it possible to "change" reality, but which remained only an interpretation, limping behind that reality. Benjamin's incomparable capacity for seeing the whole from the detail worked this time to his disadvantage. His view of the whole became obstructed by the absurdity of now autonomous details.

Along with almost all immigrants of German descent living in Paris at the outbreak of the war, Benjamin was first interned in the Stade Colombe. I met him there on one of the stone benches that served as our home for ten days and nights. The straw that was strewn about had long become putrid and smeared with *paté de foie,* an inexpensive liver paté, which, spread on bread, was our sole nourishment. Since there was almost no water to wash with, the paté clung to our faces and hair and penetrated every pore. (A description of life in the notorious Stade Colombe can be found in the relevant literature.)

In the gray of dawn on the tenth day, we were assembled in the courtyard and divided into groups for transport to different camps. I had made plans with Benjamin and some other friends to try to stay together at all costs. This custom would prove vital on later occasions. So it was that we were transported in the same bus under military guard through the streets of Paris to the Gare d'Austerlitz and from there in sealed cars to Nevers. We reached Nevers toward evening and were forced to march the two-hour distance to the camp. Benjamin, for whom walking was difficult, had met a young man who carried his suitcase and who later, in the camp, was to serve him as a disciple ministers to a venerated master. In this relationship of the younger to the older man—in the young man's care for this physically frail individual, helpless in all things practical—there was an almost biblical respect for the spiritual in a time of plagues and dangers. This was how I imagined a prophet, protectively led through the crowds by his disciple.

It was already dark when we arrived at the completely bare castle and were assigned to various floors and rooms. I lost sight of Benjamin, but I knew that the young man would take care of him. There were no lights, no beds, not a single table or chair in the castle—not even a nail, on which we could hang our things. We lay down on the floor exhausted and slept immediately.

The next morning the French commander called us into the courtyard and gave a speech. He was as much at a loss as we were, which was not really so remarkable. The decision to intern the immigrants who had sought asylum in France had been made at the last minute, and no one had been prepared for it. The German-Russian treaty and the invasion of Poland had left the military officials no time to interrogate the immigrants with respect to their political reliability. Since the communists were attempting to defend the Hitler-Stalin Pact ideologically by referring to Czechoslovakia, which had been abandoned by the Western powers, they were transformed overnight from Hitler's enemies to his allies. This explains some of the injustices that so greatly incensed us then.

But of course there were also other reasons, i.e. the French military's lack of money and French refusal to recognize any German opposition [to Hitler]. For the readers of the *Action Française,* there was no difference between those Germans who supported and those who opposed Hitler. All were equally worthy of attack. In an ambiguous case, one took the easy way out, no matter how sloppy, and let things take their own course.

At this point something rather ironic occurred, about which very little has been written: the organizational genius of the prisoners, who never ceased being German during their incarceration, won out over the French disorganization. "German" hard work, "German" order, cleanliness, and a sense for discipline and obedience took control of the camp inmates, otherwise hampered by their Jewish self-reflection. A *wandervogel* spirit behind barbed wire swept rooms with straw brooms, hung wash out to dry, organized lectures comparing Freud and Jung, Lenin and Trotsky. A community that began to function was soon fashioned from the void; from chaos and helplessness emerged a society.

Suddenly there was also a man who told everyone what had to be done. No one knew how it had happened, except that he had proposed the right thing at the right moment. He had been a manager in a department store, and there was a certain indefinable air about him that we call "authority." He had learned to give orders and choose the right people for the job. At his command, the construction of a latrine began. A conduit was laid, and also a lighting circuit. We obtained a soup kettle from the soldiers' kitchen, and straw was strewn about the rooms. Someone found blankets, and we fashioned eating and drinking utensils from old tin cans by rubbing them clean with dirt. A man who collected stamps was appointed postmaster, and a painter, famous for his dinner parties in Parisian ateliers, was appointed cook.

Shortly after this, Benjamin began to hold a course outdoors "for advanced students," charging a tuition fee of three Gauloises or a button. I could not take part in the course because, despite all my attempts to obtain a doctor's excuse, I was assigned to a work party that was supposed to build a concrete airport runway. Benjamin would look at me sadly as I reported for work detail at dawn and strode out into the snow in the same street shoes and the same—now tattered—summer clothing I had worn on our arrival at the Stade Colombe. During this time he coined the term "the proletarianization of the Jews" as the next stage of the Diaspora; the word "Auschwitz" did not yet exist in our political vocabulary. One evening as I stood with him at the barbed wire and watched the sheep grazing on the other side, he said, "Just to sit once more on the terrace of a café and twiddle my thumbs—that's all I wish for." Several months later, when I was temporarily released and went to see him in his apartment in Paris, he was not twiddling his thumbs at all—he was sitting at his desk, writing.

The Gauloises that were willingly paid as a lecture honorarium were not the only form of currency in the camp. There was a nail currency, a pencil currency, a button exchange, depending on what was in greatest demand at any given time. There were "official" exchange rates, quoted according to the principle of supply and demand: five cigarettes for one nail, or one nail, two cigarettes, one pencil, and a button for a little notebook. There were honest people who bought only what they needed, and others who "speculated" by hoarding cigarettes or nails and thus driving up the price.

There were also gangsters and thieves in this "society," which was a mirror of that other society and allotted each the place due him on the basis of his talents, his stupidity or cleverness, and his ambition or lack of initiative. One incident that Benjamin was very concerned about seemed to him symptomatic: two men from the film industry had the idea of proposing a film "Vive la France" to the commanding officer. They had to travel to Nevers every day, they explained, to do research in the city library. The commanding officer was enthusiastic and provided them with armbands that permitted them to leave the camp unmolested. They were the envy of the six hundred undernourished men who received them at the gate with threats and curses, as they returned to the camp each evening smelling of wine, with the taste of the "cuisine française" on their tongues, to discuss in whispers on the straw the first-class restaurants in which they had dined.

One day Benjamin took me aside. "It's about the armband," he whispered. "No, don't laugh. I have a plan." He wanted to propose to the commanding office the publication of a literary journal—"naturally on the highest niveau"—a camp journal for intellectuals that was to show the country exactly who they had locked up as "the enemies of France." "Come to my room tomorrow at four o'clock," he said, "we'll hold our first editorial meeting."

Benjamin lived in a lean-to at the foot of a circular stairway, which made a sort of roof over his layer of straw. From a piece of old burlap his disciple had made him a curtain, which allowed him to evade the eyes of others. A holy man in his cave, watched over by an angel. As I entered at four o'clock and pulled the curtain aside (not without first announcing myself to the angel, then serving as his secretary), two others were already squatting on the straw. The editorial meeting began. We drank contraband schnapps from thimbles, procured by the angel from the soldiers, and discussed what the journal should contain. Benjamin was very serious, almost ceremonious. He seemed to have little sense of the macabre comic element in the undertaking. "Gentlemen, it's a question of the armband," he reiterated again and again, as if this were a valid argument for defending a contestable philosophical standpoint. The armband had become for him a symbol of survival itself. It was the detail from which the whole could be manipulated.

When asked what I was thinking of writing for the first issue, I proposed a subject that I knew would win his approval: "The Emergence of a Society from Nothingness"—a sociological study of the camp, with examples taken from our own world of experience, from the first groundbreaking for the latrine to the cultural superstructure we were about to create with this journal. My proposal was accepted unanimously, and Benjamin entered it in a little notebook, where he noted all the articles for the first issue.

We met twice a week for "editorial meetings" in Benjamin's shed, which we could enter only by crawling on all fours, where we drank soldiers' schnapps from thimbles and read aloud our articles, scrawled with pencil stubs on packing paper. I can't remember the topic of Benjamin's own article, perhaps because it was still in preparation. I believe it would have been a very good, even significant, journal that would have found its way out of the camp and into the world at large. Unfortunately the first issue was never published; we never got our armbands. A few weeks later the camp was dissolved. Some of us, Benjamin

and I among others, were released to Paris thanks to a ministe-
rial decree arranged by the French PEN-Club, only to be arrested six weeks later when the Germans invaded France. This
time we were not successful at remaining together.

I met him on the street in Marseilles during the cease-fire. "I'm
escaping tomorrow through the Pyrenees," he said. That was
the last I heard before Benjamin, while staying at an inn on the
Spanish border, on the threshold of freedom—and prevented
from crossing it only by a tragic mishap—took his own life.

Translated by Deborah Johnson

Benjamin in Ibiza

Jean Selz

The name of Jean Selz first crops up in a letter Benjamin wrote to Scholem from Ibiza in July 1932. It is mentioned in connection with an amusing and unlikely story:

My stay there ended up lasting a week longer than planned. Indeed, a somewhat improvised celebration even materialized, and it owed its verve not so much to the characters in the repertoire with whom you are acquainted as to two French people who have recently arrived on the scene: a married couple I found quite delightful. Since this affinity was reciprocated, we remained to-gether—with only slight interruptions—until my departure. Our time together was so riveting—right up to midnight of July 17, when my ship was to sail for Mallorca—that when we finally arrived at the quay the gangplank had been removed and the ship had already started to move. I had of course already stowed my baggage on board. After coldbloodedly shaking hands with my companions, I proceeded to scale the hull of the moving vessel and, aided by inquisitive Ibizians, managed to clamber over the railing intact.*

The following May Benjamin returned to Ibiza, this time in exile from Germany, and he gave voice to his isolation in a letter:

When I let more than a week pass—as I have now—without seeing my Parisian friends in Ibiza, it puts me in a dismal state. By the way, the husband is absorbed in his ambition to translate small sections of the Berliner Kindheit. He does not know any German but is able to follow my paraphrases with superior comprehension.†

The mood of Benjamin's utterances about Selz, however, darkened slowly over time, until their contact ceased altogether. As a consequence, Selz's translations would not appear until 1954, in Les Lettres Nouvelles, and in versions slightly different from those found in Benjamin's papers. This essay is in part an expression of Selz's bewilderment at being suddenly dropped by Benjamin— one kind of idiosyncratic treatment testified to by other of Benjamin's acquain-tances.‡

It was in 1932, in the western islands of the Baleares, that I first met Walter Benjamin. It was also the year he came to Spain for the first time, crossing that fatal border where, as a German desperately trying to flee from other Germans, he was to take his own life eight years later.

I landed in Ibiza on an April morning. At first I didn't think I would like it enough to stay longer than two weeks; I was actually to remain nearly two years. Ibiza was not well known to tourists at the time, but a few Americans lived in Santa Eulalia on the east coast, and in San Antonio, on the west coast, a number of Germans were voluntarily practicing an exile that they would later be forced to endure. Between the two, in the small town of Ibiza, I was the only Frenchman on the entire island. Very few relationships were established between the Germans of San Antonio and the Americans of Santa Eulalia, yet these small harbors sheltered the homes of two writers with unusual personalities: Walter Benjamin and Elliot Paul. Admittedly, they were as sociable as a couple of bears, but I have always gotten along well with such people and therefore became acquainted with them early on.

Elliot Paul had contributed to the avant-garde review *transition* and was to enjoy a big success in the United States a few years later with his book about the civil war in Ibiza [*Life and Death of a Spanish Town*]. He was an intelligent and kindly sort of bear, but strictly an indoors one: Ibiza's countryside and its wide beaches apparently meant nothing to him. He and his wife Gertrude lived in the Fonda Cosme, a rustic, unattractive little inn. Elliot Paul almost never left his uncomfortable room, from which one could hear the rattle of his typewriter all day long, which made it even more difficult to gain his acquaintance. They both occasionally came to the large house I had rented in the upper part of town, however, and sometimes I had lunch with them at the Fonda Cosme. Elliot Paul wore a great beard, which made him look like Ernest Hemingway, and used to spend hours after the meal playing joyful popular tunes on his accordion. Gertrude Stein once wrote of him: "He could play the accordion as no one can who wasn't born in one."

Walter Benjamin was an entirely different type of bear, and

Elliot Paul and he certainly led one to believe that different species of bear don't seek each other's company. He was awkward and shy, but these qualities were like a shabby suit worn by a rich man who wants to conceal his wealth. For Benjamin, wealth meant a powerful capacity for thought: his thinking was anything but timid and his dialectical skill was remarkable. Armed with both of these, he could easily afford to appear awkward.

Benjamin's physical stoutness and the rather Germanic heaviness he presented were in strong contrast to the agility of his mind, which so often made his eyes sparkle behind his glasses. I can see him in a small photograph I saved, with his prematurely gray, closely cropped hair (he was forty years old at the time), his slightly Jewish profile and black moustache, sitting on a deck chair on the front porch of my house, in his usual posture: face leaned forward, chin held in his right hand. I don't think I have ever seen him think without holding his chin, unless he was carrying in his hand the large curved pipe with the wide bowl he was so fond of and which in a way resembled him.

Benjamin lived in a small peasant's house on the San Antonio bay called Frasquito's house, surrounded by fig trees and situated behind a windmill with broken sails. On a radio show in 1952 called "Ibiza, Its Mysteries and Myths," I told the story of Frasquito and his mill, which no one was allowed to enter: he had given it to his son and had been waiting thirty-five years for him to return from South America where he had mysteriously disappeared. Benjamin wrote a short story inspired by the Frasquito family and sent it, I believe, to the *Frankfurter Zeitung*. He still contributed to that newspaper, of which he had been the well-known literary critic, but was soon to stop signing his name to his pieces as the National Socialists continued their rise to power.

Benjamin had difficulty walking: he couldn't go very fast, but was able to walk for long periods of time. The long walks we took together through the rolling countryside, among carob, almond, and pine trees, were made even longer by our conversations, which constantly forced him to stop. He admitted that

Benjamin with the Selzes, Ibiza, 1932. Collection of Gary Smith.

walking kept him from thinking. Whenever something interested him he would say "Tiens, tiens!" This was the signal that
he was about to think, and therefore stop. There were times
when he said "So, so," as if speaking to himself, but usually it
was "Tiens, tiens," even while speaking German with other
Germans, the younger and less respectful of whom nicknamed
him Tiens-tiens as a result.

One day we were struck by the beauty and aristocratic bearing of the peasant women, whose gait imparted a particular
movement to their long, pleated skirts because of the eight or
more superimposed petticoats they wore underneath. The
large number of these petticoats was a matter of some puzzle-
ment for Benjamin, and he asked a peasant the reason for it.
The man replied: "When the women work in the field, they
have to bend over. If anyone is watching them, the petticoats
are a lot more practical." Benjamin said "Tiens, tiens" and then
found the conclusion to the peasant's words: "He's right. It is
proper to include modesty under the category of practical matters." Thus, from a small observation based on a tiny detail, his
thought always went very far, feeding the conversation with his
most personal opinions.

He loved to formulate theories. This annoyed me whenever I thought that his theories were not yet fully worked out in his mind and that he was in a sense *testing* them on me. He once expounded a strange idea in which he maintained that all words, regardless of the language they belonged to, resemble in their written form the things they designate. I was not over-whelmed. I countered with the idea that certain words in one language sometimes look like their antonym in another language. For example, the Spanish word *mas* (more) is more similar to the French word *moins* (less) than to its equivalent *plus*. This was confirmed by the headwaiter of one of Ibiza's *fondas* who, proud of his French, always asked me if I wanted *moins* when he came around with second helpings. "If the word 'saucepan' were used in a given language to designate a cat," I argued, "you would probably think that it looked like a cat." He began to think, as he did not easily admit defeat. "You may be right," he answered, "but it would only resemble a cat insofar as a cat resembles a saucepan."

He would sometimes linger over a word, considering it from all sides, and in doing so, often discovered in its individual syllables an unexpected meaning. One night at my house, he was struck by the dominance of a certain color in a room with white walls, a dominance that had occurred without any intention on my part. The color was red. Several bunches of roses, carnations, and pomegranate flowers presented an entire spectrum of reds to which was added the stark red of a peasant woman's handkerchief, made even more vivid by the light of a lamp. Benjamin was quick to give the room its definition: "A laboratory designed to extract the essence of the color red." He then uttered the German word *rot* (red). *"Rot,"* he said, "is like a butterfly alighting upon each shade of the color red." Later on his attention was drawn by the red handkerchief: "To me, it occupies a space between 'torch' and '*torchon*' (cloth)." In this manner he associated two words whose difference in meaning had drawn them away from their common etymology (*torquere*, to twist).

The reason I report these conversations is that they strike me as belonging to a unique aspect of Benjamin's mind, representing more than a mere far-fetched expression of his thought: they represent a method for discovering truth in which one can recognize his love of investigation, which never allowed him to neglect form in favor of content, whether in the field of historical or literary criticism. Making things relinquish their innermost secrets, forcing different words to reveal their latent correspondences as if one were creating sparks out of stones, giving them wings: such were for him some of the fundamental duties of the writer.

He knew I collected accounts of dreams, and he used to tell me his. Here is one I have saved, dated July 1932: "Emperor William II was standing trial in the Superior Court, having been accused by an old woman of causing her ruin. The old woman, dressed in rags, appeared in court with her granddaughter; in order to show how deep their misery was, she brought along the two sole objects they still owned: a broom and a human skull from which they were forced to eat and drink."

At the end of the summer I came to the San Antonio bay to move into a small, white, square house called La Casita, right on the sea, not far from the one Benjamin lived in. It was during our daily encounters and long talks on warm September nights that our friendship was sealed, one I valued highly, yet one that was to disintegrate in a most mysterious fashion.

These talks, which gradually revealed to me Benjamin's originality and depth of thought, his enormous erudition and his passion for all forms of literature, philosophy, linguistics and popular art, usually took place on the porch of La Casita. We rarely spoke of politics. He knew I disagreed with his ideas, partly derived from Marxism (though of a distinctly anti-Stalinistic variety: he was a great admirer of Trotsky). We spoke mostly of literature, and he taught me a great deal about German literature. He liked to talk about Goethe, Stefan George, and Kafka, whom he had known and whose small photograph he possessed.

I read to him everything I wrote, and he did likewise. Sometimes he would read from his tiny notebooks on which he wrote in such a small handwriting that he never found a pen that was fine enough, which forced him to write with the nib upside down. He owned many tiny notebooks, not only for taking notes, but also for writing down the titles of all the books he read. Yet another one was reserved for excerpts from his readings, destined later to become epigraphs. He liked to use the reverse sides of the letters he received from his closest friends for his manuscripts. He was maniacal about everything that touched his work; and yet, what really did not touch his work? He seemed incapable of showing interest in anything that did not provide fuel for his literary preoccupations. In this regard, he was the consummate type of the exclusive intellectual. If anything didn't go his way, if somebody arrived whom he didn't like, for example, he turned very red, sat in his armchair in a great hermetic ball like a porcupine, and nothing could make him come out of his shell.

Autumn came, accompanied by violent rainstorms, and the evenings grew cool enough to warrant the pleasure of building a fire. Entire trees carved into huge logs were delivered unto the flames of the fireplace of my small house. One evening, as I was building the fire with some of those fire starters bought in the San Antonio grocery, which were called *demonios economicos*, Benjamin observed me with rapt attention. He examined the manner in which this little scaffolding was constructed in the hearth: first an "economic demon," then a few pieces of wood coal, followed by small logs, and finally by large ones. As the fire began to submerge the entire structure, Benjamin said: "You're working just like a novelist." I looked at him in mild astonishment. "Yes," he continued, "for nothing resembles a novel more than a log fire. The whole careful construction, piece by piece, one supporting the other in perfect balance . . . what is it destined for? Destruction. And so with the novel. All its characters support one another in perfect balance, and the true purpose of the novel is to destroy them." He did not elaborate further that evening on the necessity he saw for the novel to destroy its heroes. Why should this be necessary? I was to learn the answer to that question twenty years later while reading the remarkable essay Benjamin wrote called "The Storyteller," published by Adrienne Monnier in the July 1952 issue of the *Mercure de France*. In that essay he takes up once again his

Jean Selz

comparison to the log fire and speaks of the solitude of the reader of novels:

In this solitude of his, the reader of a novel seizes upon his material more jealously than anyone else. He is ready to make it completely his own, to devour it, as it were. Indeed, he destroys, he swallows up the material as the fire devours logs in the fireplace. The suspense which permeates the novel is very much like the draft which stimulates the flame and enlivens its play.

Further on, he speaks of the novel's protagonist:

The "meaning" of his life is revealed only in his death. But the reader of a novel actually does not look for human beings from whom he derives the "meaning of life." Therefore he must, no matter what, know in advance that he will share their experience of death. (*Illuminations,* 100f.)

"The Storyteller" is the only one of Benjamin's published works that mentions the name of Ibiza. He reports the stern warning given, along with the time, by the clock of Ibiza's cathedral (and not by a sun dial, as he mistakenly wrote): *Ultima multis,* the last hour for many.

I seem to remember that Benjamin left Ibiza before the end of the fall. The dark clouds that had begun to gather over Germany filled him with anxiety. I stayed in Ibiza until December and returned to Paris after a ski trip in a primitive part of the Spanish Pyrenees, not far from Andorra. I had no intention of spending more than three months in Paris; my only desire was to return to Ibiza.

At the end of March 1933 I received a letter from San Antonio sent by Dr. Felix Noeggerath, an old friend of Benjamin's who had studied at the University of Munich with him and was spending the winter there. He wrote:

All of our thoughts have been taken up for months by the events which, after being predicted for so long, have finally become real. You know I am speaking of Germany. . . . Each letter I receive from there carries more sad news. The last one came from our friend Benjamin, who almost doesn't dare leave his house—and he has good reason not to.

A few days later, Benjamin arrived in Paris from Berlin. I asked him about Germany, and he said that from now on, whenever a German spoke of culture, it was good to feel a gun in one's pocket. I offered him hospitality, and we took the train together to Barcelona on April 4. We stayed there for a few days before taking the boat to Ibiza. We spent the evenings in the Barrio Chino which was still the extraordinary place it had been before the Spanish Revolution. A frenzied population inhabited its streets and nightclubs that no longer exist: the One-Armed Man with its flamenco dancing, El Sacristan and La Criolla with their pretty young boys dressed in evening gowns, and the Sevilla with its naked singers. In the grimy streets, young children would brazenly try to sell "hot watches" that had just been stolen.

In Ibiza I moved back into my house on Conquista Street, in the upper part of town, with its flower garden that produced tobacco and pomegranates. Benjamin went back to his little San Antonio bay, where I was to visit him many times.

It was during this spring that Benjamin read to me his childhood memories, which he collected into a series of short texts entitled *Berliner Kindheit um Neunzehnhundert.* He translated as he read. His knowledge of French was extensive enough to enable me to penetrate most of the time along the steep paths of his thought. Many passages remained obscure, however, because he couldn't find the French equivalents of certain words and expressions. This led me to undertake a French version of *Berliner Kindheit* with the help of his subtle yet precise explanations. It was a long and difficult task. Pierre Klossowski, who later worked with Benjamin on a translation of his essay "The Work of Art in the Age of Mechanical Reproduction," knows the philological nightmares his translators were forced to endure; for Benjamin never allowed the slightest discrepancy in the words chosen to translate his own. Whenever we had to admit that a word he used had no equivalent in French, his sadness and discouragement put one in a cruel predicament. We spent hours discussing the slightest words, and even commas, of his texts entitled "Wintermorgen," "Schmöker," "Loggien," and I spent more hours writing and rewriting them until they were deemed worthy of his final approval.

What I am now about to tell can only be understood if one recalls the particular atmosphere that reigned over Ibiza during the summer of 1933. While the spring of that year was filled with the indescribable peace that we had known the previous year, the summer was something entirely different. Many people suddenly began to visit the small island, and some of them were not the least bit pleasant. Among the political refugees who came from Germany in increasing numbers, there were some certified Nazis who, as we were later to learn, were spying for the Gestapo. They gave themselves away during the Civil War by turning over to a German cargo ship all the anti-Hitlerian Germans who had not been able to leave the island. One could also meet those international drifters whom the sea of misfortune always seems to carry away from the continents and wash up on the shores of every island in the world. Didn't the rumors have it that the little "agricultural engineer" who settled in the village of San Vincente and was inexplicably shot by the government militia in 1936, during the first days of the Spanish revolution, was none other than Vilain, the murderer of Jaurès? I don't know whether the unease that took hold of people's minds that summer was entirely attributable to the presence of too many strange visitors, but one did learn the most surprising things about the most unassuming people, and scandals broke out in every corner of the island, showing that its magical atmosphere had definitely been tainted.

My house on Conquista Street was often full in those days. People came to eat, work, sleep, or just to break in. Although it was difficult to exclude the undesirable ones, I saw with pleasure a small group of writers and artists. The evenings they spent in my house are linked in my memory to the scent of the flower called *Dama de noche* which filled the small garden, and the melancholy music of the Peruvian records brought over by the surrealist Andrea Gamboa, who had shocked the people of Ibiza by living with a beautiful Negro woman. I also recall the young Catalan poet Luis Frances; the sculptor Maurice Garnier, who always worried the customs officials because his bags were weighted down by the pebbles he collected on the beaches for his work; the charming Bravig Imbs, whose tragic death is well known; the Irishman O'Brien, who circled the world with his wife on a sailboat that looked like a seventeenth-century Spanish galleon. Drieu La Rochelle also came to Conquista

Street. Did he ever meet Walter Benjamin? I can't remember. But today, as I visualize them both sitting in the same part of the garden, near the well where it was coolest, I can't help associating in my mind the differences in their features, voices, and gestures, with the insurmountable ideological difference that was to separate the two men before uniting them in a common fate: suicide.

An elegant new bar had just opened up in the port of Ibiza, and it took its name from a southerly wind: The Migjorn. It soon became the favorite meeting place for foreigners. It was in the Migjorn that an event occurred one evening which was insignificant in itself, but which was to have a strange and decisive effect on my friendship with Benjamin. He usually was a paragon of temperance, but on that night his exceptionally whimsical mood compelled him to ask Toni, the bartender, to mix him a "black cocktail." Without hesitation, Toni went to work and served him a tall glass filled with a black liquid of which I never found out the frightful ingredients. Benjamin drank it down with much aplomb. Soon afterward, a Polish woman whom I will call Maria Z. sat down at our table and asked us if we had ever tried this famous gin that was a specialty of the house. The gin in question was 148 proof: I personally had never been able to swallow a drop. It was a diabolical drink. Maria Z. ordered two glasses for herself and emptied them one right after the other, without batting an eye. She then dared us to do the same. I declined her invitation, but Benjamin took up the challenge, ordered two glasses for himself, and also downed them in quick succession. His face remained impassive, but I soon saw him get up and slowly head for the door. No sooner had he left the bar than he collapsed onto the sidewalk. I ran toward him and managed to get him back on his feet with considerable difficulty. He wanted to walk all the way home to San Antonio. Seeing the unsteadiness of his gait, however, I had to remind him that San Antonio was fifteen kilometers away from Ibiza. I invited him rather to come to my house, where he could sleep in a spare room. He accepted, and we headed in the direction of the upper part of town. I soon realized how foolhardy this was: until that night, the upper part of town had never been so far up. I won't recount how the climb was accomplished, how he required that I walk three meters in front of him, then three meters behind him, how we managed to escalate those streets that were so steep that some of them stopped being streets and turned into stairways, how he sat down at the foot of one of these stairways and fell into deep sleep. . . . By the time we got to Conquista Street, dawn had started to break—that green dawn of Ibiza that doesn't seem to come from the sky, but rather from the depths of the old walls themselves, whose whiteness suddenly comes alive with a sickly tinge. Our expedition had lasted the entire night. I must have gotten up at around noon, and I went into Benjamin's room to see how he was doing. It was empty! He had disappeared, and I found a little note on the bedside table expressing his gratitude and apology.

I didn't see him again for several days. He had returned to San Antonio, and I later learned from one of his friends that he was extremely contrite about what had happened. He didn't dare see me again and wanted to leave Ibiza. Naturally I urged the friend to tell him that such things were of no consequence whatever in my mind, and that it was far from me to hold that night, which after all had been quite out of the ordinary, against him. But when I did see him again, I felt that something inside him had changed. He couldn't forgive himself for having given such a display, for which he no doubt felt genuine humili-ation and, oddly enough, for which he seemed to reproach me. Neither the affection nor the respect I held for him were able to convince him that the unfortunate effects of the 148 proof gin hadn't changed my opinion in the least. I first experienced a deep sorrow as a result, followed by a certain annoyance. We nonetheless continued our work on the translation of *Berliner Kindheit.* He no longer came readily to my house, however. One day I invited him to lunch, and he sent me a small note express-ing his regrets: "The climb will be most difficult in this heat. I think I would arrive in an exhausted state." So we continued to work intermittently in San Antonio, but soon had to stop en-tirely. Afflicted with a case of brucellosis, I had to spend several hours a day stretched out on a mat without doing anything. Benjamin, for his part, began to suffer from malaria. The idiosyncrasies of his personality were not diminished as a result, and his acerbity became more and more acute, as we were all to experience. And yet, when I think back after all these years and view our little entourage in a more objective light, I can't help discerning the figure of some evil genie working steadily to bring us apart.

Nothing gave our imaginary feud an opportunity to materialize. Yet when Benjamin left Ibiza in October, our friendship had inexplicably cooled. I did receive a friendly letter from him after his departure, but only one. At the end of the year, I returned to Paris.

I was to see him only one more time, at the Café de Flore in March of 1934. He was living in the Palace-Hôtel in Saint-Germain-des-Prés. I wanted to finish the work we had already undertaken, and we exchanged a few letters concerning two new texts from *Berliner Kindheit* that I was in the process of finishing: "Zwei Blechkapellen" and "Schmetterlingsjagd." We were supposed to meet on April 20. The day before, I received a note canceling our appointment. "It is with great bitterness," he wrote, "that I find I must submit to the malevolent constellation which seems to have been ruling over us for some time. I'm writing you these lines a few hours before an unexpected departure."

He did not give me the reason for this departure, and I never heard from him again. Our friendship thus vanished behind the veil of mystery with which he enjoyed surrounding certain phenomena of his life and thought, and this disappearance was never to be illuminated by more than the vague glimmer of a "malevolent constellation."

Even his death was shrouded in mystery. To this day I am not certain of its details. Professor Theodor Adorno, his close friend and the executor of his literary estate, wrote me the following:

The day of Walter Benjamin's death could not be determined with absolute certainty; we think it was on September 26, 1940. Benjamin crossed the Pyrenees with a small group of emigrés in order to find refuge in Spain. The group was intercepted in Port-Bou by the Spanish police, which told them they would be sent back the next day to Vichy. In the course of the night, Benjamin ingested a large dose of sleeping pills and resisted with all his strength the care that people attempted to administer to him on the following day.

Walter Benjamin was one of the most intelligent men I have ever met in my life. He was perhaps the only one who gave me with so much force the impression that there is a depth of thought where, propelled by rigorous logical reasoning, precise historic and scientific facts inhabit a plane in which they coexist with their poetic counterparts, a plane where poetry is no longer simply a form of literary thought, but reveals itself as an expression of the truth that illuminates the most intimate correspondences between man and the world.

Translated by M. Martin Guiney

Notes

* See Walter Benjamin/Gershom Scholem *Correspondence 1933–1940* (New York: Shocken Books, forthcoming), letter 4.

† Ibid., letter 23.

‡ The most spiteful example is provided by the essays of Benjamin's childhood friend Herbert Blumenthal (later Belmore); see the bibliography.

Between Marx and Fourier

Pierre Klossowski

The "Work of Art" essay, Benjamin wrote in 1936, "should appear in the Institute's journal, and in French. The work on this translation will lie in the hands of an especially talented man [Pierre Klossowski]; nevertheless the translation will scarcely come about without impairing the text. On the other hand, in view of my present situation, publication of the French text is very desirable." The essay did in fact first appear in French, in the Zeitschrift für Sozialforschung, *and its publication was attended by various difficulties. For Benjamin the most unsettling encroachments upon the text came from the journal's editors, who insisted on deletions and terminological modifications. But Benjamin was also accurate in predicting that there would be problems in translating his essay, even though Klossowski was an experienced translator. Resolving the difficulties required a fortnight of intense consultation with Klossowski, during which Benjamin rethought some of his earlier formulations. Benjamin was surely relentless in these work sessions; he must have regarded the translation as a kind of* carte de visite—*even more, a way to establish credentials—to gain him entrance into the closed circles of Parisian literary and philosophical mavens. This experience could be the source of Klossowski's observation, in a letter to Adrienne Monnier in 1952, that conversations with Benjamin could take a passionate, if not forceful, turn. Klossowski's remarks here about Benjamin, written more than three decades after their encounter, reach well beyond the "Work of Art" essay* and render impressions of Benjamin in an altogether different intellectual constellation than the other recollections. Klossowski places Benjamin between Marx and Fourier, each of whom Benjamin had made the subject of a sheaf of notes in his* Passagen-Werk.

In September 1940 when Walter Benjamin decided to put an end to his life, persuaded that he held a losing hand—with his characteristic restraint, he had neglected all opportunities to locate safe refuge—he was undoubtedly far from thinking, even for a moment, that with a single blow he would also deprive his contemporaries of one of their most perspicacious witnesses.

A confirmed Marxist—but with an ever-wakeful suspicion of all dogmatic applications and with caustic irony for all overly zealous discriminations, denouncing numerous missteps—he was intent on safeguarding, in his vast erudition (conforming to a thoroughly lyrical sensibility), what in the past had constituted for him the "shadow of the goods to come." Among these goods to come figured the vision of a society blossoming in the *free play of the passions.* His nostalgia aspired to reconcile Marx and Fourier.[1]

I met Walter Benjamin in the course of one of the meetings of *Contre-Attaque,* the name adopted by the ephemeral fusion of the groups surrounding André Breton and Georges Bataille in 1935. Later, Benjamin was an assiduous auditor at the Collège de Sociologie, an "exoteric" emanation of the closed and secret group *Acéphale,* which crystallized around Bataille soon after his break with Breton.[2] From that moment on, Benjamin occasionally attended our gatherings.

Disconcerted by the ambiguity of the "Acéphalian" atheology, Walter Benjamin objected with the conclusions he had drawn from his analysis of the German bourgeois-intellectual evolution—namely, that in Germany "the metaphysical and poetic upward valuation of the incommunicable" (a function of the antinomies of industrial capitalist society) had prepared the psychical terrain favorable to the expansion of Nazism. He then tried to apply his analysis to our own situation. Discreetly, he wanted to hold us back from a similar downfall. Despite the appearance of an irreducible incompatibility between the German situation and our situation, he believed that we too risked playing the game of a pure and simple "pre-fascist aestheticism." He clutched at this schema of interpretation, still strongly colored by Lukács's theories, to overcome his own confusion, and sought to enclose us in this sort of dilemma.

No agreement was possible on this point of his analysis; for its presuppositions did not coincide in any respect with the

given conditions and antecedents of the groups formed successively by Breton and Bataille, particularly of *Acéphale*. In return, we questioned him with all the more insistence about what
we sensed to be his most authentic basis—his personal version
of a "phalansterian" renaissance.[3] He sometimes spoke of it as
an "esoterism" that would be both "erotic and artisan," sub-
tending his explicit Marxist conceptions. With the common
ownership of the means of production, the abolished social
classes could be substituted by a redistribution of society into
affective classes. Instead of enslaving affectivity, a free industrial
production would expand its forms and organize their exchange; in this sense, work would become the accomplice of
desires and cease to be their punitive compensation.

Translated by Susan Z. Bernstein

Notes

* Jeffrey Mehlman has detailed the mark left on Klossowski's later work by the task of
translating Benjamin's text, in a superb essay, "Literature and Hospitality: Klossowski's
Hamann," *Studies in Romanticism* 22 (Summer 1983): 329ff.

1. Klossowski is interested in Fourier's emphasis on sensual passion as a form of social
critique and sees a comparable sort of "delirious" writing in the works of Fourier and
the Marquis de Sade; both are, "in some sense, augurs of the metamorphosis of affectivity in its combat with the repressive forces of modern institutions, and also the meta-
morphoses of these repressive forces in their combat with the affects." Like Fourier,
Klossowski stresses the mutual determination of erotic passions and economic forces:
"For if this combat gives rise to a reciprocal metamorphosis of present forces, it is
because the sexual impulse, particularly the forms of sensual emotion, are immediately
related to existing economic norms" (Klossowski, "Sade et Fourier," *Topique* 4–5
[October 1970]: 79). (Trans.)

2. For a manifesto of *Contre-Attaque*, see André Breton, *Position Politique du Surréalisme*
(Paris: Editions du Sagittaire, 1935), 167–74. The manifesto describes the relation of
Contre-Attaque to Marxism; for example: "*Contre-Attaque* includes Marxists and non-
Marxists. None of the essential points of the doctrine it attempts to elaborate is in
contradiction with the fundamental notions of Marxism." (Trans.)
    The Collège de Sociologie, founded by Bataille, Leiris, and Caillois, existed from
1937 to 1939. For a critical perspective on the circumstances of these groups, see Denis
Hollier, ed., *Le Collège de Sociologie* (Paris: Editions Gallimard, 1979), in which the texts
pertinent to the activities of the Collège are collected. (Trans.)
    Acéphale, from the Greek *akephalos*, means "headless." *Acéphale* was not only the name
of this largely mysterious group, but also of a publication that appeared in 1936–37.
For the program of *Acéphale*, see Georges Bataille, *Oeuvres Complètes*, vol. 2 (Paris:

Éditions Gallimard, 1970). The fifth point in the program seems characteristic: "To realize the universal accomplishment of personal being in the irony of the world of animals and through the revelation of an acéphalous universe, play and not state or duty" (273). (Trans.)

3. "Phalanstery" is the term used by Fourier for the ideal collective dwelling units, which would house 1500–1600 people, organized on the principle of passional attraction. (Trans.)

alternative. "Walter Benjamin," 10, 56–57 (October–December 1967), 72 pp. [W. Benjamin, H. Brenner, R. Heise, H. H. Holz, H.-D. Kittsteiner, A. Lacis, H. Lethen]; "Walter Benjamin (II)," 11, 59–60 (April–June 1968), 49 pp. [W. Benjamin, H. Brenner, H. Gallas, R. Heise, W. Schütte, S. Unseld, *Frankfurter Rundschau*, the editors of *alternative*]

alternative. "Faszination Benjamin," 23, 132–33 (June–August 1980), 63 pp. [W. Fuld, A. Hillach, P. Krumme, B. Lindner, M. Lüdke, H. Nagel, G. Smith]

aut aut. "Paesaggi Benjaminiana," 189–190 (May–August 1982), 272 pp. [G. Agamben, M. Blanchot, R. Bodei, M. Cacciari, G. Carchia, J. Derrida, F. Heinle, W. Kemp, P. Klossowski, A. Moscati, A. Prete, J. Selz, P. Szondi]

Beicken, Peter and Jay Bodine, eds. "Perspectives on Walter Benjamin," *CG* 12, 3 (1979): 303 pp.

Belloi, Lucio and Lorenzina Lotti, eds. *Walter Benjamin: Tempo storia linguaggio*. Rome: Riuniti, 1983, 243 pp. [G. Agamben, R. Bodei, G. Carchia, F. Desideri, B. Lindner, F. Masini, L. Rampello, F. Rella, J.-M. Rey, G. Schiavoni, H. Schweppenhäuser, I. Wohlfarth]

Bolz, Norbert W. and Richard Faber, eds. *Antike und Moderne: Zu Walter Benjamins "Passagen"*. Würzburg: Königshausen und Neumann, 1986. [N. Bolz, J. Ebach, R. Faber, K. Garber, A. Hillach, A. Kramer, M. Löwy, I. Rüffer, C. Schulte, U. Steiner, J. Taubes, M. Voigts, I. Wohlfarth]

Bolz, Norbert and Richard Faber, eds. *Walter Benjamin: Profane Erleuchtung und Rettende Kritik*. Würzburg: Königshausen and Neumann, 1982, 298 pp. [G. Ahrens, N. Bolz, J. Ebach, R. Faber, A. Hillach, J. Hörisch, U. Rüffer, R. Thiessen]

Bolz, Norbert and Bernd Witte, eds. *Passagen: Walter Benjamins Urgeschichte des XIX. Jahrhunderts*. Munich: Wilhelm Fink, 1984, 197 pp. [N. Bolz, S. Buck-Morss, P. Ivernel, H. D. Kittsteiner, B. Lindner, B. Witte, I. Wohlfarth]

Brodersen, Momme. *Benjamin auf Italienisch: Aspekte einer Rezeption*. Frankfurt a.M.: Neue Kritik, 1982, 159 pp. [M. Brodersen, E. Fachinelli, F. Rella, R. Solmi, G. Vattimo]

————. *Walter Benjamin. Bibliografia critica generale (1913–1983)*. Palermo: Centro internationale studi di estetica, 1984, 189 pp.

Buci-Glucksmann, Christine. *Walter Benjamin und die Utopie des Weiblichen*. Hamburg: VSA, 1984, 95 pp.

Buck-Morss, Susan. *Walter Benjamin and the Dialectics of Seeing: A Study of the Arcades Project*. Cambridge, MA: MIT Press, 1988.

Bullock, Marcus. *Romanticism and Marxism*. New York: Peter Lang, 1987. [Diss., University of Oregon, 1980]

Bulthaup, Peter, ed. *Materialien zu Benjamins Thesen 'Über den Begriff der Geschichte'*. Frankfurt a.M.: Suhrkamp, 1975. [T. W. Adorno, P. Bulthaup, H. Engelhardt, K. Greffrath, P.v Haselberg, G. Kaiser, H.-D. Kittsteiner, H. Marcuse, G. Mensching, P. Missac, H. Pfotenhauer, U. Sonnemann, H. Schweppenhäuser, R. Tiedemann]

Burger, Rudolf. *Fortschritt, Aufstieg, und Verfall eines Begriffs. Bemerkungen nach Walter Benjamins Thesen "Über den Begriff der Geschichte"*. Vienna: Verband der wissenschaftlichen Gesellschaft Österreichs, 1983, 63 pp.

Bibliography

Desideri, Fabrizio. *Walter Benjamin: il tempo e le forme*. Rome: Riuniti, 1980, 357 pp.

———. *Il vero non ha finestre... note su ottica e dialettica nel Passagen-Werk di Benjamin*. Bologna: Cappelli, 1984, 41 pp.

Dieckhoff, Reiner. *Mythos und Moderne. Über die verborgene Mystik in der Schriften Walter Benjamins*. Cologne: Janus, 1987, 100 pp.

Eagleton, Terry. *Walter Benjamin or Towards a New Criticism*. London: Verso and New Left Books, 1981, 187 pp.
   M. Bullock, *Minnesota Review*, n.s. 18 (Spring 1982): 156–58; M. Rosen, *TLS* (February 4, 1983), 109–10; M. Bullock, *NGC* 39 (Fall 1986): 219–32; I. Birchall, *International Socialism* 2,16:114–24; P. Johnson, *Arena* 60 (1987): 119–35; M. Bohr, *Comment* (September 19, 1987).

Faber, Richard. *Der Collage-Essay. Eine wissenschaftliche Darstellungsform. Hommage à Walter Benjamin*. Hildesheim: Gerstenberg, 1979, 81 pp.

Figal, Günter and Horst Folkers. *Zur Theorie der Gewalt und Gewaltlosigkeit bei Walter Benjamin*. Heidelberg: FEST, 1979, 69 pp.

Frisby, David. *Walter Benjamin. An Introduction to His Social Theory*. Cambridge: Polity, 1988, c. 200 pp.

Fuld, Werner. *Walter Benjamin: Zwischen den Stühlen*. Munich: Carl Hanser, 1979, 321 pp. Revised ed., Frankfurt a.M.: S. Fischer, 1981, 333 pp.

Gagnebin, Jeanne-Marie. *Zur Geschichtsphilosophie Walter Benjamins: Die Unabgeschlossenheit des Sinnes*. Erlangen: Palm and Enke, 1978, 159 pp.

Garber, Klaus. *Reception und Rettung. Drei Studien zu Walter Benjamin*. Tübingen: Niemeyer, 1987, 201 pp.

Gavagna, Riccardo. *Benjamin in Italia. Bibliografia italiana 1956–1980*. Florence: G. C. Sansoni, 1982, 105 pp.

Gebhardt, Peter, et al. *Walter Benjamin—Zeitgenosse der Moderne*. Kronberg/Ts.: Scriptor, 1976, 145 pp. [P. Gebhardt, M. Grzimek, D. Harth, M. Rumpf, U. Schödlbauer, B. Witte]

Greffrath, Krista R. *Metaphorischer Materialismus: Untersuchungen zum Geschichtsbegriff Walter Benjamins*. Munich: Wilhelm Fink, 1981, 174 pp.

Günther, Henning. *Walter Benjamin und der humane Marxismus*. Olten: Walter, 1974, 188 pp.

Hering, Christoph. *Der Intellektuelle als Revolutionär*. Munich: Fink, 1979, 185 pp.

———. *Die Rekonstruktion der Revolution. Walter Benjamins Messianischer Materialismus in den Thesen "Über den Begriff der Geschichte."* Frankfurt a.M.: Peter Lang, 1983, 218 pp.
   J. Roberts, *TLS* (July 27, 1984), 851.

Hörisch, Jochen. *Die Theorie der Verausgabung und die Verausgabung der Theorie—Benjamin zwischen Bataille und Sohn-Rethel*. Bremen: Buchladen Wassmann, 1983, 31 pp. [includes note by Sohn-Rethel]

International Journal of Sociology. "Walter Benjamin," 7, 1 (Spring 1977), 123 pp. [A. Arato, H. Paetzold, S. Radnoti]

Jennings, Michael. *Dialectical Images: Walter Benjamin's Theory of Literary Criticism.* Ithaca: Cornell University Press, 1987, 233 pp.

Kaiser, Gerhard. *Benjamin. Adorno. Zwei Studien.* Frankfurt: Athenäum, 1974, 168 pp.
   H. W. Belmore, *German Life and Letters* 31, 4 (July 1978): 386–88.

Kambas, Chryssoula. *Walter Benjamin im Exil. Zum Verhältnis von Literaturpolitik und Ästhetik.* Tübingen: Max Niemeyer, 1983, 247 pp.
   J. Roberts, *TLS* (July 27, 1984), 851.

Kauten, Heinrich. *Rettung und Destruktion. Untersuchungen zur Hermeneutik Walter Benjamins.* Tübingen: Niemeyer, 1987, 289 pp.

Kleiner, Barbara. *Sprache und Entfremdung. Die Proust-Übersetzungen Walter Benjamins innerhalb seiner Sprach- und Übersetzungstheorie.* Bonn: Bouvier, 1980, 218 pp.

Kothe, Flavio. *Para ler Benjamin.* Rio de Janeiro: Francisco Alves Editore, 1976, 126 pp.

Leinweber, Jörg. *Mimetisches Vermögen und allegorisches Verhalten. Studien zu Walter Benjamin und seiner Lehre vom Ähnlichen.* Antiquariat J. Leinweber, 299 pp. [Diss., Marburg, 1978]

Lindner, Burkhardt, ed. *'Links hatte noch alles sich zu enträtseln . . .' Walter Benjamin im Kontext.* Frankfurt a.M.: Syndikat, 1978, 324 pp. [J. Derrida, H. Engelhardt, G. Hartung, A. Hillach, W. Kemp, B. Lindner, M. Müller, H. Pfotenhauer, G. Schiavoni, I. Wohlfarth]. Second ed., Frankfurt a.M.: Athenäum, 1985, 342 pp. [adds second essay by B. Lindner]

Masini, Feruccio. *Brecht e Benjamin. Scienza della letteratura e ermeneutica materialista.* Bari: de Donato, 1977, 207 pp.

Meiffert, Torsten. *Die enteignete Erfahrung. Zu Walter Benjamins Konzept einer "Dialektik im Stillstand".* Bielefeld: Aisthesis, 1986, 191 pp.

Menninghaus, Winfried. *Walter Benjamins Theorie der Sprachmagie.* Frankfurt a.M.: Suhrkamp, 1980, 282 pp.

———. *Schwellenkunde. Walter Benjamins Passage der Mythos.* Frankfurt a.M.: Suhrkamp, 1986, 120 pp.

Missac, Pierre. *Passage de Walter Benjamin.* Paris: Editions du Seuil, 1987, 232 pp.

Moroncini, Bruno. *Walter Benjamin e la Moralità del Moderno.* Napoli: Guida, 1984, 421 pp.

Musik, Gunar. *Die erkenntnistheoretischen Grundlagen der Ästhetik Walter Benjamins und ihr Fortwirken in der Konzeption des Passagen-Werks.* Frankfurt a.M.: P. Lang, 1985, 218 pp.

Nägele, Rainer, guest ed. "Walter Benjamin." *Studies* 11, 1 (Fall 1986).

Naeher, Jürgen. *Walter Benjamins Allegorie-Begriff als Modell: Zur Konstitution philosophischer Literaturwissenschaft.* Stuttgart: Klett-Cotta, 1977, 275 pp.

Paetzold, Heinz. *Neomarxistische Ästhetik.* Part 1: *Bloch, Benjamin.* Dusseldorf: Schwann, 1974, 196 pp.

M. T. Jones, *NGC* 8 (Spring 1976): 180–86.

Pelzer-Knoll, Gudrun. *Kindheit und Erfahrung: Untersuchungen zur Pädagogik Walter Benjamins.* Königstein/Ts.: Hain, 1986, 128 pp.

Pezzella, Mario. *L'immagine dialettica. Saggio su Benjamin.* Pisa: E.T.S., 1982, 176 pp.

Pfotenhauer, Helmut. *Ästhetische Erfahrung und gesellschaftliches System: Untersuchungen zu Methodenproblemen einer materialistischen Literaturanalyse am Spätwerk Walter Benjamins.* Stuttgart: Metzler, 1975, 161 pp.

Pullega, Paolo. *Commenti alle "Tesi di filosofia della storia" di Walter Benjamin.* Bologna: Cappelli, 1980, 165 pp.

Rabinbach, Anson, ed. "Special Walter Benjamin Issue." *NGC* 17 (Spring 1979), 208 pp.

Rella, Franco, ed. *Critica e storia.* Venice: Cluva, 1980, 235 pp. [W. Benjamin, M. Cacciari, J. Derrida, F. Desideri, G. Franck, R. Infelise-Fronza, G. Mensching, F. Rella]

Revue D'Esthétique. "Walter Benjamin," new series 1 (1981), 186 pp. [W. Benjamin, P. Bürger, M. de Launay, J. Habermas, M. Jiminez, Y. Kobry, J.-R. Ladmiral, E. Palumbo-Liou, R. Rochlitz, G. Scholem, I. Wohlfarth, P. Zima]

Ridless, Robin. *Ideology and Art: Theories of Mass Culture from Walter Benjamin to Umberto Eco.* New York: Peter Lang, 1984, 232 pp. [Diss., New York University, 1983]

Roberts, Julian. *Walter Benjamin.* London: Macmillan, 1982, 250 pp.
    J. C. Evans, *Ethics* 94, 3 (1984): 555; N. Jacobs, *New Statesman* (May 20, 1983); S. S. Prawer, *TLS* 4174 (April 1, 1983), 339; M. Bullock, *NGC* 39 (Fall 1986): 219–32.

Rumpf, M. *Spekulative Literaturtheorie: Zu Walter Benjamins Trauerspielbuch.* Königstein/Ts.: Forum Academicum, 1908, 200 pp.

Rutigliano, Enzo. *Lo squardo dell'angelo. Su Walter Benjamin.* Bari: Dedalo, 1981, 117 pp.

Salzinger, Helmut. *Swinging Benjamin.* Frankfurt a.M.: Fischer, 1973, 179 pp.
    [G. Steiner] *TLS* 6 (December 14, 1973), 1539.

Schiavoni, Guilio. *Walter Benjamin: Sopravvivere alla cultura* (Palmermo: Sellerio, 1980), 345 pp.

Schiller-Lerg, Sabine. *Walter Benjamin und der Rundfunk.* Munich: K. Saur, 1984, 548 pp.

Schmidt, Burghart. *Benjamin zur Einführung.* Hannover: SOAK, 1983, 95 pp. [includes essay by W. van Reijen]

Schobinger, Jean-Pierre. *Variationen zu Walter Benjamins Sprachmeditationen.* Basel: Schwabe, 1979, 121 pp.

Scholem, Gershom. *Walter Benjamin—die Geschichte einer Freundschaft.* Frankfurt a.M.: Suhrkamp, 1975, 299 pp. English translation: *Walter Benjamin: The Story of a Friendship,* trans. Harry Zohn. Philadelphia: Jewish Publication Society, 1981.

D. Ellenson, *Religious Studies* 9, 1 (1983): 83; P. Fry, *Raritan* II, 4 (Spring 1983): 131–52; E. Grossman, *Jerusalem Post Magazine* (May 14, 1982), 16; A. Thorlby, *TLS* 4166 (February 4, 1983), 110; R. Wolin, *Telos* 58 (Winter 1983–84): 219–27.

————. *Walter Benjamin und sein Engel. Vierzehn Aufsätze und kleine Beiträge*, ed. R. Tiedemann. Frankfurt a.M.: Suhrkamp, 1983, 224 pp.

Smith, Gary, guest ed. "Walter Benjamin: Philosophy, History, and Aesthetics." *The Philosophical Forum* 15, 1–2 (Fall–Winter 1983–84), 208 pp. [T. W. Adorno, W. Benjamin, L. Lowenthal, S. Moses, S. Radnoti, G. Smith, J. Snyder, J. Todd] Revised edition, *Thinking Through Benjamin*, Chicago: University of Chicago Press, 1989. [adds W. Benjamin, R. Sieburth]

Stern, Howard. *Gegenbild, Reihenfolge, Sprung: An Essay in Related Figures of Argument in Walter Benjamin*. Afterword by K. W. Wachter. Bern: Peter Lang, 1982, 121 pp. [Diss., Yale University, 1978]
    M. Bullock, *Minnesota Review*, n.s. 21 (Fall 1983): 138–41.

Stoessel, Marleen. *Aura. Das vergessene Menschliche. Zu Sprache und Erfahrung bei Walter Benjamin*. Munich: Hanser, 1983, 255 pp.

Stüssi, Anna. *Erinnerung an die Zukunft. Walter Benjamins 'Berliner Kindheit um Neunzehnhundert'*. Göttingen: Vandenhoeck and Ruprecht, 1977, 282 pp.
    C. C. Zorach, *The German Quarterly* 51, 3 (May 1978): 388f.

Text + Kritik. "Walter Benjamin," 31–32 (October 1971), 92 pp. [W. Benjamin, P. Krumme, B. Lindner, G. Plumpe, D. Thierkopf, L. Wiesenthal]. Second ed., July 1979, 122 pp. [adds F. Masini, H. Stern, B. Witte]

Tiedemann, Rolf. *Studien zur Philosophie Walter Benjamins*. Preface by T. W. Adorno. Frankfurt a.M.: Europäische Verlagsanstalt, 1965, 222 pp. Reprinted Frankfurt a.M.: Suhrkamp, 1973, 189 pp.
    H. W. Belmore, *German Life and Letters* 21, 4 (July 1968): 345–50.

————. *Dialektik im Stillstand. Versuche zum Spätwerk Walter Benjamins*. Frankfurt a.M.: Suhrkamp, 1983, 195 pp.

Trabitzsch, Michael. *Walter Benjamin. Moderne, Messianismus, Politik. Über die Liebe zum Gegenstand*. Berlin: Verlag der Beeken, 1985, 128 pp.

Unger, Peter. *Walter Benjamin als Rezensent. Die Reflexion eines Intellektuellen auf die zeitgeschichtliche Situation*. Frankfurt a.M.: Peter Lang, 1978, 281 pp.

Unseld, Siegfried, ed. *Zur Aktualität Walter Benjamins*. Frankfurt a.M.: Suhrkamp, 1972, 288 pp. [W. Benjamin, B. Brecht, J. Habermas, W. Kraft, A. Monnier, H. Sahl, G. Scholem, H. Schweppenhäuser, R. Tiedemann, S. Unseld]. First printed privately as *Walter Benjamin zu ehren. Sonderausgabe aus Anlaß des 80. Geburtstages von Walter Benjamin am 15. Juli 1972*, 215 pp. [without J. Habermas]
    [G. Steiner] *TLS* 6 (December 14, 1973), 1539.

Wawryzn, Lienhard. *Walter Benjamins Kunsttheorie. Kritik einer Rezeption*. Darmstadt: Luchterhand, 1973, 108 pp.
    K. P. Etzkorn, *Contemporary Sociology* 3, 4 (1974): 366.

Wiesenthal, Liselotte. *Zur Wissenschaftstheorie Walter Benjamins*. Frankfurt a.M.: Athenäum, 1973, 211 pp.

Wisman, Heinz, ed. *Walter Benjamin et Paris*. Paris: Cerf, 1986, 1033 pp. [M. Abensour, G. Agamben, E. Bavcar, A. Betz, R. Bischof, R. Bodei, N. Bolz, C. Buci-Glucksmann, S. Buck-Morss, G. Carchia, F. Desideri, H. Engelhardt, M. Espagne, W. Fietkau, M. de Gandillac, K. Garber, K. Greffrath, A. Hillach, J. Hörisch, C. Kambas, B. Kleiner, J. Leenhardt, H.-T. Lehmann, E. Lenk, B. Lindner, M. Löwy, W. Menninghaus, H. Meschonnic, P. Missac, S. Moses, A. Münster, D. Oehler, M. Pessella, H. Pfotenhauer, S. Radnoti, M. Sagnol, G. Schiavoni, M. Stoessel, H. Tiedemann, Z. Tordai, W. van Reijen, M. Werner, H. Wismann, B. Witte, I. Wohlfarth, R. Wolin]

Witte, Bernd. *Walter Benjamin—Der Intellektuelle als Kritiker. Untersuchungen zu seinem Frühwerk.* Stuttgart: Metzler, 1976, 244 pp.
  D. Wellbery, *The German Quarterly* 51, 3 (May 1978): 389f.; K. Opitz, *World Literature Today* 52 (Winter 1978): 110.

———. *Walter Benjamin.* Berlin: Rowohlt, 1985, 157 pp. Expanded edition in French, Paris: Cerf, 1987.

Wohlfarth, Irving, guest ed. "Second Special Issue on Walter Benjamin," *NGC* 39 (Fall 1986), 232 pp. [S. Buck-Morss, M. Bullock, W. Fietkau, P. Ivernel, C. Kambas, B. Lindner, H.-D. Kittsteiner, B. Witte, I. Wohlfarth]

Wolin, Richard. *An Aesthetic of Redemption.* New York: Columbia University, 1982, 316 pp.
  D. Barnouw, *The German Quarterly* 57, 1 (Winter 1984): 132–33; S. Buck-Morss, *Theory and Society*, 743–48; M. Bullock, *NGC* 39 (Fall 1986): 219–32; M. Crozier, *Thesis Eleven*, 10–11 (1984–85): 225–33; F. Feher, *NGC* 28 (Winter 1983): 170–80; P. Fry, *Raritan* II, 4 (Spring 1983): 131–52; N. Jacobs, *New Statesman* (May 20, 1983); J. W. Murphy, *Studies in Soviet Thought* 31 (January 1986): 65–67; M. Rosen, *TLS* (February 4, 1983), 109–10; L. Ulansey, *MLN* 98, 5 (1983): 1319–22.

Dissertations

This grouping excludes dissertations in languages other than English and dissertations later published as books. Abstracts of some of the following titles are published in *Dissertation Abstracts International*.

Asman-Schneider, Carrie L. "The Language of Nature and the Language of Man: The Restitution of the Mimetic and the Material in the Language Philosophy of Walter Benjamin." Stanford University, 1988.

Dobak, Annelies Maria. "The Literary Critic as Alchemist. Walter Benjamin's Allegorical Method: From Romanticism to Baudelaire." Catholic University of America, 1982, 295 pp.

Harbo, Peter. "Walter Benjamin and the Romantics." University of Massachusetts, Amherst, 1982, 237 pp.

Hendren, Anne A. "Mediation of Knowledge in Artistic Discourse: An Analysis of Works by Walter Benjamin and Marcel Proust." Cornell University, 1983, 127 pp.

Kaufmann, Lane. "The Theory of the Essay: Lukács, Adorno, and Benjamin." University of California, San Diego, 1981, 370 pp.

MacDonald, Bruce Robert. "Translation as Transcendence: Walter Benjamin and the German Tradition of Translation Theory." University of California, San Diego, 1984, 153 pp.

McBride, Eugene James. "Messianic Time and German Politics Between the Wars (1919–1940): A Comparative Analysis of the Writings of Paul Tillich and Walter Benjamin." Graduate Theological Union, 1985, 484 pp.

McCole, John. "Walter Benjamin and the Antinomies of Tradition." Boston University, 1987.

Rudbeck, Carl Reinhold. "The Literary Criticism of Walter Benjamin." State University of New York, Binghamton, 1976, 222 pp.

Wallace, Katherine Theresa. "Returning the Gaze: Walter Benjamin's Baudelaire Project." Harvard University, 1984, 187 pp.

Essays, Selections, and Miscellany in English

Adams, Robert Martin. Review of *Illuminations*. *Hudson Review* 22, 1 (1969): 165–71.

Adorno, Theodor W. "A Portrait of Walter Benjamin," *Prisms*, trans. Samuel and Shierry Weber. London: Neville Spearman, 1967, 229–41. Reprinted Cambridge, MA: MIT Press, 1981.

————. "Letters to Walter Benjamin," trans. Harry Zohn. *NLR* 81 (September–October 1973): 55–80. Reprinted in *Aesthetics and Politics*. London: New Left Books, 1977, 110–33.

————. *Aesthetic Theory*, ed. Gretel Adorno and Rolf Tiedemann, trans. C. Lenhardt. London: Routledge & Kegan Paul, 1984, passim. [Revised translation forthcoming]

Agamben, Giorgio. "Language and History in Benjamin." *Differentia* 2 (Spring 1988).

Allen, Richard W. "The Aesthetic Experience of Modernity: Benjamin, Adorno, and Contemporary Film Theory." *NGC* 40 (Winter 1987): 225–40.

Alter, Robert. "Walter Benjamin." *Commentary* 49 (September 8, 1969), 86–93.

————. "WB: the aura of the past." In Alter, *Defenses of the Imagination*. Philadelphia: Jewish Publication Society, 1978, 47–66.

[Anon.] "Philosopher-Artist." *TLS* 3111 (October 13, 1961), 681.

[Anon.] "Letter to the Editor." *TLS* (September 5, 1968), 953.

[Anon.] "Baudelaire as Contagious Conspirator." *TLS* (January 8, 1970), 31.

[Anon.] "Charles Baudelaire: A Lyric Poet in the Era of High Capitalism by Walter Benjamin." *The Times*, London (August 30, 1973), 10f.

[Anon.] "Walter Benjamin" [Bibliography]. In [anon.], *A Report on Its History Aims and Activities 1933–1938*. New York: International Institute for Social Research, 1938, 27.

Arato, Andrew and Eike Gebhardt, eds. *The Essential Frankfurt School Reader*. New York: Urizen, 1977.

Arato, Andrew. "Introduction: The Antinomies of the Neo-Marxian Theory of Culture." *IJS* 7, 1 (Spring 1977): 3–24.

Bibliography

Arendt, Hannah. "Introduction. Walter Benjamin 1892–1940," trans. Harry Zohn. In *Walter Benjamin, Illuminations*, trans. Harry Zohn. New York: Harcourt, Brace & World, 1968, 1–55. Reprinted in Arendt, *Men in Dark Times*. New York: Schocken, 1968. First appeared in *The New Yorker* (October 19, 1968), 65–156.

Aronowitz, Stanley. "History as Disruption: On Benjamin and Foucault." *Humanities in Society* 2, 2 (1979): 125–47.

Bahti, Timothy. "History as Rhetorical Enactment: Walter Benjamin's Theses 'On the Concept of History'." *Diacritics* 10 (Fall 1979): 2–17.

———. "Theories of Knowledge: Fate and Forgetting in the Early Works of Benjamin." *Studies* 11, 1 (Fall 1986): 47–68.

———. "Death and Authority, End and Origin: Benjamin's 'Storyteller' Essay and *Trauerspiel* Book." In Bahti, *Allegories of History: Literary Historiography after Hegel* (forthcoming).

Bathrick, David. "Reading Walter Benjamin from East to West." *CG* 12, 3 (1979): 246–55.

Beicken, Peter and Jay Bodine. "Walter Benjamin. A Selected Bibliographical Checklist." *CG* 12, 3 (1979): 292–303.

Beiner, Ronald. "Walter Benjamin's Philosophy of History." *Political Theory* 12 (August 1984): 423–34.

Belmore, Herbert W. "Walter Benjamin." *German Life and Letters* 15, 4 (1961–62): 309–13. [Review of *Illuminationen*]

———. "Some Recollections of Walter Benjamin." *German Life and Letters* 28, 2 (January 1975): 119–27.

Berger, John. *Ways of Seeing*. London: Penguin, 1972, passim.

———. "Walter Benjamin." *New Society* (June 18, 1970), 1067. Reprinted in Berger, *Selected Essays and Articles: The Look of Things*. London: Penguin, 1972, 87–93.

Bernheimer, Charles. *Flaubert and Kafka: Studies in Psychopoetic Structure*. New Haven: Yale University Press, 1982, 189–98.

Bewell, Alan. "Portraits at Greyfriars: Photography, History, and Memory." *Clio* 12, 1 (1982): 17–29.

Biale, David. "Benjamin's Influence." In Biale, *Gershom Scholem. Kabbalah and Counter-History*, 2nd ed. Cambridge, MA: Harvard University Press, 1982, 136–42.

Birkerts, Sven. "Walter Benjamin. *Flâneur: A Flanerie*." *The Iowa Review* 13, 3–4 (Spring 1982 (1983)): 164–79.

Bloch, Ernst. "Philosophy as Cabaret," trans. Rodney Livingstone. *NLR* 116 (July–August 1979): 94–96.

Blood, Susan. "Baudelaire Against Photography: An Allegory of Old Age." *MLN* 101, 4 (September 1986): 817–37.

Blume, Harvey. "For Benjamin: The *Theses on the Philosophy of History*." *Telos* 41 (Fall 1979): 155–57.

Brewster, Ben. "Walter Benjamin and the Arcades Project." *NLR* 48 (March–April 1968): 72–76. Reprinted in *Perspecta: The Yale Architecture Journal* 12 (1969): 161–64.

Bronner, Stephen Eric. "The Tapestry Unravels. Considerations on the Structure of Walter Benjamin's Thought." *CG* 12, 3 (1979): 201–19.

Bruck, Jan. "Beckett, Benjamin and the Modern Crisis in Communication." *NGC* 26 (Spring–Summer 1982).

Bryher (Winifred Ellerman). *The Days of Mars: A Memoir, 1940–1946*. London: Calder and Boyars, 1972, 22–24.

Buck-Morss, Susan. *The Origin of Negative Dialectics. Theodor W. Adorno, Walter Benjamin, and the Frankfurt Institute*. New York: Free Press, 1977; Hassocks: Harvester Press, 1977, 335 pp.
   G. Rose, *History and Theory* (1978): 126–35; P. Hohendahl, *Telos* 34 (Winter 1977–78): 184–87; M. Rosen, *TLS* (August 25, 1978), 955.

––––––. "Walter Benjamin—Revolutionary Writer I." *NLR* 128 (July–August 1981): 50–75; "Walter Benjamin—Revolutionary Writer II." *NLR* 129 (September–October 1981): 77–95.

––––––. "Benjamin's *Passagen-Werk*: Redeeming Mass Culture for the Revolution." *NGC* 29 (Spring–Summer 1983): 211–40.

––––––. Review of *Das Passagen-Werk*. *The German Quarterly* 57, 3 (Summer 1984): 456–58.

––––––. "The Flâneur, the Sandwich-Man and the Whore: The Politics of Loitering." *NGC* 39 (Fall 1986): 99–140.

Bürger, Peter. "Regarding the Discussion of Benjamin's Theory of Art." In Bürger, *Theory of the Avant-Garde*, trans. Michael Shaw. Minneapolis: University of Minnesota Press, 1984, 27–34.

Bullock, Marcus. "Eclipse of the Sun: Mystical Terminology, Revolutionary Method and Esoteric Prose in Friedrich Schlegel." *MLN* 98, 3 (April 1983): 454–83.

––––––. "The Coming of the Messiah or the Stoic Burning—Aspects of the Negated Text in Walter Benjamin and Friedrich Schlegel." *The Germanic Review* 60, 1 (Winter 1985): 2–15.

Callen, Don. Review of *The Origin of German Tragic Drama*. *The Journal of Aesthetics and Art Criticism* 37, 1 (Fall 1978): 103–4.

Caygill, Howard. "The Significance of Allegory in the *Ursprung des deutschen Trauerspiels*." In Frances Barker et al., ed. *1642: Literature and Power in the Seventeenth Century*. Colchester: Department of Literature, University of Essex, 1981, 207–19.

Corngold, Stanley and Michael Jennings. "Walter Benjamin/Gershom Scholem." *Interpretation* 12, 2–3 (May–September 1984): 357–66. [Review of *Briefwechsel*]

Cowan, Bainard. "Walter Benjamin's Theory of Allegory." *NGC* 22 (Winter 1981): 109–22.

Davies, Ioan. "Approaching Walter Benjamin: Retrieval, Translation and Reconstruction." *Canadian Journal of Political and Social Theory* 4, 1 (Winter 1980): 59–74.

Davis, R. G. "Benjamin, Storytelling and Brecht in the USA." *NGC* 17 (Spring 1979): 143–56.

De Man, Paul. " 'Conclusions' on Walter Benjamin's 'The Task of the Translator'." *Yale French Studies* 69 (1985): 25–48.

Demetz, Peter. "Introduction," to Walter Benjamin, *Reflections*, ed. P. D., trans. Edmund Jephcott. New York: Harcourt Brace Jovanovich, 1978, vii–xliii.

Derrida, Jacques. "Des Tours de Babel," trans. Joseph F. Graham. In Graham, ed. *Difference in Translation*. Ithaca: Cornell University Press, 1985, 165–207.

Donaghue, Denis. "Keeping the faith with broken music: the criticism of Walter Benjamin." *Listener* 84 (August 8, 1970), 184f.

Eagleton, Terry. Review of *Understanding Brecht*. *International Socialism* (May 1973), 25ff.

———. "German Aesthetic Duels." *NLR* 107 (January–February 1978): 21–37. [Review of *Aesthetics and Politics*]

Eder, Richard. "Walter Benjamin's *Moscow Diary*." *L.A. Times Book Review* (November 9, 1986), 3, 13.

Feher, Ferenc. "Lukács and Benjamin: Parallels and Contrasts." *NGC* 34 (Winter 1985): 125–38.

Fekete, John. "Benjamin's Ambivalence." *Telos* 35 (Spring 1978): 193–99.

Fietkau, Wolfgang. "Loss of Experience and Experience of Loss: Remarks on the Problem of the Lost Revolution in the Work of Walter Benjamin and his Combatants," trans. Jonathan Monroe and Irving Wohlfarth. *NGC* 39 (Fall 1986): 169–78.

Fischer, Norman. "Walter Benjamin." In Robert A. Gorman, ed. *Biographical Dictionary of Neo-Marxism*. Westport, CT: Greenwood, 1985, 64–66.

Fittko, Lisa. "The Story of Old Benjamin." In Walter Benjamin, *Gesammelte Schriften* V, ed. Rolf Tiedemann. Frankfurt a.M.: Suhrkamp, 1982, 1184–94.

Forster, Kurt. "Residues of a Dream World." In Demetri Porphyrious, ed. *On the Methodology of Architectural History*. London: Architectural Design, 1981, 69–71.

Freund, Gisèle. *Gisèle Freund: Photographer*. New York: Harry S. Abrams, 1985.

Frisby, David. *Fragments of Modernity: Theories of Modernity in the Work of Simmel, Kracauer and Benjamin*. Cambridge: Polity Press, 1985, esp. 187–265.

Fry, Paul H. "The Instance of Walter Benjamin: Distraction and Perception in Criticism." In Fry, *The Reach of Criticism*. New Haven: Yale University Press, 1983, 168–205.

Gasché, Rudolphe. "Saturnine Vision and the Question of Difference: Reflections on Walter Benjamin's Theory of Language." *Studies* 11, 1 (Fall 1986): 69–90.

Gilman, R. "Successful Failure." *The New Republic* (December 14, 1968), 27–29. [Review of *Illuminations*]

Grene, Marjorie. *Philosophy In and Out of Europe*. Berkeley: University of California Press, 1976, 136–38.

Grunfeld, Frederic V. "Ultima Multis: Walter Benjamin, Gertrud Kolmar." In Grunfeld, *Prophets Without Honor*. New York: Holt, Rinehart & Winston; Philadelphia: Jewish Publication Society, 1979, 220–63.

Günther, Henning. "Education and Childhood in Walter Benjamin." *Pädagogische Rundschau* 27 (1973): 153–67.

Habermas, Jürgen. "Consciousness-Raising or Redemptive Criticism: The Contemporaneity of Walter Benjamin," trans. P. Brewster and C. H. Buchner. *NGC* 17 (Spring 1979): 30–59.

––––––. "Consciousness-raising or Rescuing Critique," trans. Frederick Lawrence. In Habermas, *Philosophical-Political Profiles*. Cambridge, MA: MIT Press, 1983, 29–63. [Retranslation of above]

Hamacher, Werner. "The Word *Wolke*—If It Is One," trans. Peter Fenres. *Studies* 11, 1 (Fall 1986): 133–62.

Hamburger, Michael. "Scholem and Benjamin," *Grand Street* 1, 4 (Summer 1982): 128–37. Reprinted in Hamburger, *A Proliferation of Prophets*. Manchester: Carcanet Press, 1983, 285–92.

Hansen, Miriam. "Benjamin, Cinema and Experience: The Blue Flower in the Land of Technology." *NGC* 40 (Winter 1987): 179–224.

Hartman, Geoffrey H. "The Sacred Jungle 2: Walter Benjamin." In Hartman, *Criticism in the Wilderness*. New Haven: Yale University Press, 1980, 63–85.

Higgonet, Anne; Margaret Higgonet; and Patrice Higgonet. "Façades: Walter Benjamin's Paris." *Critical Inquiry* 10, 3 (March 1984): 391–419.

Hillach, Ansgar. "The Aesthetics of Politics: Walter Benjamin's 'Theories of German Fascism'," trans. J. Wikoff and U. Zimmermann. *NGC* 17 (Spring 1979): 99–119.

Hoffman, Louise E. "Walter Benjamin's Infernal City." *Research Studies* 52, 3–4 (September–December 1983): 146–55.

Hollington, Michael. "Between Two Stools: A Biography of Walter Benjamin." In James Walter, ed. *Reading Life Histories: Griffith Papers on Biography*. Nathan, Queensland: Griffith University, Institute for Modern Biography, 1981, 10–19.

Ivernel, Philippe. "Paris, Capital of the Popular Front, or the Posthumous Life of the 19th Century," trans. Valerie Budig. *NGC* 39 (Fall 1986): 61–84.

Jacobs, Carol. "Walter Benjamin's Image of Proust." *MLN* 86, 6 (1971): 910–32. Reprinted in Jacobs, *The Dissimulating Harmony*.

––––––. "I, the Juggler." *Diacritics* 5, 2 (1975): 3f. Reprinted in Jacobs, *The Dissimulating Harmony*.

––––––. "The Monstrosity of Translation." *MLN* 90, 6 (1975): 755–66.

––––––. *The Dissimulating Harmony: The Image of Interpretation in Nietzsche, Rilke, Artaud and Benjamin*. Baltimore: Johns Hopkins University Press, 1978.
    R. G. Echevarria, *MLN* 94 (1979): 1257–61; D. B. Allison, *Comparative Literature* 33 (1981): 76–78.

Jacobs, Nicholas. "Letter to the Editor." *TLS* (January 1974), 32.

———. "Walter Benjamin: The Marxist Critic." *Comment* 12, 11 (1979).

Jameson, Frederic. "Walter Benjamin; or, Nostalgia." *Salmagundi* 10–11 (Fall–Winter 1969–70): 52–68. Reprinted in Jameson, *Marxism and Form: Twentieth-Century Dialectical Theories of Literature.* Princeton: Princeton University Press, 1971, 60–83; and in *The Salmagundi Reader*, ed. R. Boyers and P. Boyers. Bloomington: Indiana University Press, 1984, 561–76.

———. "Benjamin as Historian, or How to Write a Marxist Literary History: A Review Essay." *Minnesota Review*, n.s. 2–3 (Spring–Fall 1974): 116–26.

———. "Afterword" to Jameson, *Sartre: The Origins of a Style*, 2nd ed. New York: Columbia University Press, 1984, 206–12.

Jay, Martin. *The Dialectical Imagination. A History of the Frankfurt School and the Institute of Social Research 1923–1950.* Boston: Little, Brown & Co., 1973.

———. "Politics of Translation: Siegfried Kracauer and Walter Benjamin on the Buber-Rosenzweig Bible." *Publications of the Leo Baeck Institute: Yearbook* 21. London: Seckler & Warburg, 1976, 3–24. Reprinted in Jay, *Permanent Exiles: Essays in the Intellectual Migration from Germany to America.* New York: Columbia University Press, 1986, 198–216.

Jennings, Michael. "Benjamin as a Reader of Hölderlin: The Origins of Benjamin's Theory of Literary Criticism." *The German Quarterly* 56, 4 (November 1983): 544–62.

Johnson, Pauline. "Benjamin." In Johnson, *Marxist Aesthetics.* London: Routledge & Kegan Paul, 1984, 49–67.

Josipovici, Gabriel. "WB, 1892–1940." In Josipovici, *The Lessons of Modernism.* London: Macmillan, 1977, 51–63. First published in *The Times Higher Education Supplement* (January 24, 1974).

———. "The World of Benjamin." *The Jewish Quarterly* 28, 1 (Spring 1980): 54f.

Kambas, Chryssoula. "Political Actuality: Benjamin's Concept of History and the Failure of the French Popular Front," trans. Paul Loeffler and Jamie Owen Daniel. *NGC* 39 (Fall 1986): 87–98.

Kazis, Richard. "Benjamin and the Age of Mechanical Reproduction." *Jump Cut: A Review of Contemporary Cinema* 15 (July 20, 1978), 23–25.

Kermode, Frank. "The Incomparable Benjamin." *The New York Review of Books* 13, 11 (December 18, 1969), 30–33. [Review of *Illuminations*]

———. "Every Kind of Intelligence." *New York Times Book Review* 83, 31 (July 30, 1978), 1, 24–25.

Kittsteiner, H.-D. "Walter Benjamin's Historicism," trans. Jonathan Monroe and Irving Wohlfarth. *NGC* 39 (Fall 1986): 179–215.

Koestler, Arthur. *Scum of the Earth.* New York: Macmillan, 1941, 278.

Kolakowski, Leszek. *Main Currents of Marxism: Its Origin, Growth and Dissolution. 3. The Breakdown.* Oxford: Oxford University Press, 1978, 348–50.

Laing, Dave. *The Marxist Theory of Art.* Boulder, CO: Westview, 1986, chs. 3 and 6.

Lange, Victor. "Thinking Poetically." *Atlantic Monthly* (March 1969), 138–41. [Review of *Illuminations*]

Lerner, Lawrence. "Two Marxists, Fischer and Benjamin." *Encounter* 43, 9 (September 1974): 71f., 75f. [Review of *Charles Baudelaire*]

Lindner, Burkhardt. "The *Passagen-Werk*, the *Berliner Kindheit*, and the Archaeology of the Recent Past," *NGC* 39 (Fall 1986): 25–46.

Lowenthal, Leo. "The Integrity of the Intellectual: In Memory of Walter Benjamin." *PF* 15, 1–2 (Fall–Winter 1983–84), 146–57. Retranslated by David J. Ward for *Thinking Through Benjamin*, ed. G. Smith. Chicago: University of Chicago Press, 1989. Also in *An Unmastered Past: The Autobiographical Reflections of Leo Lowenthal*, ed. with intro. by Martin Jay, foreword by Jürgen Habermas. Berkeley: University of California Press, 1987.

Löwy, Michael. "Marcuse and Benjamin: The Romantic Dimension." *Telos* 44 (Summer 1980): 25–33.

———. "Revolution against 'Progress': Walter Benjamin's Romantic Anarchism." *New Left Review* 152 (July–August 1985): 42–59.

Lukacher, Ned. "Walter Benjamin's Chthonian Revolution." *Boundary 2* 11, 1 and 2 (Fall–Winter 1982–83): 41–57.

Lukács, Georg. "On Walter Benjamin." *NLR* 110 (July–August 1978): 83–88.

Lunn, Eugene. *Marxism and Modernism: A Historical Study of Lukács, Brecht, Benjamin and Adorno.* Berkeley: University of California Press, 1982.

Madsen, Peter. "Semiotics and Dialectics," trans. John von Daler. *Poetics* 6 (1972): 29–49.

Malraux, André. "Our Cultural Heritage." *Left Review* 2, 10 (July 1936): 493.

Marshall, Donald. "Images of Modernism." *Partisan Review* 45, 2 (1978): 313–16. [Review of *Charles Baudelaire*]

Masuzawa, Tomoka. "Tracing the Figure of Redemption: Walter Benjamin's Physiognomy of Modernity." *MLN* 100, 3 (April 1985): 514–36.

Maurer, Karl W. *Philosophy and History* 7, 1 (1974): 6–8. [Review of III, IV]

McCole, John. "Benjamin's *Passagen-Werk*: A Guide to the Labyrinth." *Theory and Society* 14 (1985): 497–509.

McNamee, Donald K. "The Pioneer Ideas of Walter Benjamin: An Essay Concerning Mechanical Reproducibility and its Effect on the Work of Art." *The Structurist* 6 (1966): 47–54.

Mehlmann, Jeffrey. "Literature and Hospitality: Klossowski's Hamann." *Studies in Romanticism* 22, 2 (Summer 1983): 329–47.

Milfull, John. "The Messiah and the Direction of History: Walter Benjamin, Isaac Bashevis Singer, and Franz Kafka." In *Festschrift for E. W. Herd*, ed. August Obermayer. Dunedin: University of Otago, Department of German, 1980, 180–87.

Miller, J. Hillis. *The Ethics of Reading: Kant, de Man, Eliot, Trollope, James, and Benjamin.* New York: Columbia University Press, 1986.

Mitchell, Stanley. "Introduction to Benjamin and Brecht." *NLR* 77 (January–February 1973): 42–50; also Introduction to *Understanding Brecht.* London: New Left Books, 1973, VII–XIX.

———. "Presentation of Adorno-Benjamin." *NLR* 81 (September–October 1973): 46–52.

Moses, Stéphane. "The Gap between Word and Meaning." *Jerusalem Post Magazine* (December 3, 1971), 21.

———. "Walter Benjamin and Franz Rosenzweig." *PF* 15, 1–2 (Fall–Winter 1983–84): 188–205.

Nägele, Rainer. "Benjamin's Ground." *Studies* 11, 1 (Fall 1986): 5–24.

New Left Books. "Publisher's Note." To Walter Benjamin, *One-Way Street.* London: New Left Books, 1979, 29–42.

Norris, Christopher. "Image and Parable: Readings of Walter Benjamin." *Philosophy and Literature* 7, 1 (April 1982): 15–31. Reprinted in Norris, *The Deconstructive Turn: Essays in the Rhetoric of Philosophy.* London: Methuen, 1983, 107–27.

Owens, Craig. "The Allegorical Impulse: Toward a Theory of Postmodernism," part 1, *October* 12 (Spring 1980): 67–86.

P[ascal], R. Review of *Ursprung des deutschen Trauerspiels. Modern Language Review* 25, 1 (January 1930): 124.

Paetzold, Heinz. "Walter Benjamin's Theory of the End of Art," trans. Sue Westphal. *IJS* 7, 1 (Spring 1977): 25–75.

Parmalee, Patty Lee. Review of Asja Lacis, *Revolutionär im Beruf. Berichte über proletarisches Theater. Über Meyerhold, Brecht, Benjamin und Piscator.* NGC 4 (Winter 1975): 163–66.

Pizer, John. "History, Genre and 'Ursprung' in Benjamin's Early Aesthetics." *German Quarterly* 60, 1 (Winter 1987): 68–87.

Puppe, Heinz W. "Walter Benjamin on Photography," *CG* 12, 3 (1979): 273–91.

Rabinbach, Anson. "Critique and Commentary/Alchemy and Chemistry: Some Remarks on Walter Benjamin and This Special Issue" and "Introduction to Walter Benjamin's 'Doctrine of the Similar'." *NGC* 17 (Spring 1979): 3–14, 60–64.

———. "Between Enlightenment and Apocalypse: Benjamin, Bloch and Modern German Jewish Messianism." *NGC* 34 (Winter 1985): 78–124.

Radnoti, Sándor. "The Early Aesthetics of Walter Benjamin," trans. G. Follinus. *IJS* 7, 1 (Spring 1977): 76–123.

———. "Benjamin's Politics." *Telos* 37 (Fall 1978): 63–81.

———. "The Effective Power of Art: On Benjamin's Aesthetics." *Telos* 49 (Fall 1981): 61–82.

———. "Benjamin's Dialectic of Art and Society." *PF* 15, 1–2 (Fall–Winter 1983–84): 158–87.

Ridley, Hugh. "WB—Towards a new Marxist aesthetic," in A. F. Bance, ed., *Weimar Germany: Writers and Politics*. Edinburgh: Scottish Academic Press, 1982, 168–83.

Roberts, Julian. "Walter Benjamin." In Tom Bottomore, ed. *A Dictionary of Marxist Thought*. Oxford: Basil Blackwell, 1983, 46f.

Roditi, Edouard. "Meetings with Walter Benjamin." *Partisan Review* 53, 2 (1986): 263–67.

Roloff, Michael. Review of *Illuminations. Commonwealth Magazine* 90 (August 22, 1969), 525–27.

Ronell, Avitai. "Street-Talk." *Studies* 11, 1 (Fall 1986): 105–31.

Rose, Gillian. *The Melancholy Science: An Introduction to the Thought of Theodor W. Adorno.* Basingstoke: Macmillan, 1981.

Rose, Marilyn Gaddis. "Walter Benjamin as Translation Theorist: A Reconsideration." *Dispositio* 7, 19–21 (1982): 163–175.

Rosen, Charles. "The Ruins of Walter Benjamin." *New York Review of Books* 24, 17 (October 27, 1977), 31–40; "The Origins of Walter Benjamin." *New York Review of Books* 18 (November 10, 1977), 30–38.

Rosen, Michael. "Expressions of the Economic." *TLS* 4166 (February 4, 1983), 109–10. [Review of *Passagen-Werk*, Eagleton, Wolin]

Sandor, Andras. "Rilke's and Walter Benjamin's Conceptions of Rescue and Liberation." In Frank Baron, Ernst Dick, and Warren Maurer, eds. *Rilke: The Alchemy of Alienation*. Lawrence: Regents Press of Kansas, 1980, 223–42.

Schlossman, Beryl. "Proust and Benjamin: The Invisible Image." *Studies* 11, 1 (Fall 1986): 91–104.

Scholem, Gershom. "Walter Benjamin." *Publications of the Leo Baeck Yearbook Institute: 10.* New York: East and West Library, 1965, 117–36. Revised in Scholem, *On Jews and Judaism in Crisis.*

———. "Walter Benjamin." *Encyclopedia Judaica*. Jerusalem: Keter, 1971, 530f.

———. *From Berlin to Jerusalem*. New York: Schocken, 1980.

———. "Walter Benjamin," "Walter Benjamin and His Angel," and "Two Letters to Walter Benjamin." In Scholem, *On Jews and Judaism in Crisis: Selected Essays*, ed. Werner J. Dannhauser. New York: Schocken, 1976, 172–243.

———. "Preparatory Remarks to Lisa Fittko, 'Old Benjamin'," trans. H. Zohn. Unpublished typescript.

———. "Preface." In Walter Benjamin, *Moscow Diary*, ed. Gary Smith, trans. Richard Sieburth. Cambridge, MA: Harvard University Press, 1986, 5–8. First printed in *October* 35 (Winter 1985): 5–8.

Schwarcz, Vera. "The Domestication of Walter Benjamin: Admirers Flee from History into Melancholia." *Bennington Review* 4 (April 1979): 7–11.

Semmler, Clement. "Walter Benjamin: an original." *Sydney Morning Herald* (October 3, 1970). [illus.]

Shor, Frances. "Walter Benjamin as Guide: Images in the Modern City." *Jewish Social Studies* 44 (Winter 1982): 37–46.

Sieburth, Richard. "Same Difference: The French *Physiologies*, 1840–1842." *Notebooks in Cultural Analysis: An Annual Review* 1, ed. Norman F. Cantor and Nathalia King. Durham: Duke University Press, 1984, 163–200.

———. "Benjamin the Scrivener" and " 'N': Translators' Introduction." In Gary Smith, ed., *Thinking Through Benjamin*. Chicago: University of Chicago Press, 1989.

Slaughter, Cliff. "Against the Stream: Walter Benjamin." In Slaughter, *Marxism, Ideology and Literature*. London: Macmillan, 1981, 170–96.

Smith, Gary. "Walter Benjamin: A Selected Bibliography of Secondary Literature." *NGC* 17 (Spring 1979): 189–208.

———. "Afterword" to Walter Benjamin, *Moscow Diary*, ed. Smith, trans. Richard Sieburth. Cambridge, MA: Harvard University Press, 1986, 137–46; also *October* 35 (Winter 1985).

Smith, Paul. "The Will to Allegory in Postmodernism." *Dalhousie Review* 62 (1982): 105–22.

Snyder, Joel. "Benjamin on Reproducibility and Aura: A Reading of 'The Work of Art in the Age of its Technical Reproducibility'." *PF* 15, 1–2 (Fall–Winter 1983–84): 130–45.

Sontag, Susan. "The Last Intellectual." *The New York Review of Books* 25, 15 (October 12, 1978), 75–82. Reprinted in Walter Benjamin, *One-Way Street*. London: New Left Books, 1979, 7–28, and Sontag, *Under the Sign of Saturn*. New York: Farrar, Straus, Giroux, 1980, 107–34.

Spencer, Lloyd. "Introduction to 'Central Park' " and "Allegory in the World of Commodity: the Importance of 'Central Park'." *NGC* 34 (Winter 1985): 28–31, 59–77.

Sprinker, Michael. "The Tragic Vision: Erich Heller and the Critique of Modernism." *Salmagundi* 52–53 (Spring–Summer 1981): 124–50.

Steiner, George. "Walter Benjamin: Towards a Philosophy of Language." *TLS* 3469 (August 22, 1968), 885–87. [Review of *Angelus Novus, Briefe, Über Walter Benjamin*]. Reprinted in *T.L.S.: Essays and Reviews from the 'TLS'. 1968*. London: Oxford University Press, 1969, 193–204.

[———]. "Reply" [to Letter to the Editor] *TLS* (September 5, 1968), 958.

———. "The Marxist and the Mandarin." *Sunday Times*, London (September 16, 1973), 38f.

———. "Polemical Genius of the Frankfurt School." *TLS* (December 14, 1973), 1539. [Review of III, IV; Salzinger; Unseld]

———. "The Uncommon Reader." *TLS* 3790 (October 25, 1974), 1198. [Review of I]

———. "Introduction." In Walter Benjamin, *The Origin of German Tragic Drama*, trans. John Osborne. London: New Left Books, 1977, 7–24.

Bibliography

Stolnitz, Jerome. "On the Apparent Demise of Really High Art." *Journal of Aesthetics and Art Criticism* 43, 4 (Summer 1985): 345–58.

Sussman, Henry. "The Herald: A Reading of Walter Benjamin's Kafka Study." *Diacritics* 7, 1 (Spring 1977): 42–54.

Swann, C. S. B. "The Practice and Theory of Storytelling—Nathaniel Hawthorne and Walter Benjamin." *Journal of American Studies* 12 (August 1978): 185–202.

Szondi, Peter. "Hope in the Past: On Walter Benjamin," trans. Harvey Mendelsohn. *Critical Inquiry* 4, 3 (Spring 1978): 491–506.

Tiedemann, Rolf. "Historical Materialism or Political Messianism? An Interpretation of the Theses 'On the Concept of History'." *PF* 15, 1–2 (Fall–Winter 1983–84): 71–104.

Timms, Edward F. "Benjamin and Brecht." *Cambridge Review* (March 2, 1973), 128–31.

Todd, Jennifer. "Georg Lukács, Walter Benjamin, and the Motivation to Make Political Art." *Radical Philosophy* 28 (Summer 1981): 16–22.

————. "Production, Reception, Criticism: Walter Benjamin and the Problem of Meaning in Art." *PF* 15, 1–2 (Fall–Winter 1983–84), 105–29.

Weber, Shierry M. "Walter Benjamin: Commodity Fetishism, the Modern, and the Experience of History." In Dick Howard and Karl E. Klare, eds. *The Unknown Dimension: European Marxism Since Lenin*. New York: Basic Books, 1972, 249–75.

Wellbery, David E. "Benjamin's Theory of the Lyric." *Studies* 11, 1 (Fall 1986): 25–46.

Wellek, René. "The Early Literary Criticism of Walter Benjamin." *Rice University Studies* 57, 4 (Fall 1971): 123–34.

————. Walter Benjamin's Literary Criticism in His Marxist Phase." In Joseph Strelka, ed. *The Personality of the Critic*. University Park: Penn State University Press, 1973, 168–78.

————. "Benjamin's Moscow." *The New Criterion* (November 1986): 83–85.

Werckmeister, O. K. "Walter Benjamin, Paul Klee, and the Angel of History." *Oppositions* 25 (Fall 1982): 103–25.

Wieseltier, Leon. "The Revolt of Gershom Scholem." *New York Review of Books* 24, 5 (March 31, 1977), 23–26; "Gershom Scholem and the Fate of the Jews," ibid., 24, 6 (April 14, 1977), 27–30. [Review of Scholem, *On Jews and Judaism in Crisis*]

Witte, Bernd. "Benjamin and Lukács. Historical Notes on the Relationship between Their Political and Aesthetic Theories." *NGC* 5 (Spring 1975): 3–26.

————. "Paris—Berlin—Paris: Personal, Literary, and Social Experience in Walter Benjamin's Late Works," trans. Susan B. Winnett. *NGC* 39 (Fall 1986): 49–60.

Wohlfarth, Irving. "Perte D'Auréole: The Emergence of a Dandy." *MLN* 85, 4 (May 1970): 529–71.

————. "No-man's-land: On Walter Benjamin's 'Destructive Character'." *Diacritics* 8, 2 (June 1978): 47–65.

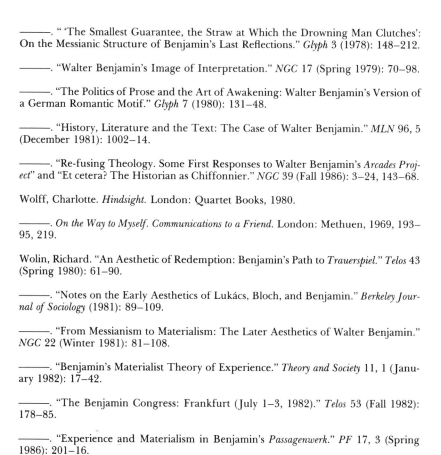

———. " 'The Smallest Guarantee, the Straw at Which the Drowning Man Clutches': On the Messianic Structure of Benjamin's Last Reflections." *Glyph* 3 (1978): 148–212.

———. "Walter Benjamin's Image of Interpretation." *NGC* 17 (Spring 1979): 70–98.

———. "The Politics of Prose and the Art of Awakening: Walter Benjamin's Version of a German Romantic Motif." *Glyph* 7 (1980): 131–48.

———. "History, Literature and the Text: The Case of Walter Benjamin." *MLN* 96, 5 (December 1981): 1002–14.

———. "Re-fusing Theology. Some First Responses to Walter Benjamin's *Arcades Project*" and "Et cetera? The Historian as Chiffonnier." *NGC* 39 (Fall 1986): 3–24, 143–68.

Wolff, Charlotte. *Hindsight.* London: Quartet Books, 1980.

———. *On the Way to Myself. Communications to a Friend.* London: Methuen, 1969, 193–95, 219.

Wolin, Richard. "An Aesthetic of Redemption: Benjamin's Path to *Trauerspiel.*" *Telos* 43 (Spring 1980): 61–90.

———. "Notes on the Early Aesthetics of Lukács, Bloch, and Benjamin." *Berkeley Journal of Sociology* (1981): 89–109.

———. "From Messianism to Materialism: The Later Aesthetics of Walter Benjamin." *NGC* 22 (Winter 1981): 81–108.

———. "Benjamin's Materialist Theory of Experience." *Theory and Society* 11, 1 (January 1982): 17–42.

———. "The Benjamin Congress: Frankfurt (July 1–3, 1982)." *Telos* 53 (Fall 1982): 178–85.

———. "Experience and Materialism in Benjamin's *Passagenwerk.*" *PF* 17, 3 (Spring 1986): 201–16.

Wright, Kathleen. "The Place of the Work of Art in the Age of Technology." *Southern Journal of Philosophy* 22, 4 (Winter 1984): 565ff.

Zimmermann, Ulf. "Benjamin and *Berlin Alexanderplatz.* Some Notes Towards a View of Literature and the City," *CG* 12, 3 (1979): 256–72.

Contributors

Theodor W. Adorno (1903–69) used Benjamin's *The Origin of the German Trauerspiel* as a text for his first seminar in 1932. He coedited Benjamin's two-volume *Schriften* in 1955 with Gretel Adorno. Volume 20, the final volume, of Adorno's own *Gesammelte Schriften* was published in 1986.

Ernst Bloch (1885–1977) first met Benjamin when they were both self-exiled in Switzerland during World War I. Bloch's *Werkausgabe* encompasses seventeen volumes, and an edition of his *Briefe 1903–1975* has also been published. His monumental *Principle of Hope* has recently been translated.

Jürgen Habermas, Professor of Philosophy at the University of Frankfurt, is the leading representative of the Frankfurt School tradition of social thought. His most recent works to appear in English are the two-volume *Theory of Communicative Action* and *The Philosophical Discourse of Modernity.*

Hans Robert Jauss is Professor of Literary Criticism and Romance Philology at the University of Konstanz. Two of his books have been translated: *Toward an Aesthetic of Reception* and *Aesthetic Experience and Literary Hermeneutics.*

Pierre Klossowski translated Benjamin's "Work of Art" essay into French for its first printing (*Zeitschrift für Sozialforschung,* 1936); he also translated a portion of Benjamin's essay on Goethe's *Elective Affinities,* under the title "L'angoisse mythique chez

Goethe" (*Cahiers du Sud*, 1937). A volume of Klossowski's work has appeared in English as *Robert Ce Soir and The Revocation of the Edict of Nantes*.

Hans Mayer was working on a book on Georg Büchner when he became cursorily acquainted with Benjamin at the Collège de Sociologie. Mayer's *Outsiders: A Study in Life and Letters* has appeared in English; two volumes of his lectures have recently been published in German.

Winfried Menninghaus, Associate Professor in the Institute for General and Comparative Literature at the Free University of Berlin, has published two books on Benjamin: *Walter Benjamins Theorie der Sprachmagie* and, most recently, *Schwellenkunde: Walter Benjamins Passage des Mythos*.

Pierre Missac (1910–86) was a regular contributor to *Cahiers du Sud* (which also published Benjamin and Bloch) and *Critique*. His *Passage de Walter Benjamin* appeared posthumously.

Charles Rosen, noted concert pianist and critic, teaches at the State University of New York at Stony Brook. He has written *Romanticism and Realism* (with Henri Zerner)* as well as *Arnold Schoenberg, The Classical Style,* and *Sonata Forms.*

Hans Sahl is a novelist, poet, essayist, and translator who lives in New York. He has recently published two autobiographical works: *Memoiren eines Moralisten* and *Die Wenigen und die Vielen.*

Gershom Scholem (1897–1982) is best known to English-speaking readers for his books *Major Trends in Jewish Mysticism, The Messianic Idea in Judaism, Sabbatical Sevi, On Jews and Judaism in Crisis, From Berlin to Jerusalem,* and *Origins of the Kabbalah.* He coedited Benjamin's *Briefe,* and he is the author of *Walter Benjamin: The Story of a Friendship.*

Hermann Schweppenhäuser, coeditor of Benjamin's *Gesammelte Schriften* and Professor of Philosophy in Lüneburg and Frankfurt, has published books and essays on critical theory, Heidegger's theory of language, and aesthetics.

Contributors

Jean Selz is an art historian. His book *Le dire et le faire* includes a second recollection of Benjamin, "Une expérience de Walter Benjamin." He collaborated with Benjamin on the translation of portions of *Berliner Kindheit* into French.

Peter Szondi (1929–71) held the first chair for comparative literature in Germany, established in 1965 at the Free University of Berlin. Five volumes of his lectures and two volumes of other writings have been published posthumously.

Rolf Tiedemann is the Director of the Theodor W. Adorno Archive, Frankfurt, and principal editor of the collected writings of both Benjamin and Adorno. He is the author of *Dialektik im Stillstand* and *Studien zur Philosophie Walter Benjamins* and has recently edited *Adorno-Noten,* Scholem's *Walter Benjamin und sein Engel,* and Benjamin's *Sonette.*

Irving Wohlfarth, Professor of Comparative Literature at the University of Oregon, has written numerous essays on Benjamin and Adorno in English, French, and German.

Index